Adobe Photoshop™ Handbook

2.5 EDITION

Adobe Photoshop™ Handbook

2.5 EDITION

David Biedny

Bert Monroy

2.5 Edition Update by

Mark Siprut

Adobe Photoshop™ Handbook, 2.5 Edition

Cover art by Erik Adigard
Book composed and produced by Sybil Ihrig, VersaTech Associates

Published in the United States by Random House, Inc., New York, and simultaneously in Canada by Random House of Canada, Limited.

Manufactured in the United States of America

First Edition

0 9 8 7 6 5 4 3 2 1

ISBN 0-679-79128-0

The authors and publisher have used their best efforts in preparing this book, and the programs contained herein. However, the authors and publisher make no warranties of any kind, express or implied, with regard to the documentation or programs contained in this book, and specifically disclaim, without limitation, any implied warranties of merchantability and fitness for a particular purpose with respect to programs and/or techniques described in the book. In no event shall the authors or publisher be responsible or liable for any loss of profit or any other commercial damages, including but not limited to special, incidental, consequential or any other damages in connection with or arising out of furnishing, performance, or use of this book or the programs.

Trademarks

A number of entered words in which we have reason to believe trademark, service mark, or other proprietary rights may exist have been designated as such by use of initial capitalization. However, no attempt has been made to designate as trademarks or service marks all personal computer words or terms in which proprietary rights might exist. The inclusion, exclusion or definition of a word or term is not intended to affect, or to express any judgment on, the validity or legal status of any proprietary right which may be claimed in that word or term.

New York Toronto London Sydney Auckland

Contents at a Glance

Contents

CHAPTER 3

Input 83

CHAPTER 5

Image Selection and Masking 155

C H A P T E R 6

Image Processing *187*

CHAPTER 7

Advanced Photoshop Techniques 249

CHAPTER 8

Output 287

CHAPTER 10

Case Studies 335

Foreword

The goal for Adobe Photoshop 2.5 was to deliver powerful, professional features that make this version easier and faster to use than previous releases. Customers using Adobe Photoshop 2.5 around the world (in eight native language versions) tell us that we have succeeded in these goals.

When Photoshop 2.0 was introduced two years ago, printers received 80% of their customers' layouts in the form of paper mechanicals. Today, over 80% of the layouts arrive as digital mechanicals or final film. QuarkXPress, Adobe Illustrator, Adobe typefaces, and high-resolution PostScript imagesetters let designers produce full-color pages and most of their page elements on the Macintosh. Photoshop 2.0 provided the missing piece of the digital page with the capability for editing on-screen CMYK photographic images and producing high-quality digital four-color separations.

The Macintosh and Adobe Photoshop also helped lead an equally significant revolution in the tools of creativity, and Photoshop made it possible to realize any creative vision. In the hands of today's innovators, these tools have broadened the definition of fine art to include digital art and photography.

The new generation of Photoshop, beginning with Version 2.5, will accelerate the revolution for the way images in all media are created and produced. Beneath the streamlined interface, Photoshop 2.5 incorporates new technology that makes the program more flexible than ever before. The plug-in architecture lets developers extend and customize Photoshop's features to meet specialized creative and production needs.

Adobe Photoshop users can choose from a huge selection of plug-in and add-on products as their needs change and grow.

The architecture of Adobe Photoshop 2.5 was designed so that almost any operation (not just filters!) can use another processor to complete the operations more quickly than can the computer's CPU alone. Only Adobe Photoshop 2.5 provides such comprehensive image-processing acceleration. It and saves time and money while making more creative experimentation possible—even in schedule-driven production environments.

Adobe never stops improving Photoshop. In August, 1993, Adobe began automatically shipping a free 2.5.1 update to all registered Photoshop 2.5 owners. Free updates are the best reason to buy and register software; just do it, if you haven't already!

With this book Mark Siprut has revised and improved the original ground-breaking work by David Biedny and Bert Monroy to explore the many new features and uses of Adobe Photoshop 2.5. He takes an approach that helps users on all levels, whether new, intermediate, or expert. The book's many graphics and illustrations make it a great way for everyone to get to know the program and get the most out of the new features. Even the new capabilities of Version 2.5.1 are covered in this edition of the *Adobe Photoshop Handbook.*

If you do not own a copy of *Adobe Photoshop 2.5*, you can use the *Adobe Photoshop Handbook 2.5 Edition* to get an overview of what is possible with this powerful software and how it can help you in your work. If you have already purchased Adobe Photoshop 2.5, you can use this book as a valuable reference to help you enhance your creative powers and increase your technical expertise.

Jeff Parker
Product Marketing Manager
Adobe Systems Incorporated

Preface

If you are familiar with the first edition of this book, you'll notice that we've made many changes for this new publication, the most obvious of which are the illustrations (they have all been replaced), the addition of a chapter on input, new case studies, and expanded information on one of Photoshop's most powerful features, channel operations. We've also included plenty of enhanced tips, techniques, and artwork from the world's top Photoshop experts, including Kai Krause, Bill Niffenegger, Nick Fain, and others.

Photoshop 2.5 is a much more refined program than its predecessor; this book reflects its complexity and depth. If you're just starting out with Photoshop, you'll find discussions and techniques that will help you quickly produce quality work. If you've already spent some time in the Photoshop universe, you'll appreciate the expert perspectives and advanced techniques that augment the latter half of the book.

However, we have not written a replacement for the Adobe Photoshop User Guide. We know that there are mini-manuals for many programs which, if you ingest the whole book and take copious notes, eliminate the need for the original program documentation. This is not intended for that purpose.

The User Guide included with Photoshop is excellent; it describes, in technical detail, functional aspects of the program (in some cases, more than most people need or want to know). Our goal in writing this book was to share with artists like ourselves the techniques and tips we have found most useful over the years, and to describe the new features of version 2.5. We hope this book will complement and augment the documentation, explaining how Photoshop's features work together and how the program can be incorporated into the larger picture of visual communication.

We will look at many arenas in which Photoshop can be applied: photography, print production, animation, video, illustration, fine arts, and more. Depending on your job, some of the program features may be more useful than others; for example, different filters may be appropriate for special animation effects but not for corporate newsletter production. Channels, arguably one of the most potent and misunderstood of Photoshop's capabilities, are demystified in Chapter 5, "Image Selection and Masking." We show how to input images from a variety of sources such as scanners, Photo CDs, 2-D and 3-D illustration programs, and video; how to manipulate and edit these images; and then how to output them using color digital printers, offset lithography, on-screen presentations, video, and more. And of course, we show how to create those wonderful special effects for which Photoshop is so famous.

We wrote this book with the Photoshop artist in mind. You can learn almost any program by methodically plowing through each and every command in sequence, but in Photoshop the tendency is to play with the features, creating "happy accidents." Many of the techniques described in the following chapters were discovered this way, and we encourage you to explore (as long as you keep backups of your master graphics files!).

Photoshop illustrator Nick Fain offers the following advice:

"Learn Photoshop thoroughly, especially where it applies to your particular area of production before beginning contracted projects. There will always be continued on-the-job learning, but perils lurk in profusion for the unprepared. A portfolio of at least 10 challenging images, output successfully on high-resolution imagesetters, and executed according to plan, should be the minimum goal of any novice before offering a service.

"The electronic medium is like any other creative discipline. Learn the basics, master the tools, be objective, and strive for versatility and original solutions. It is an insult to those who spent careers mastering 'traditional' media if computers are used to produce mediocre results in a jiffy. Cutting corners and lowering standards is like using an automated assembly line to build cheap, ugly cars that no one wants, just to meet a quota. Photoshop gives users the power to create magical images which are limited only by our resourcefulness and imagination. Remember: Every pixel counts!"

Although we have structured this book for random access, you may want to read it sequentially the first time around, especially if you are new to Photoshop. We also suggest that you keep the Adobe Photoshop User Guide handy for further reference.

Photoshop is a vast software universe, complete with silicon galaxies and black holes. Hang on for one wild rocket ride! If you have not already been converted, you may soon join the ranks of Photoshop enthusiasts like artist Eve Elberg, who enthuses about Photoshop's capabilities in her Chapter 10 case study:

"The image took me about a day to create. It went quickly because I had performed these tricks before, and I knew where my images were stored. Basically I pulled material from my library and applied some magic. This is the power of Photoshop; by simply varying one or two elements and tactics, the permutations are frighteningly endless!"

Acknowledgments

Updating and revising a handbook on Adobe Photoshop was no easy task. The entire arena of visual communication is in a tremendous state of flux, and technologies change weekly. Many people helped with this revision, contributing artwork and tips, locating facts, and chatting about Photoshop over the phone and on line (CompuServe and America On Line).

Special thanks to Michael Roney, a patient and understanding editor.

More special thanks to Anna Stump for copy editing, creative suggestions, and moral support.

Thanks also to Kai Krause for his Chops contributions to Chapter 7 and overall support of our effort; to expert Steve Werner of Rapid Graphics, San Francisco for help in revising Chapters 3 and 8; and to Rapid Graphics for output tests. Robert Arena of Bug Press, Arcata, California, also deserve special thanks for output tests and feedback. Joseph Bellacera has our gratitude for color print testing and rotoscope drawing.

Bruce and Sharon Powell of Synergy provided animation and multimedia expertise for Chapter 9. Photographer Andrew Rodney offered feedback on digital photography, provided the "Dog in Bowl" photo, and created many of the filters effects for Chapter 6.

Ralph L. Mittman and Racquel Aceves were a great help on Chapters 4 and 6, and Mark Crosten sacrificed many hours researching and drafting new information for the features chapters.

Thanks also go to Doug Ridgeway, Loughton Smith, John Esser, Larry Kuhn, Susan Kitchens, Julie Sigwart, Christ Swetlin, Linnea Dayton, Paul McAfee, Nick Fain, Carol McClendon, Lior Saar, Jeff Parker, Rita Amladi, and Steve Guttman.

Sybil and Emil Ihrig of Versatech Associates in Escondido, California provided invaluable professional expertise on book layout. Optronics' Bob Janukowicz offered resources for creating the color pages, while Rosa Deberry King applied her formidable skills creating the color separations.

Ryan Thrash and Lynda Weinman did a super job on the tech review, while Random House's Jean Davis Taft and Tom Dillon labored long and hard coordinating book production.

Special thanks to the talented artists who contributed their beautiful images to the book's Color Gallery section: Joe Bellacera, Alan Brown, Adam Cohen, Michael Colanero, Eve Elberg, Nick Fain, Diane Fenster, Louis Fishauf, Mark Gould, Francois Guerin, Kai Krause, Fran Milner, Bert Monroy, Bill Niffenegger, Elaine O'Neil, Andrew Rodney, Chris Swetlin, Howard Tiersky, Ellen Van Going, and Marc Yankus.

We also appreciate the use of the CD Folios Sky Vol. 1 Digital Photo Collection (Maile sky) in the color section; Photo Disc, World Commerce and Travel Vol. V (Eiffel Tower) for interpolation example in Chapter 2; Varden Studios for "Prisoners"; Sarah Everding for "Kulture"; Ellen Landweber for "Ant Stomp"; Merrill Nix for "Boats" and "Dogs"; Michael Roney for "Boats"; Anna Stump for "Fieldbrook Store"; Joseph Tracy for "Earth Photo"; and Cher Threinen-Pendarvis for "Lightning Dancer."

Of course, we couldn't have thoroughly explored Photoshop and produced this book without the following products, which were made available to us by their manufacturers: SuperMac 19-inch Dual Mode Color Display, and Thunderstorm and Thunder II Accelerator cards from SuperMac Technology; Wacom ArtZ ADB Digitizing Tablet from Wacom Technology Corp; and Fujitsu Dynamo 128 megabyte magneto optical drive from Fujitsu Computer Products of America.

The following companies also provided assistance: Aldus Corporation, Andromeda Software, Inc., Electronics for Imaging, Equilibrium Technologies, Fifth Generation Systems, Fractal Design Corporation, Gryphon Software, HSC Software, Imspace Systems,

Kodak, Light Source, Macromedia, Quark, Inc., Savitar, Second Glance Software, Specular International, Strata, Total Integration, Inc., and Xaos Tools.

Last but not least, thanks to David Biedny and Bert Monroy for their initial vision and continuing support.

Mark Siprut
San Diego, California
October 1993

CHAPTER 1

Welcome to Photoshop

This book is for anyone excited about the rapidly changing world of digital imaging. Whether you have just purchased your first copy of Adobe Photoshop, are trying to find out more about the program before buying it, or are upgrading from a previous release, there's something here for you.

Photoshop brings the capabilities that used to be found only in high-end paintbox systems down to the level of the Mac, with few compromises or strings attached. In only a few years, Photoshop has become the standard image editing program for photographers, designers, illustrators, and fine artists.

With the advent of large image libraries on CD-ROM, and digital photographs, every photographer, whether amateur or professional, will easily have reason to use Photoshop. Special effects previously done in the darkroom and that took hours of valuable time and many sheets of costly film can now be done in minutes using Photoshop (Figure 1–1). Likewise, Photoshop's incredibly deep feature set and large library of powerful third-party plug-ins have made it an indispensable tool for commercial designers and fine artists working in digital media.

Figure 1–1
Special effects that used to take hours to do in the darkroom can now be done in minutes.

A New Generation

Photoshop belongs to a new generation of Macintosh graphics programs—it is sophisticated on a level previously associated with the high-end computer graphics world. The tools found in Photoshop have their counterparts in high-end color-publishing and graphics systems, such as Scitex and Quantel PaintBox, that traditionally have been used to produce four-color magazines and television graphics. Photoshop has the ability to communicate with the high-end prepress world via Pixar and Scitex CT formats, which are directly supported as an output option. Macintosh screen resolution, once a limiting factor in a Mac-based paint program, is no longer a restraint; Photoshop has the ability to work in virtually any resolution the user desires.

With the maturation of the Windows operating system on DOS-based computers, many Macintosh applications have appeared on IBM-compatible PCs. Photoshop 2.5 falls into this category—it has been written to work on the PC in an almost identical fashion to the way it works on the Mac. So this book applies to you PC users, too.

NOTE: Previously Photoshop was written in Object Pascal language which was only readable to the Macintosh. Version 2.5 has been rewritten in C++, which is easily translated to other platforms, such as Windows, Silicon Graphics, and Sun Microsystems. This new language provides an easier path for Photoshop's growth and addition of features. The program now has an enhanced "open architecture," which allows third-party software companies to create "plug-ins" to augment many functions and tools even beyond the Acquire, Export and Filters menus.

***Tip*: Many of the painting tools found in Photoshop differ substantially from painting tools found in other Macintosh graphics software.**

A Unique Look and Feel

In many ways, Photoshop does not have the same "feel" as other Macintosh color bitmapped programs. Several of the features found in Photoshop have their roots in high-end paintbox systems, such as the Quantel PaintBox and Images II graphics system. Some of Photoshop's methodologies will take some getting used to—the way you use standard selection tools such as the Lasso and Marquee is distinctly different from anything that you might be familiar with from other color paint programs. However, you'll find Photoshop's interface and tool set to be deep, elegant, and powerful—one of the finest (some would say *the* finest) software implementations in the Mac universe. This approach lends to the power of the program. You could compare it to a car with either a manual or automatic transmission—the same engine performs more efficiently with a manual transmission, while the automatic sacrifices performance for ease of use. The payoff, of course, is in the substantial leap of power you will get when using Photoshop. This is not just another color paint program.

The Speed Issue

There's an old computer adage many of you might be familiar with: "You can never have enough processing speed or RAM." Macintosh owners are especially sensitive to the realistic limitations of the current generation of hardware. Ask them if they think their computers are fast enough, and listen to their responses. You may as well be asking them if they think they have too much money in their bank accounts.

As you work with Photoshop and begin to explore some of its more powerful capabilities, you may find that some of the program's operations are not as fast as you might like them to be: If you load a 3 × 5 inch, 300-ppi color scan into your trusty 8-megabyte Macintosh IIci, and you choose to color-separate the image by switching into CMYK display mode, you might find yourself tapping your fingers on your desktop (the real one, that is) and grumbling about "wanting it done before sometime tomorrow." Some of the filters take time to complete their processing (and in some cases, with large files, an unbearably long time), some of the dynamic effects (such as free rotate and distort) may seem to take ages to do their thing, and in general you might question just how slow Photoshop appears to be.

This speed issue has recently become less of a problem with Photoshop 2.5's optimized code rewrite, the introduction of System 7's 32-bit addressing scheme, and larger SIMMS chips, which allow you to install more RAM in the Mac. It is not unusual now to operate with at least 20 to 30 megabytes of RAM. A Quadra 950 can accommodate up to 256 megabytes of RAM. Accelerated 24-bit video cards and add-on DSP (digital signal processor) accelerator cards, which are specific to Photoshop functions, can increase speed even further. Some cards claim to accelerate operations by as much as 3600 times.

Main Features

Photoshop is capable of feats that put it into a class all its own.

Variable Resolution

Photoshop can import graphics files scanned or created at virtually any resolution. Unlike most Macintosh color-bitmapped programs, which are limited to the resolution of the standard Macintosh screen (72 dots per inch), Photoshop's tools work at all resolutions. Photoshop can also handle any resolution output format, ensuring compatibility with output devices available today and into the future. The only limitation is the amount of memory that the user's hardware can handle.

Variety of File Formats

Photoshop can open and save more file formats than most other Macintosh graphics packages (Figure 1–2). Besides allowing you to work with almost all of the graphics formats found in the Macintosh world, Photoshop also supports formats found in the Amiga, IBM PC, and higher-end environments. The ability to support Scitex and Targa formats opens a plethora of possibilities in terms of output options and integration with high-end prepress systems. In fact, Photoshop can handle more formats than any other microcomputer-based graphics program we've seen or used. Many of the limitations of the clipboard and scrapbook in converting different graphic-image file formats have been resolved in Photoshop.

Plug-Ins

Photoshop's open architecture allows the use of software extensions called plug-ins, which enhance a wide range of program features—including filters, Export, Acquire, and processing functions. Photoshop 2.5 comes with numerous plug-ins, and third-party software publishers offer scores more. Photoshop 2.5.1 additionally includes a folder called Optional Extensions, which contains yet more plug-ins that can enhance and customize various features; however, most of these involve performance trade-offs or conflicts.

Masks and Layers

One of the major limitations of Mac bitmapped programs is that there has been no way to properly maintain layers, or levels, normally associated with illustration programs and object-oriented design software. The multichannel aspects of Photoshop allow you to have up to 16 channels (each channel or layer can contain 8 bits of information). Normally, when working with a 24-bit color image (which takes up 3 of the 16 channels for the red, green and blue components that make up the 24-bit image), you can have up to 13 channels saved along with the image file. Each channel contains an 8-bit image mask, which can be

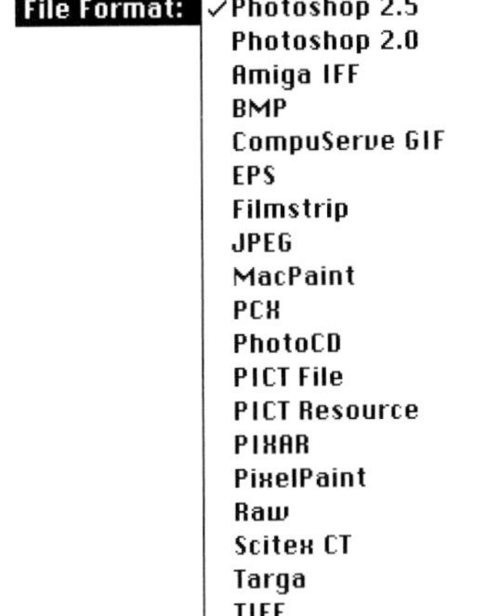

Figure 1–2
Photoshop can open and save numerous file formats.

created from any color or object in the RGB 24-bit color image. A channel can be thought of as analogous to a plate for an individual color in the printing process (Figure 1–3).

Extra channels can be added to an image to edit and store selections (masks). These additional channels, sometimes called "alpha channels," have their roots in the world of video. The next time that you watch television, take note (especially during commercials) of graphics or titles which appear to be suspended over live video, either as opaque or transparent images. This is accomplished with video alpha channels—live masks that are implemented in the hardware of the special effects devices used in video production. The alpha channels in Photoshop are essentially the same, except that they're made to work with static, still images (Figure 1–4).

***Tip*: While working with 24-bit color images, each channel contains 8 bits of information. Channels are not color; they only contain grayscale information. When you copy something into a channel, Photoshop automatically strips color hue information from the pasted image, leaving a precise anti-aliased mask that will perfectly match the color image.**

Figure 1–3
The channels can be viewed and manipulated independently of each other.

Figure 1–4
An image with its channel being used as a mask in order to paste in the sky

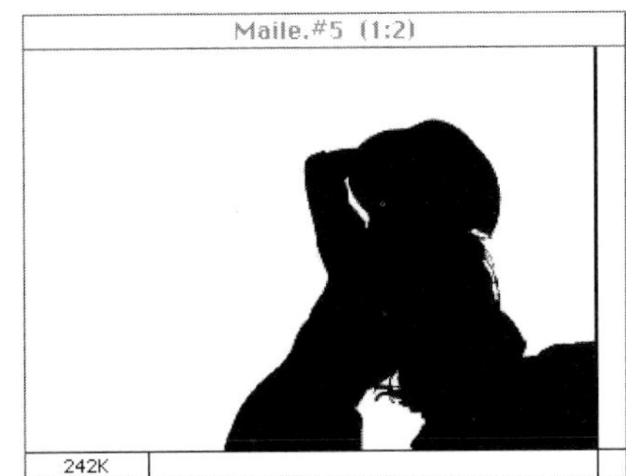

By using channels, you can create a bitmapped image with specific portions of the image—colors or objects in any combination—saved as separate layers. You can process any of the channels independently, with all of the program's tools and filters.

***Tip*: Channels aren't free: they occupy memory. In a 24-bit RGB color image, each channel is one-third the size of the overall color file size. The more channels you make in a file, the bigger the file gets for disk storage.**

Remapping to Any Color Palette (RGB-to-Indexed Color Conversion)

One of the biggest challenges facing Macintosh multimedia artists and animators is to get the most out of the limitation of 256 colors on the screen at any one time. Photoshop can convert a 48- or 24-bit color image into a 256-color image with the highest possible onscreen quality. It can make optimum use of the standard Macintosh system palette, or create a custom palette based on the colors it finds in the original color file. Users can choose from multiple dithering schemes, or choose to convert to less than 256 colors. (If you want the best possible quality in displaying a color image on a 4-bit, 16-color Mac graphics cards, Photoshop can do it.)

No Screen Redraw

A unique feature of Photoshop is that you can open menus and access the program's tools while the screen is being redrawn without having to wait for the redraw to finish. When working with large, high-resolution images, this time you save can be quite substantial.

DirectSetEntries on Real-Time Color Controllers

Many of the currently available 24-bit color display boards, such as those in the RasterOps and SuperMac lines, offer hardware support for DirectSetEntries. This allows color and brightness changes to occur in real time. Photoshop's color correction and processing controls work in real time with these display boards, allowing you to see changes on the screen interactively with the controls. As you drag a color correction slider, the screen is updated instantly.

Support for Multiple Open Documents

Photoshop was one of the first high-resolution Macintosh graphics programs to support multiple open documents. Full editing functions (cut, copy, and paste) are supported between documents. Undo is specific to each document. If you make a change in an image file—access another image file and manipulate it—chances are that you will be able to undo the last action applied to the first file. This doesn't always work; it depends on the size of the images in question, as well as the available amount of RAM. But when it does work, it's wonderful. Colors and palettes selected and open in one document apply to all other open documents. This is great for using the colors in one image as a palette for another.

Color QuickDraw Anywhere

Photoshop was also one of the first color Macintosh programs capable of handling full 24-bit color images on a black-and-white Macintosh. Even though the ROMs of these machines do not include color QuickDraw, you can work with color files and save your work, which can then be viewed on a color Mac at a later time. If you have a limited number of color Macintoshes in a production environment, and you need to process large numbers of color scans (for example, cropping 300 color scans to a predetermined size), Photoshop and a Classic or SE with 3 megabytes of RAM can be used instead of a costly Quadra. In fact, this capability extends to processing 24-bit color files—Photoshop is not reliant upon 32-bit QuickDraw for any of its functions, including working with 24-bit images. Imagine opening a 24-bit color file on a Mac SE, adjusting the brightness, and saving the changes back to the 24-bit file without 32-bit QuickDraw anywhere nearby. Quite a trick!

Virtual Memory

Although the more RAM the better, Photoshop doesn't rely on gobs of RAM memory in order to work with large images. By using a hard disk to "emulate" RAM memory, you can manipulate images much larger than the available RAM in your computer.

Tip: Photoshop likes hard-disk space. Lots of it! Make sure that you have at least four times the size of the document in free space on your hard disk. The more space you can spare, the better.

Virtual memory is built into Apple's System 7; however, Photoshop gives you these capabilities independent of System 7. If for some reason you have not yet upgraded to System 7 you'll still have virtual memory capabilities when using Photoshop.

Tip: If you are working in System 7, turn off Virtual Memory when working in Photoshop.

Photoshop's virtual memory can take advantage of multiple hard disks or drive partitions. In the Preferences dialog, select your fastest hard disk or partition as the primary scratch disk and another hard disk or partition as your secondary scratch disk. When the primary scratch disk is completely utilized for virtual memory, Photoshop switches to the secondary scratch disk to prevent out-of-memory errors. See Chapter 2, "Setup and Document Management," for how to specify scratch disks for virtual memory.

Anti-Aliasing

Anti-aliasing is a technique used to enhance the "softness" of hard edges by minimizing the pixel contrast. It is built into all of Photoshop's tools (with the exception of the Pencil tool), including type, and can be applied to the edges of selections (Figure 1–5).

Figure 1–5 Anti-aliasing demonstrated. Examples with (left) and without (right) anti-aliasing

Support for 48-Bit Color

Photoshop 2.5.1 now supports 48-bit color input from high-end scanners and digital cameras, such as those manufactured by Leaf Systems. This type of image has 16 bits of color information per channel (instead of the usual 8 bits), resulting in enhanced tonal detail and better suitability for output to large-format media such as posters. However, only Photoshop's Curves and Levels features are currently enabled in 48-bit mode. To use any other features, including the toolbox and menu items, you need to reduce the "working" image data to 24 or 8 bits. The original bit depth can be preserved by saving the file in Photoshop 2.5 or TIFF format.

Anti-Aliased Typefaces

When creating text in Photoshop, you can specify that the type appear on the screen with anti-aliasing. Anti-aliasing is a process by which harsh edges can be made to appear very smooth on the screen by the use of lighter and darker shades of an object's color. Essentially, the edges of an object are blended with the background to simulate a smooth transition between the foreground and background objects. Photoshop supports anti-aliasing through three methods:

1. System 6.x: Any screen face with larger sizes installed in the system can be drawn on the screen with anti-aliased edges. For example, if you have a 24-point screen face installed in your system, you can create smooth 12-point text on the screen. Photoshop accomplishes this by using the larger installed sizes to create optimized versions of the smaller faces.
2. System 7.0 or higher: Multiple font sizes are not necessary if TrueType fonts are being used.
3. If you are using ATM (Adobe Type Manager), you can create smooth type of any size and color from the Adobe printer fonts in your system folder. ATM is a program that allows you to have smooth, optimized screen representations of any Adobe typeface in most programs; when combined with Photoshop, these faces are fully anti-aliased.

Sophisticated Color Correction Control

Photoshop gives you absolute control over every aspect of an image. Not only will you have the standard brightness and contrast controls found in grayscale programs, such as the Aldus Digital Darkroom, but you will also have control over each individual color component in the image in ways you've always wanted (and, in some ways, never imagined). All color correction and enhancements features can be applied to entire images or to specific portions of an image. See Chapter 6, "Image Processing," for information on color correction and manipulation controls.

Color Separations

Photoshop can fully color-separate a color image, breaking it down into its four primary components—cyan, magenta, yellow, and black—which a printer uses to create four-color-process printing plates. While most programs with this capability separate the file only at printing time, Photoshop does the separation in software, and displays the separated layers and the composite on the screen. This allows you to preview the effects of the separation process and manipulate the individual plates before sending them to the output device. Using the Desktop Color Separation (DCS) format, you can export images to other programs like Adobe Illustrator, Aldus FreeHand, Aldus PageMaker, or QuarkXPress to be separated on pages with full text and illustration art in place. See Chapter 8, "Output," for information on color separation issues.

Duotones

In addition to process color separations Photoshop can make spot color separations of black-and-white images as duotones (two colors) tri-tones (three colors), and quadtones (four colors). Pantone, Trumatch, and other spot separation models are supported for making color choices. See the examples in the color section and in Chapter 7, "Advanced Techniques," for more on duotones.

Wide Variety of Image-Processing Features

The image manipulation and enhancement features found in Photoshop stand alone in the Macintosh world. The variety of filters, image processing tools, and controls for every aspect of an image can be almost overwhelming (Figure 1–6). Besides the built-in filters, Photoshop accepts third-party "plug-in" filter modules that, when placed in the plug-ins folder or the same folder as the program, appear in the standard filter menu. Many Image controls, such as the Color Balance, Brightness and Contrast, Posterization, and Hue/Saturation, work in "real-time" on 8- and 24-bit displays. As you change the settings, the screen display responds by displaying the changes instantaneously.

Compatibility with Illustration Programs

Photoshop can open and import an object-oriented Postscript file from Adobe Illustrator and turn it into a raster file (bitmapped). Vector paths can be created in Photoshop and exported to be used in a Vector program. See Chapter 8, "Output," for a discussion on working with Adobe Illustrator and Aldus FreeHand.

Object-oriented PICT files can be imported via the Acquire submenu under the File menu.

Figure 1–6
An image with a variety of filters and curves applied.

Who Uses Photoshop?

The audience for Photoshop is a large one, indeed.

- Photographers: The darkroom, with all of its polluting chemicals and tedious processes, will be a memory for most photographers using Photoshop. With the advent of digital cameras and Kodak's Photo CD technology, photographers can now manipulate images on the computer quickly and at a moderate cost.
- Video and Animation Artists/Producers: Frame-by-frame manipulation as well as global processing can be performed on filmstrips imported into Photoshop. These QuickTime movies can then be played on other computers or output to videotape.
- Desktop Publishing and Corporate Communications: Desktop publishers will find Photoshop to be an invaluable production tool for enhancing and manipulating both grayscale and color scanned images—and Photoshop also boasts color separation capabilities.

- Service Bureaus: Photoshop allows service bureaus to offer services far beyond their typesetting roots. One major new service is color separations, providing the film for engravers. This has always been a costly process; a service bureau can now handle it at a fraction of the traditional cost.
- Advertising: The first major use of Photoshop in this industry has been in the creation of full-color comprehensives. Traditionally, "comps" have been done by hand at an enormous cost in time, money, and legibility. For better results, high-end systems have been employed at an even higher cost. Photoshop puts that capability in the hands of the art director, designer, and the board artist. The production department has more control over the final production phases, thus reducing costly and time-consuming redos.
- Multimedia and Animation: Photoshop has a strong position in this fast-growing field, encompassing entertainment, training, and education. The labor-intensive process of creating visuals for animation is greatly simplified. Some of the special-effects filters can create animations that are simply mind-boggling. The ATM-based anti-aliased text is unequaled for smooth onscreen type for use in animated presentations, and Photoshop works well with such multimedia programs as Macromind Director and Adobe Premier.
- Fine Arts: The vast array of tools and special effects open the door to unseen corridors of the imagination. The filters alone allow endless hours of experimentation to create striking and exotic visual fantasies. Photographs can be manipulated to create special effects never before possible with a microcomputer. Artists who complain of the digital look of computer imagery from paint programs can now create images of superb clarity and complexity.
- Scientific and Medical applications: Many of the image-processing features in Photoshop (such as the convolution, high-pass, and sharpening filters, multichannel mathematics, and the ability to read raw multiple-channel data files from sources such as satellite data) will appeal to professionals working in many scientific fields.
- Manufacturing: Technical drawings and product photographs can be created and manipulated for manuals and visual aids in production.

Minimum System Requirements

We've all read the boxes and manuals before: "To use Adobe Photoshop, you need: An Apple Macintosh II computer with a 68020 processor (or any later model) with a minimum of 3 megabytes (MB) of application random-access memory (RAM); Apple system software 6.0.7 or higher; and 32-bit QuickDraw, version 1.2 or higher." Now, we don't know about you, but saying you can run Photoshop with the setup mentioned above, while quite possible with low-resolution images, is like saying you can get from New York to L.A. on foot. Yes, you can, but it's going to take a heck of a long time.

Obviously, you have to start somewhere and Adobe has duly noted the hardware to do just that. But we'd like to think (hope!) that most of you aren't running Photoshop with the "minimum configuration." We also realize that most of you aren't going to be running Photoshop on Quadras with 256 megabytes of RAM; 2 gigabytes of hard disk space; 21-inch color-calibrated, accelerated monitors; and DSP boards—although some might call that the "minimum configuration"!

There is no doubt that Photoshop is a powerful piece of software, and is able to gobble up all the computing resources and money you can throw at it. It is also true that Photoshop can run, whisper if you will, on a minimally configured machine and can scream on one that is maxed out. The bottom line is that if you spend a lot of time using Photoshop, it makes no sense to use it on a poky system. This section of the book will help those who can now only whisper to yell a bit louder. Those who already scream can gloat as they turn to the next chapter.

Practical Recommendations

The first rule of computers is that they are never fast enough. We've seen people nearly throw a fit while using Photoshop because applying some filters might take about 120 seconds. Now seriously, how much of a difference is 2 minutes going to make in your life? Well, it could make a whole lot of difference if your job requires you to apply that same filter 30 times a day. That adds up to 60 minutes! One hour per day! Five hours per week! One hundred fifty. . .well, you get the idea. The point is that having the fastest machine possible can really result in some astonishing time savings, so you can have more time to work, but let's be optimistic here. The faster your Mac, the faster Photoshop will work.

Adobe recommends that, at least, you use a Mac with a 68020 processor. This means a Macintosh II or an LC. At least. More realistically, we would recommend using a Mac with, at least, a 68030 processor. And we'll even better that: To make the best use of Photoshop and to greatly reduce your waiting time, use the fastest Mac you can afford. This means a Mac based on one of the 68040 processors, including the Quadra series and those in the Centris line. If you can't afford to rush out and buy a Quadra, consider adding a CPU accelerator to your machine. Accelerators are discussed in this chapter after the sections on displays and disk drives.

RAM

Lots and lots of random-access memory (RAM) is as important as having a fast computer. You see, when you are working on an image in Photoshop, the program looks at how much memory your image takes and multiplies that number 3 to 5 times. For example, if the image you are working on is 1 MB in size, Photoshop will want to have available 3 to 5 MB of memory in order to give you the opportunity, for example, to make use of the Undo command. If you have a computer with 4 MB of RAM installed, you can see that Photoshop could easily take all of that RAM, and more, just to work efficiently with a relatively small 1-MB image. And that doesn't include RAM that needs to be used by the System! Adobe recommends that you have a minimum of 3 MB of RAM available to be allocated to Photoshop. This, as you can see, is not very much at all.

VIRTUALLY SPEAKING

So what happens if you only have 3 MB of RAM available and you still want to use Photoshop? Well, as we mentioned previously, Photoshop has a very well designed method for using what is called *virtual memory*. Virtual memory means that when Photoshop uses up all the RAM it has been allocated and still needs more, the program will temporarily use part of your hard disk as a sort of "pseudo-RAM." The problem with using hard disk space as RAM is that accessing it is not done nearly as efficiently nor as fast as your computer can access RAM. So if you have only 3 MB of RAM allocated to Photoshop and 25 MB free on your hard disk, Photoshop will gladly take all the RAM and, when it needs it, will treat the 25 MB of disk space as RAM. However, accessing your hard disk as RAM is relatively slow and will eventually cause you to pull your hair out if you routinely work with multimegabyte images as your RAM quickly fills and your hard disk light starts to blink and blink and blink and blink. . . .

The best way to allow Photoshop to run faster, short of buying a new, faster computer, is to have as much RAM as you can afford. Since many images can easily be 4 to 20 MB in size, Photoshop could easily eat up 12 to 100 MB of RAM! First, decide what you can afford and buy wisely. A few companies make special cards, which can be installed in Macs with NuBus slots, that have a number of extra slots in which RAM can be installed. These cards allow users to add up to 256 MB of RAM! While the cards are relatively inexpensive, adding 256 MB of RAM is not! But if you need the ultimate setup, that is the way to go.

MEMORY SOURCES

There are a number of sources for RAM, some substantially less expensive than others. Shop around for the best deal you can get from a reliable vendor. Some earlier Macs, like the IIcx or older, cannot recognize more than 8 MB of RAM without installing a special INIT, such as Mode 32 or the appropriate Apple System Enabler.

RAM DISKS

If you have a lot of RAM available, consider using some or all of it as a RAM disk. RAM disks are created by setting aside a portion of available RAM to act as a temporary hard disk. RAM disks can be created using third-party software or by using Apple's System 7.1 operating system. The advantage of using a RAM disk is that it allows the computer to access stored data much faster that it can be accessed from a hard disk.

A RAM disk will appear on your Mac desktop just like a hard disk's icon would. Adobe recommends that if you set up a RAM disk, you put the Photoshop application and all associated files on it. This will speed your work because it will take the Mac much less time to access image data.

USING MORE THAN 100 MB OF RAM

Users who regularly work with images that might require more than 100 MB of RAM will definitely want to consider adding it to their machines but the Macintosh (through System 7.0.1) will not allow allocation of more than 99,999 KB via the "Get Info" box. How do you get around this limitation? By using a programming application called ResEdit. ResEdit is available from Apple, from a number of online services like CompuServe, and from Mac user groups. To use ResEdit to allocate more than 100 MB of RAM to Photoshop, do the following:

1. Launch ResEdit and then Open the Photoshop application.
2. Open the Size resource.
3. Open the resource with an ID number of 0.
4. Scroll to the bottom of the window containing lots of radio buttons.
5. Enter the amount of RAM you want allocated to Photoshop in the Size field. The number you will enter will be in bytes. To convert the number of desired megabytes to bytes, multiply by 1,048,576.
6. Save the changes.
7. Quit ResEdit.

CAUTION: ResEdit should only be used by advanced users! Changing something you are not completely familiar with might, at least, corrupt the software you are trying to change to the point that you will have to reinstall it from the original floppies! Always make a backup copy of the file you want to change before opening the file with ResEdit. This gives you a fully functional backup in case you corrupt the file.

ALLOCATING RAM

You can see how much total RAM you have installed in your system by selecting "About This Macintosh..." from the Apple menu when you're in the Finder. The total amount of installed RAM is shown in kilobytes (KB) after the words "Total Memory." RAM is allocated to Photoshop, and other applications, through the Get Info command under the Finder's

File menu. The info box for Photoshop has an area in the bottom-right corner that allows you to specify how much of the available RAM you want Photoshop to be able to use. So, if you have 8 MB (8,192 KB) of RAM in your computer, you can probably allow Photoshop to use up to 7 MB (7,168 KB) or less, depending on how lean your System file is, how many INITs and Extensions you are running, and how many fonts you have installed. You enter the amount of RAM in KB that you want to allocate to Photoshop by clicking the mouse cursor in the Current size box and typing in the amount. One megabyte equals 1,024 kilobytes. You can do the math if you want to be picky, but we usually just enter whole numbers, so to allocate 7 MB, we would simply enter 7000.

Screen Display

Since Photoshop is a program that you will be using to work on images, you will want to be able to view them with the best possible quality.

QUIBBLES ON BITS

Twenty-four-bit color, or photo-realistic color, makes available 16,772,216 colors to any of a monitor's pixels at any given time. Since the human eye can discern substantially less than 16.7 million colors, 24-bit color is more than adequate for the display of images at the highest quality. Photo-realistic color requires a 24-bit display card or a Mac capable of 24-bit on-board video output. Twenty-four-bit display cards are available from a wide variety of manufacturers at an even wider variety of prices. However, the Quadra series of Macs has the ability to run a monitor at the 24-bit level without using a separate video card. The Quadra 700, 900, and 950 can, with 2 MB of video RAM (VRAM) installed, support 24-bit color on 12-, 13-, 14-, and 16-inch monitors from Apple and a number of third-party vendors.

COLOR IN THE FAST LANE

A number of very sophisticated 24-bit display cards are available for the Macintosh. Some include specialized circuitry to speed up the drawing of images to the screen. Generally, Photoshop does not benefit greatly from super-fast or accelerated video cards. If you are looking to speed up Photoshop functions, consider adding RAM or buying a faster computer before investing in an accelerated video board.

CHANGING MODES

An alternative for those without the money to spend on a 24-bit system is to work in a color mode that allows the display of up to 32,768 colors per monitor pixel. This mode is called 16-bit color. Most people can't tell the difference between an image displayed on a monitor in 16-bit and 24-bit color, and many of the newer Macs support 16-bit color through their built-in video circuitry. For example, the Performa, Quadra, and Centris all support 16-bit color on at least the Apple 12-inch color display.

CRAZY EIGHTS

If you can't work in 24- or 16-bit color, you can get away quite well with working in what is called 8-bit color. Eight-bit color allows any given monitor pixel to display one of up to 256 colors. Obviously, this severely limits the amount of color an image can contain and, therefore, the image will be displayed in a *dithered* mode. Dithering means that Photoshop will make the best use of the colors available to display an image so that it looks as good as possible. Unlike the difference between 16- and 24-bit displayed images, it is usually quite easy to see the difference between an image viewed in 8-bit color and 24-bit color. Most of the recent Macs support 8-bit color on-board on a variety of monitor sizes.

IT'S ALL BLACK AND WHITE

Don't forget that you can work with Photoshop on a screen which only displays black-and-white or grayscale images. Color images can be manipulated with Photoshop on a black-and-white or grayscale monitor just as if you were working on a color monitor. You just can't, obviously, see what you're doing in color. Photoshop, by the way, also happens to be a superb image manipulation program for noncolor images, and works quite efficiently on systems with monochrome displays.

Sizing Things Up

That brings us to monitor size. It can be safely said that when it comes to monitor or screen size, bigger is better. While larger monitors are definitely more expensive, the time you save in scrolling images up and down, not to mention the comfort gained from not straining to look at a dinky 9- or 12-inch screen, will be appreciated. Nineteen-, 20- and 21-inch monitors are *de rigeur* for Photoshop pros. The range of choices in these and the popular 16- and 17-inch sizes are numerous and you should do your homework before deciding what's best for your needs—and pocketbook. Mac-specific magazines run frequent tests of large monitors, and display cards, and are a good source of information. However, the ultimate decision rests in your eyes. Try to see in person the differences in monitors you might be considering. It's difficult to make a wise choice sight unseen, especially if it's something you'll be looking at for hours on end.

Disk Drives

You can never have enough hard disk space and your hard disk is never fast enough. Are we being redundant here or what? First it's a fast computer and then it's oodles of RAM. Now you want a huge, quick hard disk, too? Well, sorry, but it's true. As mentioned above, if you are lucky enough to have enough RAM to enable Photoshop to contain your images, the capacity and speed of your hard drive become less important. But, if you're like most of us, Photoshop will be forced to use your hard disk for virtual memory. If you have a slow, low-capacity hard disk, you will be limiting not only Photoshop's speed, but the maximum size of the images you can work with. Not that it's bad. In fact, most of us aren't throwing around 40-MB files, so we can handle a little waiting in exchange for having money to pay the bills. But if you want Photoshop to work as fast as it can when using its virtual memory scheme, it will help to have a large, fast hard drive.

Scheming

Photoshop's virtual memory scheme is very well done. With version 2.5, you can select a primary and, if you need it, a secondary *scratch disk.* A scratch disk is what Photoshop calls the hard disk(s) it uses to hold data temporarily.

What can you do to speed up virtual memory, no matter the size and speed of your hard disk? Here are some tips:

1. Set the System Disk Cache in the Memory Control Panel to the lowest number possible.
2. Under System 7, also make sure you have Virtual Memory turned off in the Memory Control Panel.
3. Defragment the drive used for virtual memory by Photoshop with a hard disk utility like Norton Utilities' Speed Disk.

4. Don't use removable hard disks like Syquest or Bernoulli. Because these types of disks get rougher treatment than fixed hard disks, they are a bit less reliable. Their speed also leaves something to be desired, especially in comparison to a good fixed hard disk.

Drive Types

Today, there are a variety of media to use for storing data. All of the devices and technologies have their own peculiarities and features, and we will go over these briefly below.

MAGNETIC

This is the kind of disk most people have associated with their computers, either inside their Mac or as an external device. Magnetic disks use rapidly spinning platters of machined aluminum with a magnetic coating. Data is read from or written to the platters in millionths of a second by tiny heads attached to quickly moving arms. The speed of the platters and the speed with which the arms move across the platters generally determine a hard disk's speed in transferring data.

Magnetic hard disks are a relatively inexpensive, fast storage medium. Their cost per megabyte generally declines as you move to larger capacities, and the larger capacity disks are generally the fastest.

ARRAYS

Arrays are simply two or more magnetic hard disks attached via some controlling circuitry to act as one. Disk arrays, as they are sometimes called, are the fastest possible medium for storing large amounts of data, short of having enough RAM to do it—although the contents of data stored in RAM are lost as soon as the computer is turned off. Disk arrays are expensive, but those with a need for speed will want to look closely into this solution.

OPTICAL

Optical drives use a laser to read and write data onto media similar to a Compact Disk. Optical drives, called WORM (write once, read many times) drives, can store a large amount of data onto a super-stable, removable, CD-like platter. The drawback is that they are slow and once you store something using a WORM drive, it's there for good and cannot be changed, although it can be retrieved as many times as you like. WORM drives are used to store data you want to keep for a long time, and which you will want read-only access to. WORM drives have fallen out of fashion recently with the advent of optical technology, which allows you to write and read from the same type of CD-like disk. These drives, called magneto-optical drives, are described below.

MAGNETO-OPTICAL DRIVES

Magneto-optical drives are, like their name implies, a hybrid of magnetic and optical technology. They use disks that have tiny particles of metal embedded in them. The polarity of these particles can be altered by a laser which gives these drives the capability to store lots of data safely and to change it just like a magnetic hard disk. Magneto-optical drives are expensive compared to magnetic disks and are not as fast, although the gap is closing between the two varieties.

CD-ROM

A technology which is going through an explosion now is the CD-ROM. CD-ROM stands for Compact Disk–Read Only Memory. These discs look just like regular audio CDs, but they can hold over 600 MB of data. Unlike WORM drive disks, to store data, they require expensive hardware and software. However, the CD-ROM is not widely used as a personal storage medium, but as a way of distributing large amounts of data inexpensively to people who own CD-ROM drives. Stock photographs, typefaces, patterns, textures, and even software are being distributed safely and economically via CD-ROM formats, the most famous of which right now is Kodak's Photo CD system. People with color and/or black-and-white negatives or slides can send them to Kodak and have them scanned and stored on a special type of CD-ROM called a Photo CD. This medium is great for those without the money to purchase their own scanners, because it allows them to unload that time-consuming task onto someone else. Furthermore, the scan quality is excellent and should satisfy all but the most demanding applications.

Hardware capable of allowing individual users to make their own CD-ROMs is also on the market and will certainly be an area to watch in the future.

CPU Acceleration

If you can't afford to purchase a new, fast computer, you might want to consider how you could speed up the one you already own. It's sort of like putting a Porsche engine in a Geo.

The most common type of acceleration is to replace the Central Processing Unit (CPU) you're using now with a newer, faster version. Apple offers upgrades for some computers in which all of the Mac's circuitry is replaced. In some instances, a new case is included. Apple upgrades tend to be expensive, however, and a number of third-party suppliers have stepped in to satisfy those with more modest means.

HOW DOES IT WORK?

In Apple's case, the entire motherboard in an older machine is swapped for one with newer circuitry and a newer CPU. This must be done by an authorized Apple technician, and you will be without your Mac while the surgery is done. With third-party vendors, users can install many of the upgrades themselves and realize the same, or sometimes better, benefits.

THIRD-PARTY OPTIONS AVAILABLE

There are a number of companies that offer acceleration solutions for speeding up your Mac. DayStar Digital, for example, has a complete line of user-installable cards and replacement CPU chips. Radius, Applied Engineering, Tech Works, and others provide a myriad of alternatives at widely differing prices. In some cases, a user can simply slide a small circuit board into the Processor Direct, or NuBus, slot of a Mac and end up with a substantial speed increase. Other solutions require that the CPU chip itself be removed from the motherboard and replaced by a new one. This alternative is a bit more complicated than simply sliding in a board; but any evenhanded, patient user should be able to complete the task with little difficulty.

It is best to check out Mac-related magazines for advice when it comes to the specifics about CPU acceleration. The market is constantly changing and new products appear at a dizzying pace. Just be sure that you are aware of any compatibility issues with software you may own. As always, look before you leap.

Photoshop-Specific Acceleration

A relatively recent option available to Photoshop users is the ability to greatly increase the speed at which certain specific functions of Photoshop are accomplished. For example, companies like DayStar Digital, SuperMac, RasterOps, Newer Technology, Radius, and Spectral Innovations offer NuBus cards with specialized chips that will supposedly speed the application of some Photoshop filters by as much as 2000 percent! With the version 2.5 rewrite (discussed earlier), more of Photoshop's functions were opened up for third-party acceleration by DSP or RISC cards. Those who are considering the purchase of a card specifically for acceleration of Photoshop functions should be careful to compare any included software among manufacturers, since it is the software that allows the acceleration to take place.

HOW DOES IT WORK?

We're glad you asked. All of the above cards use custom-designed chips that can process specific instructions very quickly—more quickly than the Mac's main CPU can. By using special software provided by the card makers, some processor-intensive tasks, like the application of the Unsharp Mask filter, can be handled by these special high-speed chips instead of by the main CPU. It's like having a separate engine for each wheel of your car. Just think how fast you could go if each tire had it's own power source instead of just one engine for all four! The choice of the type of chips to use and the special software distinguishes these cards from each other.

DSP VS. RISC

The most common chip used for Photoshop-specific acceleration is called a Digital Signal Processor (DSP) chip. Used by the telephone company for years, these speed demons have made the jump to the Mac. DSP chips do a superior job of handling the kinds of calculations required for many of Photoshop's most complicated functions. Some boards even use two DSP chips that work together for the fastest possible results.

The other type of chip used is called a Reduced Instruction Set Computing (RISC) chip. These fast microprocessors are more efficient than today's generation of microprocessors because they require less internal code, or instructions, to get things done. RISC chips are easily programmable and have a potential impact across a wide variety of applications besides Photoshop.

Plug-Ins

While many of these boards are similar in the way they increase speed or in the type of chips they use, the software that accompanies the boards is the key to making them work. Version 2.0 of Photoshop allowed these companies to provide software with their boards that sped up many filter functions, like Sharpen, Sharpen More, Unsharp Mask, Blur, Blur More, Gaussian Blur, Resize, and Custom. With version 2.5 of Photoshop, many more functions are available to be accelerated by these boards.

HOOKS AND GRABS

The software is the key here. The hardware is more or less the same. Writing the software "hooks" that can "grab" certain functions and speed them up is the problem. Fortunately, Adobe has been very good about providing key portions of the Photoshop code to board vendors so that they can write the special software needed to accomplish the desired acceleration. This means that once you purchase one of these boards, updates that are provided via software as the hooks are the only things that change. That being the case, this leaves open the possibility that more software companies will allow these special hooks to be written for their programs so that they can take advantage of the sometimes incredible acceleration the cards offer.

IS IT WORTH IT?

If time is money to you, these boards are definitely worth it. We've seen a function such as an Unsharp Mask filter take over 2 minutes to be applied to a 6-MB image in Photoshop and less than 10 seconds using an acceleration board! We blazed through the revision of this book using the Thunder II card from SuperMac.

Before you buy, take a look at test results completed by the major Mac publications. While the hardware doesn't differ greatly among these boards, the software does. Adobe has come up with a scheme in which software accompanying these boards is given a special label—if it was written to conform to Adobe standards.

AVAILABLE PRODUCTS OVERVIEW

Provided below is a synopsis of some of the features of Photoshop-specific acceleration boards available at press time. We've used some of them and have included some personal comments where appropriate.

SuperMac ThunderStorm The ThunderStorm and Thunder II DSP boards use two AT&T chips to speed up Photoshop functions and filters. Storm Technology Inc., the image compression and decompression specialists, developed the board which will also accelerate the compression and decompression of images using Storm's Picture Press software. SuperMac includes software plug-ins to accelerate many of Photoshop's filters.

Radius DSP Booster The DSP Booster is available as a daughtercard for the Radius Rocket 68040 accelerators. Using two AT&T DSP chips, the DSP Booster speeds up Photoshop functions through software plug-ins provided by Radius. The card will also accelerate many of the Rocket's tasks and Radius promises to use the DSP Booster for other color publishing, CAD, and video applications.

DayStar Digital Charger The Charger is a dual DSP NuBus card that we used on a IIfx, a IIci, and a Quadra 950 with great results. The DayStar card is the same card as the SuperMac ThunderStorm which was developed by Storm Technology. DayStar includes a set of plug-ins and Storm's PicturePress software at no charge. According to DayStar, the Charger will also work with software modules developed by other manufacturers that support the SuperMac ThunderStorm and the Storm Technology PhotoFlash boards.

RasterOps PhotoPro The PhotoPro is a RISC-based acceleration board we used on a IIfx and a Quadra 950. RasterOps makes both a NuBus version and a daughtercard version that connects to certain RasterOps display boards. If you're short on NuBus slots and have one of the compatible RasterOps display boards, the daughtercard version is a good idea. The PhotoPro board comes with the requisite software plug-ins to speed up certain Photoshop functions and will also accelerate the compression and decompression of QuickTime PICT images.

Spectral Innovations Lightning Effects We didn't use the Lightning Effects II board by Spectral Innovations, but it is a NuBus-based DSP board with the same software plug-ins that accelerate Photoshop functions and filters as well as image compression and decompression.

Newer Technology Image Magic We didn't use this board, either, but Newer Technology's Image Magic DSP board uses one AT&T DSP chip for acceleration of Photoshop functions and filters.

Printers

What good is Photoshop if what you see on your screen can't be printed out in some fashion? While working in Photoshop is fun, having a print in your hands completes the circle. There are a number of options available for producing hard copy and a brief description of them follows.

DOT MATRIX

Who can forget about the good, old ImageWriter? Well, this dot-matrix printer, which uses small pins striking against a ribbon, is still a very viable way to output images created in Photoshop. In fact, it may be just the thing to add that special, retro-computer flair to your prints. While most dot-matrix printers produce black-and-white output, single-color and even four-color ribbons are available. Adobe even provides an ImageWriter color export module to print to an Apple ImageWriter using a color ribbon. If you're into economy, or maybe art, try using a dot-matrix printer with Photoshop.

LASER

With resolutions from 300 to 600 dots per inch (dpi) and even higher, laser printers are a decent output device for black-and-white and even grayscale images. Apple and Hewlett-Packard, for example, offer the ability to print images on their latest laser printers using a number of shades of gray to achieve remarkable quality. If you put out a newsletter or other publication that uses black-and-white photos, consider trying to output your halftones to your laser printer. Photoshop has numerous controls for adjusting the quality of halftones, and you might be surprised at what you can get away with.

INKJET

Inkjet printers are a couple of steps above the dot-matrix printer with color ribbon mentioned above. However, the quality of inkjet output can rival that of thermal wax printers described below. Inkjet printers use tiny jets to spray different color ink onto plain paper to produce full-color output. The prices of color inkjet printers is very near what a good dot-matrix printer would cost in some cases, so being able to afford decent color printing is certainly possible.

THERMAL WAX COLOR

Thermal wax color printers are perhaps the least expensive way to get a good, color image output on paper. Using special color-impregnated ribbons to produce their slick prints, thermal wax printers are available from many manufacturers at prices that rival regular laser printers. Thermal wax printers generally require that a special paper be used. This paper is sometimes flimsy and shiny, but recently some companies are touting their printers' ability to use good, laser bond paper. Thermal wax printers excel at producing transparencies because of the way they transfer color to the media. With color becoming more and more popular, the prices for thermal wax printers have fallen sharply.

PHASE-CHANGE COLOR

Phase-change color printers are a relative newcomer to the color printer field. Using colored wax sticks instead of ink or ribbons, phase-change printers produce excellent quality prints on a variety of plain paper or transparencies up to 11 by 17 inches in size. One drawback to phase-change printers is that they generally don't do a great job on transparencies.

DYE-SUBLIMATION COLOR

Dye-sublimation printers produce some of the best color output you will ever see. The quality of a print produced by one of these printers rivals prints produced in a traditional darkroom. Using expensive ribbons and special paper, dye-sublimation printers are used by those who require the best possible output, at the highest cost per page. Dye-sublimation printer prices have been steadily falling, so if you need the best, check them out.

OTHER HIGH-END PRINTERS

Photoshop is also used by newspapers, magazines, book publishers, and printers to produce high-quality color images. To get those images requires specialized, expensive output devices such as large printing presses. There also exist high-end inkjet printers, which are used to make color proofs of things like advertisements and newspaper pages before they are printed; they run anywhere from $30,000 on up.

Other Output Devices

Photoshop is a valuable tool for producing color separations via high-resolution output devices like imagesetters. Imagesetters can output Photoshop files onto paper or film at resolutions above 2000 dpi. Photoshop is also a valuable tool for producing 35mm and larger color slides for presentations and other uses.

IMAGESETTERS

Imagesetters are specialized machines, optimized for high-resolution output of images and text. They are usually used by those who handle images that will be printed by a printing press. Imagesetters produce the pieces of film or paper which will be used to make plates that will be used on a press. Resolutions of 1200 to 2500 dpi are very common in the imagesetter world, with higher numbers possible. If you are using Photoshop to output to an imagesetter, you should get to know the output device you are using very well. Special software might be required for you to add to Photoshop so that it can properly prepare your image for output to an imagesetter.

FILM RECORDERS

Film recorders are machines that are dedicated to producing prints or slides for use in presentations of some sort, or film for conventional color separations. These machines use film cameras and special imaging chips to expose an image to the film in the camera. The film is then developed. Film recorders also produce images using large-resolution numbers—some up to 16,000 dpi! A variety of film recorders from various manufacturers are available. Their price is usually determined by their resolution and their speed. If you make a lot of presentation slides, a film recorder might be a good investment, especially since having slides made by a service bureau can be expensive over time.

CHAPTER 2

Setup and Document Management

Introduction

You will discover that Photoshop is full of menus, dialogs, and controls for an exhaustive selection of tools and features. Navigating through this maze can take some time and requires a certain degree of patience.

This chapter looks at some of the more important concepts of Photoshop, including the display modes, program preferences, and the process involved in creating and saving files. Do not be overwhelmed by the sheer number of options in the program. If approached methodically, Photoshop has a very logical organization and way of working.

General Organization

When you begin using Photoshop, your first impression may be that you are in one of the most complicated graphics programs you have ever seen. That is probably true; you don't often see graphics programs quite this dense (though programs such as Macromedia Director certainly come close). This is the price one pays for power.

Some software, such as Director and Microsoft Word, have Short/Full or Beginner/Expert modes. These modes toggle certain features that the beginner might find confusing or intimidating. Once familiar with the basic operations of a program, you can then turn on the full, or expert, menus to access all of the features of the software. Photoshop does not offer a similar set of modes; all of the program's features are always there, whether you need them or not. However, after you spend some time with Photoshop, you'll find that it's more straightforward that you might have imagined.

The Menus

The Menus in Photoshop

File: Contains all of the pertinent file functions (New, Open, Place, Save, Close, etc.), as well as menus (Acquire and Export) for any external drivers or plug-ins (such as JPEG compression routines, scanner drivers, printers), preferences, and printing functions.

Edit: There are basic editing functions (Cut, Copy, and Paste); special paste modes; Fill, Pattern, and Crop commands; access to System 7 Publish and Subscribe; and controls for compositing images.

Mode: Various display modes allow for the processing of images in black-and-white, additive color (red, green, and blue), subtractive color (cyan, magenta, yellow, and black), Lab color, and indexed color systems.

Image: Controls image processing, multichannel effects, dynamic effects (such as flipping, rotating, scaling, distorting), resizing and resampling, histogram, and trap.

Filter: Numerous filters for enhancing, sharpening, blurring, manipulating and distorting images.

Select: Special features that apply to the selection tools, including access to channels.

Figure 2–1
The Photoshop Menus

File Edit Mode Image Filter Select Window

Window: New windows of a document; zoom controls; rulers; palettes to control brush sizes, channels, colors, and paths; and an information window.

For a full discussion of the menus, see Chapters 4, 5, and 6 (Figure 2–1).

Screen Display Management

By default, the tool palette is automatically opened when Photoshop is opened. Other palettes can be opened by selecting the commands under the Windows menu. The palettes available are Brushes, Channels, Colors, Info, and Paths. See Chapter 4, "Using the Tools and Palettes," for a full discussion about palettes.

At the bottom of the main tool palette you will find three small icons that control the screen display mode (Figure 2–2).

The default mode is the left-hand icon, which displays the menu bar and all open document windows. When you click on the middle icon, the current active document fills the screen and the menu bar remains visible. When you click on the icon to the absolute right, the menu bar disappears, expanding the current active document to fill the whole screen.

***Tip*: You can temporarily make the tool palette and any other open palette (window) invisible by pressing the Tab key on your keyboard; this toggles the palettes on and off.**

Assuming that you have enough memory, try working with more than one document open at a time. Open a new image by selecting New or Open under the File menu, or switch the active document by opening the Window menu, and choose another open document from the list of open files at the bottom of the Window menu. Or simply click anywhere on the window of an open document and it will move to the front as an active document.

You can zoom into and out from an image by using the magnifier tool in the main tool palette. Simply click the magnifier where you want to zoom in, and press the Option key to use the magnifier to zoom out, or away. You will know whether you are zooming in or out because the

Figure 2–2
Screen display mode icons on the tool palette

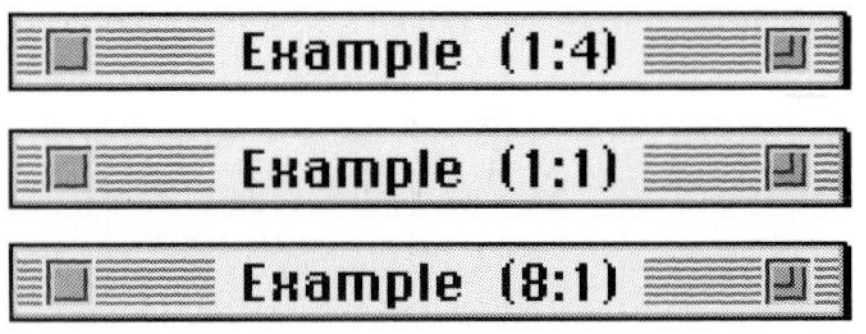

Figure 2–3
The Title Bars showing the zoom factor of 1:4 (reduced to 25%), 1:1 (actual size), and 8:1 (800% magnification)

magnifier icon will contain a "+" character when zooming in and a "–" character when zooming out. When the character disappears from inside the zoom tool, you know that you are as far as you can go. The maximum magnification and reduction ratios are 16:1 (1600%) and 1:16.

Zoom controls are also located in the Window menu. You can use these instead of the magnifier tool, but you will probably want to use the keyboard equivalents [Command-+ (plus) for magnification, Command- – (minus) for reduction], instead of the magnifier tool.

Other keyboard shortcuts for zooming and scrolling are: Command, Spacebar and click with the mouse on the area to zoom in; Option, Command, Spacebar, and click on the area to zoom out; and Spacebar and press and drag with the mouse will scroll (Hand Tool).

***Tip*: To zoom in on a particular area to the maximum magnification possible in the current window size, select the zoom tool and then press and drag a rectangle on the desired area. Double-clicking on the zoom tool will restore the 1:1 view of the image.**

The current magnification ratio is displayed in the title bar of a document's window: as you zoom in and out of a document, the ratio is updated in the title bar (Figure 2–3). This ratio represents the relationship of the screen resolution to the image resolution. That is, at a 1:1 view the resolution of the screen and the image are matched. Photoshop is using every pixel of the monitor to represent every pixel of recorded information in the image. A high-resolution image will appear very large at a 1:1 view and a low-resolution image will appear smaller. Zooming in and out only changes the view of an image, not its size.

T*ip*: If you are working on a document and wish to create multiple views of the image, you can choose the New Window command from the Windows menu. This is useful for creating multiple, simultaneous magnification views of a working document. If you paint in one view, the other views are updated immediately after you release the mouse button.

Document Size Indicator

In the lower-left corner of a document window is a numerical readout of the size of the document, in kilobytes (Figure 2–4).

Most of the time, this is the size of the document as saved on disk. We've found that in certain cases, such as 24-bit PICT files, the disk size is smaller than the size that appears in the size indicator.

T*ip*: In the case of 24-bit PICTs, a 640 × 480 image might take up 379K on disk, but when opened into Photoshop, the size indicator displays a size of 900K (the size of a 640 × 480 RGB image). If you manipulate the image without resizing it, and save it back to disk as a 24-bit PICT, the size will be reduced back to the original incoming PICT file size.

PREVIEWING PAGE SIZE

If you press and hold on the size indicator number, a Page Preview window pops up and displays a dummy of a full page (as specified in the Page Setup dialog). It shows a bounding box of the total area occupied by the document. Even if you have two separate elements on two extreme sides of the document, the bounding box is drawn based on the defined size of the document (Figure 2–5).

If your image is larger than the current page size, you'll notice that the bounding box extends off the edge of the page (Figure 2–5). Be careful, the image will print cropped. Photoshop cannot tile an image for multiple-page registered output, a capability found in many page layout programs. You will have to take Photoshop images into Aldus PageMaker, QuarkXPress, or another program that has tiling capabilities.

Anything selected in the Page Setup dialog is reflected in the miniature page view, including crop and registration marks, calibration bars, negative output, and emulsion type (Figure 2–6).

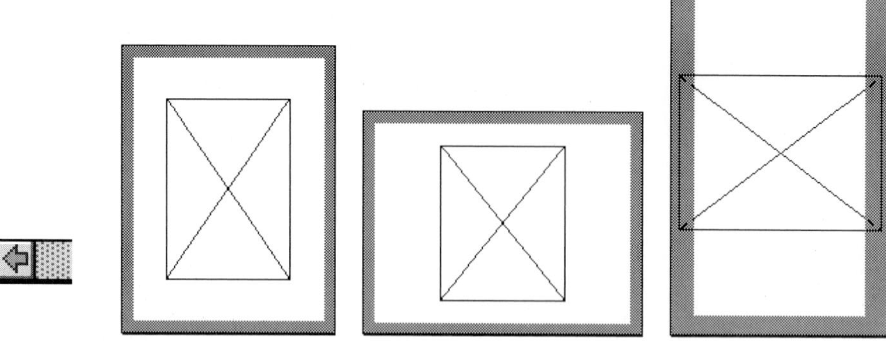

Figure 2–4
The Document Size Indicator is in the lower-left corner of a document window.

Figure 2–5
The Page Preview pop-up display appears by pressing on the Document Size Indicator in the lower-left corner of a document window.

OTHER SIZE PARAMETERS

If you press the Option key while pressing on the size indicator, the Page Preview display is replaced by a numerical readout that includes information on the resolution, size, and number of channels in the document (Figure 2–7).

The size of the image is displayed in both pixels and any other units selected in the Units dialog found in the Preferences command under the File menu.

The size and resolution of the document can be controlled in the Image Size dialog under the Image menu. If you need some extra space to work with around an image, go to the Canvas Size dialog also under the Image menu. Image Size and Canvas Size are explained in Chapter 6, "Image Processing."

Rulers

You can turn on Photoshop's onscreen rulers by choosing the Rulers command under the Window menu. The measurement units used in the rulers display are set with the Units submenu found in the Preferences command under the File menu. You can set the units individually for the vertical and horizontal rulers. The available units are inches, centimeters, picas, and points (and in the case of the width, columns, discussed in the next two sections, "Setting Preferences" and "General Preferences."

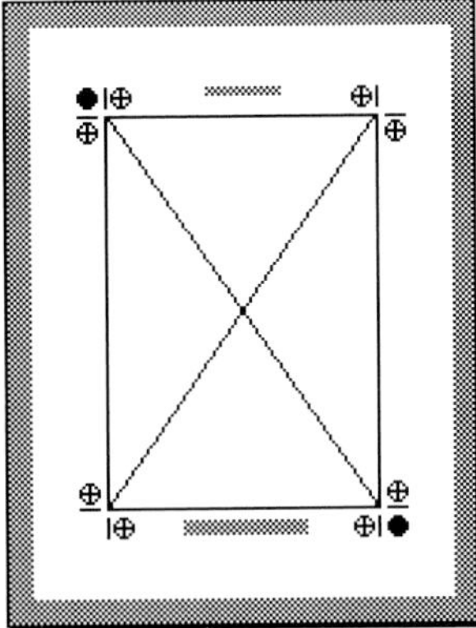

Figure 2–6
The Page Preview pop-up display will display crop marks, registration marks, and calibration bars which are turned on in the Page Setup dialog.

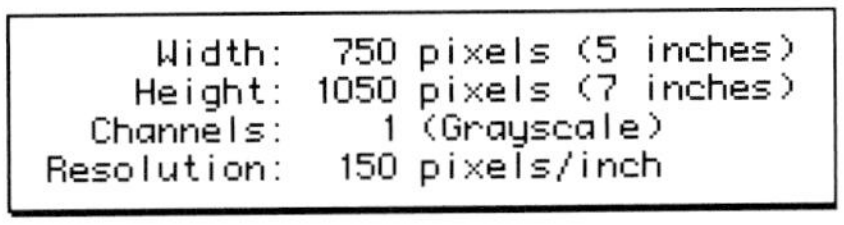

```
     Width:  750 pixels (5 inches)
    Height: 1050 pixels (7 inches)
  Channels:    1 (Grayscale)
Resolution:  150 pixels/inch
```

Figure 2–7
A numerical readout appears if you hold the Option key down while pressing on the Document Size Indicator.

You can also change the ruler's origin points by dragging from the upper-left corner where the two rulers meet (Figure 2–8). This control works exactly as its equivalent in many other Macintosh design programs. Press the pointer in this area, drag to the new desired zero origin location, and release the mouse button. Double-clicking on the upper-left corner where the two rulers meet will restore the origin point of the rulers.

Setting Preferences

Photoshop remembers a variety of your default settings by creating a Preferences file which is stored in your Preferences folder. If you look in the File menu, you will see the Preferences submenus (Figure 2–9). In the Preferences dialog boxes, you can adjust controls that affect the behavior of various aspects of the program. These settings control general display options, keyboard function keys, assigning scratch disks for virtual memory, color separation setup information, calibration options, display options, tool options, ruler units, and options for exporting information from the Clipboard.

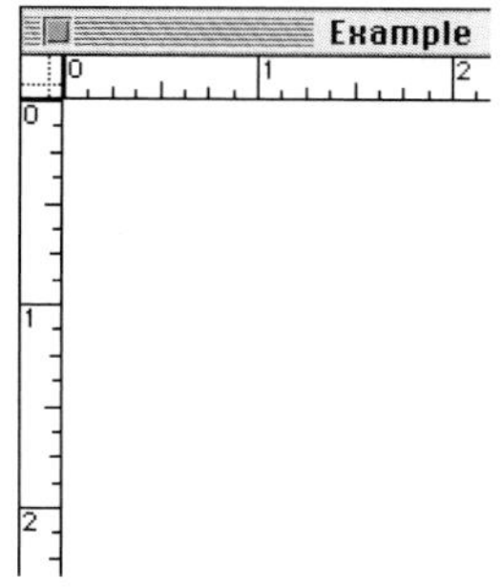

Figure 2–8
The Ruler's zero origin point can be changed by pressing and dragging from the upper-left corner of the rulers.

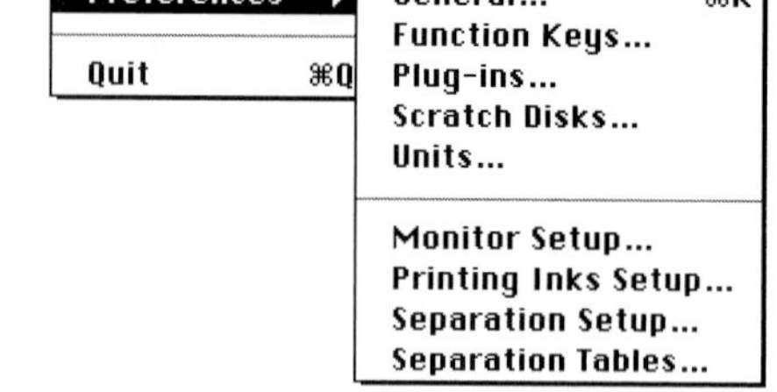

Figure 2–9
The Preferences submenus, found under the File menu

NOTE: Be aware that once you set or change any of the preferences, the settings affect all future documents that are opened in Photoshop.

Some of the preference settings affect only how a document is viewed on the screen, some affect the output only and some affect both. Be aware of what the settings are actually doing.

General Preferences

General Preferences has a variety of settings that affect how documents are viewed and manipulated (see Figure 2–10).

COLOR PICKER

You have your choice of either the standard Apple Color Picker or the Photoshop Color Picker. The Apple Color Picker allows you to select colors from a color wheel, which is the same in all Macintosh applications. The Photoshop Color Picker offers much more control in the selection of colors. For example, it alerts you of colors that cannot be printed. Colors may be selected from a choice of several color systems: HSB (hue, saturation, and brightness), RGB (red, green, and blue), CMYK (cyan, magenta, yellow, and black), Lab (luminance and chroma), or Custom Color Palettes. See Chapter 4, "Using the Tools and Palettes," for more on selecting and using colors.

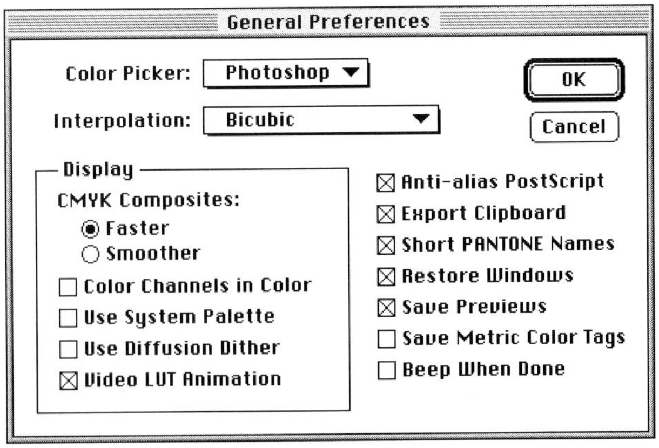

Figure 2–10
The General Preferences dialog box

INTERPOLATION

The process of interpolation is how Photoshop determines the color of added or deleted pixels when an image is resampled, rotated, or has had any special effects applied. All of the dynamic effects in Photoshop, including resizing (both the interactive resizing controls and the Resize command in the Image menu), distortion, perspective, and rotation commands are tied into the interpolation settings. The quality and speed performance of these features are directly affected by the interpolation mode selected in the Preferences dialog:

- **Nearest Neighbor** is the fastest of the methods, yielding the lowest quality. If you use this when distorting or resizing an image, you'll immediately notice that the image is recalculated with a large amount of distortion.
- **Bilinear** is a medium-quality method, with the quality residing somewhere between nearest neighbor and bicubic.
- **Bicubic** is the slowest of the methods, but gives you the highest-quality results. This method is the default setting when you run the program.

Here are three examples, using the Distort commands, of the differences in quality when using the three modes (Figure 2–11).

Display

There are several options that control how documents are displayed on the monitor. These display options do not affect the output data; they affect only what you see on the screen.

Nearest Neighbor

Bilinear

Bicubic

Figure 2–11 These examples show Nearest Neighbor, Bilinear, and Bicubic interpolation methods. They had Scale, Skew, Perspective, Distort, and Rotate commands applied to them.

CMYK COMPOSITES

When working in CMYK Color mode the computer has to temporarily convert the pixels of the image to the red, green, and blue primary colors of the monitor. With the Faster option selected, the screen is drawn almost as fast as when working in RGB Color mode. These colors and values will be less accurate than if you select the Smoother option. Obviously, the latter is going to take longer.

COLOR CHANNELS IN COLOR

When you view individual Lab, RGB, or CMYK channels on the screen, you may choose to have them represented as grayshades or in the actual color of the channel. For example, when looking at the red, green, and blue channels of a 24-bit color image, you can view the channels in their actual colors—the red channel displayed in shades of red, for example. Viewing a channel in grayshades is important because it is sometimes difficult to view a channel in its actual color—yellow is a perfect example. Viewing channels without colors enabled allows you to precisely view the color saturation (by looking at corresponding gray values) of a given channel.

If you're using a grayscale monitor or black-and-white system, this setting will have no effect on your display.

USE SYSTEM PALETTE

When working with Photoshop on a system with an 8-bit video display, you can force the display to always use the standard Macintosh System palette to display all visible windows. When working with multiple 24-bit Photoshop files, each time you select a different document window, you will notice that the colors in each of the other document windows "go crazy" for a few moments. This happens because Photoshop is calculating an optimized 256-color palette to best represent the 24-bit data in the active document. When this happens, the colors in the other open documents are remapped to the colors in the current active palette, resulting in a fun, but useless, color effects show. By activating "Use System palette," you are effectively forcing Photoshop to use the standard Apple 256-color default palette to represent all of the open documents. The result is that you will have a less accurate 8-bit representation of an image's 24-bit data, but all of the open windows will show consistent color.

Be sure to use this option if you are using an 8-bit video display and you plan to work with multiple color files at one time. If you've opened files from any program that can create and save images with custom 256-color palettes, you will notice that as you click on each different window the colors in the other windows will redraw, and much of the time they will look very odd. This is because the custom color palette for the currently selected window overrides all other palettes. This redrawing becomes more noticeable depending on how many documents are open at once, and on the resolution of the images. The big problem you'll run into here is that if your open documents are high-resolution images, screen redraw might become quite bothersome (the higher the resolution of an image, the longer it takes to redraw the image on the screen).

***Tip*: One way to know that a custom palette is being used by the foreground window is to check the little colored apple used by the desk accessory menu. If its colors aren't the normal rainbow, a custom palette is being used, and the normal rainbow colors are being replaced by the custom colors in the active palette.**

USE DIFFUSION DITHER

By selecting this option, color transitions in an image will be enhanced when using an 8-bit video display. Dithering gives the illusion of a color or value in between adjacent pixels.

The "Use System Palette" and "Use Diffusion Dither" controls will have no effect if you are running Photoshop in 24-bit display mode with a 24-bit video card. In this case, many different 256-color palettes can be handled simultaneously without palette remapping.

VIDEO LUT ANIMATION

With "Video LUT Animation" on, while using the image-processing controls (the Map and Adjust commands), and with the preview button not selected, all open Photoshop documents will show changes as they are being made in real-time. If the preview box is selected, the adjustments will show only in the active document. With "Video LUT Animation" off, when using image-processing controls with the preview button deselected, open windows will not show changes as they are being made. If the preview box is selected, the adjustments will show only in the active document.

ANTI-ALIAS POSTSCRIPT

When placing or pasting a postscript vector image (e.g., Adobe Illustrator) into Photoshop, this option will improve the quality of an image as it is being rasterized. Because it takes more work, this function will slow down the operation.

EXPORT CLIPBOARD

By deselecting this option the clipboard will be emptied when switching applications or when quitting Photoshop. If you want to copy and paste between programs, leave this on.

Tip: Every time you open a desk accessory while in Photoshop, or switch to another program, the clipboard is processed according to the clipboard export option you've selected. If you have a large image on the clipboard, this conversion process can become quite annoying, as it makes you wait until the conversion is done before proceeding. If you need to access a peripheral desk accessory while in Photoshop or if you want to work in another program, you will want to abandon "Export Clipboard." Obviously, if you want to copy and paste between programs, leave it on.

SHORT PANTONE NAMES

This preference is important to use if you are planning on exporting duotones, tritones, or quadtones to other programs and you are using Pantone names for the colors (see Figure 2–12). If you do not use Short Pantone Names the colors will not output on the corresponding plates when making separations in other programs because the names will not have the same spellings (unless you manually specify the spelling in each of the programs). See Chapter 7, "Advanced Photoshop Techniques," for more on creating duotones, tritones, and quadtones, and see Chapter 9, "Output," for printing considerations.

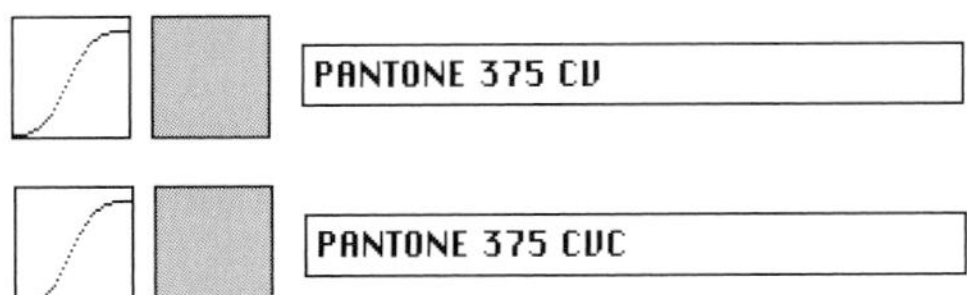

Figure 2–12
Use the "Short Pantone Names" option to avoid costly output mistakes.

RESTORE WINDOWS

Select this option if you want Photoshop to remember the position of all your open windows the next time you open it; otherwise only the default windows (toolbox and Brushes palette) will open.

SAVE PREVIEWS

When running System 7, this option will show thumbnail images of the documents as icons in folders on the desktop. This is helpful for remembering what they look like without opening them.

SAVE METRIC COLOR TAGS

Photoshop version 2.5.1 enables you to save files with EFI Color metric color tags, assuring color consistency between Photoshop, QuarkXPress, and numerous output devices.

BEEP WHEN DONE

This reminder will tell your computer to beep when an operation is completed. You may then continue to work on your machine. This is helpful when performing time-consuming tasks, letting you read or daydream.

Function Keys

Many Photoshop operations can be simplified by the use of the function keys. If you are working with a keyboard that has function keys, you can use the preset key assignments, or you can modify them or create additional key assignments. The preset assignments can be changed and additional ones can be created in order to make use of all the function keys.

To assign a command to a function key, click on the text box next to the function key number and then choose the desired command or type it in. (Remember, spelling counts.) Additional function keys can be assigned by selecting the shift option (Figure 2–13).

Plug-Ins

This preference allows you to change the folder location of the plug-ins. You must restart Photoshop to execute this change.

Scratch Disks

When the RAM (random access memory) runs out of working space, Photoshop uses a designated hard disk to assist in temporarily storing data and computing information.

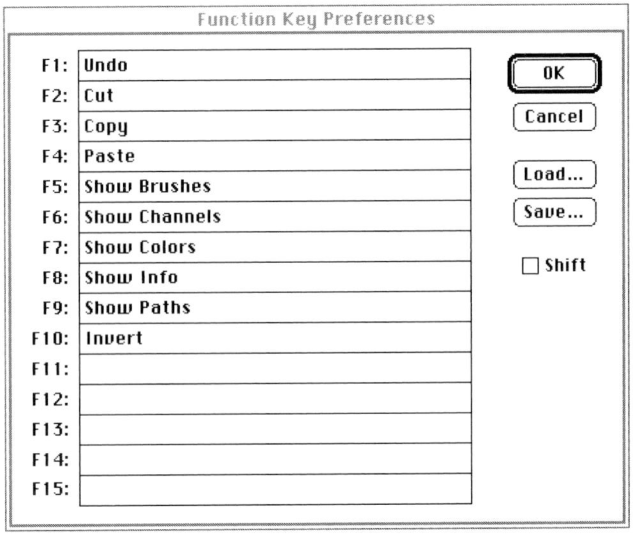

Figure 2–13
Function keys can be assigned to most commands.

Tip: The process of using disk space for RAM, called virtual memory, is built into System 7. Virtual memory needs to be turned off in the Memory control panel for Photoshop's virtual memory to work correctly.

Virtual memory in Photoshop can be assigned to any hard disk attached to your Mac (Figure 2–14). The default scratch disk for virtual memory is the startup disk, but any disk on your system can be used. You can even assign a secondary disk to use in case the primary one becomes overloaded. It's a good idea to use your fastest hard disk and make sure to leave as much space free as possible.

Units

You can specify ruler units in pixels, inches, centimeters, points, and picas. These units apply to any dialog box or window that uses measurements.

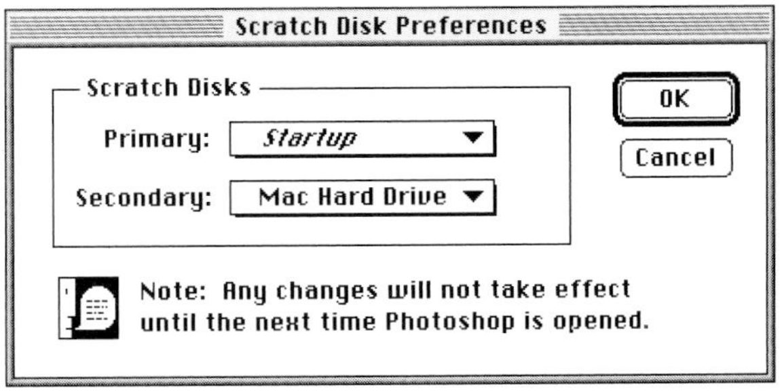

Figure 2–14
Virtual memory can be assigned to any hard disks on the SCSI chain.

The Column size and gutter controls allow you to "simulate" multiple-column layouts within Photoshop. This is especially useful because you can create comprehensive layouts without needing to use a page layout program. By setting a fixed column and gutter size that corresponds to the related settings in your page layout program, you can crop images with the assurance that the ratio of the cropped image will match the column specifications in the receiving page layout program. You can specify columns as a measurement unit in the cropping tool control dialog when resampling an image and when setting up output size in the size/rulers dialog in the Page Setup command (Figure 2–15).

Monitor Setup

The Monitor Setup dialog balances several factors that affect how colors and values are seen on the monitor (Figure 2–16). It also affects the conversion of colors between modes. Monitor Setup should only be used as part of the calibration process.

> **NOTE: Monitor Setup, Printing Inks Setup, and Separation Setup are all part of the calibration process. See Chapter 8, "Output," for more information on calibration.**

Printing Inks Setup

Printing Inks Setup affects the conversion to CMYK Color mode (see Figure 2–17). It also adjusts the colors and values when printing to a CMYK postscript printer and you are outputting from other than the CMYK mode. Its function is to adjust for the dot gain and color gamut of the final printing device (offset printing press or digital printer).

Selecting "Use Dot Gain for Grayscale Images" will adjust the monitor to reflect the selected dot gain, but will not affect the output.

Separation Setup

This preference controls the amount of black that is generated in the black plate when converting to CMYK Color mode (Figure 2–18). It also affects the black generation when printing to a CMYK postscript printer when outputting from other than the CMYK mode.

The Separation Type buttons toggle the choice GCR (Gray Component Replacement) or UCR (Undercolor Removal). The black generation can be set to None, Light, Medium, or Maximum. A custom setting is also possible.

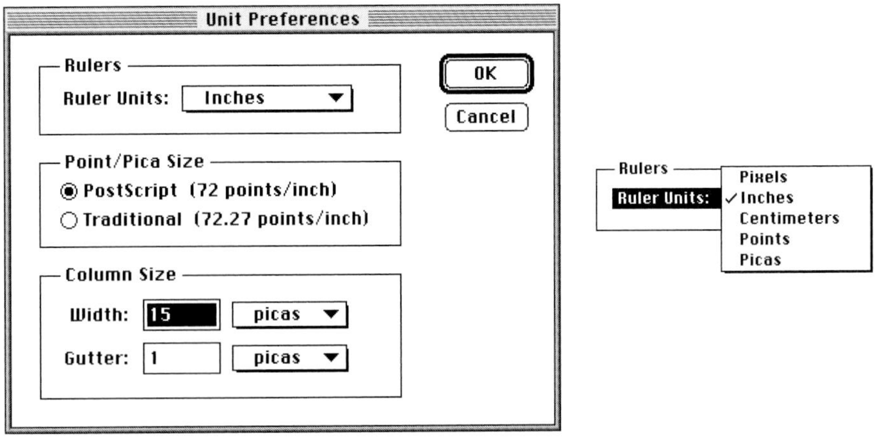

Figure 2–15
The Unit Preferences dialog

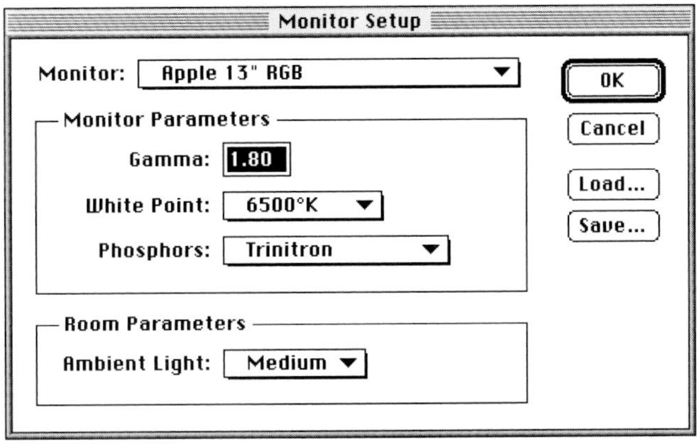

Figure 2–16
The Monitor Setup dialog

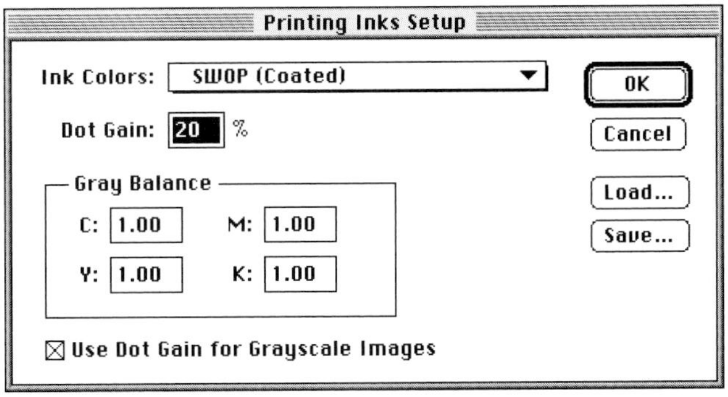

Figure 2–17
The Printing Inks Setup dialog

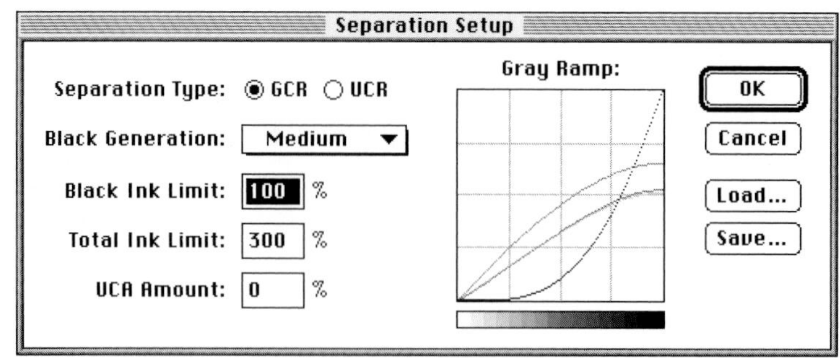

Figure 2–18
The Separation Setup dialog controls the generation of the black plate when converting to CMYK Color mode.

Separation Tables

If you print images to a variety of output devices or different paper stocks, Separation Tables (see Figure 2–19) can be used to save and then load the settings made in Separation Setup and Printing Inks Setup.

Color tables can be built with Apple's ColorSync matching system, which is now part of System 7. We found that scanning with Ofoto, the ColorSync tables created with Ofoto could be accessed via Separation Tables.

Tip: Don't adjust Monitor Setup, Printing Inks Setup, or Separation Tables in the middle of a project unless you are sure about what you are doing. Generally these settings are adjusted as part of the calibration process or after consultation with your printer and/or service bureau. See Chapter 8, "Output," for more on calibration, working with a service bureau, and printing.

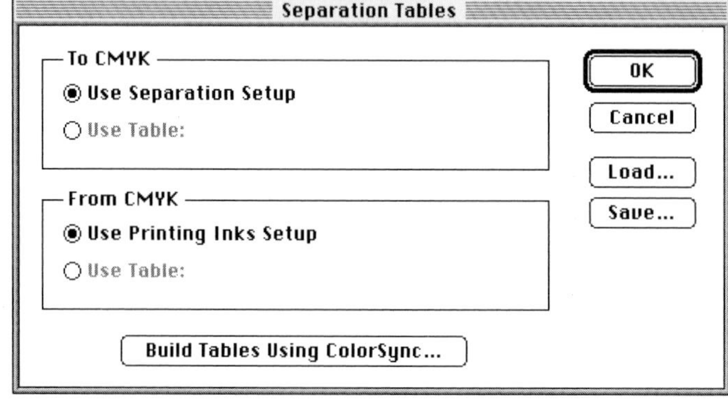

Figure 2–19
The Separation Tables dialog

Display Formats and Modes

The most basic features of Photoshop are the display modes available from the Mode menu. Different display modes are used to represent different types of images on the screen, and to allow you to change the image on the screen in various ways, such as the CMYK mode, used to convert images for prepress output. For example, you will use the different display modes for the following:

Mode
Bitmap...
Grayscale
Duotone...
Indexed Color
RGB Color
CMYK Color
Lab Color
Multichannel
Color Table...

- Editing grayscale images
- Creating and manipulating duotones
- Working with color images and creating color separations
- Preparing images for optimized screen display quality
- Creating and using masks with color and grayscale images
- Working in the fully featured native Photoshop format
- Working with imported Photo CD images

Before we discuss the various display modes, it's important to understand some basic concepts regarding how Photoshop deals with its world.

In Photoshop, every pixel of a grayscale image (8 bits) has a brightness value ranging between 0 and 255; 0 is black, 255 is white, and the values in between correspond to the grayscale spectrum of 256 tones.

Every mode consists of a composite representation of distinct channels that create the image. Each channel is actually a grayscale image with 256 tones. These values are assigned color values which combine with other channels to create millions of colors. For example, in RGB mode there are three 8-bit channels with 256 tones in each channel. This totals 24 bits, yielding 16,777,216 colors.

Every pixel of a color image on a 24-bit monitor (the screen uses RGB to display colors regardless of the mode that you are in) consists of a mix of red, green, and blue tones. A pixel with a value of 0 for each of the RGB tones is black, while 255 for each of the RGB values results in a white pixel. A pixel with a red value of 255 and blue and green values of 0 is red, while values of 255 for both red and blue and 0 for green yield magenta.

> **NOTE: At this point it's important to clear up a mistake most people make when talking about "32"-bit color. There are only 24 bits of data dedicated to the color information found in an RGB image. The other 8 bits are dedicated to an alpha channel. Photoshop is an exception to this rule—it implements its own alpha channel mechanism, resulting in the ability to have multiple 8-bit channels assigned to each file. Because of this ability, a Photoshop file can actually have more than 32 bits per pixel. A CMYK color document has 4 channels, each with 8 bits of data, which also equals 32 bits. The term "32-bit file" is most often applied to exporting a video alpha channel, which is only supported by some video cards.**

Photoshop can have up to 16 channels in one document. When in RGB mode, the first three channels are reserved for red, green and blue. In CMYK mode the first four channels are reserved for cyan, magenta, yellow, and black. The remaining channels can be used as masks or to select and isolate parts of an image. Channels can be added to all of the modes except for the Bitmap mode.

***Tip*: Not all of the filters and image-processing features in Photoshop work with all of the display modes. For instance, if you want to process an imported 8-bit PICT file through most of Photoshop's special effects, you'll need to convert the indexed image to RGB, manipulate the image, convert it back to indexed color, and then save it in PICT format for exporting. When working with grayscale images, the only features that will not work are those specifically relating to color.**

To view and manipulate individual channels or combinations of channels, use the Channel palette in the Window menu. Notice that the "eye" indicates that you are viewing a channel and the "pencil" indicates that you can manipulate the selected channel. See Chapter 5, "Image Selection and Masking," for more on channels.

***Tip*: It is possible to view one channel and to manipulate another. But be careful. We have found that it is quite easy to accidentally work in the wrong channel unintentionally.**

The Display Modes

Bitmap

Black-and-white bitmaps are the most fundamental form of Mac graphics. You'll need black-and-white bitmaps if you work with HyperCard or are creating images to be used on a black-and-white computer (Mac SE, Classic, etc.). Another use of the Bitmap mode is to create dithered patterns and custom halftone screens for special effects. The Bitmap display mode is a simple black-and-white 1-bit display. All color and grayscale information is removed from the image when it is converted to Bitmap mode. To convert a color image to Bitmap mode, you must first convert it to a grayscale image, which simply removes the hue information, leaving the saturation and brightness values intact.

Normal MacPaint bitmap images are limited to 72 ppi, while the bitmap display mode in Photoshop allows you to have higher-resolution black-and-white images. When converting a color or grayscale image to bitmap mode within Photoshop, you can choose the output resolution used for the conversion process (Figure 2–20). The different settings result in various image sizes and dot densities.

To convert an image to bitmap mode:

1. Open a 72-ppi grayscale screen image.
2. Press and hold on the size indicator in the lower left-hand corner of the image window. Take note of the actual size of the image.
3. Select the bitmap display mode from the Mode menu. The Bitmap dialog will appear (Figure 2–20).
4. Specify 150 pixels/inch as the output resolution.

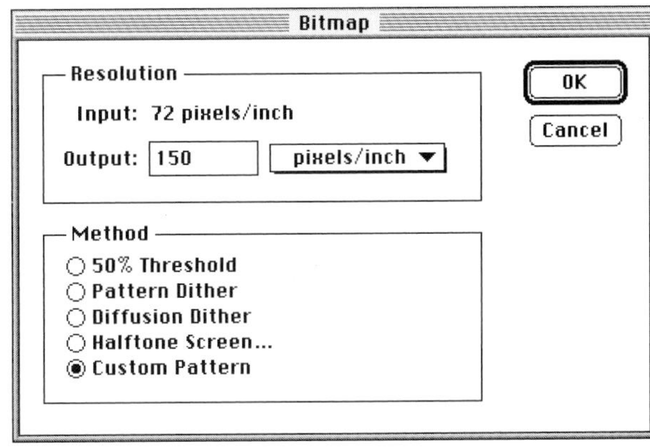

Figure 2–20
In the Bitmap dialog the output resolution and the dithering method can be set.

Note that the image seems to have been magnified in its window. In reality, the image is the same size, but at a higher pixel density. Press and hold on the size indicator in the lower-left side of the image window, and observe that the image is the same size as the original grayscale image.

The default settings in the Input and Output fields correspond to the resolution of the image being converted. You can specify the units for output to be either pixels per inch or pixels per centimeter by pressing on the pop-up menu button on the right-hand side of the units field. To change the input units, select the Image Size option under the Image menu and then change the unit format in the New Size area.

***Tip*: With the Bitmap mode, you have full control over the characteristics of the halftone dots used to draw the image to the screen, as well as special dithering modes for optimized screen-display of the bitmapped image. This mode is good for creating images with a jagged or aliased look, which is sometimes desirable as a design effect. It is also good if you wish to process an image through a custom halftone screen and then convert the halftone image back into RGB Color mode for special effects.**

When converting a grayscale image (Figure 2–21) to Bitmap mode, you can apply one of five types of dithering or halftone screens to the image:

50% Threshold: This converts the image into a high-contrast, non-textured bitmap. When analyzing the grayscale image, pixels with a value of 128 or higher are converted to white, and those with values of 127 or lower are converted to black. (Compare Figures 2–21 and 2–22.) This is called a line shot in conventional photography.

Pattern Dither: This conversion method "clumps" the grayscale values into geometric groups of black-and-white dots as in Figure 2–23.

Diffusion Dither: This is one of the most visually pleasing conversion modes. The look is reminiscent of the grainy look of early Macintosh-scanned images produced with the Koala MacVision digitizer. This is usually the preferable conversion option when preparing images for viewing on a black-and-white screen (Figure 2–24).

Figure 2–21
The original grayscale image

Figure 2–22
50% Threshold

Figure 2–23
Pattern dither

Figure 2–24
Diffusion dither

Halftone Screen: This conversion method allows you to process an image through a variety of halftone screens. While this technique is usually used when printing an image, this conversion method allows you to create printed halftone effects on the Mac screen (a very helpful visual effect), as well as to "pre-halftone" an image for optimized printing on a non-PostScript printer. Using this technique, you can print custom halftones on any non-PostScript printer—something which has been quite impossible until the arrival of Photoshop.

When choosing this conversion method, you are presented with a dialog box containing the halftone options (Figure 2–25). You may enter specific halftone screen frequencies, which are measured in lines per inch, as well as the screen angle of the halftone. Different screen frequencies are used depending on the final output applications. For example, when preparing an image for output to a 300-dpi non-PostScript printer, a frequency value between 53 and 75 lines per inch and an angle value of 45 degrees will produce the best results. There are also six types of dot shapes, each producing a different effect (Figure 2–26).

Tip: You can save settings to your disk and then load them later for use with other images.

Custom Pattern: This option is used when you have predefined an area of an image as a pattern. Normally, this is done to create a custom fill or painting pattern for use with the painting tools (see Chapter 4, "Using the Tools and Palettes"). When used in conjunction with the Bitmap mode, you can create gorgeous custom mezzotint effects (Figure 2–27 and Figures C–25 and C–26 in the Color Section). This conversion option is discussed in Chapter 7, "Advanced Photoshop Techniques."

Tip: The Custom pattern conversion option is only available if you have defined a custom pattern during the current work session. Make sure that the pattern image size is as large as the image that it will be applied to; otherwise the pattern will be tiled to fill the entire image area.

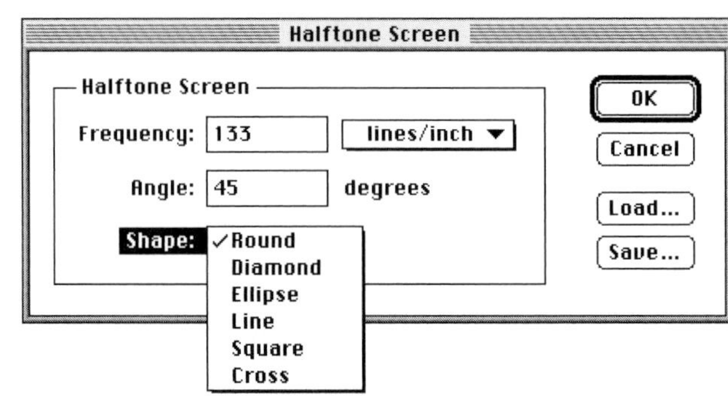

Figure 2–25
The Halftone Screen dialog allows you to set the screen frequency, angle, and shape.

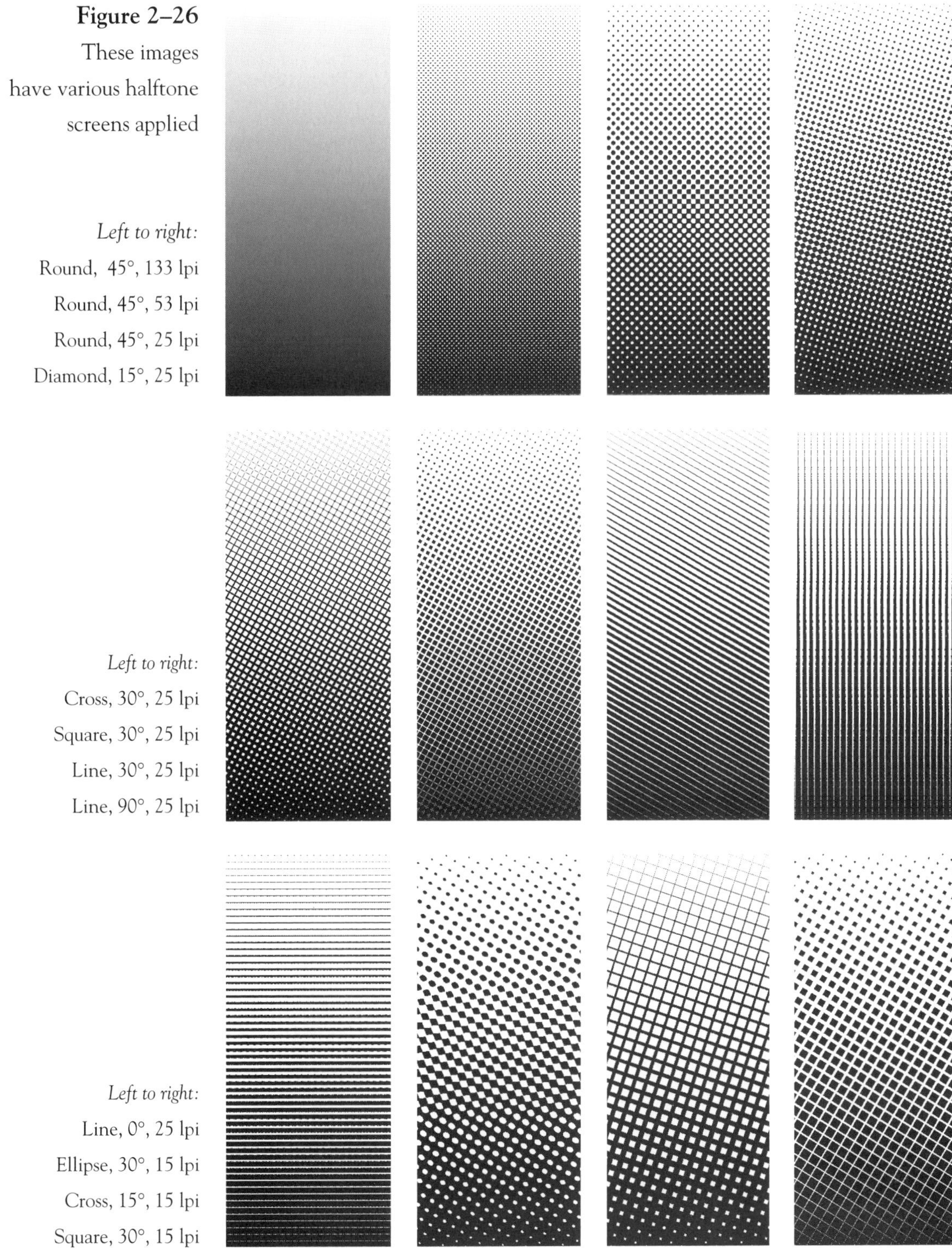

Figure 2–26
These images have various halftone screens applied

Left to right:
Round, 45°, 133 lpi
Round, 45°, 53 lpi
Round, 45°, 25 lpi
Diamond, 15°, 25 lpi

Left to right:
Cross, 30°, 25 lpi
Square, 30°, 25 lpi
Line, 30°, 25 lpi
Line, 90°, 25 lpi

Left to right:
Line, 0°, 25 lpi
Ellipse, 30°, 15 lpi
Cross, 15°, 15 lpi
Square, 30°, 15 lpi

Figure 2–27
Custom Halftone screen applied

When you convert a bitmap image into Grayscale mode, you have the option of specifying the size ratio to be used in the conversion process (Figure 2–28). Essentially, this controls the actual size of the resulting image. When the default setting of 1 is used, the resulting image is the same size as the original bitmap image. If you enter a value of 2, the resulting image will be scaled down 50% with respect to the size of the bitmap image.

***Tip*: You can convert a 1-bit black-and-white scanned picture into an enhanced grayscale image by scanning at multiples of the desired size, and using the multiple as the size ratio when converting the black-and-white image into grayscale mode. Photoshop averages the groups of black-and-white pixels and creates "artificial" grayscale dots.**

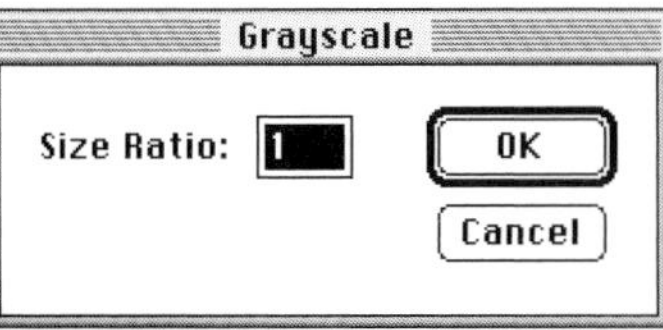

Figure 2–28
Use this dialog box when converting to Grayscale from Bitmap.

Grayscale

The Grayscale mode uses up to 256 shades of gray for each pixel in the image. When color images are converted to grayscale, all hue information is removed from the image, leaving the brightness and saturation values intact. Grayscale images can be obtained by scanning a black-and-white image, opening a Photo CD file created from a black-and-white negative, or converting a color image to Grayscale mode.

Tip: You can use the Grayscale mode to slightly enhance the apparent quality of 4-bit, 16-gray scans by opening a 4-bit TIFF file, converting it to full Grayscale mode, and applying a single pass of the Blur filter.

The manipulation tools and filters work in Grayscale display mode but the controls for manipulating color values are unavailable. For example, the Hue/Saturation and Color Balance controls are disabled when you are working in Grayscale mode.

Tip: It is important to understand the Grayscale mode because individual channels in the other modes function in the same way.

Duotone

Duotones, tritones, and quadtones are used in offset printing to increase the tonal range and to add color to black-and-white images. The monitor can display up to 256 shades of gray but the printing press can only reproduce about 50 tones of gray (or an ink color). By printing the same image two times in register, the range of tones increases, rendering a richer, more saturated image.

Duotones can take advantage of custom color inks such as those manufactured by Pantone and Toyo. Since the ink colors are not necessarily process colors and can vary so much, Photoshop does not break each hue out as a channel but treats the duotone as a single 8-bit channel. The separation to individual plates happens only at the time of printing. The selection of the colors and manipulation of the tonal curves takes place in the Duotone dialog, which appears whenever Duotone is selected from the Mode menu (Figure 2–29) The colors and tonal curves for the various plates are simulated as a composite on the screen. See the duotone examples in the color section.

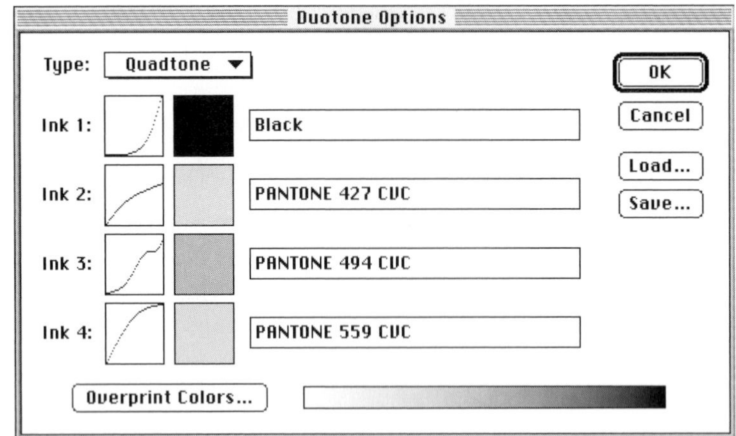

Figure 2–29
In the Duotone dialog you can specify colors and tonal curves for monotones, duotones, tritones, and quadtones.

Tip: It is possible to view individual plates as channels by converting to Multichannel mode. Be sure to save your document before doing this because you will need to revert back to the Duotone version. The Multichannel mode will not print the duotone correctly.

Duotones can have very subtle tonal scales as well as extremely brilliant colors. See the examples in the color section and check out Chapter 7, "Advanced Photoshop Techniques," for more on duotones.

Indexed Color Mode

The Indexed Color mode is used when you want to limit the number of colors used to display an image (Figure 2–30). Typical applications include on-screen presentations and multimedia animation. An indexed color image has a specific color lookup table, or fixed palette. There are five types of color palettes that can be used when converting to Indexed Color mode.

The Exact palette is an option only when there are 256 or fewer colors in the image being converted. In this case Photoshop matches the colors in the palette to the colors in the image exactly.

The Standard System palette (8-bit) or uniform palette (less than 8 bits) consists of a predetermined set of colors that are supposed to be supported by any application following the standard Apple programming guidelines. Object-oriented PostScript software such as Freehand and Adobe Illustrator use the standard System palette to display their entire color range on 8-bit displays. By dithering, or mixing, the colors

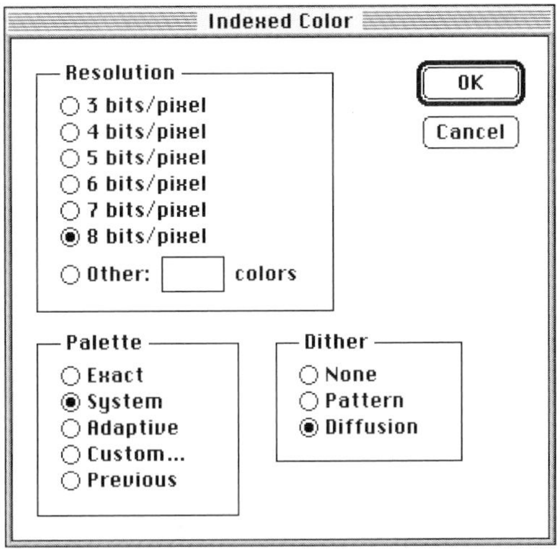

Figure 2–30
The Indexed Color dialog that appears when converting to Indexed Color mode allows you to choose the pixel depth, palette, and diffusion dither.

in special patterns, it is possible to simulate intermediate shades of the colors, resulting in more colors than are actually in the palette.

Adaptive palettes are optimized to best represent the colors found in an image. When converting a 24-bit image to 8-bit indexed color, Photoshop analyzes the colors in the 24-bit image and creates a 256-color palette that best represents the colors found in the 24-bit file. An image with an 8-bit adaptive palette tends to look very much like the 24-bit image onscreen. We've fooled more than one person into believing that adaptive palette 256-color images created by Photoshop were actually 24-bit images.

With the Custom palette your own color table can be created. Color tables can be saved for future use and previously created tables can be loaded.

The Previous palette is handy when converting more than one document that needs to have the same palette. Once a palette is applied to an image, subsequent conversions to Indexed mode have the Previous palette as an option.

To prepare images for screen presentations, it is preferable to use adaptive palettes. It is often helpful if multiple images use the same palette. The problem is that some programs have problems dealing with custom palettes and expect images to be mapped to the Apple system palette. Programs such as Macromedia Director have the ability to import and work with different palettes. See Chapter 9, "Animation," for specific tips on moving palettes and images into Macromedia Director.

When you convert an RGB image into Indexed Color format, you can determine how the colors in the original image will be represented on the screen and the type of color palette that will be generated (Figure 2–30).

You can determine the number of bits dedicated to each pixel, which determines the number of colors in the color palette. Four-bit color can use up to 16 colors per pixel, while 5-bit color yields 32 colors (2 to the fifth power). Odd numbers, such as 3, 5, and 7, are useful for saving images in some of the more esoteric modes, such as Amiga IFF and CompuServe GIF formats. The indexed color depths most used on the Macintosh are 2, 4, and 8 bits.

The palette and dithering options allow you to specify the type of palette that will result from the format conversion—either adaptive, system (8-bit), or uniform (4-bit)—and the type of dither employed.

The Exact palette is useful only when there are less than 256 colors in the RGB image. In this case, no dithering is employed to create intermediate shades. In our experience with the program, we found that the Exact option is rarely available with detailed color images containing a variety of shades. System (256 colors) or Uniform (16 colors) palettes conform to the Apple standard color palettes for those respective color depths; and programs written to Apple's design specifications are supposed to utilize these fixed color palettes. Adaptive palettes are created when Photoshop analyzes the colors, found in the 24-bit RGB file, and creates an optimized set of colors that best represent the values found in the 24-bit file. Clearly, adaptive palettes yield the most true representations of the color range when RGB files are converted.

We find that regardless of the palette used, the diffusion dither tends to yield the smoothest attainable image. The pattern dither is useful for a certain effect, and the None option results in a heavily "quantized" appearance that is far from the original RGB image.

To view the currently active palette, select Color Table in the Mode menu (Figure 2–31). This option is only available when in Indexed Color mode.

You can save and load custom color tables using the Load and Save buttons in the right-hand side of this dialog. You can also change individual colors in the table by clicking on the desired color, which opens the color picker. If you change a color in the color table, all occurrences of that color in the image file will be updated to reflect this new color.

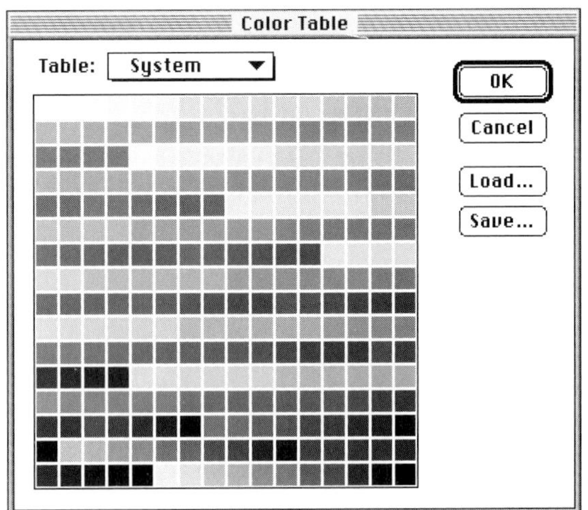

Figure 2–31
The Color Table allows you to edit the colors and make custom palettes for a document. Color tables can be saved and then loaded in future documents.

You can also create gradients between two colors by selecting a range of colors in the table. You will be asked to specify beginning and ending colors, and Photoshop will automatically create the blend using the number of color cells selected. This technique can be used in Director to create a smooth transitions when cycling colors.

The black body, grayscale, and spectrum color palettes are built into Photoshop. Selecting one of them replaces the current palette with the chosen palette.

The **Black Body** color palette has its origins in physics. This table displays a transition of colors based on the nature of how heat is radiated from a body (like light radiating from a star). As the body heats up, it goes from black to red to orange to yellow to white. If you were to heat a bar of iron over a hot fire, that would be the order of colors as the bar becomes increasingly hot. Desktop publishers probably won't get too much use from this color table, but scientists might find it useful for image analysis problems.

Grayscale replaces the color range with a smooth 256-shade transition of grays from black to white.

Spectrum is a color table based on the colors that make up white light. If you observe light passing through a prism, you'll see a smooth transition between violet, blue, green, yellow, orange, and red.

RGB Color

RGB (red-green-blue) Color mode is the normal Photoshop working mode. Usually when you open a color scanned image into Photoshop (regardless of whether it's a TIFF or PICT file), you'll find yourself in the RGB display mode. RGB is also one of the default modes when new documents are being created. RGB mode gives you access to the full capabilities of all of Photoshop's tools and filters.

A 24-bit RGB image can be described as three separate 8-bit images, one each of red, green, and blue, superimposed one on top of another to provide the full color spectrum. RGB Color mode shows the three 8-bit channels superimposed, but you can also view the separate color components of an image by choosing them from the Channel palette in the Window menu. Each channel can be viewed and manipulated in its appropriate color or in gray values. This choice is available in the General Preferences dialog in the File menu. All of Photoshop's image processing commands and filters can be applied to any of the separate color component channels of an image.

When the monitor is running on a 24-bit video display card, RGB Color mode is displayed on-screen with the full 24-bit color range. On an 8-bit system, a pattern dithering scheme is used to display the image with the best possible 8-bit quality. All tools work at a full 24 bits, regardless of the pixel/bit depth of the video card driving the monitor.

CYMK Color

CMYK (cyan-magenta-yellow-black) Color mode is used for processing four-color separations of a color image. Printers use four process colors, cyan, magenta, yellow, and black, to create the full range of printable colors.

When using CMYK mode, you can see either the value of each of the layers as a black plate with the corresponding tonal densities or represented by the actual colors of the layers. Use the Color Channels in Color button in the General Preferences dialog to toggle this feature.

When working in CMYK display mode, you can have a window showing a live RGB view that interactively displays the changes made to individual CMYK channels. Typically, you will start either from Lab or RGB mode and convert to CMYK in order to output four separate layers, or plates, which are used to generate printing plates.

The process separation resulting from the conversion to CMYK mode is controlled by the parameters found in the Monitor Setup, Printing Inks Setup, Separation Setup, and Separation Table dialog boxes found in Preferences. These settings should be set before you start working and should not be changed in the middle of a project.

For more information on converting to CMYK mode and creating color separations for four-color process printing, see Chapter 8, "Output."

Lab Color

The Lab Color mode is based on visual color perception using a standard created by the Commission Internationale de L'Éclairage (CIE). International standards for color measurements were established by this organization in 1931. Color values are defined mathematically so that they can exist independent of any device. Lab colors will not vary among different monitors and printers, as long as they are calibrated correctly.

> **NOTE: The HSB and HSL Color modes were replaced by the Lab Color mode in Photoshop 2.5. However, you can still use HSB and HSL with a plug-in available through America On Line and various other commercial and private bulletin board systems (BBSs).**

Before this color model was available, conversions between RGB Color and CMYK Color were a problem because the range (gamut) of colors available in RGB do not match the gamut available in CMYK. Lab color gives users a way to create consistent color documents on different color devices. It is used in the conversion from RGB to CMYK Color modes, introduced in Photoshop 2.5. If you print with Postscript level 2 printers, you can print directly from the Lab Color mode.

Lab Color is made of three channels: a channel for *luminance* or lightness, which controls the tonal range in the image and two channels to control chroma;. an **a** channel, which controls the range from green to magenta; and a **b** channel, which controls the range from blue to yellow. Since the values (lightness) in an image are separated from the colors it is possible to adjust the lightness (or tones) without affecting the actual color components of the image. After adjusting any of the channels, the image can be converted back to the original RGB or CMYK Color modes. See Chapter 7, "Advanced Photoshop Techniques," for some special effects that can be done with the Lab mode.

Kodak uses Photo YCC, which is another implementation of CIE device–independent color. When opening a Photo CD document, the image can be imported directly into the Lab Color mode. Since Lab

Color is the standard reference for other Color models, it is safe to switch back and forth between Lab Color and RGB Color mode, or between Lab Color and CMYK Color mode.

Tip: Do not switch back and forth directly between RGB and CMYK Color modes. This will adversely affect the colors.

Multichannel

The Multichannel mode is probably the most "generic" display mode in Photoshop. Documents in Photoshop can consist of up to sixteen 8-bit channels, each essentially containing grayscale information. In an RGB document, three of the 16 channels are used for the three RGB layers, leaving 13 other 8-bit channels that can be used as alpha channels. If you delete any of the component channels of an RGB or CMYK image, the image will be converted automatically into the Multichannel display mode. Also, when converting to Multichannel mode any color names will be replaced by numbers.

The Multichannel mode consists of any number (up to 16) of grayscale channels that can be displayed individually or as a composite. When viewed as a composite each channel will appear in the color set in Channel Options (a hierarchical submenu in the Channel Palette). You can use the Multichannel mode to view duotone color plates in grayscale but not for printing duotones. The Multichannel mode is also used as a transition to convert duotones to the Scitex CT file format.

Tip: If you are working with groups of grayscale images that are similar sizes, you might want to create a single multichannel Photoshop document with a different image in each of the channels. Using this technique, you can keep up to 16 related documents together in one file.

Tip: To save a duotone image in the Scitex CT format, convert from Duotone to Multichannel, add blank channels so that there is a total of four. Convert the image to CMYK mode and then save it in the Scitex CT format.

Calibration

Before you start working seriously in Photoshop you probably will want to calibrate your system. The intent of this process is to try to get the color and tonal qualities of the prescanned original, the display, and the final output to match each other as closely as possible. You will quickly learn that colors on the monitor do not match colors in printed output. Actually, they will never match perfectly. A basic problem is that the monitor uses projected light, which is composed of the additive primary colors (red, green, and blue), and printed output reflects light by optically mixing the subtractive primary colors (cyan, yellow, and magenta, plus black). Chapter 15 in the Photoshop 2.5 manual describes a basic method of calibration. See Chapter 8, "Output," for more on calibration options.

There are third party calibration systems available. We have been using Kodak ColorSense Color Manager to calibrate a Quadra 800. It is designed to coordinate color information between a variety of devices, such as scanners, digital cameras, monitors and output devices. Some scanning software can be calibrated to particular output considerations. We have been using Ofoto (scanning software) with a Hewlett-Packard ScanJet IIC to do this quite successfully. Cachet from Electronics for Imaging provides calibration using its EFIColor color management system.

Color management also has become more controllable with the introduction of Apple's ColorSync in System 7, the Lab (CIE) standard that is built into Postscript Level 2, and other third party user-friendly calibration and color management (such as EFIColor) systems.

Creating New Documents

When choosing the New... command from the File menu, the dialog box shown in Figure 2–32 appears in order to set the characteristics of the new document. The clipboard image can then be pasted directly into the new document without it needing to be cropped.

***Tip*: You can change the resolution or size of an image at any time by selecting Image Size under the Image menu.**

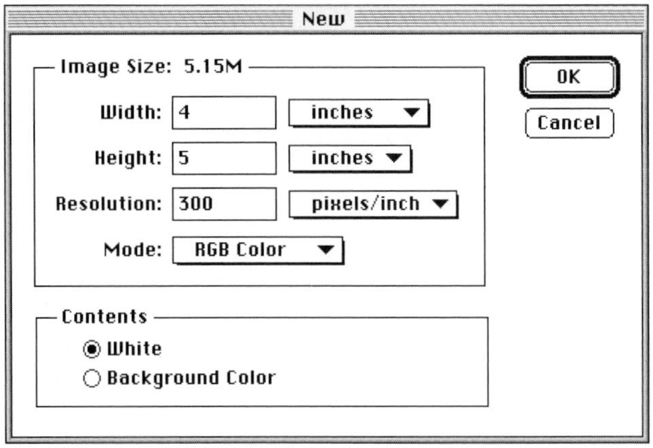

Figure 2–32
The New dialog gives you the opportunity to set the size, resolution, and mode of a new image.

The image size is specified by separate height and width values. By pressing on the units field, immediately to the right of the height and width values, you can specify the measurement in units of pixels, inches, centimeters, points, or picas. The width units can also be specified in terms of columns.

A new document can be opened in the Bitmap, Grayscale, RGB Color, CMYK Color, and Lab Color modes. If there is an image in the clipboard, its mode will automatically be reflected in the New dialog.

The default image resolution is 72 pixels per inch, which is the Macintosh screen resolution. You can specify a different default resolution if you know that you will want to work with images at a higher resolution. Resolution can be specified in terms of pixels per inch or pixels per centimeter. Set the units by pressing on the field to the immediate right of the resolution value. Also note that you can create a new file with a specified background color.

Opening Existing Documents

In our experience with Photoshop, we've come to refer to it as the "universal can opener," since it can open and save in a number of graphics formats. Most Mac users will be familiar with many of the formats found in the hierarchical format menu in the Save and Save As dialogs, but to many some of them won't be familiar. Each format has specific uses

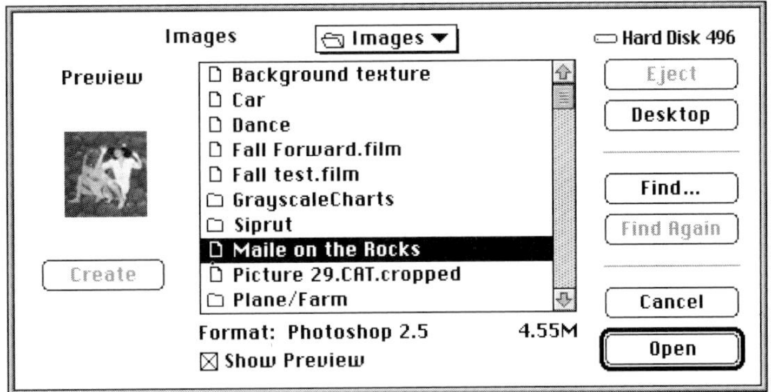

Figure 2–33
The file formats Photoshop can open directly

(Figure 2–33). For a description of file formats, see "Photoshop File Formats" later this chapter.

Using the Open command in the File menu, Photoshop can directly open 19 different file formats. These include:

- Photoshop 2.5
- Amiga IFF
- CompuServe GIF
- Filmstrip
- MacPaint
- Photo CD
- PICT Resources
- PixelPaint
- Scitex CT
- TIFF
- Photoshop 2.0
- BMP
- EPS (Encapsulated PostScript)
- JPEG
- PCX
- PICT
- PIXAR
- RAW
- Targa

For a description of each of these, see the section "Photoshop File Formats," later in this chapter.

The Open As... command is useful for opening file formats not normally used in the Macintosh environment, such as TIFF files or Targa files that are created on the IBM PC. Use the Open As... command if the file cannot be opened or recognized when you use the Open command. The default format in the Open As... command, called Raw, is a generic format that can be used to open files that are likely to appear if you work with different types of computers. We have successfully used the Open As, Raw command to open and view some great space shots that we got from a CD-ROM disk of assorted image files from the Voyager missions.

Kodak Photo CDs can be opened directly into Photoshop. After selecting the desired file, the Photo CD dialog box will appear. Select the appropriate Color mode and resolution. If you plan on using the image to create color separations, select the Lab mode. Grayscale will remove all color information. For on-screen presentations select RGB mode. See Chapter 3, "Input," for a full discussion on Photo CD technology.

Adobe Illustrator files can be opened or "placed" into already open documents. Photoshop rasterizes the mathematically oriented vector graphics into a grid of pixels at the selected resolution. Upon selecting an Illustrator EPS file, the EPS Rasterizer dialog box will appear. Select the appropriate size, resolution, and mode. Normally you would want to select Anti-aliased and constrain proportions.

Acquire

The plug-in modules accessible from the Acquire command under the File menu allow Photoshop to be able to work with other file formats such as anti-aliased PICT (which imports object-oriented PICT files) and TWAIN. The Acquire command also provides an avenue to access scanners, video frame grabbers, digital cameras, and more (Figure 2–34).

Saving

Photoshop was originally conceived as a file-format translation program and, as a result, it can save images in most of the formats you're likely to ever want or need. The Save and Save As dialogs each contain a pop-up menu of the output file formats (Figure 2–35).

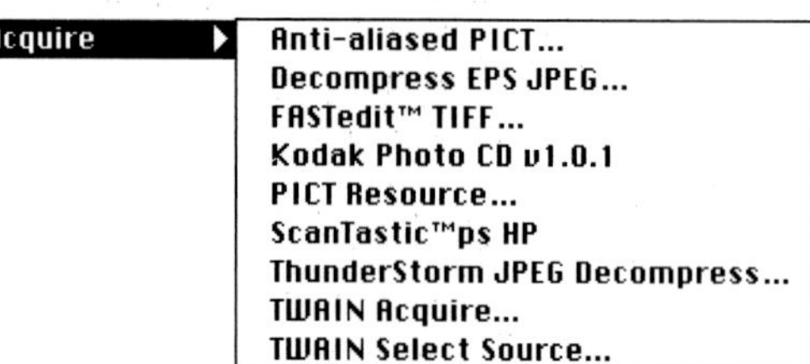

Figure 2–34
The Acquire submenu allows access to various graphic file formats and input devices.

Tip: Each of the different display modes presents you with different options when saving a file. You'll notice that at times some of the file formats in the Save dialog aren't available, depending on the display mode you're in when you select the Save command. Photoshop is smart in knowing what saving options will logically work based on the display mode. For example, to save a file in Scitex CT format, you need to be in CMYK display mode. If you're working on an image in Photoshop's normal RGB mode, you won't be able to save an image as a MacPaint file without first converting the display mode to Grayscale and then to Bitmap mode. See "Photoshop File Formats" below for more on saving in the proper mode and file format.

After you choose the file format you wish to use for output—and name the document—pressing the Save button will bring you to a dialog that lists the options associated with the selected format.

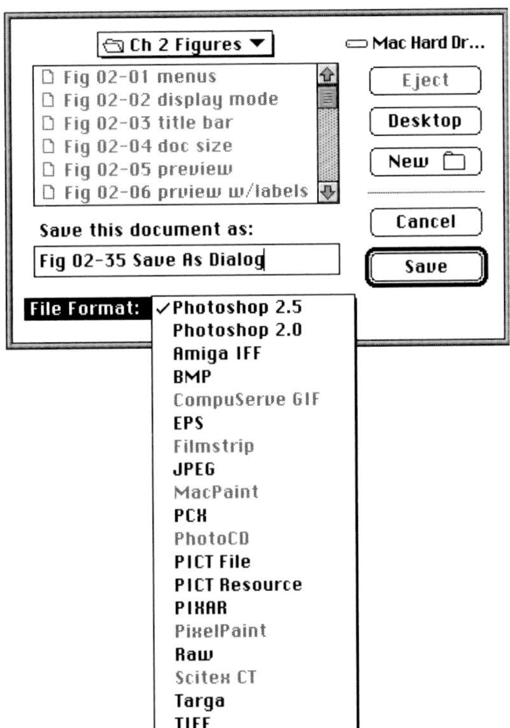

Figure 2–35
The file formats that Photoshop can save to

To get an idea of how large a disk file a saved image will create, look in the lower-left corner of the image window. The number there, which displays the amount of RAM an image occupies, typically indicates the amount of disk space the file will occupy when saved to disk.

***Tip:* If an image doesn't fit on a floppy disk, Photoshop will automatically segment the file into multiple "chunks" and will prompt you to insert as many disks as needed to save it. When opening an image saved in this fashion, Photoshop asks you to insert the disks with the segments, and rebuilds the single-image file.**

As a general rule, you should always try to use the native Photoshop format for saving images, regardless of the mode you are working in, the video card in your machine, or the model Macintosh being used. The image will always retain the full color information it started with, whether imported into Photoshop as a 256-color indexed image or as a 24-bit scan file. Also, save the document in the appropriate format (such as TIFF, EPS) only as the final step when the intent is to use the image in another program.

Photoshop File Formats

Photoshop 2.5

The native Photoshop 2.5 format is preferable for saving either grayscale or color images that you don't plan to export to another application. This is the only format that supports all of the display modes. When you are working in Photoshop, files can be opened and saved much faster than any other file format. This format ensures that all channels and pen paths are saved with the main image. (See Chapter 5, "Image Selection and Masking," for more information on channels).

Photoshop 2.0

Save a file in this format if you need to open it in Photoshop 2.0. This format will retain all of the features available in Photoshop 2.0. Note that you cannot save in this format while in the Lab mode, because the Lab mode does not exist in version 2.0.

Amiga IFF

The Amiga Interchange File Format (IFF)/Interleaved Bitmap (ILBM) File Format is the standard raster file format for the Commodore Amiga. Use this format to transfer images between the Mac and the Amiga. Some paint programs on IBM computers also support this format.

BMP

The BMP format is common on IBM and PC-compatible computers. When saving to this format, the BMP Options dialog box will appear. Select the appropriate operating system (Windows or OS2) and pixel bit depth (Figure 2–36).

CompuServe GIF

The CompuServe GIF format is a raster file format that allows color bitmapped images to be moved around multiple computer platforms. It was developed in order to allow CompuServe users with different computers to exchange bitmapped and scanned artwork.

The GIF file format uses indexed color. The documents contain a color map of up to 256 colors, which is used to maintain optimal colors for the translated image. In addition to the Indexed Color mode, Grayscale and Bitmap modes can be saved to this file format.

This format is useful for saving or opening files to or from CompuServe, a public telecommunications service. The GIF format was created because it can be highly compressed to lessen download and upload times. A number of microcomputers can read this file format.

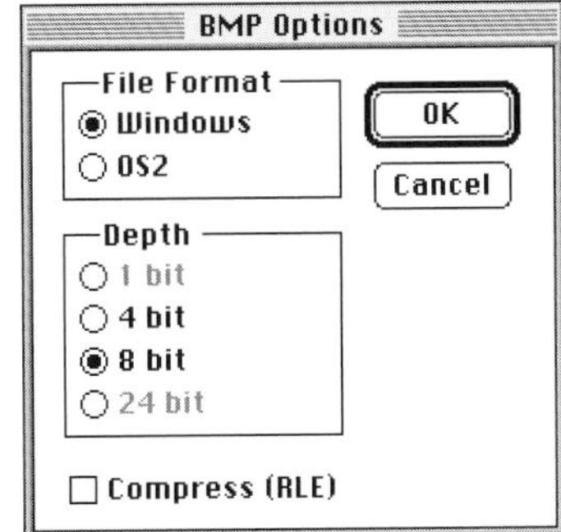

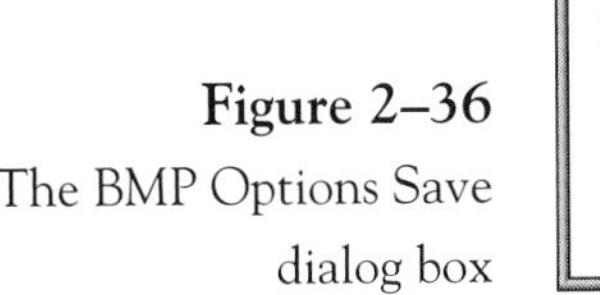

Figure 2–36
The BMP Options Save dialog box

EPS (Encapsulated PostScript)

EPS (Encapsulated PostScript) is one of the most useful formats for exporting color images to page layout programs. Using this format you can place color images into programs, such as AldusPageMaker, QuarkXPress, and Adobe Illustrator, for incorporation into full-page layouts. Photoshop will also open and import EPS files.

***Tip*: If you primarily use grayscale images in your layouts, then you should stick with using the TIFF format; a grayscale image saved in the EPS format is appreciably larger than its TIFF counterpart.**

An EPS file, like everything in the Macintosh universe, is made up of two "forks," or different types, of information. In the case of an EPS file, a "data" fork holds the actual PostScript code portion of a graphic image, and a "resource" fork contains the PICT resource for Macintosh screen representation. When printed to a PostScript printer, only the image's data fork PostScript is sent to the output device.

When saving an EPS file, you can choose to create either a 1-bit black-and-white or an 8-bit color screen preview of the image, or no preview at all (in which case, when imported into a page layout program, the image is represented by its bounding box).

The ASCII and Binary options are used, depending on what program you plan on taking the EPS file into. Most programs recognize binary EPS files. An ASCII file is twice as large as an equivalent binary file and, therefore, occupies more disk space and takes longer to save and print.

***Tip*: Although most programs will accept binary code, make sure that the program you are placing the file into will accept it. Some programs, especially older versions (such as Aldus PageMaker) will accept only ASCII code.**

The halftone screen and transfer (dot gain compensation) values set in the Page Setup dialog can be saved with an EPS file. These values will override any screening or dot-gain compensation utilized by the program importing the image. For example, if you move an EPS file saved with custom halftone information into Adobe Separator, the saved halftone information will override Separator's default halftoning values.

***Tip*: Normally you would not set the halftone screens and transfer function in Photoshop. These are usually controlled in the final output program.**

If you are in the bitmap display mode, and choose to save the image in EPS format, you also have the option to make the white areas of the black-and-white image transparent. Normally the white areas will appear opaque when placed over another image in another program.

If you decide to save a file in EPS format while in the CMYK display mode, a check box for the Desktop Color Separation option becomes visible in the EPS Save Options dialog (Figure 2–37). When this is chosen, the image is saved to disk as five separate files: four files representing the CMYK separations, and a plain EPS file that serves as a screen and low-resolution print preview. You can place a full-color bitmap into other programs and separate it on a page with text and other art in place. Photoshop was one of the first graphics programs to support this powerful capability.

Photoshop can open or import vector EPS files from Adobe Illustrator at any resolution. The object-oriented postscript file is rasterized into the bitmapped nature of Photoshop.

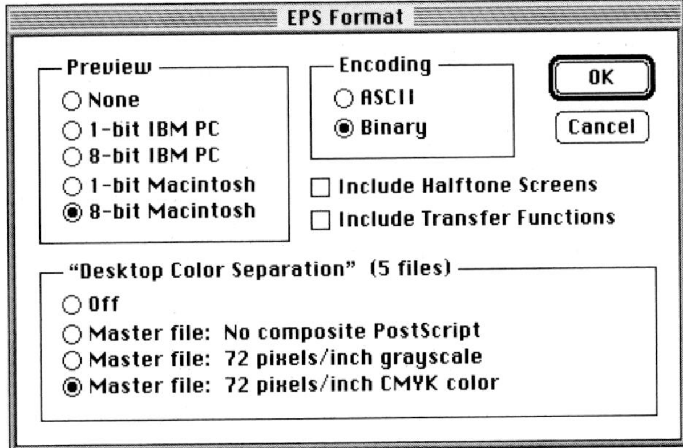

Figure 2–37
The EPS Options Save dialog in CMYK mode

Tip: Photoshop will import Adobe Illustrator and other Photoshop EPS files without any problem. To import an Aldus FreeHand EPS, use Altsys EPS Exchange to save it into an Adobe Illustrator EPS format and then open it in Photoshop. See Chapter 8, "Output," for more options on working with Illustrator.

Filmstrip

QuickTime movies exported from Adobe Premiere in this format can be opened, manipulated, and then saved in the Filmstrip format. Photoshop can now be used for *rotoscoping* (the traditional animation technique of tracing or drawing on individual frames of a film), special effects, and adding elements to movies. Individual frames or entire filmstrips can be manipulated (Figure 2–38). Any audio associated with that movie will not be transferred; and as long as the number of frames in the filmstrip has not been changed, you can add the sound again in Adobe Premiere. See Chapter 9, "Presentation Graphics, Video, and Animation" for more information on filmstrips.

JPEG

The Joint Photographic Expert Group (JPEG) format compresses files by streamlining the way data is stored. If the proper level of compression is chosen, data that is not necessary is discarded, yielding an image with an imperceptible difference in quality. Since data is actually removed from the file the JPEG compression format is refereed to as "Lossy," because after compression and decompression the image will not match the original. Also, decompression is automatic when a JPEG file is opened.

When saving into the JPEG format a dialog box will appear giving you an Image quality choice for the compression (Figure 2–39). Be aware that greatest amount of compression produces an image with only fair image quality, and the least amount of compression produces an image with excellent image quality. See Chapter 3, "Input," for more information on JPEG.

NOTE: Repeatedly compressing and decompressing a single file can result in a degradation of image quality.

Figure 2–38
A filmstrip document window in Photoshop

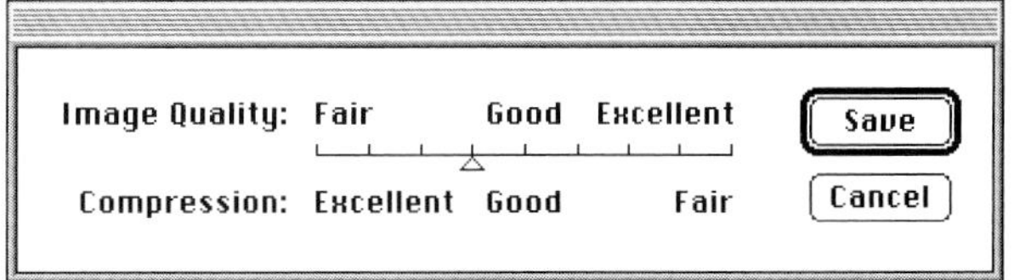

Figure 2–39
The degree of compression in the JPEG format has a direct relationship to the image quality.

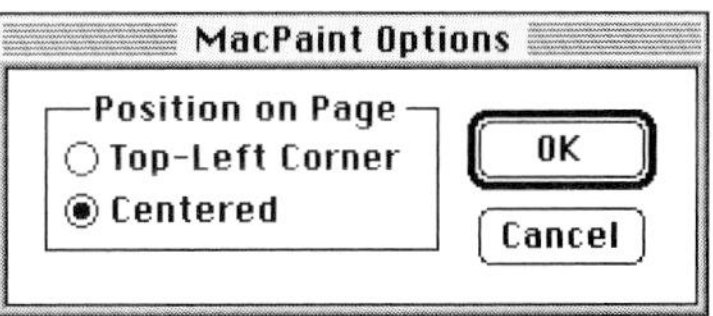

Figure 2–40
You can control the position of an image in the MacPaint Options dialog when saving to the MacPaint format.

MacPaint

MacPaint is the original Macintosh bitmapped format. Black-and-white images in 72 pixels per inch can be saved from the Bitmap display mode as MacPaint files. The size of this image is limited to 8 × 10 inches, which is 576 × 720 pixels. You can specify that the image appear either in the center or top-left corner of the MacPaint document (Figure 2–40).

MacPaint is supported by most programs; it is good for ImageWriters, for importing files into HyperCard, for Mac screen dumps, and when you absolutely want that crude neomodern digital look.

PCX

The PCX format is common on IBM and PC-compatible computers. It was established for PC Paintbrush by Zsoft. The PCX format can be saved from the RGB Color, Indexed Color Grayscale, and Bitmap display modes only.

Photo CD

The Photo CD format was established by Kodak to be used with the new CD technology. Kodak Photo CDs can be opened directly into PhotoShop, but PhotoShop cannot save into the Photo CD format. Once a Photo CD file is opened it must then be saved into another format, which usually should be the native Photoshop 2.5 format.

Photo CD files can be opened into Lab Color, RGB Color and Grayscale modes at a variety of resolution choices (Figure 2–41). See Chapter 3, "Input," for more information on Photo CDs.

PICT

PICT is probably the principal general-purpose file format for graphics on the Macintosh. There are two different types of PICT files—PICT I and PICT II. PICT I was the original format for object-oriented graphics programs (such as MacDraw). PICT II came out at the same time that the Macintosh II was introduced. It was made to support complex object files and color bitmapped images (of up to 24 bits of color depth). PICT II files are supported by many color-bitmap and page layout programs.

Although the PICT format can be opened or imported by most programs, it is not recommended for use in programs where the final output will be color separations. The TIFF or EPS formats are best for color separations (see Chapter 8, "Output"). PICT Files are good for on-screen presentations, movies, and animations. (See Chapter 9, "Presentation Graphics, Video, and Animation.")

***Tip*: If you import an object-oriented PICT file into Photoshop, it will automatically get converted into a 72 ppi bitmap. In order to get the best results, you might try enlarging your original image in the source program, and then reduce it in Photoshop. For example, if you're starting with a design in MacDraw, double the image's size in MacDraw, import the image into Photoshop, and then reduce the entire document by 50%.**

When saving from RGB Color mode you can choose between 16 bits per pixel and 32 bits per pixel. At 32 bits per pixel JPEG compression options become available (Figure 2–42). When saving from Grayscale mode, you have your choice of 2, 4, or 8 bits per pixel. At 8 bits per pixel JPEG Compression options become available (Figure 2–43).

When saving to the PICT format from the Indexed Color mode there is no choice as to the pixel depth or palette. These settings are determined by the palette in use, which was established at the time of conversion to the Indexed Color mode.

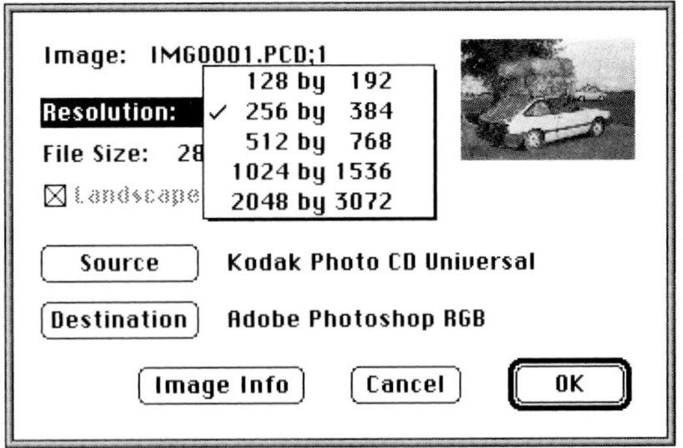

Figure 2–41
You can open Photo CD files into the Lab Color, RGB Color, and Grayscale modes at a variety of resolution choices.

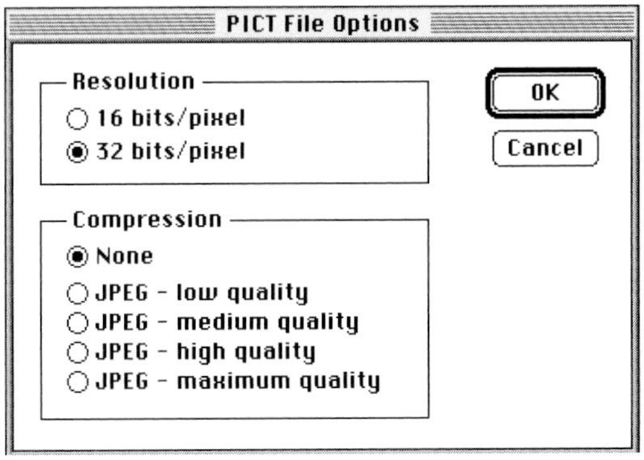

Figure 2–42
Saving to the PICT format from RGB Color mode

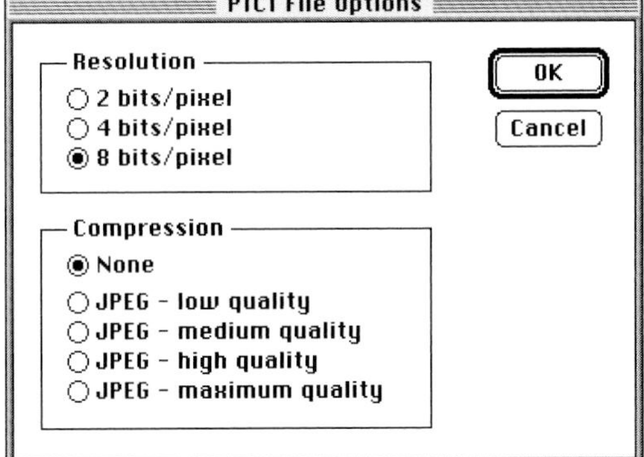

Figure 2–43
Saving to the PICT format from Grayscale mode

***Tip*:** When you want to save a document as an indexed color file with a custom color palette, you need to convert the image to the Indexed Color display with the mode at 8 bits per pixel and with the Adaptive Palette selected before saving it. For the best results, if you need to save an image with the system palette, use the diffusion dither option with the System Palette selected when converting the image from RGB to the Indexed Color mode.

When saving a PICT file from Bitmapped mode there also is no choice for pixel depth. The image will always be 1 bit per pixel, which is black and white with no gray tones. Also, PICT files cannot be created from Lab Color, CMYK Color, Duotone, or Multichannel modes.

PICT Resource

This format is used to create custom startup screens and to create PICT resources for inclusion in an application (only programmers need apply).

When you save a file as a PICT resource, you can specify the resource ID (0 for startup screens), resource name, and resolution. The resolution and compression options are the same as the PICT format options (Figure 2–44).

PIXAR

The PIXAR format is designed to transfer files to and from the high-end PIXAR computer workstations. Only the RGB Color and Grayscale modes can be saved in the PIXAR format.

PixelPaint

You can save images in the PixelPaint format in order to open the file in PixelPaint and PixelPaint Professional. You can choose the document size (in pixels) and the position of the image on the page (Figure 2–45). The PixelPaint format does not recognize 24-bit color, so make sure to convert color images to the Indexed Color mode before saving. PixelPaint will recognize and use a custom palette that is created by using the Adaptive option when converting to indexed color. Only the

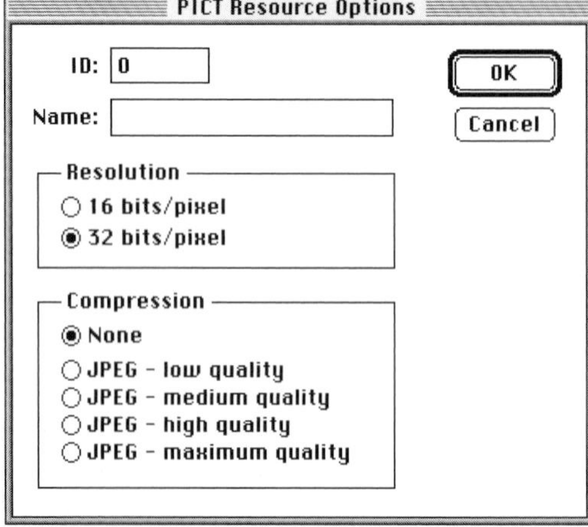

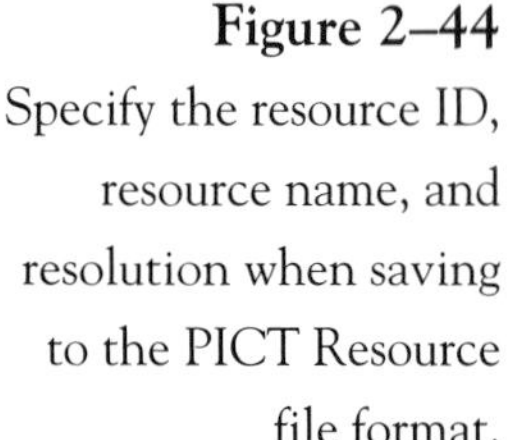

Figure 2–44
Specify the resource ID, resource name, and resolution when saving to the PICT Resource file format.

Indexed Color, Grayscale, and Bitmapped modes can be saved in the PixelPaint format.

Raw

Raw format is a generic raster format, primarily for use in exporting images to other programs and types of computers. Binary code is used to describe pixels. All colors and channels are retained. The file type, file creator, and header can be indicated, as well as whether the color order is to be interleaved. You can save to the Raw format from any mode except for the Bitmapped mode. Refer to the Photshop manual for more information on how to specify information in the Raw format (Figure 2–46).

Scitex CT

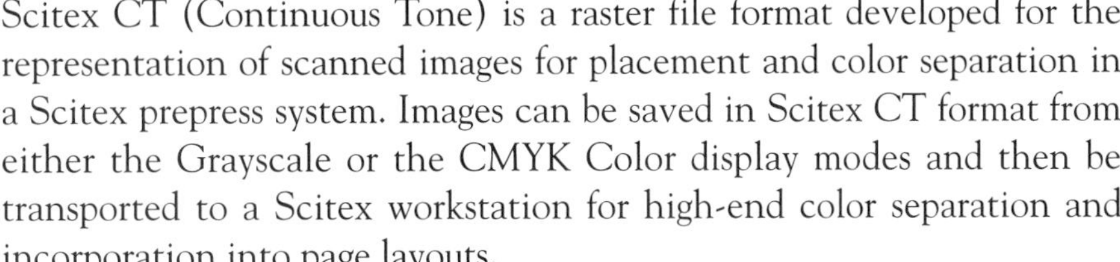

Scitex CT (Continuous Tone) is a raster file format developed for the representation of scanned images for placement and color separation in a Scitex prepress system. Images can be saved in Scitex CT format from either the Grayscale or the CMYK Color display modes and then be transported to a Scitex workstation for high-end color separation and incorporation into page layouts.

The Scitex CT format can handle high-resolution images; it does not save channels or paths, and works only from the CMYK Color and Grayscale modes. When imported into Photoshop, a Scitex CT image automatically opens into the CMYK Color mode. Also, Scitex CT file format requires special software for transfer to a Scitex system. Photoshop can save in the format, but not transfer.

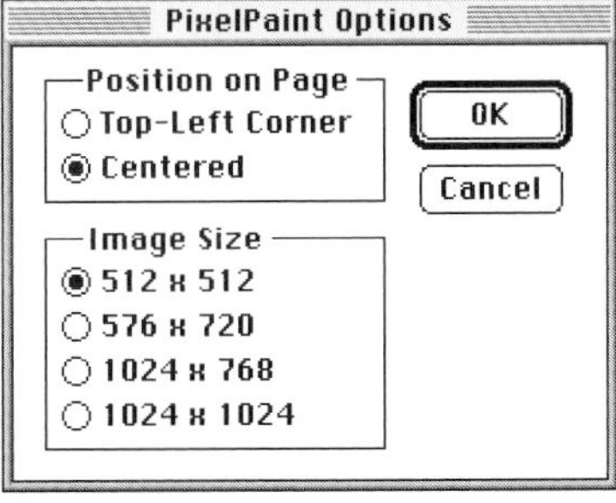

Figure 2–45
When saving to the PixelPaint format, you can choose the document size (in pixels) and the position of the image on the page.

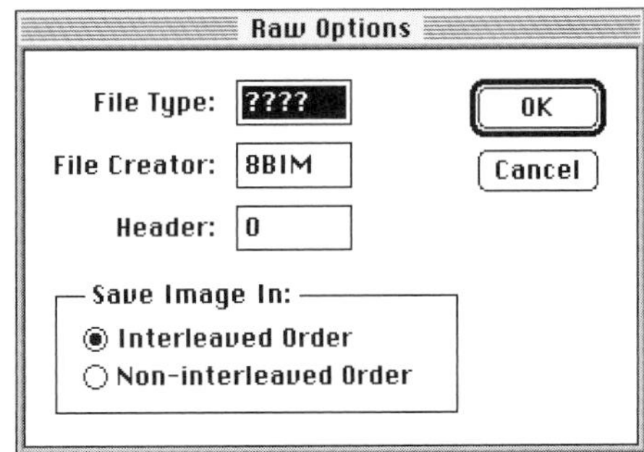

Figure 2–46
The file type, file creator, and header should be indicated as well as whether the color order is to be interleaved when saving in the Raw format.

Targa

Targa is the most common format found in higher-end PC-based paint systems. We've decided to share a written description of the Targa format and file transporting written by John Simon, manager of the MFA Computer lab at the School of Visual Arts in Manhattan. Play it, John.

> In the IBM PC world, the Targa format is the standard for paintbox programs built to utilize the TrueVision Targa and Vista video boards. We were successful in opening compressed and uncompressed TGA files over a TOPS network, working on the file in Photoshop, and then saving the changes back to the PC-based file without ever having the Targa file reside locally on the Macintosh hard disk.
>
> TGA files can contain either 16, 24, or 32 bits (in 32-bit files, the 8-bit alpha channel is in fact implemented for an overlay layer) of color information per pixel (Figure 2–47). Some programs expect the 24-bit RGB file to include an alpha channel, even though the alpha channel isn't recognized; hence the 32-bits per pixel option. Targa files can also be saved while in Indexed Color mode and Grayscale mode.

TIFF

TIFF (Tag Image File Format) was developed by Aldus to allow page layout programs to import and print continuous tone images (scanned grayscale graphics) as screened halftone images. Aldus originally developed the format for its own PageMaker software, and then made the format specifications available for other software companies to incorporate into their software. In doing so, Aldus was able to establish a format that continues to be the standard for transferring scanned images among various programs and between multiple computers. The TIFF format is readily supported by Macintosh, Intel/IBM PC-type machines, and other computers, such as the NeXT system.

TIFF was optimized specifically for scanned images, which are always raster (bitmap). It does not support vector (object-oriented) graphics, so it is not an efficient format for line art. TIFF files can be saved from all of Photoshop's modes (with channels and color properties included) except from the Multichannel mode. While most people think that there is only one type of TIFF file format, in actuality there are a variety of TIFF subformats and variations. Most are supported by current software. For example, one variant of the TIFF format involves a built-in level of lossless file compression (LZW encoding), which some scanner software can output but some older page-layout programs don't support. Photoshop can import some types of LZW-compressed scanned images, and can save images with LZW compression (Figure 2–48). If you want

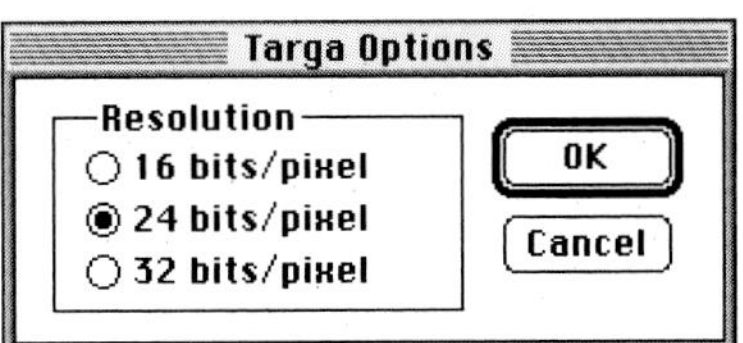

Figure 2–47
The Targa Options dialog allows for the pixel depth to be set when saving TGA files.

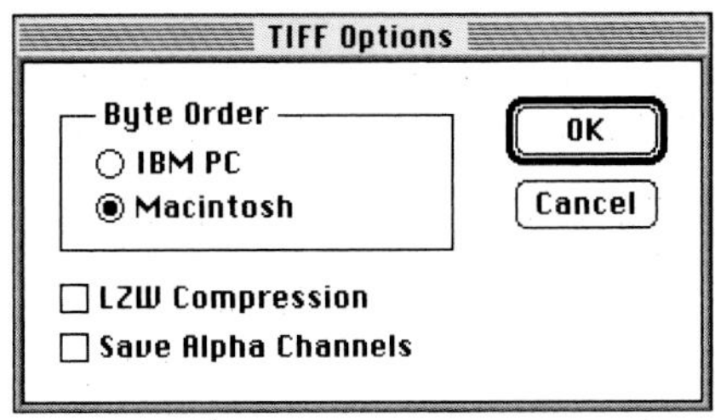

Figure 2–48
The TIFF Options dialog allow you to save in either Mac or IBM PC formats, to select LZW compression, and to save channels

to export LZW TIFF images from Photoshop, make sure that your page-layout program will support compressed TIFF files.

***Tip*: When saving a TIFF file you have the option to save any channels in the document. If you are saving the image in the TIFF format, in order to import and print it in another program, there is no reason to save the channels. Be sure to save another version with the channels in case you want to use them later.**

The TIFF exists on both Mac and PC platforms. When saving a file from Photoshop, you have the option to select for IBM PC or Macintosh formats (Figure 2–48). You can use one of the many available file translation utilities or networking systems to move Photoshop between platforms. File transfer is facilitated if the Macs and PCs are networked together with a networking scheme such as TOPS.

Export

In addition to saving in the above formats, the Export command under the File menu accesses plug-ins that offer the ability to save, transfer, and print images in a variety of modes and methods. For example, by using the Export command you can print to a film recorder, print to a non-PostScript printer, or save a pen path in order to use it in Adobe Illustrator.

CHAPTER 3

Input

In the mid-1980s, when the Macintosh was first employed as a graphics tool, the only choice an artist had for input was a black-and-white scanner, a black-and-white video camera that created a coarse dithered pattern to show tones, or pixels painted on the screen with the mouse through a paint program. The only option for output was a rather rough print from a dot matrix printer or a finer rendition from a black-and-white laser. Although constrained with what we now consider primitive technology, the early Mac artists had imagination and creativity, and produced pieces that attracted a great deal of attention.

Today, color scanners, monitors, and printers are commonplace. The range of choices a Photoshop user has for input and output is immense and growing constantly. This chapter will discuss a variety of input methods and devices that are useful for getting images into a Macintosh. They include:

- Scanners
- Digitizers and frame grabbers
- Electronic photography
- CD-ROM technology (digital stock photos and Photo CD)
- Graphics tablets

We will also discuss what you need to know about source images, resolution, and special input considerations for preparing files for a film recorder. Finally, because of the large files that input devices produce, we will discuss alternatives for compressing your documents.

Just about everyone using Photoshop will eventually require one or more input devices, depending on the type of work they are doing and the types of image sources they have access to. Below is a discussion of some of the essential criteria for selecting the right type of input device.

Scanners

It has been said that "eyes are the windows of the soul." These words also apply to the relationship between computers and optical scanners. Scanners open the eyes of the computer to a virtually unlimited world of analog (continuous tone) artwork. The scanner market is now flooded with a wide range of offerings (in terms of both capability and price), which can be confusing to the prospective buyer. Photoshop is the ultimate scanned-image processor, and everyone from the fine artist to the corporate publisher will probably end up using a scanner in conjunction with Photoshop. There are some basic issues in selecting a scanner, based on final output requirements and budget factors.

Bit Depth and Resolution

The amount of information that a scanner can absorb is expressed as its bit depth and resolution. Most desktop units work with variable resolutions between 72 and 600 pixels per inch (ppi) and with anywhere from 4 to 24 bits of color/grayscale information. (Some newer scanners can now capture 48 bits of information, which Photoshop 2.5.1 can import.) If you plan on doing grayscale scanning exclusively, then 8 bits is all you will need, while most color scanners do 24 bits of color data. You can use Photoshop to strip resolution and color depth away from an image as desired, but keep in mind that although you can "downsample" an image while retaining image integrity, you should scan at high resolutions, rather than use Photoshop's resampling command to convert a low-res image into high resolution. Slide scanners typically scan at higher resolutions than desktop flatbed scanners.

Film Scanning

If your original images are photographic film transparencies (anywhere between 4 x 5 to 8 x 10 inches), you will not be able to use a standard flatbed scanner for scanning. Most flatbed scanners are made to handle images or printed matter on opaque paper or stock. Film allows light to shine through, requiring a mirror attachment of some sort, which shines the light back into the scanner. Some of the more expensive flatbed color scanners offer mirror options, while most of the lower-priced desktop color scanners don't. Most of the grayscale scanners on the market don't have a mirror option either; look for scanners that can handle medical X-rays, as these inherently can handle other types of film as well.

Slide Scanners

If your original artwork exists in 35mm slide format, or if you need to create high-res scans on the desktop, you will probably end up looking at a slide scanner. Slide scanners are typically in the $2,000–$20,000 price range, depending on the types of film accepted and the output resolution. Slide scanners made by vendors such as Leaf Systems, Eastman Kodak, Pixelcraft, and Nikon have higher-resolution photoreceptors than flatbed scanners—from 2,000 to 6,000 ppi.

> **NOTE: Some of you might think that you can scan slides on a cheaper color flatbed scanner with usable results. We would like to tell you that it does not really work. In addition to having a lower resolution, the optics of flatbed scanners are designed for the narrower dynamic range of prints.**

Nikon and Leaf Systems have produced slide scanners which have won high praise. In particular, the Nikon LS-3510AF and LeafScan 35 are excellent models in the middle of the price range. For an economical slide scanner check out the Nikon CoolScan. Introduced in the spring of 1993 with a resolution of 2700 ppi and priced as low as $2,195, it can be purchased either as a separate unit or installed in your computer.

Grayscale or Color

This choice seems fairly obvious: If you do not use color images, then a grayscale scanner is all you need. Any color scanner can also do grayscale (either directly, or by stripping the color out of an image using Photoshop). There are a number of companies releasing reasonably good, low-priced desktop color scanners ($1,200–$3,500).

While scanners in this price range can produce very acceptable color images for screen presentation and low-end color separation work, the old computer axiom "GIGO" (garbage in, garbage out) still holds true. If you want to create exacting color separations for magazine or high-end publishing, these just won't do the job. Some of the scanners have slight problems with specific colors. The specific color that presents problems is referred to as the "drop-out" color, and may consist of just one or two shades of a particular color family.

Flatbed or Sheet-fed

Scanners come in two paper-handling varieties: *sheet-fed* and *flatbed.* Sheet-fed scanners pass the paper through a stationary scanning element; while the element in a flatbed scanner moves as the paper remains motionless. The flatbed mechanisms work much like a standard photocopier. If you plan on scanning artwork from books or other bound sources, flatbeds allow the artwork to be scanned without cutting or otherwise damaging the original bound materials. Sheet-fed scanners can handle only single-sheet nonbound art, and tend to be sensitive to heavier paper weights. (The maximum paper weight that can be handled on a specific scanner varies from unit to unit.)

If you need to use a sheet-fed scanner to input bound artwork, simply create a photocopy from the original artwork, and scan the photocopy. If your photocopier has reduction capabilities, artwork can be scaled before being scanned; however, image quality can vary depending on the photocopier.

Color flatbed scanners which seem to merit looking at at the time of this writing include the Agfa Arcus on the higher price side and the Hewlett-Packard ScanJet IIc on the inexpensive side. Both produce excellent results within their price ranges.

Drum Scanners

One of the realistic limitations of Photoshop is the quality of scanned source files. While desktop scanners are typically useful for a variety of color printing applications, the final reproduction method might dictate the use of expensive, professional scanners and output systems.

For critical prepress applications, use Photoshop with images scanned on high-end drum scanners. These days color service bureaus are competing with traditional color prepress houses in providing scans that can be saved in formats such as TIFF and Scitex CT, which Photoshop can read directly. If you are working or planning to work in this capacity, we should remind you that file sizes get quite large (30–75 megabytes is an "acceptable" file size). At this point, Photoshop's performance is limited by the CPU, so expect more frequent coffee breaks during most filtering and correction functions. Also, realize that optical storage is a viable archival investment.

More affordable drum scanners from Optronics (the ColorGetter), Screen (the DT-S1015 and ISC-2010), Howtek (the Scanmaster), and Danagraf North America (the ScanMate) are appearing in the $30,000–-$70,000 price range. They will deliver prepress-quality source scans and, when coupled with a calibrated monitor and well-maintained imagesetter, can be used as the makings of a viable high-end Mac-based color separation system.

Software

Most desktop scanners today are provided with software plug-ins for Adobe Photoshop. Adobe is not, and will not be, the supplier of these modules. You will have to inquire about the availability of a driver from the scanner manufacturer. After you install the plug-in, following the instructions provided with the software, normally the scanner settings are accessed by choosing Acquire from the File menu and then selecting the scanner module from the Acquire submenu.

One such plug-in we have used to drive a Hewlett-Packard ScanJet IIc is ScanTastic from Second Glance Software. It provides control of resolution, bit depth, scaling, brightness and contrast, and transfer curves for each of the RGB channels. Scanned images automatically become an open Photoshop document without the need of saving and then importing the scan.

While using a plug-in for scanning is the preferred route, any scanner (and supporting software) that can provide TIFF or PICT images is, by definition, compatible with Photoshop.

Some software packages like Ofoto from Light Source Computer Images Inc. offer calibration and automated control of the scanning operation. It can be set up to scan for specific output needs. Other scanner-to-final-output calibration and color-control programs include Color Encore from Southwest Software, ScanMatch from Savitar Color Communication, Color Sense from Kodak, Cachet from Electronics for Imaging, and Agfa Fotoflow. For more information on calibration, see Chapter 8, "Output."

Cameras, Digitizers, and Frame Grabbers

Digitizers or Frame Grabbers

Video digitizers were among the first input devices to hit the Macintosh world, years ago. Although scanners have replaced digitizers as the preferred method of input, the former are still quite popular for situations that specifically warrant their use. Here are two examples:

- Importing pictures of real-world three-dimensional objects into the computer without having to photograph them and then scan the photographs
- Grabbing images from video sources, such as videotape, camcorders, or still video cameras

The resolution of images which come from video is fixed at approximately 640 by 480 pixels, and color fidelity is generally poor, so the image captures may not be of print quality.

The actual difference between a digitizer and a frame grabber is that a typical frame grabber has onboard RAM memory for storing at least one (if not more) digitized images. A digitizer simply allows you to grab a frame of video and bring it into computer RAM.

Digitizers and frame grabbers that use NuBus cards are the preferred device for video input, and typically are offered as 8-bit grayscale, 8-bit grayscale/color, 16-bit grayscale/color, and 24-bit grayscale/color. Typically, the software included with these devices offers the ability to save images in either PICT or TIFF format. Check with the board manufacturer for availability of a Photoshop plug-in.

Digital Cameras

A newer technology is provided by various forms of electronic photography. There are two main camera types: *analog to digital*, often referred to as still video cameras, and *direct digital* cameras.

A good example of the still video camera is the Canon RC-570, which records the images as analog information (using the NTSC standards) on 2-inch floppy disks. The standard "video format" means the images can be played back on TV. To digitize the images, you use an optional video-digitizing board and software. The camera has the advantage of relatively low cost ($1,500–$7,500) and convenience. The quality is fine for video, multimedia, or lower-quality publication, but is probably not sufficient for medium- to high-quality needs.

Direct digital cameras are more expensive than their still video cousins, and some offer higher quality capabilities. Here the digitizing happens in the camera itself. Because of their high cost and relative low image quality (compared to scanning), they are most appreciated by newspapers that need photographs for deadline. Newspapers can live with the lower resolution because they use coarse halftone screens. The Kodak professional digital cameras use a Nikon camera body with standard lenses and a Kodak digital imaging back that can record color images at a fairly high resolution. With a digital storage unit (a small, portable hard disk), the camera can be used in the field and then be plugged into a Macintosh SCSI port for immediate import into Photoshop via the File/Acquire submenu.

CD-ROM Technologies

CD-ROM technology has existed since 1984. CD-ROM offers the ability to store and access large amounts of data (over 600 megabytes per disk) at relatively low cost. This makes it an excellent medium for the storage of high-resolution color images, as well as multimedia, voices, music, and other data that requires huge amounts of storage space.

Each year since CD-ROM was introduced, industry pundits have predicted that "this is the year of CD-ROM," but use of the medium has grown slowly. Now it appears that CD-ROM is finally taking off. Market researchers predict that in 1993—as this is being written—there will be as many CD-ROM drives sold as in all previous years combined. Apple now builds CD-ROM drives into new computer models, and nearly half of the buyers of new Macintoshes are choosing CD-ROM drives when they are offered.

To users of Photoshop, two developments in this technology provide a potentially new source of images for input: *digital stock images* and *Photo CD*.

Digital Stock Photos

CD-ROM technology is widely used for storing stock photographs in digital format. Traditionally, if you wanted photographs you either hired a photographer or licensed the use of a transparency from a stock photo agency. While the use of stock photos would be cheaper than using a photographer, it did not come cheap. You had to pay a royalty fee of between $200 and $4,000 for use of an image, depending on the kind of publication and the size at which it would be printed. Then you would have the image scanned by a color house for another $100 to $200.

Today collections of photographs on CD-ROMs are being offered for as little as 40 cents per image. Many of the initial collections are focused on nature scenes and textures and backgrounds, and their quality varies widely. Some collections are marred by poorly scanned, washed out, or dirty images. The least expensive images are relatively low resolution, suitable only for multimedia or laser-printing quality.

Other collections, sometimes sold at considerably higher cost, provide carefully chosen, well-exposed-and-scanned images which can be invaluable for high-quality projects.

***Tip*: Carefully check the license agreement that comes with an image collection. You are not purchasing the images; you are being licensed to use the images in specific ways. For example, most licenses will not allow you to resell the images or to post them on a bulletin board. Other licenses may be more restrictive. Ask the vendor if you are not sure about the reproduction rights for your specific use.**

Traditional stock photography agencies are now getting into the act and are beginning to distribute their images on CD-ROMs. These agencies aim at professional graphic artists who design books, magazines, and advertisements, and who have used their services before. Usage restrictions on these collections are much more severe. Comstock, one of the largest agencies, distributes a collection of low-resolution versions of their images on CD-ROM, but only for rough comps or for in-house publications. If you want to publish the image, you must still negotiate a royalty fee as was the case before CD-ROM. You will be supplied with the full-resolution image on a Syquest cartridge or a transparency for scanning. Comstock also maintains a bulletin board which allows users to research through libraries of images and then download them for use in projects.

To use *digital stock photographs* on CDs in Photoshop, you just need the software which comes with your CD-ROM drive. It consists of a CD-capable driver, such as Apple's CD-ROM drivers and QuickTime.

Stock photography and image library companies which take special care with their collections and offer high-quality images include Comstock, Artbeats, CD Folios, PhotoDisc, and D'pix.

Photo CD

Another of the driving forces spurring on the use of CD-ROMs is Kodak Photo CD, which makes use of the CD-ROM to store and display images that are taken by conventional photographic methods. Photo CD makes use of a proprietary, compressed image format developed by Eastman Kodak called Image Pac.

Users take color negative or slide film to their photofinisher, who is equipped with Kodak's Photo CD Imaging Workstation. Prints or slides are developed using normal processes, the film is scanned, color corrections are made based on the film type, and then the image data is written onto a Photo CD disk. Individual photographs from existing negatives or slides can be put onto a Photo CD for a slightly higher price. The photofinisher will also make an indexed color proofsheet print of the images on the disk for reference.

Prices will vary. Generally, commercial film processors who use mass production methods will digitize each slide for as little as under $1. Consumer processing labs use automatic settings when digitizing images for Photo CDs, which are averaged for viewing on monitors or television screens. Professionals usually do not want their scans corrected in such a way. If you are more concerned with quality, you should go to a professional laboratory which will charge more but which can give your slides more attention. In either case, the cost is considerably less than traditional scanning.

The Photo CD images can either be viewed on a Photo CD player, which can be connected to almost any television set, or they can be read by a CD-ROM drive connected to a computer, where they can be used as input for programs like Adobe Photoshop.

Color images are stored in YCC, a device independent color space similar to Lab, in the following resolutions:

Base/16 128 × 192 pixels (thumbnail size)
Base/4 256 × 284 pixels
Base 512 × 768 pixels (closest to TV and monitor resolution)
4 Base 1024 × 1536 pixels (the proposed HDTV resolution)
16 Base 2048 × 3072 pixels (usable printing at 133 lpi at up to 8 × 10 inches)
64 Base 4096 × 6144 pixels (Pro Photo CD format)

Kodak recently introduced the Pro Photo CD Master, a new scanner for photo processors that can scan as high as 4096 × 6144 pixels of resolution and can handle film up to a 4 × 5 inch format. This should be a boost to the use of Photo CD since most professional photographers work in larger film formats.

Photoshop and Photo CD

Photoshop 2.5 is designed to handle Photo CD easily using a plug-in distributed with the application. You can choose to open Photo CD images by choosing Open from the File menu (Figure 3–1). You are given the choice of opening a color image as RGB Color or Lab Color modes at one of the resolutions described above. In order to better preserve the colors, convert to RGB Color mode for on-screen presentations,

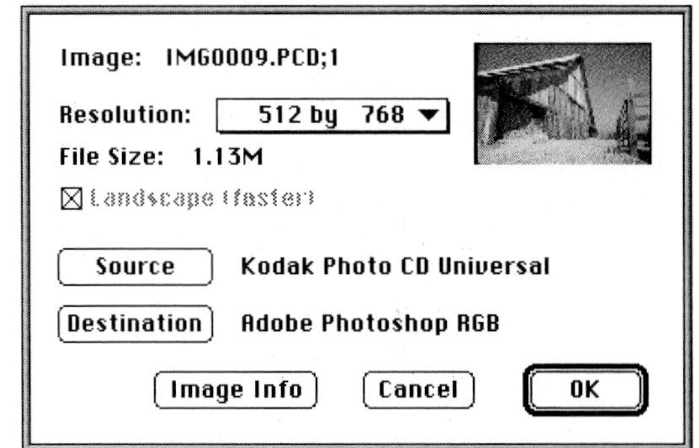

Figure 3–1
Photo CD Options dialog box

video, or RGB output, or convert to Lab mode for color separations. Click on the Image Info button to determine the film type used, and then click on the Source button to select the appropriate film type.

For more control when opening Photo CD images, use the Photo CD Acquire module supplied by Kodak (Figure 3–2). You will have more resolution options than when using the Open menu. The Kodak software gives you more options for opening in Video RGB, Photo CD YCC (which is not useful unless you want to do your own color mapping), and several choices based on different Gamma and White Point settings (which correspond to the settings found in Monitor Setup in Photoshop 2.5 Preferences). There is no option to open in Lab mode. You can view a

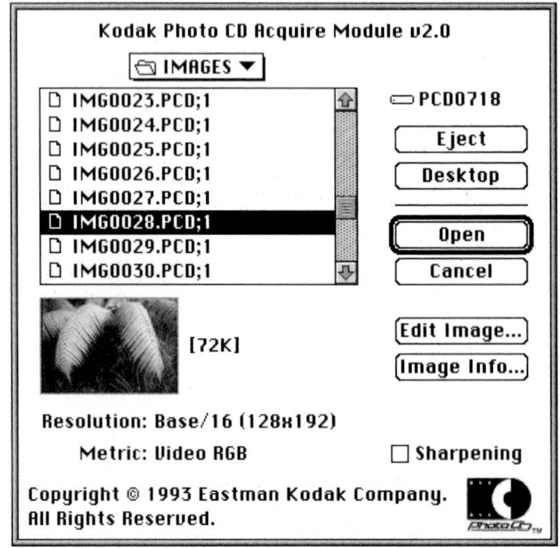

Figure 3–2
Kodak Photo CD Acquire module dialog box

thumbnail preview of the images on the disk before you open them. There are also some simple tools for cropping, zooming, and rotating images, but it usually makes more sense to do these functions within Photoshop.

Whether you use the Photoshop built-in option or the Kodak module, your images will open at 72-ppi resolution. You will want to go immediately to the Image Size dialog under the Image menu to change to the size (and resolution) that you will be using for the image.

A simple method of accessing Photo CD is to use Kodak PhotoEdge Software. It will open the files and allow simple image editing, such as sharpen, adjust tones, rotate, and crop. We have found PhotoEdge to be useful in generating proofsheets of the images on a Photo CD.

To view the images on a Photo CD, simply double-click on the Quick Time slide show that is included on the disk.

Graphics Tablets

Many Mac artists find that the mouse is far from perfect for drawing images freehand. Pressure-sensitive graphic tablets are a popular alternative to the mouse. There are many manufacturers of graphics tablets for the Macintosh but some of them are designed for other applications, such as for engineering applications. The tablets that are of most interest to artists are those manufactured by Wacom, CalComp, and Kurta. Wacom, in particular, specialized in this area early on and offers several models including the ArtZ, SD510c, and 420e, each having different choices of features. Tablets from these vendors use cordless pens for drawing, as an alternative to the clunky mouse. We enthusiastically use the Wacom ArtZ tablet in our work.

Photoshop 2.5 supports the use of pressure-sensitive digital tablets in many painting tools. Double-click on the following tools to set options for how the tablet's pen will affect the use of the tool:

Pencil	to vary size, color, or opacity
Airbrush	to vary color or pressure
Paintbrush	to vary size, color, or opacity
Rubber stamp	to vary size or opacity
Smudge	to vary size or pressure
Blur/Sharpen	to vary size or pressure
Dodge/Burn	to vary size or exposure

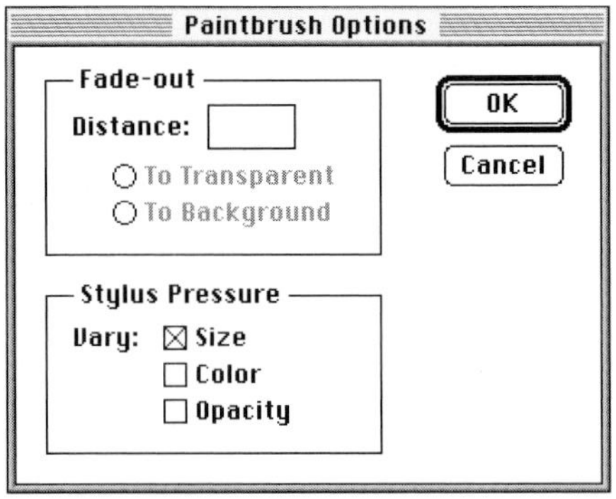

Figure 3–3
Paintbrush Options dialog box showing stylus pressure options

For example, using the Paintbrush tool, if you select the size option (Figure 3–3), when you apply downward pressure to the pen against the tablet, the width of the brush interactively increases. Reducing pressure reduces the width. It's a very cool way to simulate real paintbrush strokes.

Tablets are available in a variety of sizes, resolutions, sampling rates, and pressure levels. A tablet can connect either to the ADB connector (used by the mouse) or to a serial port. The key in purchasing a graphic tablet is to try out tablets, and to pick one which matches your purposes. For example, you might not need the largest (and most expensive) tablet if you are only using it to trace small pieces of artwork.

Then just plug it in and play!

The Process of Digitizing Images

Once you have chosen your source of input, you must think ahead to plan how you intend to use the images you are going to create. Output and input are integrally related in Photoshop. In particular, you must do three things *before you do your input:* (1) You must calibrate your system so that you can achieve consistent and predictable results. (2) You must understand that the quality of your source image and how skillfully it is scanned will have a significant effect on your final result. (3) You must understand the concepts of resolution and file size so that you can create a file that will be appropriate for the output method you intend to use. Chapter 8, "Output," describes four steps you should take to calibrate your system. The second and third points are discussed below.

Source Images, Scanning Skill, and Quality

Whichever image source you choose, the GIGO (garbage in, garbage out) axiom mentioned earlier applies when it comes to choosing a source image for input. Whenever possible, choose the best image you can find as the source for your scan or other input. You will save yourself a great deal of time and will end up with a better result if you have a photographer shoot an extra roll of film to get a well-exposed and well-developed image than to try to correct a bad image in Photoshop—even though Photoshop gives you tremendous capabilities to do that.

If at all possible use original film for scanning rather than a print. The dynamic range of film is much higher than it is in prints. And the ability of photographic paper to record all the tonal information contained in a negative is far less then the ability a good scanner has to read it. By the time a print is made, a great deal of data is lost. Therefore, a scanned print will record far less digital information than scanned film. For example, a typical black-and-white negative may be able to record 12 stops of tonal information, but a print may only be able to record 8 stops of information.

An equally important factor is the skill of the scanning operator. A bad scan made on a drum scanner may be worse than a good scan made on a less expensive scanner. If you are doing the scan yourself, learn the techniques necessary to do good ones. Teaching you scanning, however, is beyond the scope of this book. Courses on desktop scanning are now offered by color service bureaus and arts schools that teach computer graphics. There are also several books about scanning available. If you purchase drum or desktop scans, make sure the operator is skilled in scanning for the output you want to do. For example, an image would need to be scanned differently for output through a film recorder than if it were being color-separated digitally.

Pixels and Resolution

Whether your source is a scanner, frame grabber, digital camera, or Photo CD, the basic "atom" of information in Photoshop is a pixel. Photoshop works with a fixed grid of bit-mapped information. On the Macintosh the pixel is square (this is not always so on other platforms). The resolution of the pixel grid is defined either when the information is sampled by the scanner or other image source, or when you create a new Photoshop document. In the scanning software, it's defined by the scanning resolution. When you open a new document, resolution is defined as pixels per inch or pixels per centimeter.

Another way to measure resolution is to use the number of pixels in each dimension. The advantage of this method is that the number is not keyed to a particular unit of measure. Images for film recorded on slides or transparencies are usually measured this way. Certain file formats, like Targa and Photo CD, do not record resolution information in the file. Photoshop will open these files as 72 ppi and in dimensions that may be huge. You can then adjust to the size and output resolution you desire.

As mentioned earlier in this chapter, the amount of information recorded by the scanner or other input source is called its bit depth. This can represent black-and-white (Bitmap mode), grayscale (Grayscale mode), or color information (RGB, CMYK, or Lab mode). For color images, if your input source is a desktop scanner, the input will be in RGB mode. If you have purchased a drum scan from a color service bureau, it will usually already be converted to CMYK mode. If you receive a Photo CD, which uses the YCC format as its native color space, you may open it either in Lab or RGB mode, as described above.

Choosing an Appropriate Resolution

It is very important that you choose a resolution that will be appropriate for the image's intended use. If you create an image which has too low a resolution, it will appear "pixelated" or coarse when it is printed or displayed. Pixelated means that you can see the actual pixels which make up the image. On the other hand, if you create an image with too high a resolution, you will slow down the process of producing the image at every stage. The file size will be much larger than necessary, so Photoshop will require much more of your computer's RAM, thus slowing down all operations, especially if the program has to use the scratch disk for virtual memory. The larger file will also be much larger to transport, and it will print more slowly.

Resolution and File Size

The size of the file you create is a product of three factors: (1) the dimensions of your image, (2) the bit depth of your image, and (3) the resolution of your image.

The first factor is pretty simple to understand. If you double the size of an image in both dimensions, the area of your image (width times height) will be four times as large. So, the file size will quadruple.

Grayscale images contain 8 bits of information for every pixel. RGB images record 8 bits for each red, green, and blue channel, so each pixel requires 24 bits of information. Thus RGB images are three times as large as grayscale images with the same dimensions. If you convert from RGB to CMYK, you go from three channels of information to four (from 24 to 32 bits), and your file size increases by one-third.

Finally, it is important to understand the relationship between resolution and file size. If your resolution is twice as high as necessary, you will quadruple your file size! And since Photoshop's RAM requirements are related to file size, you will need four times as much resolution to manipulate the document.

To make things easier, you can use Photoshop to handle the complexities of figuring out how large a file is going to be. Choose New from the File menu (Figure 3–4). Enter the dimensions of the image that you want to use. Select the mode you will be working in, either Bitmapped, Grayscale, RGB, CMYK, or Lab. Then enter a value for resolution. Photoshop will calculate the file size.

What Is the Right Image Resolution?

If you are creating an image that will only be displayed on a computer screen, such as for a presentation or video project, your choice is easy: You should choose 72 ppi, the standard Macintosh screen resolution.

If your final output is to a 300 ppi laser printer, your image will need to be halftoned for printing. (See Chapter 8, "Output," for a discussion of the digital halftone process.) The usual rule of thumb is to choose a

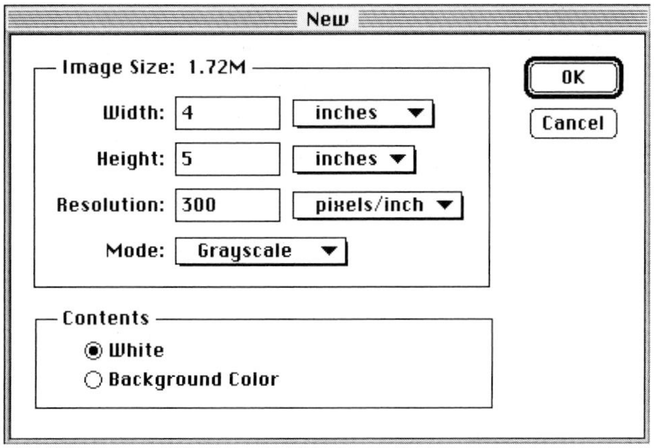

Figure 3–4
New dialog box

resolution which is between 1.2 and 2 times the lines per inch of the halftone. The normal halftone for a laser printer is between 53 and 75 lpi, so a resolution between 100 and 150 ppi would be appropriate.

Less expensive digital color printers may use a halftone dot for imaging, so their output is relatively coarse. Use the same formula as above to calculate resolution (lpi x 2 = resolution). Higher quality digital color printers are continuous tone (each pixel can be any of over 16 million colors), but they are still relatively low resolution. Usually an image resolution between 150 and 200 ppi is adequate for imaging. On the very highest quality printers, you might go up to 300 ppi but your file size will be much higher.

If your image is to be sent to a high-resolution imagesetter for film output—whether in grayscale or a color separation—you need to use the "twice the screen frequency" formula. You first need to find out from your printer what screen frequency is required for the press and paper that will be used for reproduction. For a photograph for magazine reproduction, you will need to refer to the specifications provided by the magazine. For example, if your image will be reproduced at 150 lpi, an image resolution of 300 ppi should work just fine. If your image is being prepared for a film recorder, other rules apply. See the discussion in Chapter 8, "Output."

Preparing Images for a Film Recorder

Sometimes you may be preparing artwork in Photoshop which you would like to have imaged on 35mm or larger film. For example, you could be preparing an image for a slide presentation, or you may wish to image a transparency that can be scanned by the drum scanner in a color prepress house. There are several advantages to creating a transparency. Since it is continuous tone, it can be scanned to different sizes and screen frequency requirements. One other advantage of producing a transparency is that a predictable light source is all that is required for viewing it. Also, the format is well understood and easily handled by graphic arts professionals.

The film recorder consists a cathode ray tube (CRT) attached to a camera back. The recorder produces a continuous tone image on slide film or a negative of a particular size. There are film recorders of different qualities. The better ones address a larger and higher pixel count with a smaller spot size (the size of the pixel on the CRT).

Slide film recorders always image in RGB, so you should prepare your image in Photoshop in RGB mode. If you are beginning with a drum scan, have it stored on disk in RGB (not converted to CMYK as the scanner's color computer would normally do for color separations).

***Tip*: The software which drives film recorders can vary. Some film recorders have a Photoshop plug-in, so the Photoshop bit-map information can be sent directly to the film recorder. Other software would convert a Photoshop file to PostScript before sending it to the film recorder. Because of these differences you should consult with your film recorder service bureau to prepare your file to their specifications.**

Critical issues for preparing images in Photoshop for film recording are their resolution and aspect ratio. Like other issues of resolution, it is important that you consider the output resolution on the film recorder at the time the image is being created or digitized. Film recorders record images at fixed output resolutions. Each resolution is recorded on a pixel grid of a fixed size (*x* pixels wide by *y* pixels high). If your image is smaller than or equal to the height and width of the pixel grid, you can output at that resolution.

The resolution you choose depends on the quality requirements of your job and your ability to handle the file size which must be created. Another factor is that the price of a slide or transparency is higher for higher resolutions. Ideally you should create your image at the exact pixel size of the resolution you intend for output. The chart below shows the pixel dimensions of each resolution and the approximate file size for a 24-bit (RGB) image. The resolution choices (2K, 4K, and 8K) refer to the number of pixels on the long side of the image:

35mm Slides

Resolution	Pixel Dimensions	File Size
2K	2048 x 1364	8.0 MB
4K	4096 x 2728	32.0 MB
8K	8192 x 5456	127.9 MB

4 x 5 and 8 x 10 Transparencies

Resolution	Pixel Dimensions	File Size
2K	2048 x 1536	9.0 MB
4K	4096 x 3072	36.0 MB
8K	8192 x 6144	144.0 MB

Images can be enlarged for film recorder output, either in Photoshop or as the file is being imaged by the film recorder. In Photoshop this will be done by interpolation (see Chapter 2, "Setup and Document Management"). As with output for prepress, outputting a low-resolution image at a high resolution on a film recorder will not give it any more detail or resolution; it will only create a larger file size and cost more.

35mm slides have an aspect ratio of 3:2; 4 x 5 and 8 x 10 transparencies have an aspect ratio of 4:3.If your image does not match the aspect ratio and pixel dimensions of the recorder resolution, the film recorder service bureau can either crop the image or resize the image to fill the film area in one dimension. The other dimension will show unexposed film. For a slide presentation, cropping the image to match the aspect ratio of the slide is usually the best choice.

Compression

Once you scan and begin working with an image, you'll usually want to store it in the most efficient way possible while also preserving its quality. That is one reason why compression is such a crucial issue in the world of high-res color. Compression allows you to make optimum use of your hard disk space, both for working with and archiving large images. There are various options for image compression from within Photoshop or with digital signal processor (DSP) chips that are found on NuBus boards, which greatly speed up the process.

JPEG

JPEG (Joint Photographic Expert Group, the name of the committee which developed the format) is a standard method for compressing color bitmapped images. It is based on the Discrete Cosine Transform (DCT) algorithm, which analyzes 8 x 8 or 16 x 16 pixel areas of an image (independent of resolution), and performs a sophisticated "averaging" of the values in the cell. The result of this operation is that the image size is dramatically decreased.

JPEG is known as a "Lossy" compression system. There are both non-Lossy (Lossless) and Lossy compression schemes. Lossy compression sacrifices a level of detail and reproduction quality. The JPEG compression format allows you to specify the compression ratio. The higher the compression factor, the more data that is stripped out of the image, resulting in increasingly poorer quality in the final image.

In general, images meant for prepress are candidates for lower compression ratios; high-quality color separations require as much original information as possible. Images meant for video output are candidates for much higher compression ratios. For example, graphic arts professionals find compression ratios of between 10 and 20 produce good compression with very high quality for prepress, while ratios between 25 and 40 can be used for video applications. Of course, these numbers may vary with your particular hardware. If you are lucky enough to be dumping images to a digital video format such as D1, or even HDTV, you will want to stick to prepress compression ratios. We do not expect that many of you will run into this problem.

JPEG compression is now supported directly within Photoshop. When you choose Open from the File menu, you can open a JPEG compressed file. When you choose Save from the File menu, JPEG is one of the format choices. If you choose JPEG format, you are presented with a dialog box (Figure 3–5) where you can choose one of nine levels of image compression labelled from Fair to Excellent. Choosing "Excellent" compression creates a poorer image quality. There are now many software and hardware products that perform JPEG compression. Theoretically Photoshop should open them all, but this will probably not be the case for some time. (This is not unlike the TIFF format in the first few years it was used, where different software wrote different "flavors" of TIFF.)

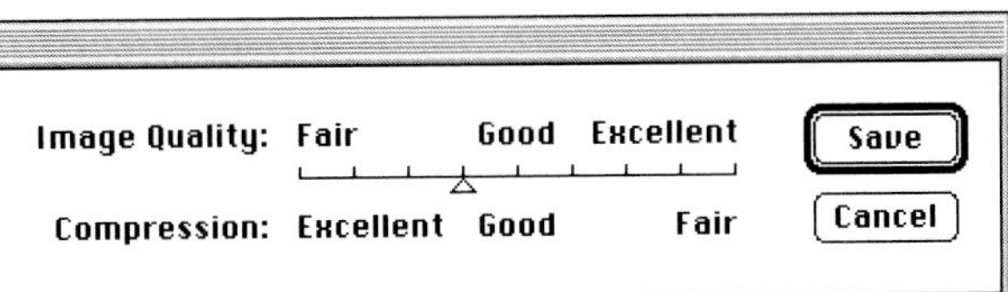

Figure 3–5
JPEG Save Options dialog box

***Tip*: Be sure to do tests to determine the levels of compression that work best for your image. The level of compression possible may also vary with the image content. An image with an extreme amount of detail (a sailing ship with rigging, for example) might not be a good candidate for compression.**

Compressing and decompressing a JPEG file in Photoshop is slow because the conversion is done entirely in software. If JPEG compression is important to you, you should consider buying a NuBus board, which has a DSP chip that can do JPEG compression and decompression much faster. You can purchase a dedicated JPEG board, but a better choice these days is to buy a multipurpose DSP board, which is designed to speed up many Photoshop operations. These boards work with any Macintosh with a NuBus slot. Each product will have a software plug-in or plug-ins that replace certain filters in Photoshop. DSP cards, which are certified as "Adobe Charged," utilize Adobe's own algorithms for the filters, and produce effects identical to the Photoshop software.

Besides speed, another advantage of buying a DSP board is that the JPEG implementation is usually more accurate. With some JPEG software implementations, if you repeatedly compress and decompress an image, it will progressively lose quality. Graphic arts professionals report the best implementation of JPEG is that developed by Storm Technologies, an early pioneer in the JPEG arena. Their JPEG, running on DSPs from SuperMac and Daystar, does not lose any more information after the second iteration; other implementations, notably those built into QuickTime, will lose quality with successive compressions.

***Tip*: Even with a good JPEG implementation, it is probably wise to minimize the number of times you compress an image. Save in JPEG once you've done all of the desired manipulation and you want to save a final compressed version on disk.**

Another JPEG compression alternative, which is also available in Photoshop, is a built-in Export plug-in module for writing an EPS file in which the image is compressed. This feature is only useful if you are sending the image to a PostScript Level 2 printer. On a PostScript Level 1 printer the EPS will not print at all. PostScript Level 2 printers have the ability to decompress a JPEG image on the fly. Transmission and printing times will reportedly be faster. (We did not have a chance to test this because at this writing PostScript Level 2 imagesetters were not available.)

To use this feature, choose Export from the File menu and choose the Compress EPS JPEG module (Figure 3–6). You will see the same choices for image compression and quality that you see in the JPEG Save dialog. The resulting EPS file can be placed in a page layout program like QuarkXPress or PageMaker. Unfortunately, there is no option to save a preview image with the EPS file, so all you see in the layout program is a gray box; however, it will print properly to a PostScript Level 2 printer. (Storm's PicturePress application, which comes with its DSP boards, gives you numerous compression and file format options.) To open an EPS JPEG file, you must choose Acquire from the File menu and choose the Decompress EPS JPEG module.

Non-Lossy Compression

There are several software products that can compress Photoshop images (as well as other files) using non-lossy (lossless) compression. The three most popular are StuffIt Deluxe, DiskDoubler, and Compact Pro. Each product has their advocates and each will do a serviceable job of compressing Photoshop files.

Lossless compression is always an alternative if you or the person who will be receiving your image (like a service bureau) has concerns about quality loss from JPEG Lossy compression. The compression ratios from these products are much lower than those from Lossy compression.

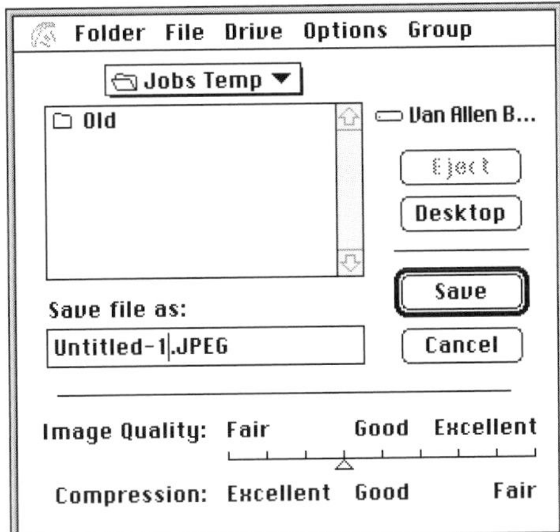

Figure 3–6
JPEG EPS Save Options dialog box

Tip: **If you are sending compressed files to an output provider always check ahead to make sure that they can decompress the files in the format that you're providing. Most compression software can now write files as ".sea" files (self-extracting archives). If you do this, all your recipient has to do is double-click on the file for the image to be decompressed.**

With your input choices made—the knowledge of how to choose an appropriate resolution and how to store your images—it is time to turn to the tools available in Photoshop, which is the topic of the next chapter.

CHAPTER 4

Using the Tools and Palettes

The most obvious fixtures of Photoshop are the drawing and selection tools, which are found in the toolbox on the left side of the screen. In this chapter we will concentrate on painting tools, typographic controls, and color selection options that are supported by the toolbox, along with the *floating palettes* that can be moved to any position on the screen.

The floating palettes, including Brushes, Channels, Colors, Info, and Paths, are used when editing and painting images. They are accessed under the Windows menu (Figure 4–1). This chapter will provide a complete description of the Brushes, Colors, and Info palettes. Chapter 5, "Image Selection and Masking," includes detailed information on the Channels and Paths palettes, as well as on the selection tools—the Elliptical and Rectangular Marquees, Lasso, Magic Wand, and Pen.

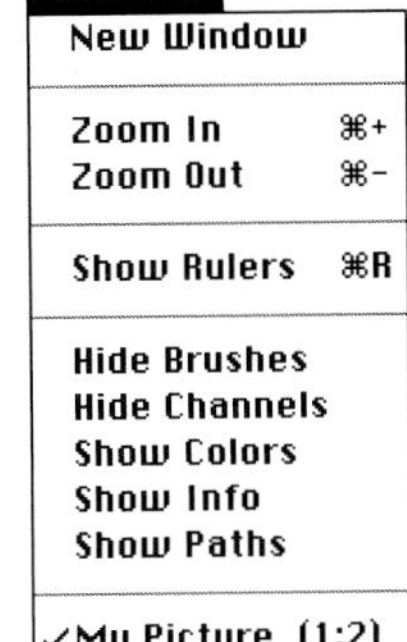

Figure 4–1
The Windows Menu showing the available palettes

When you first begin working with Photoshop, you probably should use the tools and palettes in their default state before changing their settings. Remember, each tool and palette has many working modes and options, so proceed patiently.

Working with Palettes

There are a number of shortcuts and helpful hints for speeding up your work with any of the palettes. In general, you will work with more speed if you keep your most-used palettes open in an unobtrusive place on the desktop. Of course, if you are working with a smaller monitor, the palettes may get in the way. You can alternatively collapse and grow the palettes by clicking on the zoom box in the upper-right corner of the palette windows.

To make all the palettes disappear, including the toolbox, press the Tab key. Press Tab again to make them all reappear. To hide individual palettes, select the palette's Hide command from the Window menu (Figure 4–1) or click its close box. The commands associated with a palette are accessed by pressing on the small black triangle near the upper-right corner of its window. This is referred to as a pop-out menu (Figure 4–2).

> **NOTE: When a palette is open, the Windows menu will display a command to "Hide" the palette; when a palette is closed, the menu will display a command to "Show" the palette.**

To make open palettes reappear in the same positions when you close and reopen Photoshop, make sure the Restore Windows option is

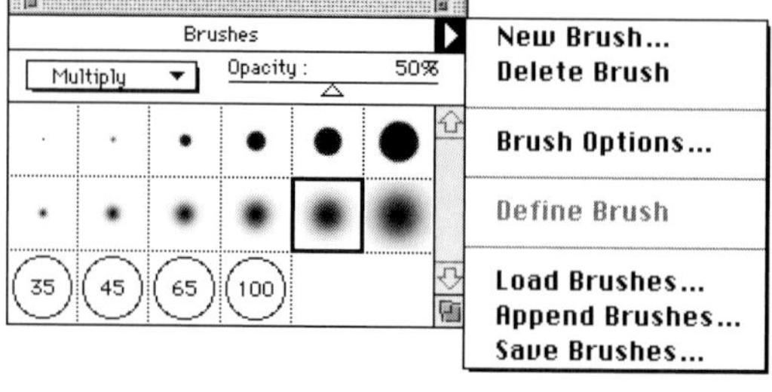

Figure 4–2
The Brushes palette with its pop-out menu

checked in the General Preferences dialog box. You can access the General Preferences by pressing the Command key and the letter K.

If you have a keyboard with function keys, you can make the palettes appear without using the Show command in the Window menu. Photoshop comes with some commands preassigned to function keys. To change these assignments, select Function Keys from the Preferences submenu under the File menu.

The preassigned function keys for the palettes are:

Show Brushes:	F5
Show Channels:	F6
Show Colors:	F7
Show Info:	F8
Show Paths:	F9

Brushes Palette

The Brushes palette (Figure 4–2) allows you to select brush sizes, create and delete brushes, define brush options, and save and load sets of brushes. It also controls the characteristics of most of the tools in Photoshop. The Mode and Opacity settings even work with floating selections. A more complete description appears later in this chapter under the heading "Using the Brushes Palette with the Tools."

Channels Palette

The Channels palette (Figure 4–3) shows the names of all the channels currently in use by a document. Channels can be made visible or invisible, as well as editable or uneditable, with the Channels palette. An eye icon indicates that the channel is visible; a pencil icon indicates that a channel is active and can be edited. It is possible to view one channel while working on another channel, ensuring perfect registration. Multiple channels can also be edited simultaneously.

***Tip*: Pay attention to which palette is active. It is easy to accidentally edit the wrong channel. For quick access to a channel, use its keyboard shortcut shown on the right side of the palette.**

Selecting the Quick Mask mode will add a temporary channel to the Channels palette. Under the Select menu, channels can be loaded as selections via the Load Selection submenu and selections can be saved

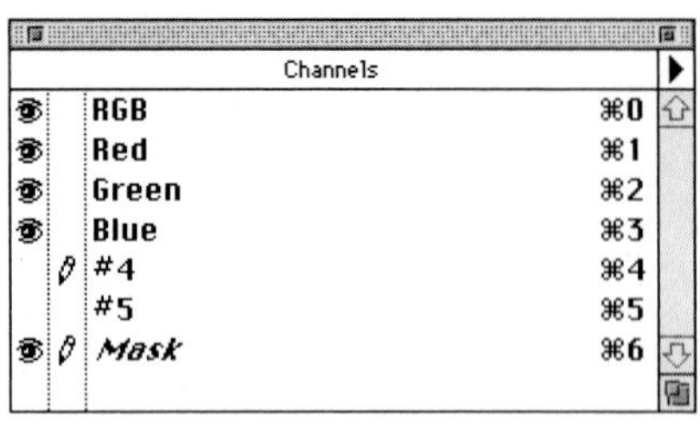

Figure 4–3
In the Channels palette, an eye indicates a visible channel; a pencil indicates an active channel.

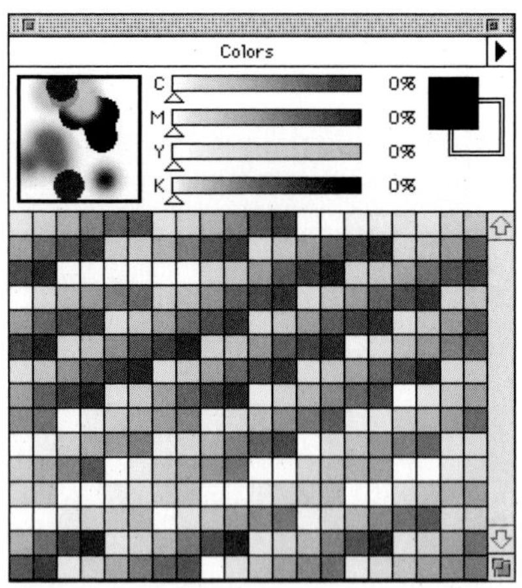

Figure 4–4
The Colors palette

as channels via the Save Selection submenu. A discussion of channels and the use of the Channels palette appears in Chapter 5, "Image Selection and Masking."

Colors Palette

The Colors palette (Figure 4–4) allows the selection of foreground and background colors from the RGB (Red, Green, and Blue), HSB (Hue, Saturation, and Brightness), CMYK (Cyan, Magenta, Yellow, and Black) and Lab (Lightness and Chroma) color models, as well as the Grayscale model. You can mix your own custom colors by using many of the painting tools in the scratchpad, which is in the upper-left area of the palette. Custom palettes created to assist in specifying printing ink colors, such as the ANPA, Pantone, Toyo, Focaltone, and Trumatch color systems, can be loaded into the Colors palette. You also can create your own custom palettes, then save and load them into future projects. A complete discussion of the Colors palette appears later in this chapter in the section "Color in Photoshop."

Info Palette

The Info palette (Figure 4–5) provides information about various image parameters, including the precise position of the pointer and the color values of pixels. Use the Info palette to measure angles of rotation, size, and distance, depending on the tool in use. These values are expressed in the *x* and *y* coordinates of the pointer's position using the current ruler units. The Scale command causes the height and width of a selection to appear, as well as the amount (percentage) of change. Use the information in the Info palette as an on-screen densitometer and tape measure.

***Tip*: Leave the Info palette open at all times. Once you get used to it, it will help you control color output and the size and position of elements.**

An important aspect of the Info palette is the color information, which is displayed in two modes simultaniously. Usually the first color shows the current display mode data and the second the desired destination mode data. This gives you access to color values prior to actually converting a document. The color values for pixels can be shown in Grayscale, RGB, HSB, CMYK, and Lab modes. An exclamation point next to a CMYK color value indicates a nonprintable process color.

To change the color modes for the readouts and the measurement units, select the Options pop-out menu (Figure 4–6). Use the Info palette to show the before and after effects of color adjustments to individual pixels.

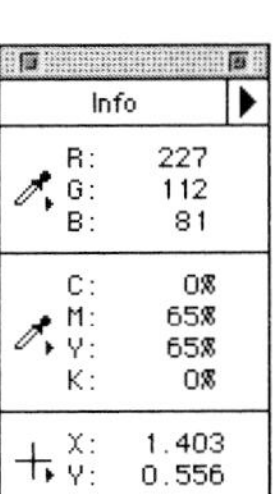

Figure 4–5
The Info palette

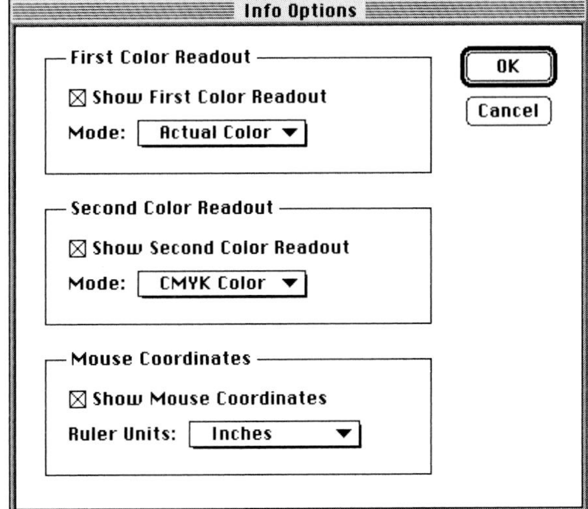

Figure 4–6
The Info Options pop-out dialog box

> **NOTE: The values in the second color readout (especially when converting to CMYK Color mode to make separations for printing) are affected by the Printing Inks Setup and Separation Setup submenus in the Preferences selection under the File menu.**

Paths Palette

The Paths palette (Figure 4–7) allows you to use the Pen tool to draw precise, smooth-edged vector paths. The Pen tool is similar to the Pen tool in Adobe Illustrator and Aldus FreeHand. Paths made in either Photoshop or Illustrator can be swapped easily. The accurate paths can be converted to selections for more precision, as opposed to using the Lasso tool to define a selection. Paths can be saved and then recalled for editing or exporting. Exported paths can be used as clipping paths to mask a Photoshop image that will be used over other images or colors in another program. A complete discussion of the Paths palette is contained in Chapter 5.

Using the Tools

Main Toolbox

The Main Toolbox (Figure 4–8) contains icons for selection and painting tools, as well as for access to the Color Picker for color selection (covered later this chapter under "Color in Photoshop"), the screen display modes (covered in Chapter 2), and the Quick Mask mode. The Quick Mask mode, a new feature in Photoshop, is used for creating and editing temporary masks. More information on masks and their use with the Quick Mask feature can be found in Chapter 5. The Toolbox can be made to disappear and reappear (from the screen), along with any other open floating palettes by pressing the Tab key on the keyboard.

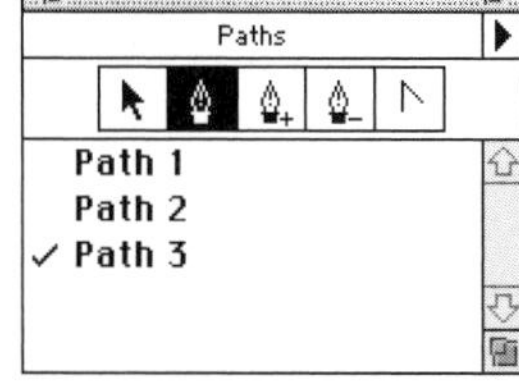

Figure 4–7
The Paths palette

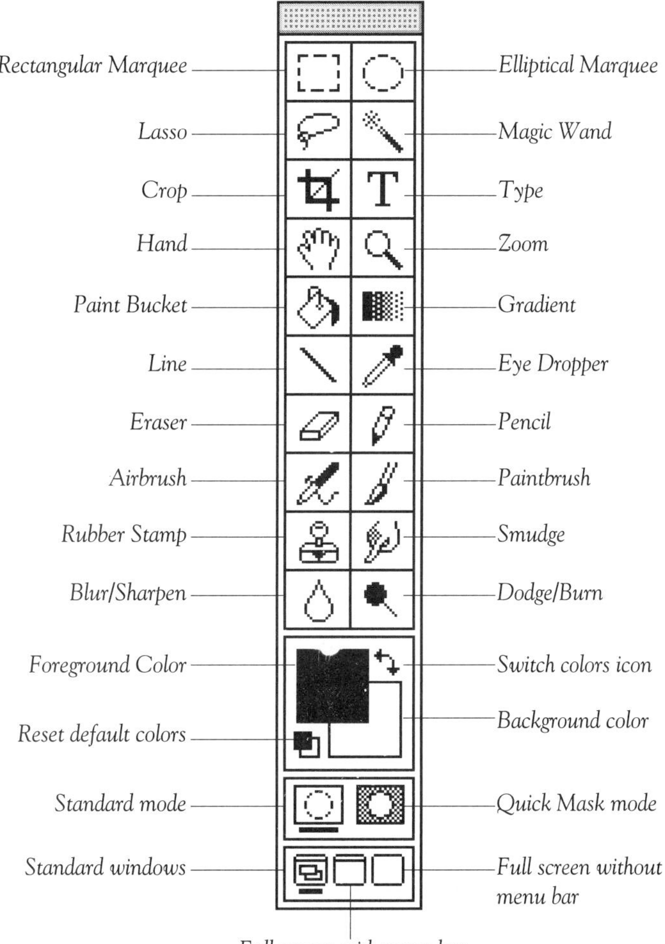

Figure 4–8
The Main toolbox

Common Tool Factors

Here are some factors that apply to the operation of most of the tools.

- Each tool has a unique icon. When using a tool on the screen, your cursor will usually be represented by the specific tool icon. To provide maximum accuracy when using most of the tools, you can replace the tool icon with a precision crosshair. The center point of the crosshair is the "hot spot"; the effect of the tool is centered on the crosshair's hot spot. Note that the crosshair for the Eyedropper tool differs from the crosshair used by the rest of the tools. If you prefer to use the actual tool icons, Figure 4–9 shows the hot spots of each tool.

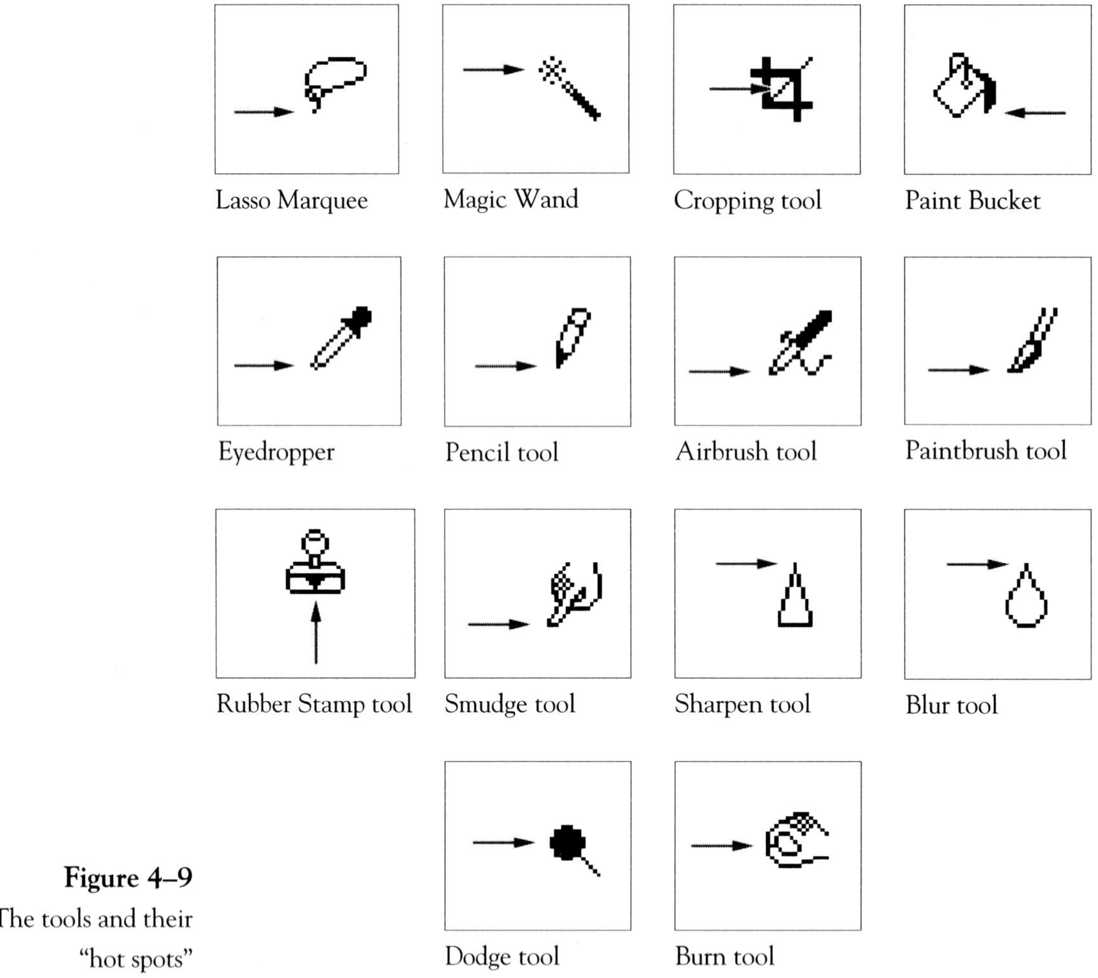

Figure 4–9
The tools and their "hot spots"

***Tip*: To use a crosshair instead of the tool icon, press the Caps Lock key on your keyboard. While the Caps Lock key is activated, the crosshair indicator is active for all tools. If you decide that you like using the crosshair feature, just remember that if you save a file while the Caps Lock key is depressed, the letters WILL ALL BE CAPS when you start typing the name of the file.**

- While using the drawing tools, you can temporarily change the current tool into an Eyedropper if you want to select a new foreground color from a color found in the image by pressing the Option key. Clicking on a color will make that color the active foreground color.

***Tip*: While using the Eyedropper tool, you can click on image windows other than the one you are currently working within in order to pick up colors not found in your working document. Using this capability, you can make a document with your preferred color palette, and select colors from this document at any time.**

- If you want to use a tool to draw a straight line (or in the case of the softening or sharpening tools, to apply the effect in a straight line), choose the tool and click once where you want the effect of the tool to start. Then hold down the Shift key and click an end point. The result will be a straight line between the two points.
- Hold down the Shift key while painting to constrain movements to 90 degree increments; release the Shift key to continue in the freehand mode. Holding down the Shift key while painting with the Line tool will constrain its movement to 45 degree increments.
- If you press a number from 1 through 0 before using a tool, you will set the Opacity (transparency), Pressure, or Exposure (depending on the tool in use) from 10 to 100 percent. For example, before you paint with the Paintbrush, press the 4 key and your painting Opacity will be set to 40 percent.
- Double-clicking on most tools in the toolbox will open the tool's Options window (Figure 4–10), allowing you to modify controllable parameters that affect the way the tool works. For example, in the Paintbrush or Airbrush Options window you can specify the Paint Fade-Out rate and Stylus Pressure options. The Fade-out rate determines the distance the tool can go before the "ink" flow gradually runs out.

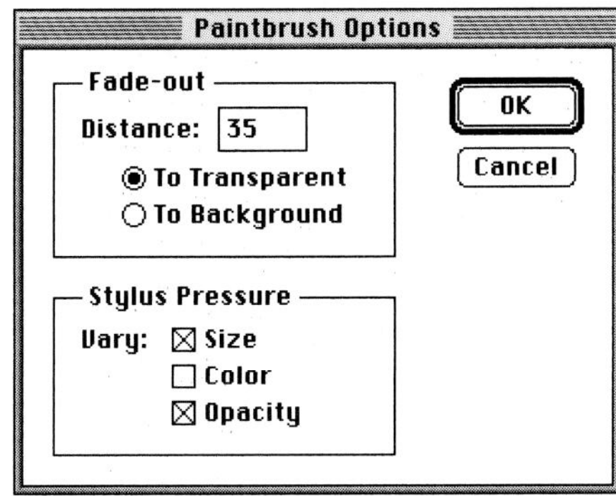

Figure 4–10
Setting a Fade-out rate and Stylus Pressure options in the Paintbrush Options dialog box

- If you're working on a floating selection with an editing tool, you can hold down the Command key to invoke the arrow, which will let you move the selection without switching tools manually.

Control the use of a cordless pen on a pressure-sensitive digitizing tablet, such as the Calcomp, Kurta, and Wacom tablets, in the tool's Options window. You have the option to set the variation in pressure to affect the size, color, and opacity of the tool. Set the stylus pressure options for the Pencil, Paintbrush, Airbrush, Rubber Stamp, Smudge, Blur/Sharpen, and Dodge/Burn tools. The Wacom ArtZ ADB Tablet was used to create illustrations and experiment with various effects in the production of this book.

Tip: **The brush size in the Brushes palette also affects the dynamics of the stylus. Try using larger brush sizes. If a small brush size is selected the range of the tools will be limited.**

Using the Brushes Palette with the Tools

The expanded Brushes palette controls the selection of brush shapes and parameters. Brushes used for painting and editing appear in this palette. In the Brushes palette, you also can control the Opacity and Modes settings for most tools and functions in Photoshop. From the Brushes Palette and its pop-out menu (Figure 4–2), you can create and delete brushes, define brush options, and save and load sets of brushes.

To access the Brushes palette, select Show Brushes from the Window menu. This floating window can now be collapsed to save screen space by clicking on the zoom box in the upper-right corner of the palette while leaving the pop-out menus still available.

The brush shape for a selected tool is shown in the Brushes palette. To choose a Brush shape, click on the desired shape. Numbers inside a circle (diameter) indicate a brush too large to be shown in the palette. The Brushes palette now includes the ability to change most of the parameters previously accessed in the individual tool dialogs.

Adding, Editing, and Removing Brushes

By selecting the pop-out menu, you can create new brushes or edit existing brushes. Any new brushes will appear in the lower part of the palatte window. You can also delete brushes if you no longer use them.

Select New Brush from the Brushes palette pop-out menu to create a new brush. The New Brush dialog box will appear (Figure 4–11). This dialog box is the same if you double-click on any existing brush in the Brushes palette.

The lower-left preview shows the current brush angle and roundness. The lower-right preview displays the brush stroke. As you change the settings the previews will simultaneously show the effects.

The Diameter slider changes the brush size from 1 to 999 pixels. The hardness slider reflects a percentage of the brush's diameter (0–100%). The Spacing options control the distance between brush marks. Specify the spacing with a percentage of the brush's diameter from 1 to 999. The higher the value entered, the more space to be added between brush marks. Click the check box next to Spacing to turn off its function. With Spacing off, the mouse will be sensitive to the speed at which it is moved, causing it to skip more pixels at faster speeds (Figure 4–12).

The Angle option is like varying the tilt of a brush in your hand as you paint. It is measured as an angle from the horizontal. The Roundness option varies the shape as an oval anywhere from a circle to a straight line. A 100% setting will be a perfect circle.

A brush may be deleted by selecting it in the Brushes palette and then choosing Delete Brush from the pop-out menu.

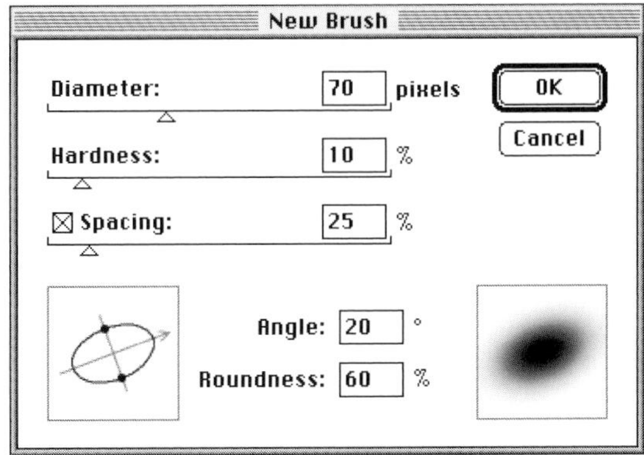

Figure 4–11
The New Brush dialog box

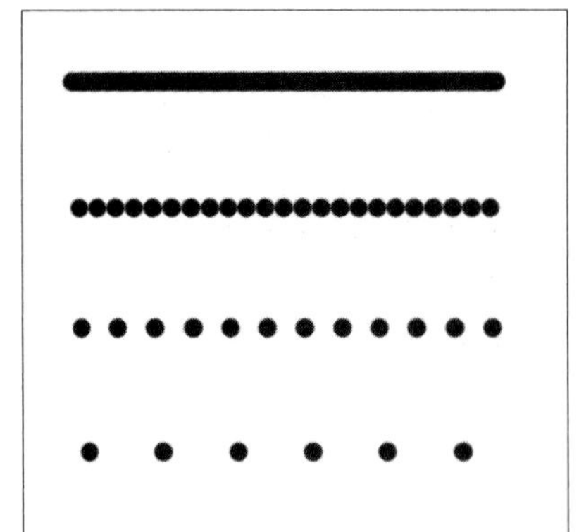

Figure 4–12
Spacing set to 25%, 100%, 200%, and 400%

Custom Brush Shapes

Create custom brush shapes by selecting parts of an image. A selection with soft edges (light gray) will simulate an anti-aliased brush. Although a custom brush can be made from any selection, they are usually better against a white background.

Use the Define Brush option from the Brushes palette pop-out menu after making a selection to create a custom brush (Figure 4–13).

Options for custom brushes can be set in the Brushes palette pop-out menu or by double-clicking on the brush's icon (Figure 4–14). Spacing and Anti-aliasing are the only options. Large brushes cannot be anti-aliased.

Saving Brushes

You can now save a palette of brushes and then load them for use with any other document. Although the Brushes palette can hold as many brushes as you need, it will be more efficient if you group and create your own personal sets of brushes. The Save Brushes and Load Brushes commands in the Brushes palette pop-out menu allow you to do what their names say.

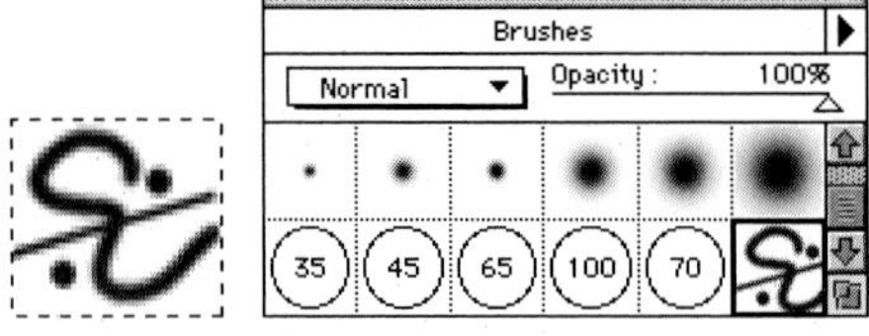

Figure 4–13
A Custom brush defined from a selection of an image

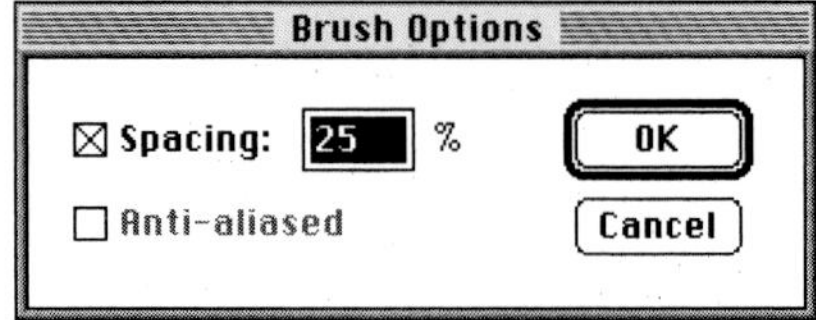

Figure 4–14
The Brush Options dialog for a custom brush; Anti-aliasing is not available for larger brushes.

Brushes stored in a file can be added to the current palette with the Append Brushes command. Remember, you can always load the Default Brushes file in the Brushes & Patterns folder, which is installed with Adobe Photoshop, to return to the original set of brushes.

Opacity, Pressure, and Exposure Controls

The Opacity Slider control appears when the Type, Paint Bucket, Gradient, Line, Pencil, Paintbrush, and the Rubber Stamp tools are selected. The percentage of opacity will determine the transparency of the paint being laid down by a particular tool in relation to the underlying image (Figure 4–15). For example, when a solid black is the Foreground color and the Opacity is set at 30%, the result will be a 30% black blended over the parts of the image that the tool is passed. Opacity can also be controlled with the number keys on the keyboard. By pressing a number from 1 through 0 before you use the tool, you will set the transparency from 10 to 100 percent. For example, before you paint with the Paintbrush tool, press the 4 key and your painting opacity will be set to 40 percent. Be aware, however, that this sets the opacity for that tool until it is changed again.

The control for setting the pressure appears when the Airbrush, Smudge, and Blur/Sharpen tools are selected. Pressure controls the "force" with which a tool is applied to the surface. For example, in the case of the Smudge tool, a higher pressure setting will spread paint farther (Figure 4–16). With the painting tools, higher settings result in more paint applied to each stroke.

Figure 4–15
A brush stroke with the foreground color set to 100% black and the opacity set to 30% over a 10%, 25%, and 50% black panel

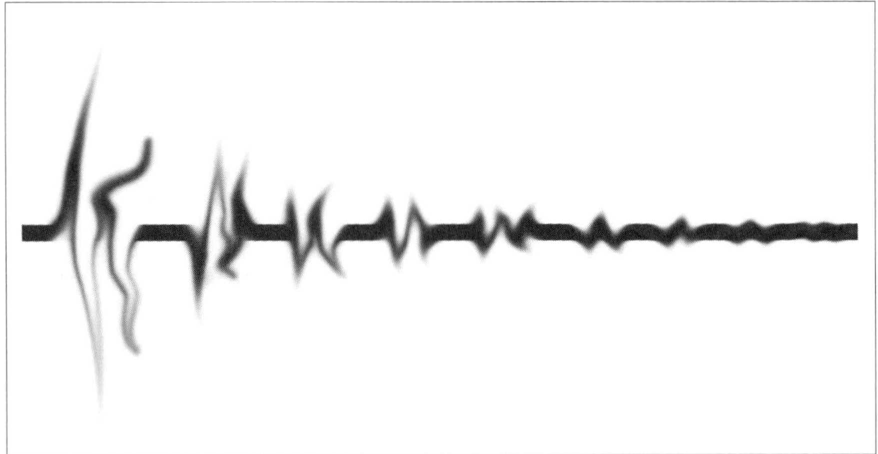

Figure 4–16
A black line distorted with the Smudge tool at different pressure settings going from 90% to 10% left to right at 10% increments

Exposure is used by the Dodge/Burn tool. A higher number equals a stronger effect. For example, to dodge more heavily with the Dodge tool, set the Exposure number to a high value. The exposure can be set to affect either the highlights, midtones, or shadows.

Painting and Editing Modes

Another new capability in the Brushes palette is to control pixels that are affected by a painting or editing tool. The modes also apply to the Fill and Composite Controls discussed in Chapter 5. Each of the tools allows you to apply color (or value) in one of ten modes, which are chosen from a pop-up menu in the Brushes palette (Figure 4–17). The mode choices will change depending on which tool is selected in the Main toolbox. The modes are: Normal, Darken, Lighten, Hue, Saturation, Color, Luminosity, Multiply, Screen, and Dissolve.

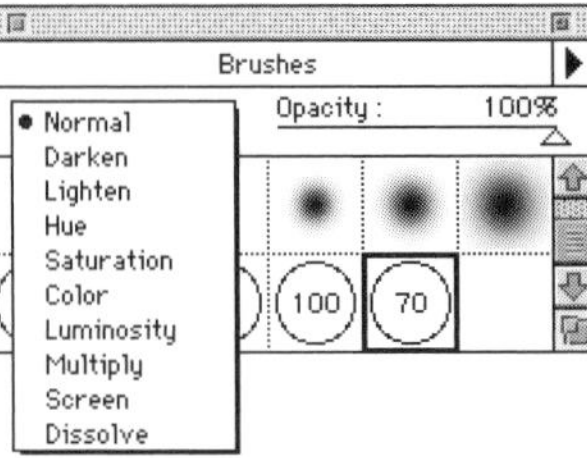

Figure 4–17
The mode choices in the Brushes palette

The **Normal** mode is the default setting for all the tools. When selected, the current foreground color is applied as a solid, opaque color fill. **Darken** mode applies a tool only to pixels lighter than the current foreground color, while pixels darker will not change. **Lighten** mode applies a tool only to areas that are darker than the current foreground color. Lighter pixels will not change.

The Lighten and Darken modes are also found within other features of the program, such as the Composite Controls dialog and the Fill command. They work much the same way; the brightness of the foreground color sets the sensitivity, or threshold, of tinting and pasting a selected region or masked area.

Use **Hue** mode to change pixels to the foreground color. The saturation and luminosity values are left unchanged. Only the saturation values of pixels you paint will change in the **Saturation** mode.

Use the **Color** mode for tinting or changing colors. In this mode, only the hue component (or actual "color") is applied to the image, leaving the values untouched. When colorizing grayscale images, use the Color mode to apply "transparent" tints of the current foreground color. The luminosity of the image remains intact, while the hue and saturation values of the pixels change.

The **Luminosity** mode is the inverse of the Color mode. When you paint or fill in the Luminosity mode, only the lightness of the pixels change, while the color values are unaffected. The **Multiply** mode darkens the image by multiplying the color values when painting or filling areas. **Screen** mode lightens the colors in an image and tints them in the direction of the foreground color. The Screen mode does the opposite of the Multiply mode.

The **Dissolve** mode works like the Airbrush tool in the original MacPaint program by randomly replacing the original pixel colors with the foreground color. This dithered effect is most effectively created by setting the Opacity to a low percentage and selecting a large brush shape and painting with the Paintbrush or Airbrush tool.

Tip: **If you encounter a problem with tools that do not seem to be drawing on the screen when used, check your mode settings (Darken, Lighten, etc.) to make sure that you are not using a setting that prohibits the tool from applying paint as expected.**

Individual Tool Overviews

Rectangular, Elliptical Marquee, and Lasso Tools

Use these tools to make freehand or constrained selections of all or parts of an image. Each has its own particular characteristics and uses, depending on what you're trying to do.A more detailed discussion of the selection tools appears in Chapter 5, "Image Selection and Masking."

Magic Wand Tool

The unique and powerful Magic Wand tool is also used to make selections. By looking at the color similarities between adjacent pixels, the Magic Wand tool allows the selection of areas without trying to trace outlines with other selection tools. A complete discussion of the Magic Wand tool also appears in Chapter 5.

Cropping Tool

As the name implies, this tool eliminates unwanted parts of an image. The Cropping tool is an expanded version of the Crop command found under the Edit menu. With the Crop command, you use the rectangular selection tool to select the part of the image that you want to keep, then select Crop from the Edit menu. But by using the Cropping tool, you can determine the resolution of the final cropped image, and adjust the cropping area with the resizing handles before actually completing a crop.

To use the Cropping tool, drag the Cropping tool over the area to be cropped (Figure 4–18); the very center of the tool is the "hot spot." Four handles will appear at the corners of the selection after releasing the mouse button. Drag the handles independently to redefine the selected area. Move the cursor into the selected area to transform it into scissors and then Click. You also can double-click on the Cropping tool to open the Cropping Tool Options dialog box (Figure 4–19).

***Tip*: When cropping an image, the selected area will be the new image size. If you want white space around an image, it is better to erase the unwanted perimeter, or place the newly cropped image on a larger canvas. See the discussion of Canvas Size in Chapter 6, "Image Processing."**

By entering values into the Width and Height fields (which can be specified in a variety of units selectable from the pop-up menus next to the fields), you can crop images to a predetermined size. The resolution

Figure 4–18 Image before cropping, showing handles before cropping, and image after cropping

Figure 4–19 The Cropping Tool Options dialog box

Cropping Tool Options

Width: 4 inches
Height: 6 inches
Resolution: 300 pixels/inch
OK
Cancel

field allows you to specify the final resolution of the cropped image. You can crop and resample the image in one step.

If you want to crop and rotate an area in one pass, press the Option key while pressing on a resizing handle. You can now rotate the Cropping tool, using the selected handle as the central rotation axis. When you click inside the cropping area, the image is automatically rotated and cropped.

Type Tool

Like most other bitmapped graphics programs, Photoshop allows you to create bitmapped type for use in illustrations. But unlike other raster programs, in Photoshop you can create type in a variety of resolutions and it can be anti-aliased, or smoothed against the background (more on this in a moment). Using the special effects filters, you can also create outrageous display faces in myriad colors and textures.

When you select the Type tool and click anywhere in the active document window, the Type Tool dialog appears (Figure 4–20). Specify the font and size, leading (line spacing), letter spacing, alignment (justification), and style. You can create type in sizes between 4 and 960 points or pixels. You specify type size in either pixels or points by pressing on the pop-up menu next to the size number field.

You enter text by typing in the text field in the lower portion of the dialog. Standard Macintosh editing techniques apply here; and, although the Edit menu is not available while you are in the Type tool window, the keyboard equivalents for Cut, Copy, and Paste (Command X, C, and V, respectively) function on highlighted text.

Up to 255 characters can be typed in a text field, all of which must have the same style specifications. To create blocks of type with different styling, make multiple blocks of type and combine them manually. (After all, no one ever claimed Photoshop to be a page-layout or typographical-effects program!) The text will appear as a floating selection so that you can move it around the screen. You can delete it by pressing the Delete key on your keyboard (which will not disturb the image behind it), or by using any of Photoshop's tools or controls to modify it.

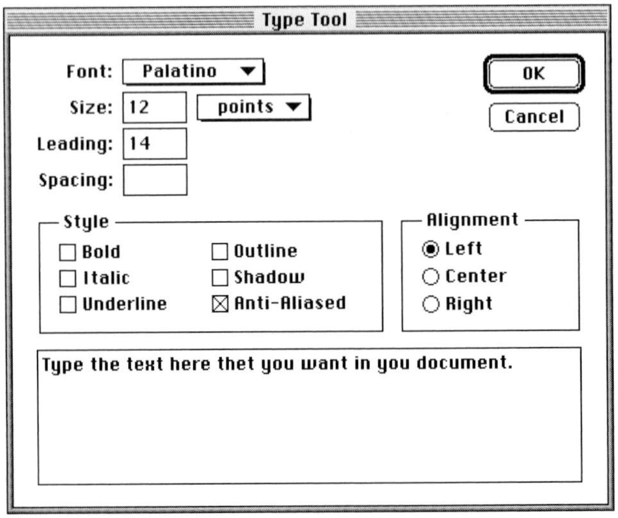

Figure 4–20
The Type Tool dialog box

To create and manipulate text:

1. Select the desired color for your text (the current foreground color), and click the Text tool on an image.
2. Type in some text, choose your font size and style. Click OK.
3. The type will appear on the image as a floating selection, which is filled with the current Foreground color. To change its color, click on the current Foreground color and pick another hue. Select the Fill command from the Edit menu. You can also press the Command and Delete keys on your keyboard for a quick fill using the current Foreground color. You can continually change the color of the type as long as you do not deselect it (if you click anywhere on the background image outside of the text, the text will be deselected and become part of the surrounding pixels).
4. Choose the Scale, Skew, Perspective, or Distort command from the Effects command in the Image menu. Handles appear on the four edges of the type. Press and drag on a handle to manipulate the text. Experiment with it!

Any Photoshop command or filter can be applied to selected text for endless visual experimentation and fun. You can change the color of text by using the Hue/Saturation controls in the Image menu; you can apply strange filters, paste bizarre textures into or behind type; or you can discover a new kind of elemental particle. Just about any visual phenomenon is possible.

***Tip*: While the text is still selected (immediately after creation), you can open the Composite Controls dialog (Edit menu) and change the way that the text interacts with the underlying image. For example, using Composite Controls, you can vary the transparency of the text, allowing the background to show through; or, by using the Color/Lighten/Darken modes, you can apply the type as a tint or drop it out of the background.**

Photoshop enhances scaled sizes of all Type 1 fonts for maximum on-screen quality by using the Adobe Type Manager (ATM) software. It uses the printer description files in the System folder as a foundation to calculate and draw screen fonts (Figure 4–21). In conjunction with

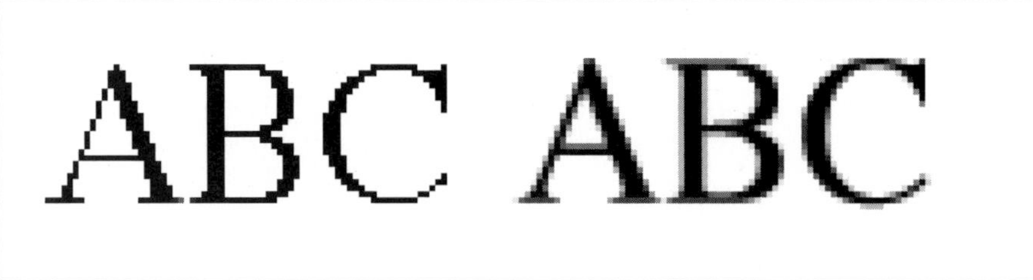

Figure 4–21
Normal bitmapped type (left) and anti-aliased type (right) using Adobe Type Manager (ATM)

ABC ABC

Photoshop, ATM opens the doors to a wide world of smooth, high-quality, anti-aliased, bitmapped type.

> **NOTE: Remember, Photoshop text is not normal outline PostScript text when you save and print it. Do not expect to achieve the quality of normal object-oriented text typically produced by illustration programs such as Illustrator and FreeHand.**

If you are running ATM normally with the rest of your system, it will automatically be used by Photoshop. To get the highest quality type, though, make sure to activate the anti-aliased checkbox in the Type Tool dialog box.

***Tip*: If you want to see the way type will look on a background without deselecting it, use the Hide Edges command in the Select menu (Command-H). Even though the "marching ants" selection effect is hidden, the type remains selected and can be moved into a new position.**

When creating large-sized type, it is preferable to specify the size in the text creation dialog, as opposed to stretching the type with the dynamic stretching command. Stretched type is much coarser than large sizes that are specified in the text creation dialog.

To deselect individual characters in a floating text block, you can either hold down the Command key and drag the lasso around the character or characters you do not want selected, or you can hold down the Shift and Command keys and drag the lasso around the characters you want to remain selected.

Hand Tool

Use the Hand tool to move an image that is too large to fit in the active window. To use the Hand tool, select it in the toolbox and move the cursor into the active image area. By pressing and dragging, you can move an image in the window so that you can see the rest of it. As you drag, you may need to continue to move the hand outside of the active window to see more.

Tip: **By double-clicking on the Hand tool icon in the toolbox, you will return the magnified detail of an image to fit entirely within the document window.**

Zoom Tool

The Zoom tool and the zoom commands in the Windows menu are used to magnify and reduce your view of parts of an image when you need to work on small details or see the entire image. When using the Zoom tool you are not changing the actual size of a document, just how you are looking at it.

The magnification factor of an image is shown in the document's title bar (Figure 2-3). Photoshop allows magnification and reduction up to 16 times the original view of a document. For example, if 4:1 is shown in the title bar, the magnification factor is 4. This means the image is being viewed at four times the original size, or 400 percent. If 1:4 is shown in the title bar, the view of the image is reduced four times, or 25 percent. A 1:1 view of a document, or 100 percent, is calculated based on the resolution of your screen and of the image, not on the dimensions of the document. Since screen resolution is usually about 72 pixels per inch, documents having a high image resolution will show up larger when viewed on-screen than those with lower image resolutions.

To use the Zoom tool, click on its icon in the toolbox and move the cursor into the active image area. You will notice that inside the circle of the magnifying glass icon, a plus symbol appears. With each click of the mouse, the view of the image will magnify by a factor of 2. Now, hold down the option key while clicking on the mouse and the symbol inside the circle of the cursor will change to a minus sign. Click on the mouse and the view of the image will reduce by a factor of 2.

The area of the image you magnify or reduce will be centered around the point you click. When you cannot magnify or reduce the view of an image any further, the circle of the cursor will appear blank.

Tip: By double-clicking on the Zoom tool icon in the toolbox, you will return to a 1:1 view. While in any other tool, press and hold the Command key and the Spacebar to go immediately to the magnifying Zoom tool or press and hold the Option key and the Spacebar to reach the reduction Zoom tool.

By pressing and dragging the Zoom tool cursor in an image, you can select an area to magnify up to a factor of 16, depending on the size of the area you select. You can also magnify and reduce your view of a document by selecting Zoom In and Zoom Out, found under the Window menu. These commands will change your view by factors of 2.

Paint Bucket Tool

Mac enthusiasts have grown to know this tool; it uses the currently selected color to fill the area over which it is applied. When you click on a particular color, it will fill the color area with the current foreground color.

Unlike its predecessors in other paint packages, the Photoshop Paint Bucket has Tolerance and Anti-aliased settings, which are available in the Paint Bucket Options dialog (Figure 4–22). They are accessed by double-clicking on the Paint Bucket tool. In most other paint programs, the bucket will fill only the color over which it is used. The Tolerance setting determines additional values that will be filled. The higher the tolerance setting, the farther a dropped Paint Bucket will spread. Let's say an image area is made up of three or four similar colors. If you have used the bucket in other programs in this situation, you know the bucket will

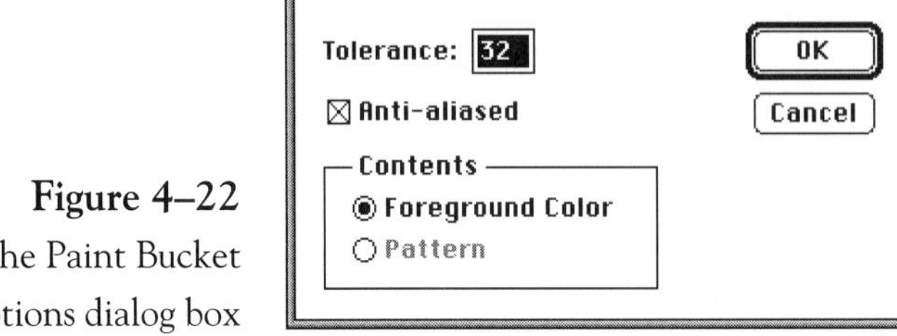

Figure 4–22
The Paint Bucket Options dialog box

fill only tiny portions of the area, or only one of the three or four colors. With the Tolerance setting, the bucket can be set to fill the entire area.

The Anti-aliased setting will make the outside edges of the fill appear fuzzy. In general, the higher the resolution setting, the smoother the edge. The Contents options fill the selection with the foreground color or with a defined pattern. The Modes and Opacity settings in the Brushes palette will also control how the color is applied with the Paintbucket.

Gradient Tool

This useful tool will assist you in creating realistic images. Unless an object is bathed on all sides with spotlights, no object in real life is a solid color to the viewer. If you study your surroundings closely, you will notice that all the objects in a room, for example, including the walls, are made up of gradients of color. The surface color of any object will diminish in intensity as it moves away from the light source. Even the subtlest of gradients will add dimensionality to an object.

***Tip*: To create realistic 3-D objects with shading, you might want to create them in a 3-D illustration program such as Raydream Designer, StrataVision 3-D, Swivel 3-D, MacroMedia 3-D, or Alias Sketch, and then import them into Photoshop.**

Gradients are attained by selecting a starting and an ending color. The starting color is created in the Foreground color box. The ending color is in the Background color box. If red is selected as the foreground color and blue as the background color, the result will be a range of purple shades that blend from red into blue.

The Gradient tool is also applied to create large gradient areas such as skies. This effect is traditionally achieved with an airbrush. Use the Gradient tool in a press-and-drag fashion. The first press of the mouse button lays down the foreground color. Dragging the mouse with the button depressed will produce a line that follows the movement of the mouse. The length of the line will determine the smoothness of the transition from one color to the next. The direction of the line will determine the direction of the fill. Releasing the mouse button will activate the fill, and at that point the background color will be used.

The Gradient tool's application of a fill can be modified to create some unusual effects. There are two types of fills: *linear* and *radial*. The linear fill will create fills where the transition is in straight lines that follow the direction in which the fill was applied. The radial will make a fill of concentric tones, from the foreground color out, as in a sunburst effect.

In both types of fill, the Midpoint Skew can be defined within the Gradient Options dialog box (Figure 4–23). This sets up the point at which there is an even mix between the foreground and background colors; 50% is the default. A lower percentage will set that midpoint closer to the starting point. For example, 25% will set the midpoint one-quarter of the way from the start to the end of the fill. A higher percentage sets it away from the start.

You also can select one of three Style options in the Gradient Options dialog box. The Style option determines how the fill makes the transition from the foreground color to the background color. The Normal option makes the transition in the same color space as the original image using the intermediate gray levels between the two chosen colors. The Clockwise Spectrum option makes the transition between the two colors using the intermediate hues that lie between the two colors moving clockwise around the color wheel. (See the Apple Color Picker in Figure 4–37.) The Counterclockwise Spectrum works the same as the Clockwise Spectrum option except that the transition between the two colors will be in counterclockwise direction around the color wheel.

A Mode for the effects of the Gradient tool, as well as the Opacity settings, may be selected from the pop-up menu in the Brushes palette.

To create a clear blue sky for instance, use the Gradient tool as follows:

1. Select the starting color of a rich blue in the foreground color.
2. Select a lighter shade of blue in the background color box. This will serve as the color along the horizon, which usually appears to be lighter.

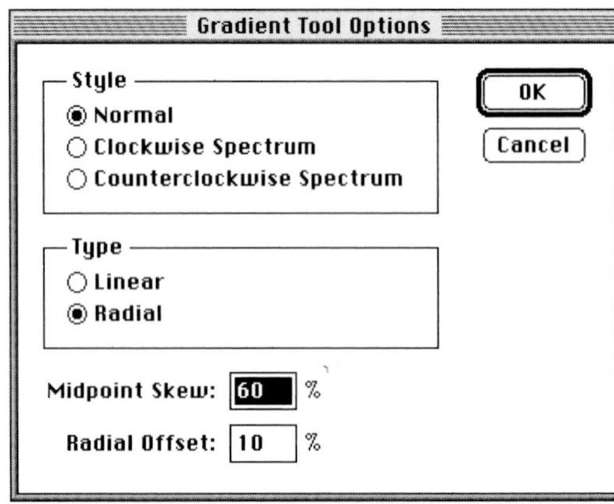

Figure 4–23
The Gradient Tool Options dialog box

3. With the Gradient tool, press and drag from the top down.
4. Release the mouse upon reaching the bottom of the sky area and the fill will be applied.

Line Tool

This tool's function dates back to the early MacPaint days. In Photoshop, it has undergone some evolutionary changes. The line weight can be specified in pixels and the resulting line will be anti-aliased. Place arrowheads at the tips, on either end or both. Modify them into various shapes and styles by adjusting their width, height, and concavity in the Line Tool Options dialog box (Figures 4–24 and 4–25).

***Tip*: You also can use the Line tool to measure distances in the document. To do this, define a line width of 0 in the Line Tool Options dialog box and choose Show Info from the Window menu. As you drag the pointer, the Info palette displays the *x* and *y* coordinates of the starting point, the change in *x* and *y*, the distance, and the angle.**

Eyedropper Tool

Select colors from open documents for the foreground and background colors with the Eyedropper tool. As you click the mouse button on parts of an image, the colors detected will be shown in the foreground color box. Click anywhere on an image with the Eyedropper tool to select a foreground color from an image. Hold down the option key and click to select a background color. You may also select colors from images in inactive windows with the Eyedropper tool.

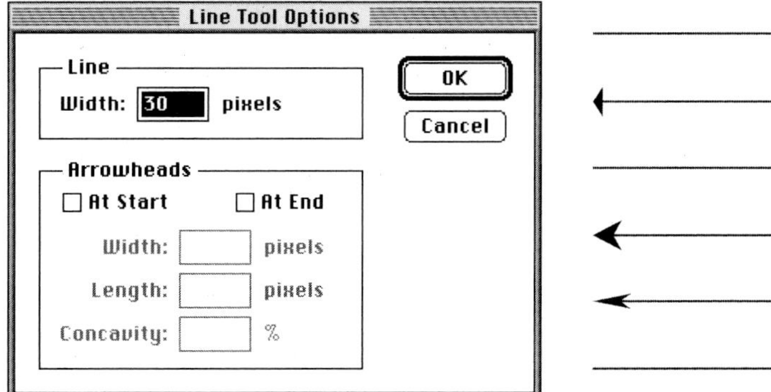

Figure 4–24
The Line Tool Options dialog box

Figure 4–25
Examples of different arrowheads

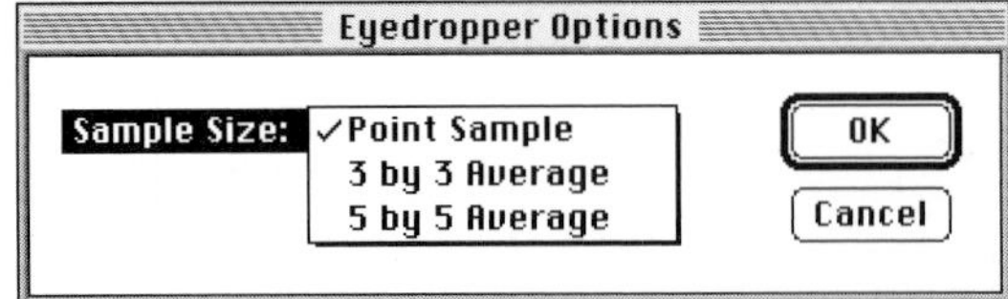

Figure 4–26
Eyedropper Options dialog box showing the available sample sizes

You can change the area the Eyedropper tool uses to select a color through the Eyedropper Options dialog box (Figure 4–26). The pop-up menu in the dialog box has three options. The Point Sample option reads the exact value of any one pixel. The 3 by 3 Average option takes a 3-pixel by 3-pixel area and averages the values within. The 5 by 5 Average option does the same thing as the 3 by 3 option but with a 5-pixel by 5-pixel area. To see information about the pixels, use the Info palette in conjunction with the Eyedropper tool, and use the Point Sample option.

Eraser Tool

Press and drag the Eraser tool over any portion of the image to erase it. If the current background color is other than white, the Eraser will erase to that color.

***Tip*: Change the background color of a page by to setting the Background color in the Toobox and double-clicking the Eraser tool. This is much faster than filling a background with a different foreground color using the Paint Bucket tool or Fill command.**

If you press the Option key, the Eraser becomes the Magic Eraser. This turns the normal Eraser into a reverting tool. As you erase with the Magic Eraser, the image reverts to its last saved version on disk, regardless of the changes made to the image since the last time it was saved. The Magic Eraser will not work if the image has been resized or resampled.

***Tip*: The Rubber Stamp tool also has the ability to selectively revert areas of an image to the last saved version of a document. The difference is that the edges of the Magic Eraser tool are hard and jaggy, while the Rubber Stamp has anti-aliased edges. See the section on the Rubber Stamp tool for more information.**

Figure C–1
The grayscale "Boats" by Michael Roney was converted to Lab mode and colorized by filling areas with the **a** and **b** channels active and the Lightness channel inactive.

Figure C–2
The colors only were then inverted with the **a** and **b** channels active and the Lightness channel inactive.

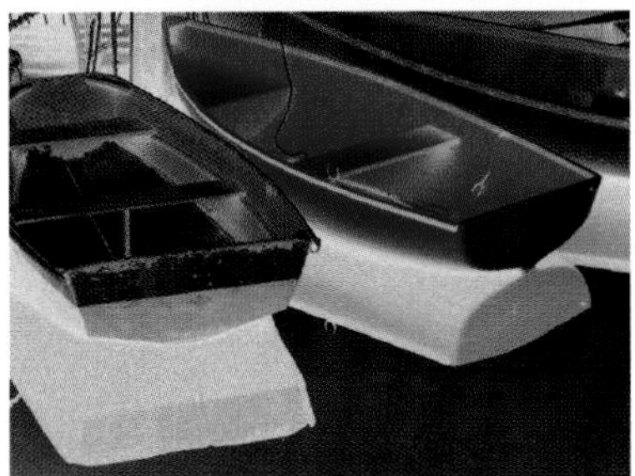

Figure C–3
This time, only the *values* in the colorized photograph were inverted with the Lightness channel active and the **a** and **b** channels inactive.

Figure C–4
The curves in the Curves command dialog box were dramatically altered for the **a** and **b** channels only on this photograph by Mark Siprut.

Figure C–5
This time, the values were dramatically altered with curves in the Curves command dialog box for the Lightness channel only.

Figure C–6
Bill Niffenegger used the Variations command to make a color cast and saturation test for a color separation test sheet. For the above, he used: (1) More Saturated; (2) just right; (3) Less Saturated; (4) More Blue to the Midtones; (5) More Green to the Midtones; (6) More Red to the Midtones.

A variety of filters, both native to Photoshop and plug-ins, were used to create these effects on Andrew Rodney's photograph, "Dog in Bowl."

Figure C–7 Emboss and Trace Edges

Figure C–8 Pinch

Figure C–9 Aldus Gallery Effects Volume 1, Dry Brush

Figure C–10 Aldus Gallery Effects Volume 1, Mosaic

Figure C–11 Aldus Gallery Effects Volume 1, Splatter

Figure C–12 Aldus Gallery Effects Volume 2, Glowing Edges

Figure C–13 KPT (Kai's Power Tools) Texture

Figure C–14 KPT Find Edges and Invert

Figure C–15 Andromeda 3-D Box and Sphere on Grid

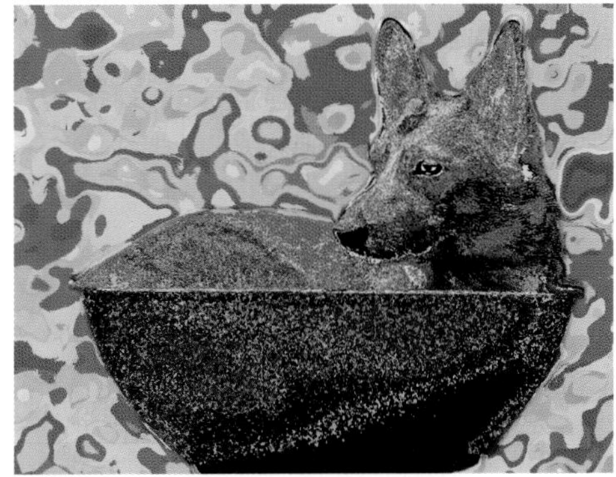

Figure C–16 Second Glance Chrommassage

Figure C–17 Xaos Tools Paint Alchemy Oil Canvas

Figure C–18 Xaos Tools Paint Alchemy Bubbles

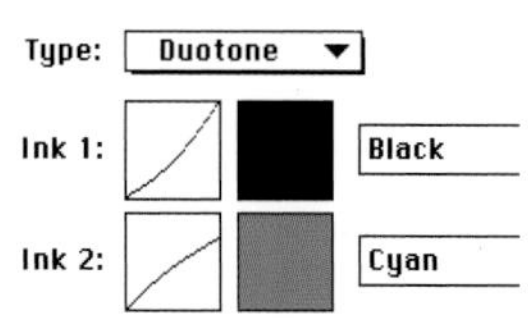

Figure C–19
The duotone curves shown above were applied to the grayscale photograph "Boats" by Merrill Nix.

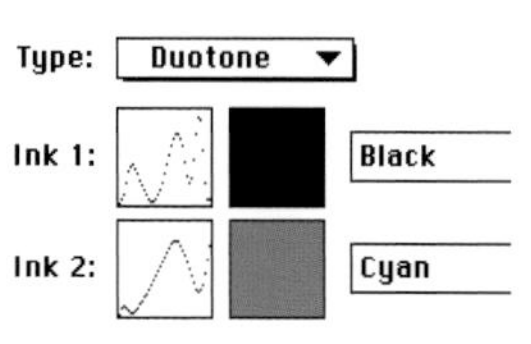

Figure C–20
The curves for this duotone were modified more dramatically.

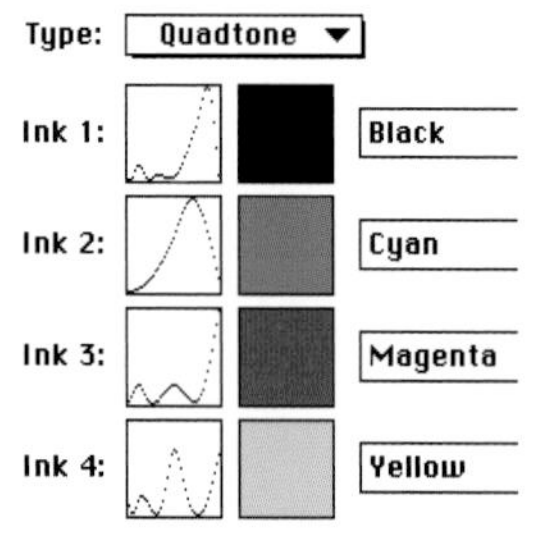

Figure C–21
The above curves resulted in this Quadtone.

Figure C–22
"Fieldbrook General Store" by Anna Stump began as a scanned ink drawing, which the artist then used as a template for overpainting. She applied the Aldus Gallery Effects Watercolor filter as the last step.

Figure C–23
Francois Guerin created "Iced Tea" by painting without a template. After sketching loosely, he filled the shapes with colors, then used the Airbrush tool for transparencies, the Blur tool to blend colors, and the Gaussian Blur filter for softness.

Figure C–24

Three different techniques were used to modify these full-spectrum, 20% tint blends. *Left*: the Gaussian Blur filter (set to 3 pixels) was applied to each of the CMYK channels, as explained in Chapter 8. The center and right strips were created with the help of two halftone screen alternative techniques described in Chapter 7: "Dithered Pixels" (*center*) and "Mezzotint" (*right*).

Figure C–25

Mark Siprut created "Billy" using the Molten Metal technique described in Chapter 7.

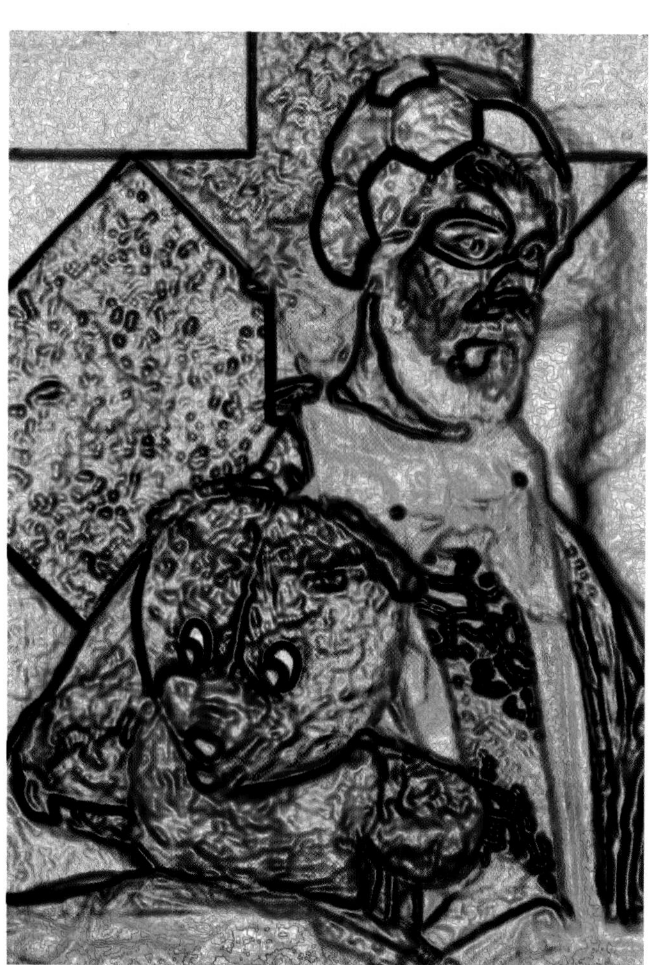

Figure C–26
Mark Siprut created "Maile" using the "Dithered Pixels" technique explained in Chapter 7, "Advanced Photoshop Techniques." The sky (courtesy of CD Folios) was pasted into the background by defining the figure as a mask.

Figure C–27
On this version, Siprut used the "Mezzotint" technique described in Chapter 7, "Advanced Photoshop Techniques."

Figure C–28
This animation sequence, created with the rotoscoping technique explained in Chapter 9, "Animation," uses a series of images from Adobe Premiere saved in the Filmstrip format. After opening the file, each frame is traced and colorized. Then, the file is saved back to the Filmstrip format. Adobe Premiere opens the file and plays it with the original timing and soundrack.

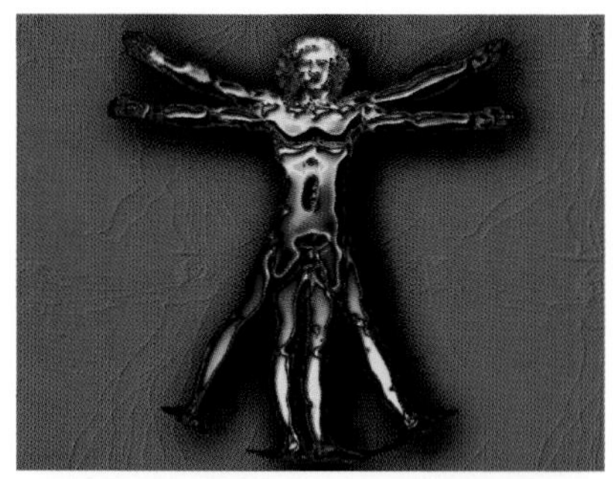

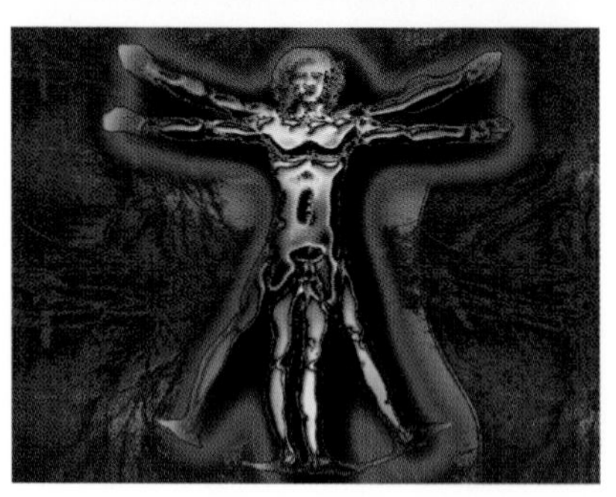

Figure C–29
To create the "Leonardo Pix" series, Kai Krause used various channel operations (Chops), as well as masking, Levels, Curves, and filters. For a detailed explanation of the processes used to create these images, refer to Chapter 7, "Advanced Photoshop Techniques."

Pencil Tool

The Pencil tool works like the pencil found in almost every Macintosh graphics program. As you drag it across the screen, it paints with the Foreground color. The Pencil tool is not automatically anti-aliased. By double-clicking on the Pencil tool in the Main toolbox, the Pencil Options dialog opens (Figure 4–27).

You can set the pencil to automatically erase specific colored pixels to the background color by selecting the Auto Erase option in the Pencil Options dialog box. The Auto Erase feature gives you the illusion that the pixels are being erased, but what really happens is that they are being replaced by pixels of the background color. First you must draw a line with the selected foreground color. If you start the next line on the previously drawn line, it will change to the selected background color. If you draw any where other than on the previously drawn line, it will continue to fill with the foreground color.

The Fade-out rate controls how far you can draw with the pencil before it fades out. Pressure-sensitive digitizing tablets with cordless pens also are supported by the Pencil tool. Simply set the stylus pressure to vary the size, color, and opacity.

***Tip*: When using a pressure-sensitive drawing tablet, you can vary the width of the Pencil tool by pressing down on the stylus. If you use a Wacom tablet, you might wonder how it works with the Pencil. The default brush size for the pencil is a single pixel, and although the pressure sensitivity should affect the pencil, at first nothing will happen. You can change the size of the Pencil tool by choosing a large brush as**

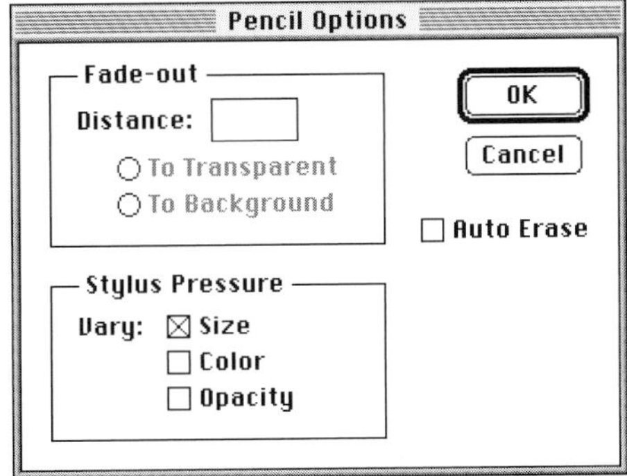

Figure 4–27
The Pencil Options dialog box

the default. The Pencil will still draw a single pixel brush, but as you press down on the stylus, the brush size will increase up to the size of the largest default size selected.

One practical use of the pencil that we have come across is to create a pattern that begins with random pencil strokes and then process it through some of Photoshop's special effects filters, as in Figure 4–28. Other uses of the pencil include pixel-by-pixel editing, or retouching precise areas of an image.

Airbrush Tool

The Airbrush is a seductive painting tool. Similar to the Paintbrush, you use this tool to apply gradual tones of color. The edges of the stroke are much softer than those of the Paintbrush, resulting in a close simulation

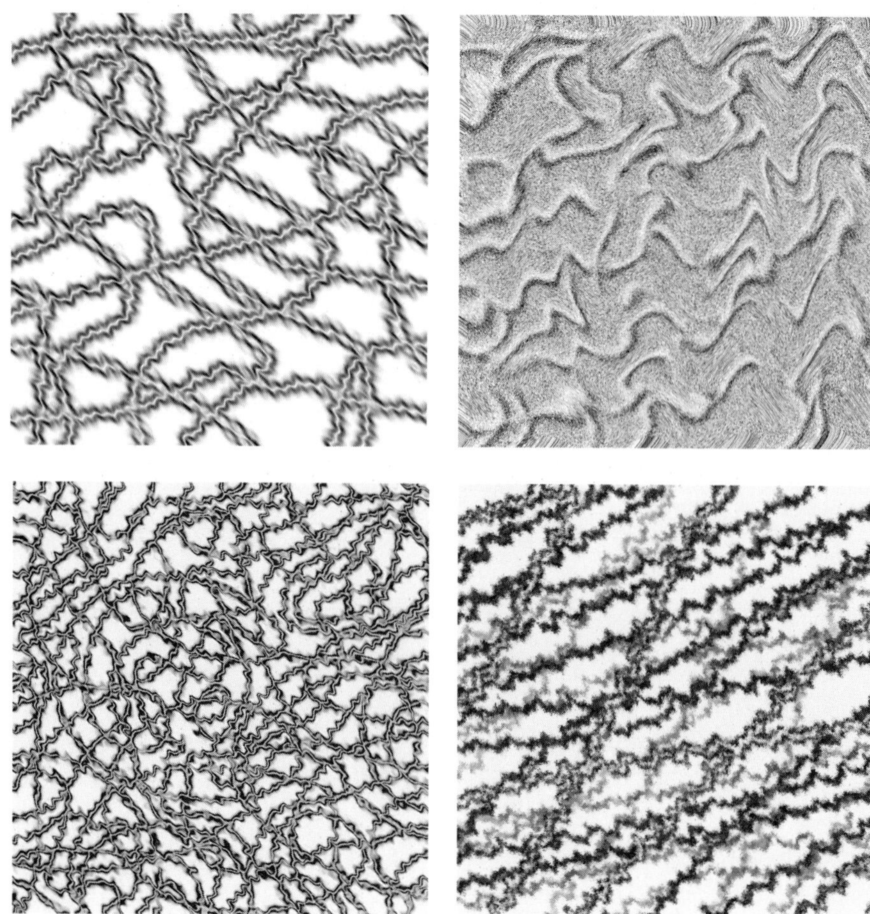

Figure 4–28
Examples of random pencil strokes processed through some of Photoshop's special effects filters

of the traditional airbrush look. Colors applied as soft, subtle sprays make it possible to add just a hint of color. Passing over a previous stroke gradually builds up the density of paint.

Some applications of this tool include adding make-up to skin tones, adding highlights and shadows to an object, and tinting areas with soft color. It can also simulate reflections on metal where tones of varying grays or colors can be sprayed, as you can with a traditional airbrush.

Double-click on the Airbrush tool to open the Airbrush Options dialog box (Figure 4–29). The Distance box controls how far a stroke will go before it runs out of ink. Unlike its real-world counterpart, it can be accurately controlled. The Stylus Pressure selections will allow a cordless pen on a pressure-sensitive tablet to vary either the color or the apparent pressure of the Airbrush tool.

Tip: In traditional methods, an airbrush is used to achieve smooth gradients for large areas such as skies. Use the Gradient tool for blends and the Airbrush tool for more detailed work.

AIRBRUSH SPARKLE RECIPE

The Airbrush tool is great for adding a little sparkle that your image might be missing, such as a starburst shimmer that gives a polished surface a high-gloss look. Here is an exercise to try out:

1. Start a new document and select Invert from the Map submenu under the Image menu. This turns the document into a black background.
2. Type a word in a large font size and bright red color.

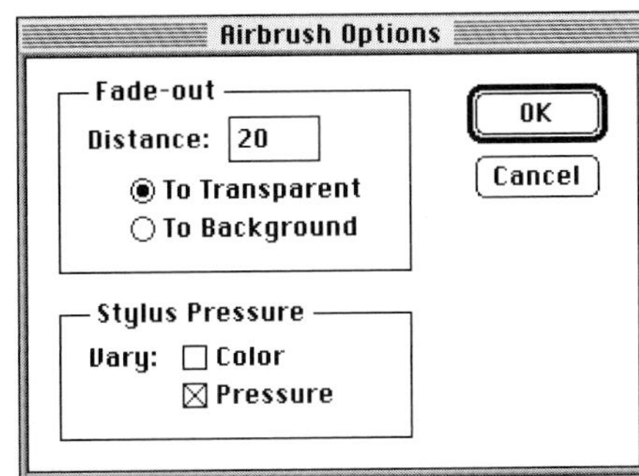

Figure 4–29
The Airbrush Options dialog box

3. Select a bright yellow color, which will become the sparkle.
4. Select the third smallest brush size in the Brushes palette.
5. Double-click on the Airbrush tool to bring up the Options window. The setting for fade-out depends on the size of the area, but for this exercise, set the Distance to 80 pixels. Click OK.
6. Hold down the Shift key and click the tool at a tip of the last letter in your word.
7. Still holding the shift key, click about 2 inches away from the first click point.
8. Release the Shift key and click one more time on the original click point.
9. Hold down the Shift key and click 2 inches away but in the opposite direction.
10. Go back to the options window and reset the Fade-out to 40, then click OK.
11. Click again on the original point.
12. Hold down the Shift key and click 1 inch away at a right angle to the previous lines.
13. Release the Shift key and click once more on the original click point.
14. Hold down the Shift key and click 1 inch away but in the opposite direction. The result should be sparkling!

Paintbrush Tool

Painting with the anti-aliased Paintbrush, you will find that smooth brush edges will blend with the background as you apply color. Set the Paintbrush Options (Figure 4–14) in the Brush Options dialog box. As in the Airbrush tool, control the fade out rate and stylus pressure for digitizing tablets in this window.

The Paintbrush tool is "smart." If you paint while dragging the cursor very fast, Photoshop will force the paint stroke to follow the exact path of the brush, even though the drawing of the stroke lags behind your quick wrist action. If you are painting already on a slower Macintosh you know about this lag.

Rubber Stamp Tool

The Rubber Stamp tool actually uses a two-step process. Think of the Rubber Stamp tool as a pixel duplication tool. First you place the Rubber Stamp tool within the area of pixels that you want to duplicate and hold down the Option key while you click on the mouse button.

Then move the cursor to the area that you want the duplicate image to be. As you press and drag in this area, you will see the image appear, duplicating itself from the selected area. A crosshair will show the source of the pixels as you paint.

***Tip*: Although the Smudge tool is perfect for small retouch areas, it is not advisable for retouching large areas of inconsistent shading. For retouching and cloning try using the Rubber Stamp tool.**

The Options dialog box (Figure 4–30) offers the choice of seven different modes to use with the Rubber Stamp, all of which are anti-aliased. The following options make the Rubber Stamp a useful tool.

CLONE (ALIGNED)

The Clone (aligned) option takes a sample of an entire image and applies that sample over another image or part of an image. You take a sample from an image by option-clicking. The Rubber Stamp tool then will start applying the sample elsewhere based upon the point at which you took the sample. The relationship of the initial sampling point is maintained, allowing you to stop and start (even change brush shapes and modes), and to continue to paint the same image (Figure 4–31). You also can clone from another file even though the other file is not an active window. The Rubber Stamp tool can pick up information from any part of the file (visible or not).

Use the clone function when you are trying to retouch an area that has a texture. Textures present a problem in retouching. Some of the more problematic textures are water, cloudy skies, skin, and any other texture made up of noncontinuous tones or shapes. The best method for working

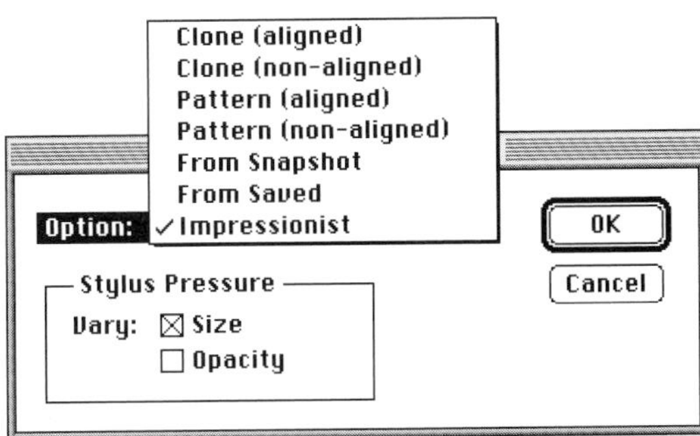

Figure 4–30
The Rubber Stamp Options dialog box showing the seven different painting modes available

Figure 4–31
An example of a cloned image created using the Rubber Stamp tool

with these textures is to use the textures themselves. A typical situation might be a boat in the water that should be eliminated. Using the Rubber Stamp with the clone option does the trick. Do the following:

1. With the option button depressed, click the cursor over an area showing the water texture (the triangle at the tool's base turns white).
2. Release the option button (the triangle at the tool's base turns back to black).
3. Move the cursor to the area to be covered; in this case over the boat.
4. The paint strokes will be the water texture. Note the crosshair, which tracks the cloning.

Recently, we discovered a problem that was ideal for this technique. A sports figure was to be in an ad, but the name of his team could not be used. The only photo available had the subject wearing his team's jersey, which had a pattern of tiny vent holes with the team name across it. With traditional methods the name would be painted out and then the pattern holes would be illustrated with painstaking attention to maintain the pattern. With Photoshop, we cloned the lower part of the jersey over the name, maintaining the overall color, hole pattern, and folds.

When retouching skin tones, it is important to note the sharpness of the image. If it is sharp, then the pores in the skin will be noticeable. If these pores are erased or smudged, the skin will appear smeared. To avoid the smeared look in your retouching, maintain as much of the original texture as possible. Use the Rubber Stamp, but be careful to clone areas very close to the section to be retouched. This is essential because the overall skin tone is not a flat color. Light illuminating soft, curved skin produces a gradient in both color and value.

CLONE (NONALIGNED)

The Clone (nonaligned) option works like the aligned option above except that no matter where you paint with the tool, it will always sample from the original point specified. This sampling occurs even if the sampling point is not visible within the working window.

The Clone (nonaligned) option is very useful for applying the same sample from an image in multiple locations in a composition.

PATTERN (ALIGNED AND NONALIGNED)

The Pattern (aligned) option allows the selection of a pattern and the repeated application of that pattern with the Rubber Stamp tool as uniform tiles.

As with the Clone Options, the Pattern Option has an aligned and nonaligned choice. The aligned choice applies a tile in a fixed position. Painting over the same area will produce the same tile in the same position. The nonaligned option paints the pattern from the center out, beginning from where the tool's hot spot begins to paint.

FROM SNAPSHOT

The From Snapshot option allows you to select all or part of an image with a selection tool, then use that selection to paint with. To use this option, you have to understand that there is an empty image buffer attached to all the images you use. To fill this buffer, make a selection and use the Take Snapshot command in the Edit menu to temporarily store the data in the buffer. You can undo any changes made to a document by creating your selection and then selecting the From Snapshot option for the Rubber Stamp tool to apply the original stored selection.

FROM SAVED

Using the From Saved option for the Rubber Stamp tool is similar to using the Eraser tool's magic eraser mode. As you paint, it restores an image to the state it was in the last time you saved it. The difference is that it uses the brush characteristics set in the Brushes palette: brushshapes, soft edges, sizes, and opacity.

IMPRESSIONIST

You can create organic-looking textures or patterns with this option. It is perfect for turning photographs into paintings. To explain this option, imagine splitting an image into two layers. The first or base layer is the last version saved of the image. The top, or paintable, layer is the image currently being manipulated.

For example, using a round brush shape that is five pixels in diameter, it has a one-pixel hot spot in the center. This hot spot looks at the color over which it passes on the base layer and then spreads that color out to the edges of the five-pixel wide brush, creating a smeared color. Passage over multiple colors creates the effect of impressionistic brush strokes.

To give a photograph an effective painterly look, use a small brush size. A larger size results in a more chaotic appearance. A very large brush will obliterate the image. However this is an excellent method for creating new patterns and textures.

Tip: Over a colorful image, pass a large Impressionist brush in short strokes to create a series of colorful swirls. Then treat the image further through the use of filters to create some unusual backgrounds.

Smudge Tool

This tool will bring you back to kindergarten and the fine art of finger painting. The concept is similar to applying a stroke in charcoal and using a finger to work it into shape. The Smudge tool pushes the color from where the mouse button is first pressed in the direction that it is dragged. Setting the pressure in the Brushes palette determines how far the color will be pushed. A low setting gives a slight push or blurring action, and a high setting can smear a color across an entire document. (See Figure 4–16 for pressure examples.)

Tip: Although the Smudge tool is perfect for small retouch areas, do not use it for retouching large areas of inconsistent shading. For retouching and cloning try using the Rubber Stamp tool.

Double-clicking on the Smudge tool will open the Smudge tool Options dialog box (Figure 4–32). In addition to the Stylus Pressure options (which only applies to pressure-sensitive digitizing tablets), Finger Painting can be selected. With this option the foreground color will be applied at the beginning of the smudge (Figure 4–33).

The Smudge tool cannot be used on a document in either the Bitmapped or Indexed color modes.

Blur/Sharpen Tool

This combination of the Blur tool and the Sharpen tool facilitates the softening or enhancement of edges. Hold down the Option key and click the Blur/Sharpen tool to switch between the two modes or double click on it to access the Blur/Sharpen Options dialog box (Figure 4–34).

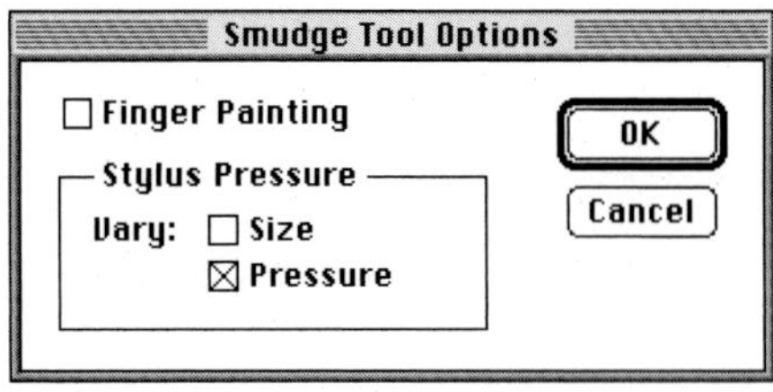

Figure 4–32
The Smudge Tool Options dialog box

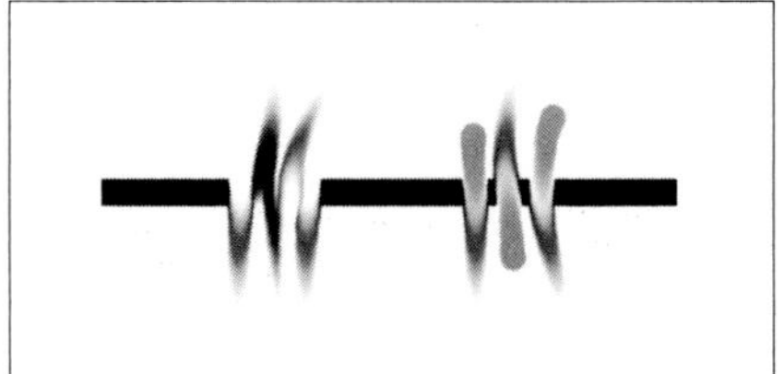

Figure 4–33
An example of normal smudging on the left, and on the right smudging with the Finger Painting option selected. The foreground color was set to 50% black.

In addition to selecting which tool to use, you can select how the stylus pressure on a digitizing pad will affect the tool.

Use the Blur tool for blurring harsh edges of an image, or areas containing undesirable details. As you apply the Blur tool to an area, the contrast between the pixels in the area decreases, resulting in an overall smoothing effect.

The Lighten and Darken settings (set in the Brushes palette) for this tool can be very useful. Use Lighten to smooth out the shadow areas of an image, leaving brighter, more detailed areas sharp and defined. Or use the dropper tool to choose a color that represents the lightest portion of a shadowed area, and set the Blur tool to Darken. It will affect only the desired areas.

***Tip*: When set at a small brush size, the Blur tool is good for softening the rough edges that are sometimes created when you place one image on top of another.**

Figure 4–34
The Blur/Sharpen Options dialog box with Blur selected as the active tool

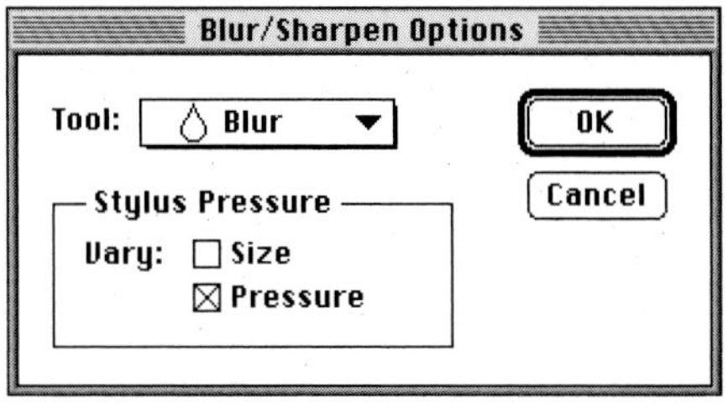

Blur/Sharpen Options
Tool: Blur
OK
Stylus Pressure
Cancel
Vary: Size
Pressure

Use the Sharpen tool to define soft edges in order to create the effect of enhanced focus, or clarity. As you apply the Sharpen tool to an area, the contrast between the pixels in the area increases, resulting in an overall sharpened effect. If you continually drag the Sharpen tool over a specific area, you will probably end up stripping away all of the intermediate values in those pixels. Although this might be used as an artistic effect, it is easily abused if the intent was only to reasonably sharpen a soft detail.

***Tip*: The artistic effect part is the fun: You can create smooth-edged, high-contrast portions of an otherwise detailed grayscale image. You can obtain similar effects by applying the Threshold control over a paint stroke, which is applied to an image through an alpha channel.**

The Blur/Sharpen tool cannot be used on a document in either the Bitmapped or Indexed color modes.

Dodge/Burn Tool

The addition of the Dodge/Burn tool to Photoshop gives control that was previously only possible in a traditional photographic darkroom. By pressing and dragging the mouse over specific parts of an image, you are given creative control over the lightness and darkness. And it is shown on the screen—with the lights on!

Traditionally, dodging and burning techniques let photographers correct unbalanced tones in a photograph by underexposing or overexposing areas to achieve a complete range of highlight and shadow details. The Dodge tool lets you lighten areas of the image; the Burn tool lets you darken areas.

The Dodge tool decreases the density of pixels in an image to lighten it. The Burn tool increases the density of pixels in an image to either subdue highlights or to darken shadows. To switch between the two modes of the tool, hold the Option key and click on the Dodge/Burn icon or double-click on it to access the Dodge/Burn Options dialog box (Figure 4–35). In addition to selecting which tool to use, you can select how the stylus pressure on a digitizing pad will affect the tool.

The Modes and Exposure options in the Brushes palette appear when using the Dodge/Burn tool (Figure 4–36). The Mode options determine how the tool will affect shadows, midtones, and highlights. The Highlights mode will modify only light pixels; Midtones will modify colors in the middle range; and Shadows will modify the dark pixels in an image.

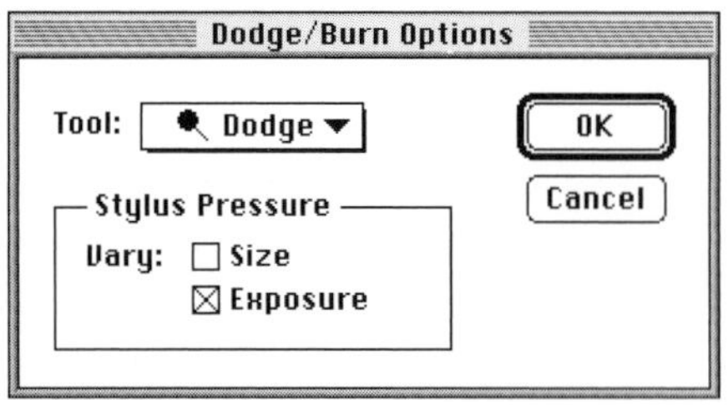

Figure 4–35
The Dodge/Burn Options dialog box with Dodge selected as the active tool

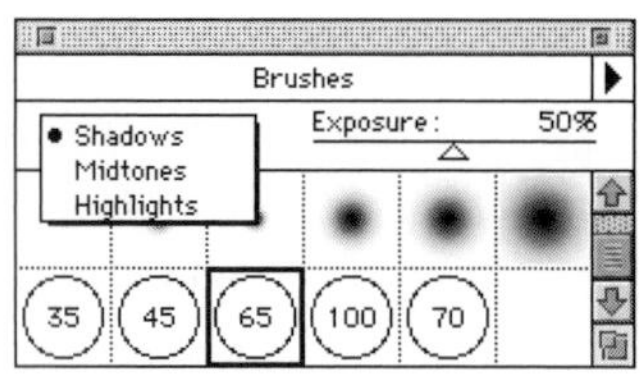

Figure 4–36
The Brushes Palette with the Dodge/Burn tool selected

When you are using the Dodge/Burn tool, you can adjust the exposure for the tool in the Brushes palette with the Exposure slider. Exposure can range from 1 to 100 percent. If you want the effect of the Dodge/Burn tool to be strong, set the slider to a higher number. If you want to effect to be weaker, set the slider to a lower number. You may also set the exposure by using the 1 through 0 number keys on the keyboard.

The Dodge/Burn tool cannot be used on a document in either the Bitmapped or Indexed color modes.

Color Controls

Just under the Blur/Sharpen and Dodge/Burn tools in Photoshop's toolbox are the controls for choosing the Foreground and Background colors, for switching between them, and for returning to the default colors (see Figure 4–8). To select a color, click on either the Foreground or Background color box and a Color Picker box will appear. For painting and filling, use the Foreground Color selection box. The Background Color selection box is the color that remains when you cut a selection out of an image, or erase from an image, or use the Pencil tool in the Auto Erase mode.

The colors in the foreground and background selection boxes are the two colors you used to create a blend with the Blend tool. Click on the Switch colors icon to swap the foreground and background colors. Click on the Default colors icon to return to the default black foreground and white background colors.

Color in Photoshop

The dynamic power of Photoshop to work in several different color models also creates a dilemma. For example, if you are creating images that you will use only for display on a computer screen or on a television, you might use RGB, HSB (Hue, Saturation, Brightness), or Lab colors. If you are working on images that you eventually intend to print on a press, then eventually you are going to have to convert your images to CMYK, grayscale, or some variant of these color models, including duotones, tritones, and quadtones.

The capability to work in so many different color models is an inherent problem, because they do not directly convert to each other. Although the conversion appears easy, the colors will not always convert properly. There is a unique range, or *gamut*, of colors in each color mode that does not exist in other modes. For example, the gamut of colors available in RGB Color mode cannot be reproduced in CMYK Color mode or on a printing press using CMYK inks. Or, the gamut of colors in RGB Color mode cannot be reproduced with video using NTSC colors.

Apple Color Picker

Colors can be selected from either the standard Apple Color Picker or the Photoshop Color Picker. Select the desired Color Picker in the General Preferences submenu under the File menu. The Apple Color Picker (Figure 4–37), common to most Macintosh programs, allows you

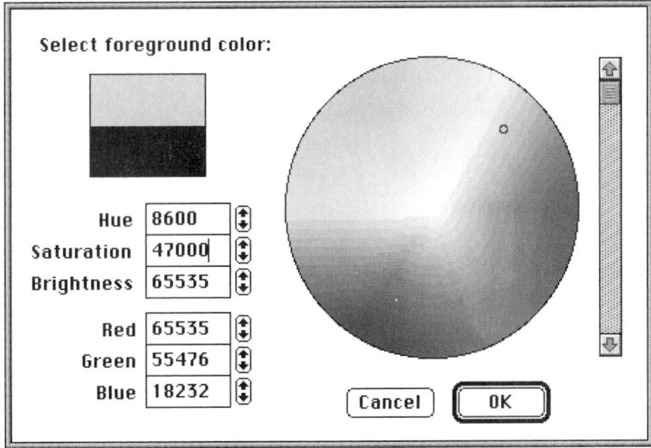

Figure 4–37
The standard Apple Color Picker

to choose colors through HSB or RGB color spectrums. You can type in values from 0 to 65,535 in the fields, but it might be more intuitive to use the color wheel in the right side of the dialog box.

Drag the mouse around the perimeter of the color wheel to change hue. Move in toward the center to change saturation. Slide the scroll bar on the right side of the color wheel to adjust the brightness. Move up for lighter values and down for darker values. The color box in the upper left splits in half, showing you the original selected color with the revised color above it.

The Apple Color Picker offers the advantage of visualizing colors based on their relationship on the color wheel. However, conversion to CMYK Color mode when using the Apple Color Picker is problematic, because it will not warn you of out-of-gamut color selections.

The Photoshop Color Picker

The Photoshop Color Picker provides for a more stable and versatile method of color selection (Figure 4–38). A simultaneous display of a color's numeric mix in the various color modes allows you to select colors based on the HSB, RGB, Lab, or CMYK color models. A color selection out of the CMYK color gamut causes a warning alarm to appear, alerting you that the color cannot be reproduced with CMYK colors, which are the process colors used in offset printing.

To access the Color Picker for color selections, switch to the Photoshop Color Picker in the General Preferences submemu under the File menu. Click on the Reset Default Colors button to return the foreground color to black and then click on the Foreground color to open

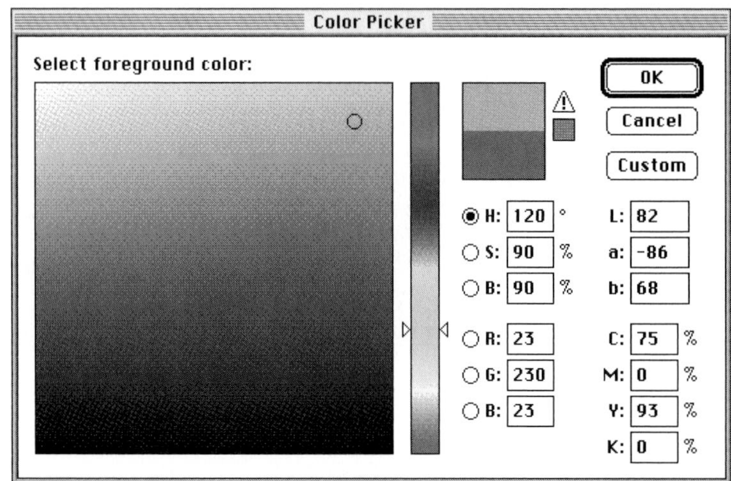

Figure 4–38
The Photoshop Color Picker with an out-of-gamut color selected

the Color Picker. The color field, displaying values of red, fills the left side of the window. Click in the upper-right corner of the color field and a color spectrum will appear in the Color slider, which is a vertical strip to the right of the color field.

Colors may be selected visually from the color field and Color slider. They display components of either the HSB or RGB color models only. Clicking on the various radio buttons changes the color display modes. The current default mode, Hue, sets the Color slider to display hues, while the Color Field displays the other two components of the color, Saturation and Brightness. The horizontal axis in this case reflects changes in saturation and the vertical axis reflects changes in brightness. Selecting the Saturation model (clicking the "S" button) displays a range in saturation in the Color slider. The color field displays changes in hue on the horizontal axis and changes in brightness on the vertical axis. To explore the other modes, follow the same system.

After selecting a desired hue, click anywhere in the color field to change its saturation and brightness. Clicking on the various radio buttons changes the display modes. The Color slider shows the range of colors in the selected component; and, as previously mentioned, the Color Field displays the other two components.

***Tip*: Work with one color component, preferably Hue, until you understand it and then move on to explore the others. Bouncing around may confuse you. We have found the first three, HSB, to be the most useful.**

Change colors at any time numerically by typing the appropriate number in the value fields. As you type in new numbers, Photoshop automatically recalculates the new color and updates the entire window. For the different modes, do the following:

- In the HSB mode, specify Hue by a color's angle (degrees) on the color wheel, and specify saturation and brightness by a percentage.
- In the RGB mode, specify a range of colors from 0 to 255 in each of the fields.
- In the Lab mode, specify Lightness (L) as a percentage, and the a and b components by values ranging from –128 to 127.
- In the CMYK mode, specify a percentage in each of the color component fields.

Tip: Learn color theory by plugging different numbers into the fields and studying the results.

The settings made in the Printing Inks Set Up and the Separation Set Up preferences submenus under the File menu affect how the color values relate to each other. Refer to Chapter 8, "Output," for more information on setting preferences. The two color swatches in the upper-central part of the Color Picker window display the original color and above it, the current selected color.

Nonprintable Colors

Many colors that can be selected in the Color Picker cannot be printed on a printing press. For example, bright neon colors require special inks. When selecting a nonprintable color, a warning appears indicating an out-of-gamut color choice. An alert triangle with an exclamation mark (!) appears in the upper right side of the Color Picker (Figure 4–38). You can click on the small color square below the exclamation mark to choose the closest CMYK equivalent as the current color. If you continue with an out-of-gamut color, Photoshop will create a color as close as possible to your selection. Although the color may print well on a color digital printer, it will not output predictably on an imagesetter that creates film separations for offset printing.

Custom Colors

The various color models in Photoshop fall into three basic categories:

- Projected light colors: HSB, RGB, Lab, and NTSC
- Process printing colors: CMYK, Pantone Process, TruMatch, FocolTone, and ANPA Color
- Spot printing colors: Pantone and Toyo Colors.

Custom printing colors can be specified in the Custom Colors dialog box (Figure 4–39) accessed by clicking the Custom button in the Color Picker.

Projected Light Colors

Components of the visible spectrum combine to make projected-light colors. To create images for display on computer monitors, for television (video), for output to a film recorder, or for printing to an RGB printer, work in the RGB Color mode and specify colors from the HSB, RGB, or Lab models in the Color Picker. For television (video) output, apply the

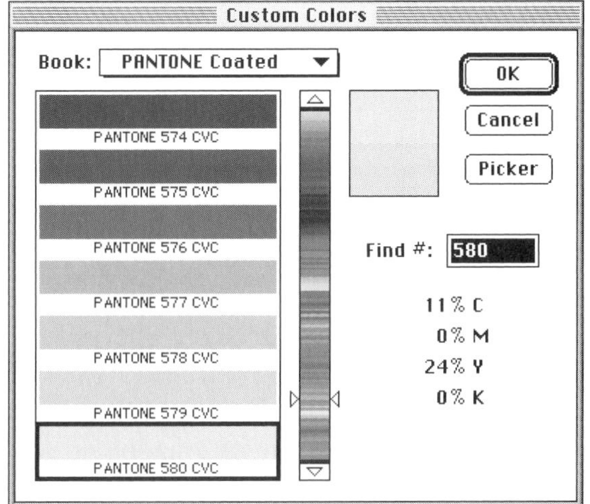

Figure 4–39
The Pantone Custom Colors dialog box

NTSC Colors filter from the Video submenu under the Filters menu to remap the colors to the appropriate palette. For more about NTSC colors, refer to Chapter 9, "Animation."

Find out what the limitations (in the gamut) are of the intended output device and then work within those parameters. The projected light colors convert into process printing colors with mixed results, and many of these colors cannot be reproduced on a printing press.

Process Printing Colors

Trumatch, Pantone Process, Focoltone, and ANPA color systems are created by mixing tints of each of the CMYK process color inks. Each of these process color systems has corresponding reference books that show swatches of the printed colors. The printed, color swatchbooks have corresponding numbers that can be specified in the Custom Colors dialog box.

Obviously CMYK process colors can be specified as percentages of each component in the Color Picker without using one of the above color systems. Refer to a swatchbook displaying CMYK tint mixes for an accurate selection

> NOTE: **Be sure to use a printed swatchbook as a reference and not depend on the monitor. The monitor uses RGB colors to display an image and cannot be trusted to match CMYK colors.**

Trumatch

The Trumatch CMYK-based swatchbook shows over 2,000 achievable computer-generated colors. The Trumatch Color Finder is organized into 50 hues, which are numbered sequentially around the color wheel. Each hue section displays up to 40 tints and shades based on saturation and brightness. The swatchbook also has a section specifically designed to specify four color grays, which are normally difficult to produce. The Trumatch system also was designed specifically for digital output. The finer screen tint increments allow for subtler variations in colors than the 5% to 10% steps available with conventional screens.

Pantone Process Colors

The CMYK-based Pantone Process swatchbook displays over 3,000 colors in the industry-standard 5% increments (with a few at 3%). You can specify a color's number in the Custom Colors dialog box or enter its CMYK percentages directly into the Color Picker.

Focoltone

The Focoltone color system, originally created for the traditional printing industry, facilitated a designer's color selection by providing combinations made with common components. The stripper at the print shop could easily eliminate or add screen tint components to make any color changes.

Focoltone's CMYK-based swatchbook displays 763 colors that can be selected in the Custom Colors dialog box or by entering its CMYK percentages directly into the Color Picker. Focoltone also provides custom color formulas to match the solid-ink process colors.

ANPA Color

The ANPA Color system in Photoshop uses the NAA Color Ink Book Vol. 8, which recently replaced the ANPA Color Ink Book Vol. 7, as a basis for color selection. The color reference book contains 41 colors created from nine base colors—the process colors plus some special spot colors. Use the reference book when specifying colors to be used in daily newspapers that print ROP color on newsprint paper. Each page in the book shows a single ink spot color (see the next section) and, when applicable, the process color mix that most closely matches it. Each color is also printed in three lighter tints, 10, 30, and 50%, overprinted by similar tints of black. You select ANPA colors in Photoshop by using the Custom Colors dialog box.

Printing on newsprint requires special consideration in color selection and output because of the highly absorbent quality of the paper. The absorbent paper causes more than normal dot gain (ink spread), which is an issue when printing halftones. See Chapter 8, "Output," for more information on dot gain.

The Spot Printing Colors

A *spot color* refers to an actual ink that a printer puts on the printing press. Select the colors that have corresponding swatchbooks in the Custom Colors dialog box. To create spot-color separations, you must work in the Duotone mode. Refer to Chapter 7, "Advanced Photoshop Techniques," for information on creating duotones, tritones, and quadtones. Photoshop converts spot colors into CMYK colors, unless specified in the Duotone mode. These converted colors may not match the original spot colors. Beware of selecting colors in this unreliable fashion.

> **NOTE: Do not depend on the monitor when selecting colors, use a printed swatchbook. The monitor uses RGB colors to display an image and cannot be trusted to match spot-ink colors.**

When working with spot colors, you must be very consistent in your color-naming conventions. If you will be exporting these images to other programs, color names must match letter for letter and space for space.

***Tip*: If you want to specify a metallic, custom pastel, or varnish ink, simply identify it with any spot color and then tell the printer how you want the plate printed. If you want to apply a varnish to a process-color separation, create a new channel with the masked area and then print it separately.**

Pantone Colors on Coated and Uncoated Paper

The Pantone Matching System (PMS) provides over 1,000 spot-color inks. This international color language provides an accurate way to specify, communicate, and match color. The Pantone company does not produce inks; they simply produce the color swatchbooks and the specifications for the ink colors. Ink companies make and sell the ink products to printers.

Ink colors vary depending on the paper they are printed on. The PMS swatchbooks display colors on both coated and uncoated paper. Colors may be selected in Photoshop for either paper type. Be careful not to switch between color selections in Pantone Coated and Pantone

Uncoated because the colors and their numbers will change as they attempt to match the color effect on the paper.

Tip: To ensure that the Pantone names match their spelling in other programs, select Short PANTONE Names in the General Preferences submenu under the File menu.

Toyo 88 Color Finder

The Toyo 88 Color Finder system consists of 1,050 spot-ink colors blended with Toyo bases and intermediates. This is the only system available in Photoshop that uses its own inks. The organization of the Color Finder into two categories, high and low chroma, has its roots in psychological research done in color perception.

The Toyo colors also seem to be brighter and more vibrant than those found in other systems. To ensure the best match, specify a Toyo Ink from a certified blender and a printer who uses Toyo inks.

The Colors Palette

Select colors quickly and logically in the Colors palette from either a set of default colors, the above-mentioned color systems, or custom color palettes that you have created. Open the Colors palette by selecting Show Colors under the Windows menu (Figure 4–40). Change the color modes to Grayscale, RGB Color, HSB Color, CMYK Color, and Lab Color using the pop-out menu on the right side of the palette. The Slider controls reflect the selected color mode. Move the sliders to vary each of the color components.

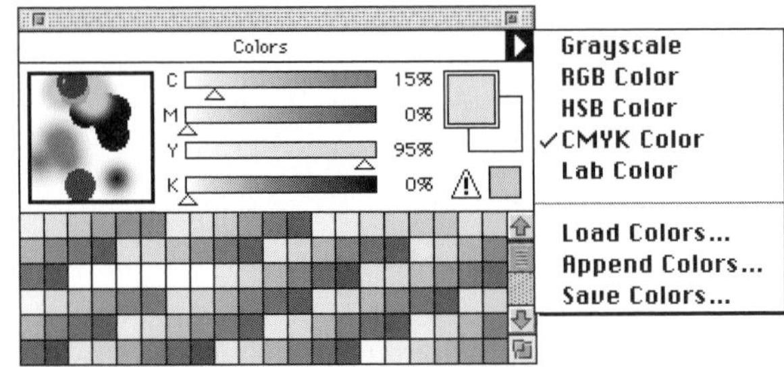

Figure 4–40
The Colors palette showing its pop-out menus and alert triangle

Below the Slider controls is a series of color swatches (cells). The cursor becomes the Eyedropper tool by passing it over the cells, allowing you to click on a color to select it as the current foreground or background color. The Foreground or Background color boxes work identically to their counterparts in the Toolbox.

Use the large scratch area as a custom-color mixing well. Any of the painting tools can be used to mix colors; it's similar to the way an artist uses a palette. Try using the Smudge tool or the Gradient tool to mix colors. The Rubber Stamp clone tool allows you to copy portions of an image into the Scratchpad. Zoom in or out for precise color selections with the Magnifier tool. The scratch pad is also a convenient place to define a custom brush shape or pattern.

To change a cell's color mix to a new color, hold the Option key to turn the cursor into the Paint Bucket tool and click on a cell. It will automatically turn into the Paint Bucket tool when it's over a new cell. To add a new color between existing cells, hold the Shift and the Options keys down and click on a cell. The new color will be added and the existing cells will move over.

If you select or mix a color out of the CMYK gamut, an exclamation point in an alert triangle will appear on the right side of the palette. Next to it will be the closest color Photoshop can simulate. Click on it and the selected color will change to this new color.

***Tip*: To create a set of consistent pastel colors using the HSB mode, set the Saturation and Brightness to fixed light values and move the Hue slider to get the desired colors. To make lighter and darker tints and shades of a fixed color, use the Saturation and Brightness sliders while leaving the Hue constant.**

To delete a Color swatch hold the Option key down to turn the curser into the Scissors tool and click on the cell.

You can create custom palettes yourself or load any of the existing custom color palettes, such as the ANPA, Pantone, Toyo, Focoltone, and Trumatch palettes. Use the pop-out menu to load and save palettes. You can combine palettes by using the Append Colors command,

Although the Color palette can hold many colors, you might create several smaller palettes for organizational purposes.

Tutorial: The Basics

A Simple Logo

By creating a simple logo (FIgure 4–41), this exercise will give you a basic understanding of the Paintbrush tool, Type tool, and Color Picker.

1. Under the File menu select New. The New image dialog box appears allowing you to set the parameters of the document.
2. Set it to 6 × 6 inches at 72 pixels per inch in the RGB Color Mode.
3. Select the Type tool and click within the window. The Type Tool dialog box will appear, allowing you to set the text specifications.
4. Select Palatino, set the size to 42 points, leave the Leading blank (we are entering only one line) and the Spacing blank; click the Bold, Anti-Aliased, and Alignment Left buttons.
5. Click in the text entry box (the lowest part of the dialog) and type in Stroke of Genius. Click OK.
6. The type appears on the screen as a floating selection. To reposition the text, place the cursor over the type (it turns into an arrow). Then press and drag it to a more desirable position. Click elsewhere on the window to deselect the type or select None under the Select menu.
7. With the Type tool selected, click just below the Stroke of Genius text. The Type Tool dialog appears again. This time use Palatino Bold Italic, 24 points, flush-left, and anti-aliased. In the entry box, delete Stroke of Genius and type Art Supplies. Click OK.
8. Position the new text off-center to the right, as shown in Figure 4–41, and deselect.
9. Select the Foreground color box to open the Color Picker. Click in the upper-right area of the Color Field to select a bright red. Click OK.

Figure 4–41
A simple logo created with the Paintbrush tool, Type tool, and Color Picker

10. Now you will create a graphic device for your logo. Double-click on the Paint Brush tool to open the Paint Brush Options dialog and set the Fade-out Distance to 30. Click OK.
11. Choose Show Brushes under the Window menu to open the Brushes palette. Select the fifth shape from the left in the top row.
12. Paint a stroke under the word Stroke and there you have it, a logo.

CHAPTER 5

Image Selection and Masking

A basic function of any graphics program is to select portions of an image to be manipulated. If you have used other Macintosh painting programs, you have probably grown accustomed to the standard Marquee and Lasso tools. In Photoshop the selection tools are more powerful and complicated than in other programs, but once mastered, they easily allow you to do what previously may have been difficult or impossible.

In this chapter you will discover how the selection tools can isolate areas as masks. These precise and complex selections can be filled, manipulated, filtered, layered, copied, or pasted into. The manipulation of selections will be covered in Chapter 6, "Image Processing."

The Selection Tools

You can select images or portions of images with one of four selection tools found in the Toolbox (Rectangular Marquee, Elliptical Marquee, Lasso, and Magic Wand), or with the Pen tool located in the Paths palette (Figure 5–1). You can then use the selection tools for the following applications:

Figure 5–1
Selection tools in the Toolbox and the Pen tool

- To create complex photomontages with multiple elements from different sources.
- To place objects against any background and create seamless and smooth edges between foreground and background objects.
- To construct on-the-fly masks for applying tint and color correction changes to specific portions of an image.
- To save selected areas as paths with a document to silhouette them against backgrounds in other programs.
- To create vignettes with soft borders around selected areas.
- To save selections as channels for future use in the current document or in combination with other documents or channels.
- To specify selections to be copied, pasted, pasted into, pasted behind, pasted with special effects, pasted at various transparencies, and filled with colors.
- To apply dynamic effects such as scale, skew, perspective, and distort.
- To alter the selected portion of an image with the many filters available in Photoshop.

Macintosh users who have followed the progress of graphics software since MacPaint can tell you that things have not changed much in all these years. The Lasso and Marquee are still the standards for selecting images on the screen. In the world of the original MacPaint and other black-and-white paint programs, screen pixels could be one of either two colors: black or white. Selecting a black-and-white image with a Lasso was a straightforward affair: The Lasso zoomed in on the black pixels, slipping over the surrounding white pixels in the process. In some of the more sophisticated implementations of this capability, the Lasso knew that white pixels inside the solid-black pixel boundaries were supposed to be transparent.

When color painting programs began to appear, the standard Lasso and Marquee went through an evolutionary stage. Programs such as Pixelpaint and Studio 8 dealt with more than just black-and-white values for pixels; the Marquee or Lasso could select portions of an image by its color components or by ignoring background colors.

Photoshop raised the capability of image selection to new heights, making the choices and processes more complex. To understand how to properly use the selection tools in Photoshop, you will need to temporarily forget how other Macintosh paint programs work in this regard. The familiar Lasso and Marquee tools found in Photoshop are far more intelligent and powerful than their counterparts in most other Mac graphics programs.

Here are some basic points to remember about the selection tools:

- Double-clicking on a tool's icon opens an option's dialog box, allowing you to control various functions of the tool.
- For selecting a specific isolated image against a solid-color background, you will probably use the Magic Wand tool. It effectively takes the place of the Lasso tool normally found in bitmapped paint programs.
- Any area is automatically masked while selected; whatever you do will only affect the selected area. Paint tools, filters, and color correction controls only work within a selection, unless nothing is selected.

***Tip*: If you are in a magnified view and your current drawing tool does not seem to be working, make sure that you do not have an area selected that is outside of your view. The tool will work only within that selected area.**

- While using any of the selection tools, you can actually adjust or move the active selection "shape" by pressing the Command and Option keys while dragging from the inside of the selected area or by using the cursor controls on an extended keyboard to nudge the shape by one-pixel increments. This moves the selection area without moving the contents of the selection.

***Tip*: By using the selection tools and the Command and Option keys, you can create "cookie-cutter" masks consisting of the shape of a selected area. By moving the custom selection area onto another part of the image and using color correction controls or filters, it's easy to generate special ghosting and shadow effects.**

- Add to and subtract from selections by using key commands in conjunction with the tools. By pressing the Shift key, add to a current selection range. For example, make a selection with the Marquee tool, add to the selection area by using the Shift key, and choose more of the image with any of the other selection tools. Use the Command key in combination with the selection tools to subtract from the current selection. Use the Command and Shift keys together to calculate and select the intersection of two overlapping selections.

Tip: The selection modifier keys work with all of the selection tools (except for the Pen tool) all of the time; you can begin selecting with one tool, and add to or subtract from that selection area with any other selection tool.

- When moving a selected image into place, deselecting it will place it over the background and make it part of the background image. If you undo the Deselect, you can delete the floating image by pressing the Delete (Backspace) on your keyboard, or by selecting Clear from the Edit menu. This will delete the floating selection and return the background to its original state. In many other Macintosh graphics programs, this same action removes the floating image while erasing the background behind it.
- As in most other Mac graphics programs, pressing Option while dragging a selection moves a duplicate of the selection, leaving the original intact. You can also select Float from the Selection menu (Command-S).
- For careful, delicate selections you should probably use the Pen tool and then convert the path to a selection.

Tip: Once you have made a selection, save it as a channel or a path. You will always be able to get it back after deselecting.

Rectangular and Elliptical Marquees

The two marquee tools—the Rectangular and the Elliptical Marquees—allow you to select portions of an image for manipulation. These two anti-aliased selection tools have similar options. Double-click on the tool's icons to open the Options dialogs (Figures 5–2 and 5–3).

Both tools have constrain parameters that allow you to select portions of an image with a predetermined selection size, as well as a fixed height-to-width ratio. The Constrained Aspect Ratio maintains the specified proportion for selecting. When you use a ratio of 1:1, the selection tool will always be constrained to perfect squares and circles. The variable ratio allows you to expand this capability by determining separate width and height values.

The Fixed Size button forces the selection to be the specified size. When you click the selection tool in the image, the predetermined Marquee appears on screen at the specified size and can be moved to the desired location on the screen. Clicking the mouse button outside the selection applies the selection.

***Tip:* If you are preparing images for boilerplate layouts, chances are that you have already created sized placeholders for graphic images that are optimized for the layout. By predetermining the size and aspect ratio of these two selection tools, you can save time you would spend moving the image back and forth between Photoshop and your page-layout program.**

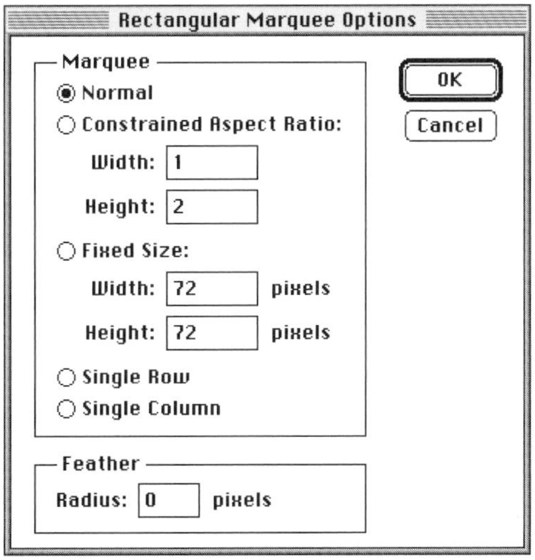

Figure 5–2
Rectangular Marquee Options dialog box

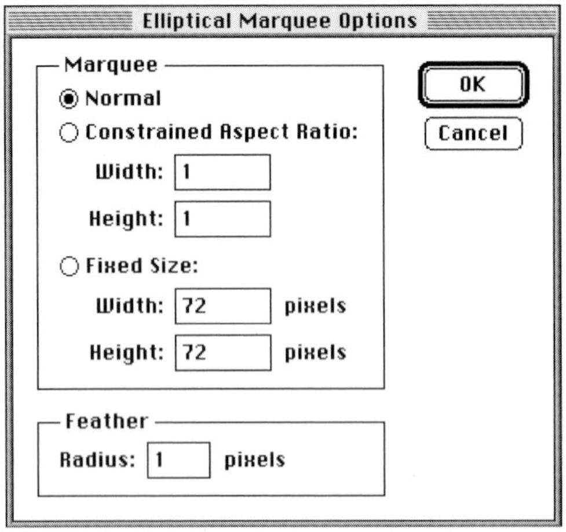

Elliptical Marquee Options

Marquee
- ◉ Normal
- ○ Constrained Aspect Ratio:
  - Width: 1
  - Height: 1
- ○ Fixed Size:
  - Width: 72 pixels
  - Height: 72 pixels

Feather
Radius: 1 pixels

OK
Cancel

Figure 5–3
Elliptical Marquee Options dialog box

Select an area by pressing and dragging diagonally from corner to corner or by holding the Option key and dragging from the center out.

The rectangular Marquee can be used to sèlect individual one-pixel-wide vertical and horizontal bands of an image. This is useful for retouching images captured with video digitizers and frame grabbers, which sometimes have signal distortion consisting of slightly shifted or offset scan lines. Once the scan line is selected, you can "nudge" it a pixel at a time in any direction by using the cursor keys on your keyboard.

Use the Feather Radius option to define how far to either side of the selection border you want the feather edge to extend. You may also define a Feather Radius by choosing Feather under the Select menu after making a selection (Figure 5–4).

The Lasso

The Lasso tool works differently from what you might expect. It does not automatically close in on an object against a solid background (the old MacPaint way). For "autoselecting" a continuous color area use the Magic Wand tool. The Lasso includes everything inside of the area created by dragging as part of the active selection.

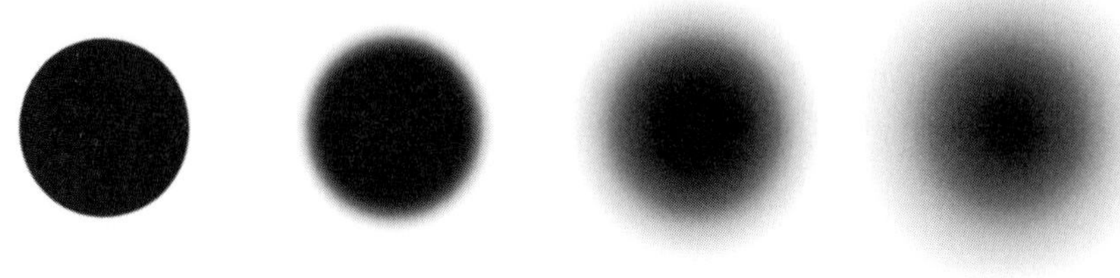

Figure 5–4
A selection filled with black with the Feather Radius settings at 1, 10, 30, and 50 pixels.

The Lasso also has an additional mode that allows you to toggle between the normal freehand mode and a "rubber-band," straight-line mode. To draw straight lines, hold down the Option key and plot points. Click at the vertices of the polygons or straight lines. When you release the Option key, Photoshop closes the current selection with a straight line between the first and last points. You may also release the Option key with the mouse button pressed down and continue making freehand selections.

Double-clicking the Lasso tool opens the Lasso Options dialog (Figure 5–5). Feathering control and Anti-aliasing controls become available.

Specify a Feather Radius to automatically avoid a harsh edge around a selection. We suggest setting this value to 1 for most basic selection tasks. If you want to create a smooth transition between your selection area and the surrounding pixels, check the Anti-aliasing box.

The Magic Wand

Use the Magic Wand to select contiguous areas of similar colors. Clicking on a color will automatically extend the selection to its borders. Select Anti-aliasing and adjust the spread factor sensitivity by double-clicking on the Magic Wand tool icon to bring up the Magic Wand Options dialog box (Figure 5–6).

The Tolerance control determines how far the selection area will spread. The values range between 0 and 255; lower values result in smaller selections and higher values result in larger selections (Figure 5–7).

Fill and Stroke

This feature allows you to fill a selection or the border around a selected area. After making a selection, choose the Fill or Stroke commands under the Edit menu to open a dialog box that specifies the fill options. In the Fill dialog (Figure 5–8), set the Contents to fill with either the

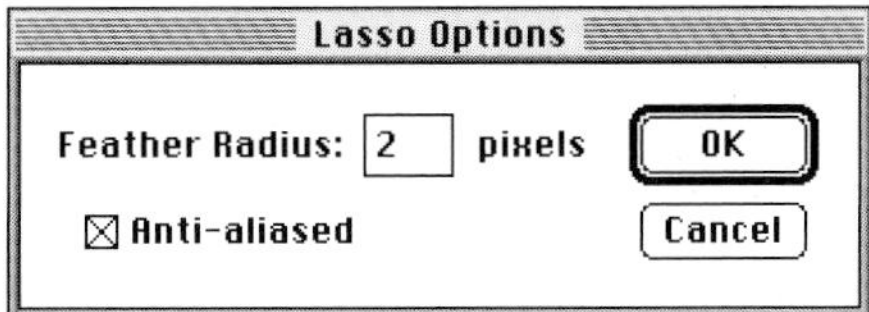

Figure 5–5
The Feather and Anti-aliasing controls for the Lasso tool

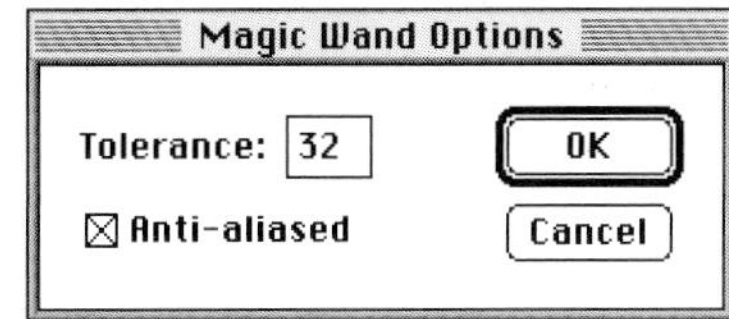

Figure 5–6
Control Tolerance and Anti-aliasing in the Magic Wand Options dialog box

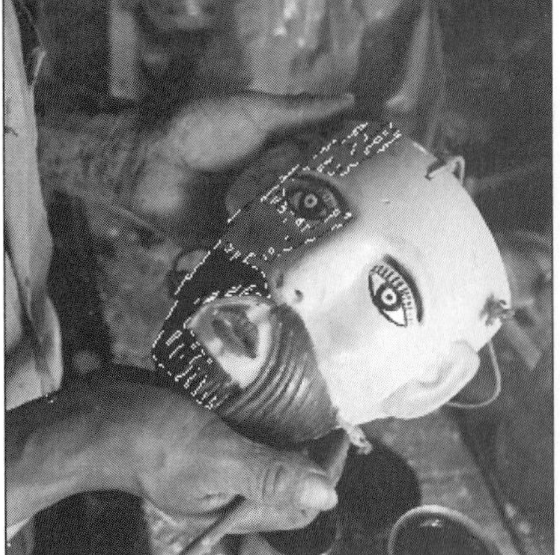

Figure 5–7
The Magic Wand tool is set to a low tolerance in the figure on the left, and to a high tolerance in the figure on the right.

Figure 5–8
The Fill options dialog box

Foreground Color, a defined Pattern, a saved version of a file, or a Snapshot. You can also set the Opacity (transparency) and fill Mode. Set the stroke Width, Location, and blending in the Stroke dialog (Figure 5–9). The Foreground color will be applied to the edge of a selection (Figure 5–10).

***Tip*: You can quickly fill any selected area with the current foreground color at 100% opacity by pressing the Option and delete (backspace) keys. This shortcut does not use any of the settings in the Fill dialog box.**

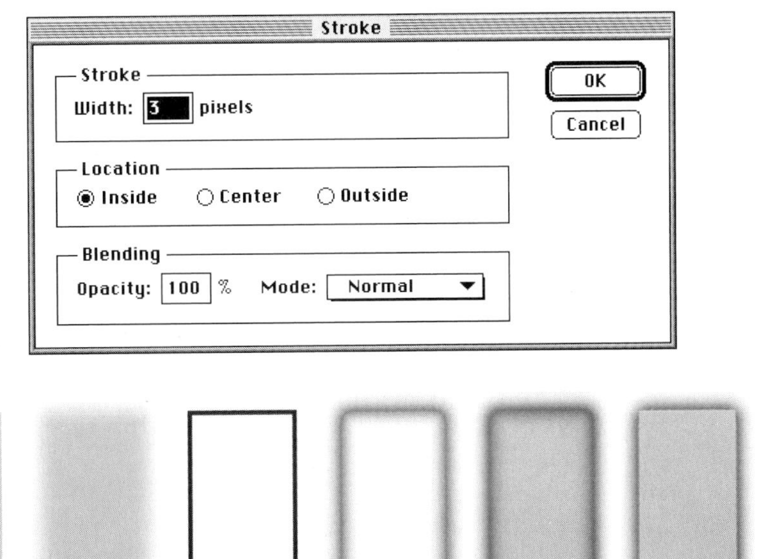

Figure 5–9
The Stroke options dialog box

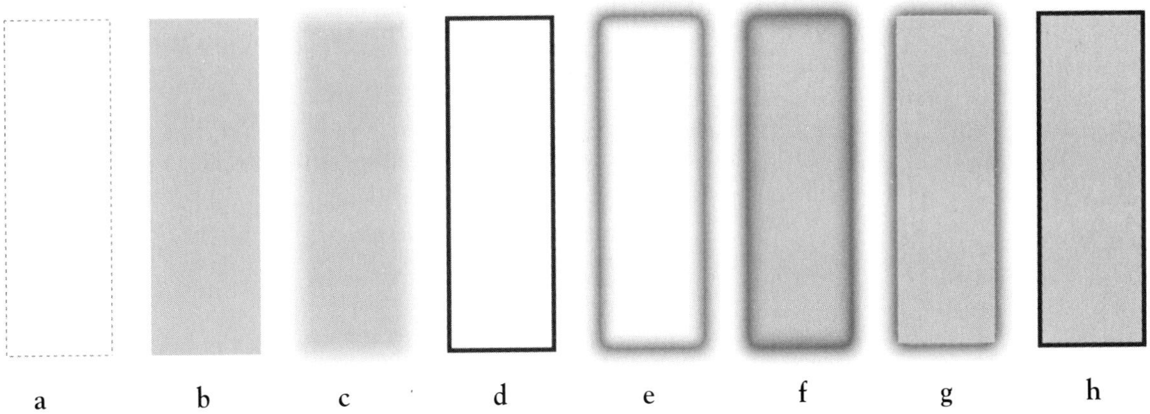

a b c d e f g h

Figure 5–10 Fills and Strokes. (a) An area selected with the Rectangular marquee; (b) filled with 30% black; (c) filled with 30% black using an 8-pixel Feather Radius; (d) no fill with a 5-pixel black Stroke; (e) no fill with a 5-pixel black Stroke and an 8-pixel Feather Radius; (f) filled with 30% black, with a 5-pixel black Stroke and an 8-pixel Feather Radius on both; (g) filled with 30% black, with a 5-pixel black Stroke and an 8-pixel Feather Radius on the Stroke only; (h) filled with 30% black, with a 5-pixel black Stroke.

Fills and Strokes use the same Mode options available for the painting and editing tools. For a description of each mode, see the section "Painting and Editing Modes" in Chapter 4, "Using the Tools and Palettes." Choose Feather under the Select menu for a soft edge.

The Pen Tool

With the Pen tool you can draw smooth vector paths that have the precision of a drawing program, which can be saved as paths or used as selection borders. The Pen tool in Photoshop works like the pen tool in Adobe Illustrator and Aldus FreeHand. Clicking or dragging the mouse along a path creates anchor points. They can be adjusted by dragging the anchor points or the direction lines associated with each anchor point.

Tip: Make sure you have the DirectBits plug-in module installed in the Plug-ins folder to speed the operation of the Pen tool.

Paths Palette

Define the Pen Tool's functions using the selections in the Paths palette (Figure 5–11). Open the Paths palette by selecting Show Paths under the Window menu.

To make a path, select the pen icon in the Paths palette and then click the beginning point of the desired line. Continue clicking to create straight lines with corner points at each click. To plot anchor points with curved lines, press and drag at the points where you want the curves to change direction. To create a closed path, click on the beginning anchor point as the last link. A small circle appears to let you know that the path has been closed. Each anchor point will have a pair of lines with direction points at the ends. Press and drag the direction points to adjust the curves. Press and drag an anchor point to move the line segment associated with it. Holding down the shift key when adding points constrains them to 45° angles.

To preview a path before setting the next point, double-click the Pen tool to open the Pen Tool Options dialog and click the Rubber Band box (Figure 5–12).

The Pen tool is great for creating selection masks with the utmost precision. By using the Arrow tool in the Paths palette, and the add point (the pen with a plus) and the delete point (the pen with a minus) tools, you can create paths around odd-shaped objects with greater

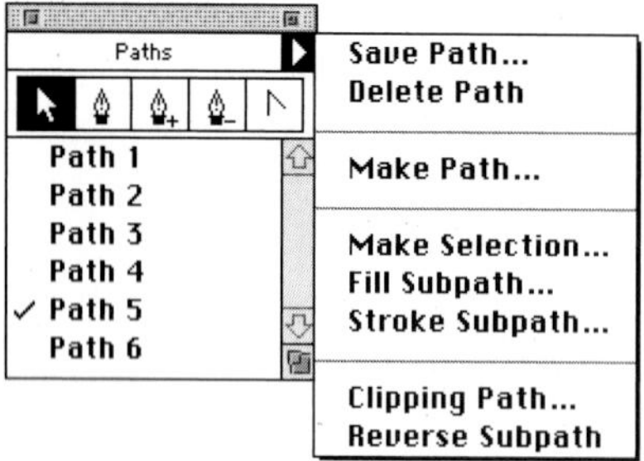

Figure 5–11
The Pen palette showing its pop-out menu

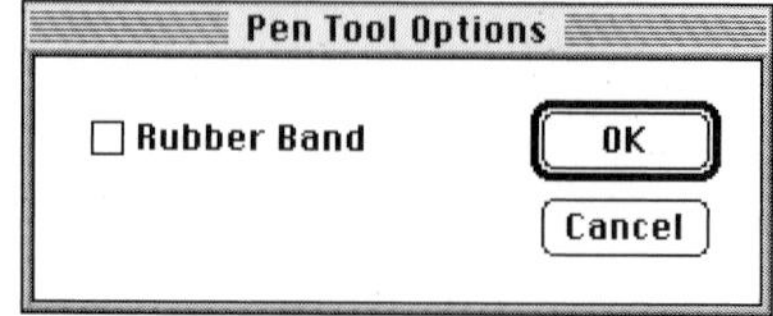

Figure 5–12
The Pen Tool Options dialog box

accuracy than the lasso tool. Use the corner point tool (at the far right) to toggle anchor points between corner and curve points.

Use the following methods for editing paths:

- To change a point between a straight corner and a curve, select the corner tool in the Paths palette (on the far right side) and click on the point you want to change.
- Hold down the Control and Command keys to switch to the corner point.
- Change the direction of a curve by dragging on the direction point handles with the corner tool.
- To move a point in a path, use the arrow tool in the Paths palette and drag the point to the new position. To temporarily change to the Arrow tool while using the Pen tool, hold the Command key.
- To add a point to a path, use the Pen + tool in the Paths palette by clicking on the part of a line you want to add a point to.
- To delete a point, use the Pen – tool in the Paths palette by clicking on the point you want to delete.
- To select multiple anchor points, hold down the Shift key and click on the points. Press and drag anywhere off a path to create a marquee to use for selecting multiple anchor points.
- Duplicate a path by holding down the Option key and dragging on a path.

Working with Paths

Choose Save Path in the Path palette's pop-out menu to add a path to the list of saved paths. These will be saved with the image in the same file format. Delete a path by selecting it in the list and choosing Delete Path in the pop-out menu. Convert a path to a selection by choosing Make Selection, or by pressing Enter on the numeric keypad. Convert a selection to a path by choosing Make Path. Paths can also be stroked and filled in the pop-out menu.

***Tip*: To retain an exact path and anchor point positions, save the path before you define it as a selection. Converting a selection to a path creates a new set of anchor points.**

To use paths from other Photoshop documents or from Adobe Illustrator, copy them to the clipboard and then paste them into the new document.

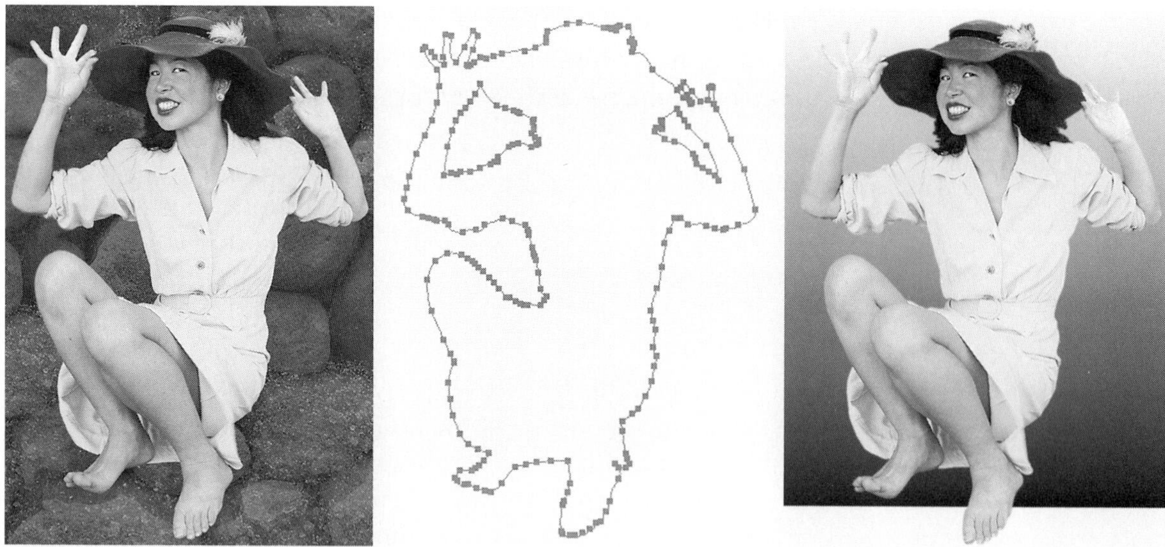

Figure 5–13 The model on the left was traced with the Pen tool and then the path (center) was saved as a Clipping Path. The image was placed into Illustrator (right) against a blended background.

Clipping Paths

Clipping paths can be used as masks in other applications, such as Adobe Illustrator, Aldus FreeHand, Aldus PageMaker, or QuarkXPress. To silhouette a Photoshop image against a background of another image, color, pattern, or type in a vector program, you must save a clipping path with the document (Figure 5–13).

Convert a saved path to a clipping path by selecting Clipping Path from the Paths palette pop-out menu. The Clipping Path dialog box opens allowing you to select the desired Path, Flatness, and Fill Rules (Figure 5–14).

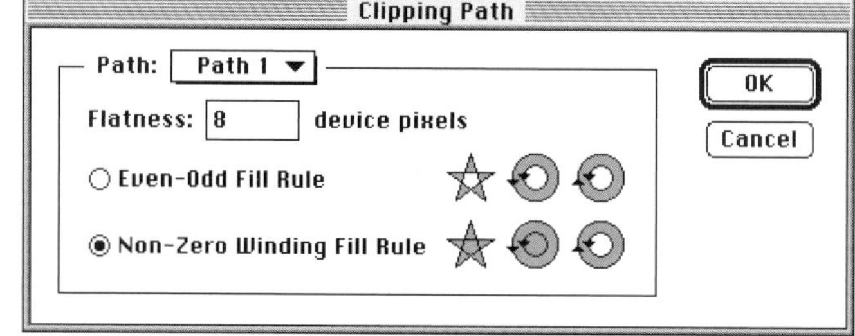

Figure 5–14 The Clipping Path options dialog box

The Flatness setting for clipping paths refers to the smoothness of the curves in the final output. The lower the Flatness value, the smoother the curve. You can enter a number from 0.2 to 100, but for high-resolution printing do not use a number higher than 8.

Use the Fill Rules selections when you include more than one path in a clipping path. They both count the number of path crossings and the direction of the stokes. The fill rules can be confusing, but you can remember it this way: In general, use the Even-Odd Rule for compound, multipart paths that may include paths enclosing other paths; and use the Non-Zero Rule for simple paths that will result in quicker printing to a PostScript printer. If undesirable results occur when using a Fill Rule, try the other rule or select one of the paths and reverse its direction by choosing Reverse Subpath in the pop-out menu.

***Tip*: To see the effects of a clipping path and any applicable fill rules, the document must be saved as an EPS file and placed into another program such as Adobe Illustrator, Aldus FreeHand, Aldus PageMaker, or QuarkXPress.**

When saving the document for use in another program, use the EPS file format to include the clipping path. More information on clipping paths can be found in Chapter 8, "Output."

Applying a Fill or Stroke to a Path

Fill a path with a color or a defined pattern by using the Fill Path command. The Stroke Path command applies a stroke to a path. These commands are similar to the Fill and Stroke commands with some useful differences.

Click on a path in the list and select Fill Path from the Paths palette pop-out menu to open the Fill Path dialog box (Figure 5–15). In Contents, select either the Foreground Color, Pattern, a saved version of a file, or a Snapshot to fill a path. In Blending, select the Opacity and fill Mode. The Fill Path command uses the same Mode options available for the painting and editing tools. For a description of each mode, see the section "Painting and Editing Modes" in Chapter 4, "Using the Tools and Palettes." Choose Anti-aliased to eliminate the jaggies.

Click on a path in the Saved Paths list and select Stroke Path from the Paths palette pop-out menu to open the Stroke Path dialog box (Figure 5–16). The tools available in the pop-up menu function identically as the

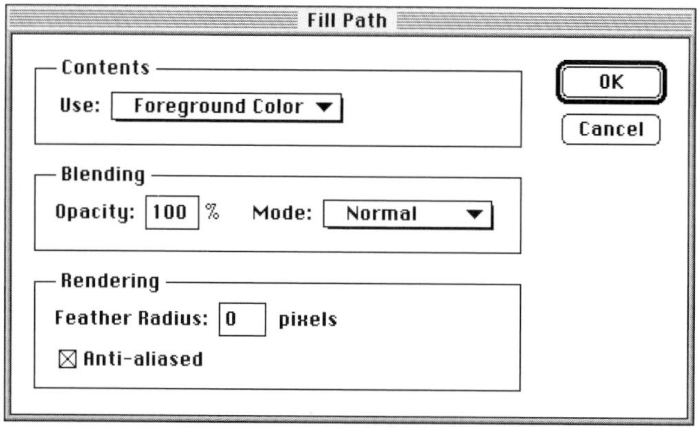

Fill Path
Contents
Use: Foreground Color
OK
Cancel
Blending
Opacity: 100 % Mode: Normal
Rendering
Feather Radius: 0 pixels
☒ Anti-aliased

Figure 5–15
The Fill Path dialog box

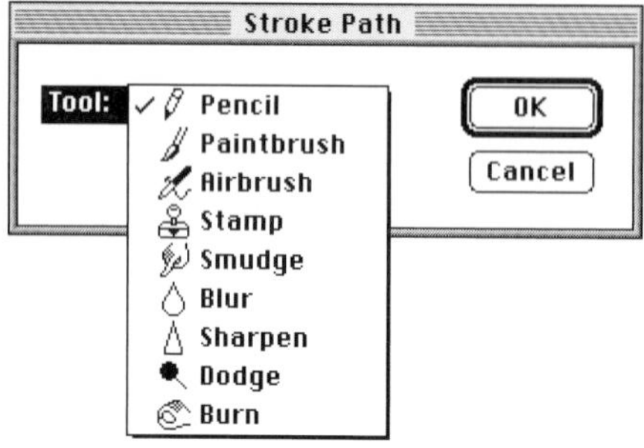

Figure 5–16
The Stroke Path dialog box options dialog box showing the available tools

Figure 5–17
Examples of the Brush, Airbrush, and Rubber Stamp tools applied to the Stroke Path command

toolbox tools with their settings controlled in the Brushes palette. The selected tool will be applied to the path (Figure 5–17).

Tip: **If you select a tool from the Toolbox before selecting Stroke Path, the Stroke Path dialog box will be bypassed and the tool will be applied automatically to the path using the settings in the Brushes palette.**

Defining Paths As Selections

Any path can be defined as a selection. A path can also be combined with or subtracted from a selected area. To convert a path to a selection, click on it in the list and pick Make Selection from the Paths pop-out menu to open the Make Selection dialog box (Figure 5–18). You can also simply press Enter on the numeric keypad. If you want to combine the converted path with a selection, select an area with one of the selection tools prior to the above step.

Specify the number of desired pixels to either side of the selection edge in the Feather Radius field and choose Anti-aliased to eliminate the jaggies. There are four options in the Operation area to define the selection border. In the Operation area, select how you want the path to combine with a selection (if selected). These options function the same as do the Command and Shift keys to combine selections with the selection tools.

Defining Selections as Paths

Convert a selection made with any of the selection tools to a path by picking Make Path from the Paths palette pop-out menu. The Make Path dialog box will open (Figure 5–19).

A number from .5 to 10 pixels in the Tolerance box determines how accurately the path will follow the lines of the selection by plotting more or less anchor points. A higher value produces a smoother path with less detail by plotting fewer points. A lower value produces a rougher path with more detail by using more points (Figure 5–20).

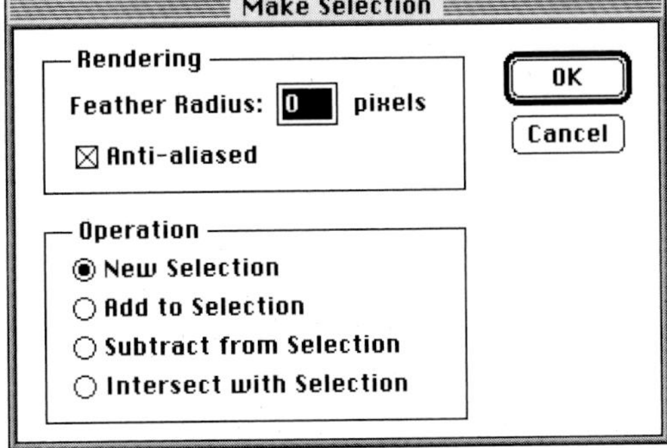

Figure 5–18
The Make Selection dialog box allows for various ways to combine a path with an existing selection.

Figure 5–19
The Make Path options dialog box showing the Tolerance control

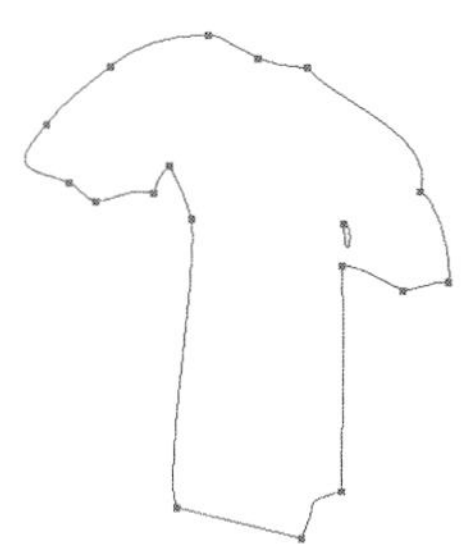
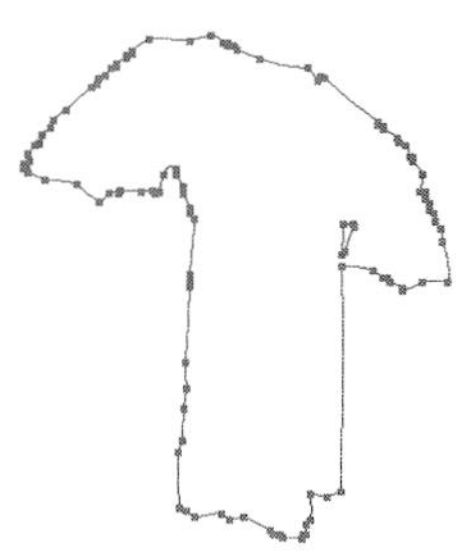

Figure 5–20
The shirt in the original image (left) was selected and converted to a path at a 5-pixel Tolerance (center) and at a 1-pixel Tolerance (right).

Tip: **Too many anchor points in a path can cause problems when outputting to a PostScript printer from a vector program.**

Select Menu

The Select menu (Figure 5–21) works in conjunction with the selection tools in the tool palette. Using the commands under the Select menu extend the selection area and create an array of "vignetting" effects. You can use the feather command, copy a selection into a channel, load a selection from a channel, select a common color throughout a document, and hide the "marching ants" of a selected area while maintaining the selection.

Select All

The Select All command (Command-A) selects the entire currently active document, regardless of the current magnification. If the entire document is not visible, the selection marquee will extend beyond the visible boundaries of the window.

Tip: **If you want to rotate or flip an entire document, do not use the Select All command to select the whole document for rotation; this will result in a cropped image.**

None

Deselect any selected area by selecting None (Command-D). Once applied, you can be sure that nothing is selected in the current document.

Tip: **You can also deselect a selection by clicking anywhere outside of the selection area (inside of the document), unless the Magic Wand tool is in use, in which case click inside the selected area.**

Inverse

Inverse selects the exact opposite of the current selection. If you are working on a selected portion of an image and decide to leave it alone to manipulate the rest of the picture, use the Inverse command. Switch back to the exact original selection by choosing Inverse again.

Hide Edges

Hide the "marching ants" animation of the selection border with the Hide Edges command (Command-H), even though the selection remains. Applications of the Hide Edges command include applying masked painting tools to a selection without seeing the selection edges, seeing how text looks immediately after creating it without deselecting the text, and previewing an area processed with any filter without the distraction of the animated selection effect. The Hide Edges command toggles to Show Edges when Hide Edges is active; the next selection will turn it off.

Feather

Feathering allows you to precisely determine how a selection's edges will blend with a background. With the Feather command, you can create variable soft edges for a selected area, resulting in believable "vignette" effects. When you choose Feather from the Select menu, a dialog appears allowing you to specify the degree of feathering (Figure 5–22). Accepted values are 1 to 250 pixels. Higher numbers yield softer edges.

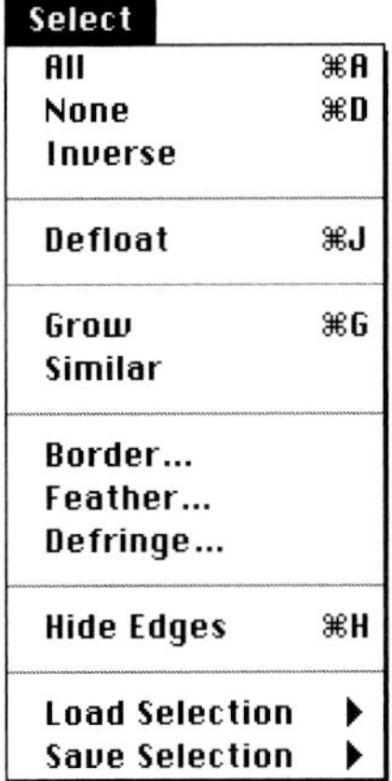

Figure 5–21
The Select menu

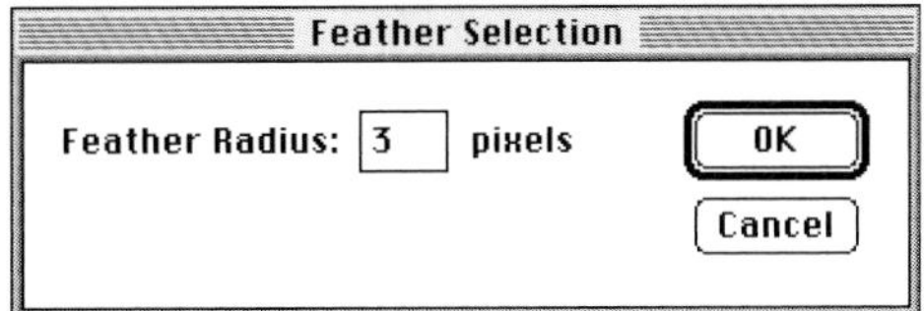

Figure 5–22
The Feather Selection dialog box

Use the Feather command alone to create everything from smooth borders to glowing halo effects (Figure 5–23) or in conjunction with other selection commands for special effects. See the technique for creating glows around objects by combining the Feather and Fringe commands in Chapter 7, "Advanced Photoshop Techniques."

Tip: Apply the feather effect to the selection tools in their options dialogs by double-clicking on the tool's icon in the Toolbox.

Defringe

A common problem when pasting a selection made with the Magic Wand tool is that the outer borders of the selection tend to display traces of left over colors and tones from the original background. Use the Defringe command to have Photoshop analyze the inner adjoining areas of a selection edge and extend the colors and values to the edge, covering the offending pixels (Figure 5–24).

Tip: Apply the Defringe command before deselecting a floating selection. Once deselected, the selected area becomes part of the background. To see the Defringe effect without deselecting, use the Hide Edges command.

Border

The Border command creates a new selection along the edge of a selection. Choose the Border command and specify the desired width in pixels in the Border dialog box (Figure 5–25). Specify the border width between 1 and 64 pixels. This selection is identical to any other selection; you can apply filters, feather it, copy it, and change its color (Figure 5–26).

Figure 5–23
Feather examples with the Feather Radius set to 5 (left), 25 (center), and 50 (right) pixels.

Figure 5–24 The sphere at left, created on a white background, shows a light edge when pasted on a darker background. The Defringe command was applied at a 2-pixel setting to eliminate the fringe and produce a smooth believable edge on the dark background.

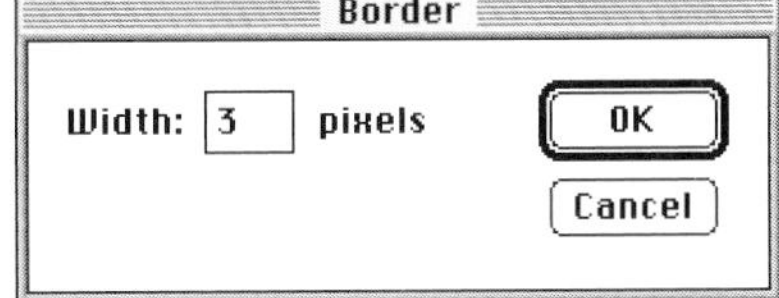

Figure 5–25
The Border dialog box

Figure 5–26
The Border command was used on a rectangular section, which was manipulated with filters and curves.

Grow

Choose the Grow command when a selected area needs to be slightly larger. By choosing Grow, the selected area expands to adjacent pixels based on color and value. The amount of additional expansion as well as the degree of anti-aliasing is based on the tolerance setting in the Magic Wand dialog box (regardless of the selection tool in use).

Similar

Choosing the Similar command causes Photoshop to search through the document and select all colors that are similar to the originally selected color or colors. As in the Grow command, set the sensitivity of the Similar command in the Magic Wand dialog box. Use this command if you want to change or manipulate a particular color in the entire document.

Float and Defloat

After making a selection the Float command becomes an option. By selecting Float, the selection can be moved without affecting the original image. A floating selection, not in its original position, has the Defloat command as an option. If Defloat is selected, the background color (usually white) will remain after the selection is moved or deleted.

***Tip*: After making a selection, hold the Option key down while dragging the selection to a new position. The original image will remain.**

Save and Load Selection

The Save Selection command converts the current selection into a new channel. View the channel by choosing show Channels under the Windows menu and clicking on the desired channel in the Channels palette. A channel can be used as a selection at any time by selecting Load channel.

The Load Selection command converts a channel into an active selection. By saving selections as channels and then loading them when needed, hours of work time can be eliminated because you do not have to reselect areas. See the "Channels" section later in this chapter for more details.

Paste Controls

The Paste Into and Paste Behind commands under the Edit menu are directly linked to Photoshop's masking capabilities. Use these commands to paste a clipboard image into or behind a selection.

After applying the Paste Into and Paste Behind commands the pasted image becomes an active selection. Any manipulation or painting tools can be applied to it before deselecting. Try some of the following options after pasting an image:

- Move the pasted selection to position it precisely.
- Save the pasted image as a channel.
- Use the dynamic controls to stretch, distort, rotate, show perspective, and skew the image.
- Apply any filter or color control to the pasted image. Modifications will affect only the pasted selection and not the surrounding area.

When you modify the pasted image, you can undo the effect without undoing the actual Paste Into or Paste Behind command. Once deselected, the pasted image becomes part of the bitmap and cannot be manipulated.

Paste Into

Use the Paste Into command to paste the clipboard image inside of the current selection area. In effect, the pasted image is masked by the boundaries of the selected area. To use the Paste Into command:

1. Copy an image into the clipboard.
2. Select an area in a document with the Rectangular marquee tool.
3. Choose the Paste Into command. If the clipboard image does not appear within the selected area, you will see its bounding box in the center of the document.
4. Move the pointer within the bounding box of the pasted image, and press and drag the image into the area of the original selection.
5. Release the mouse button when you are satisfied with the position of the pasted image. The image will appear masked by the edges of the original selection.

Solid backgrounds are likely candidates for the Paste Into command because they are easily selected with the Magic Wand Tool. All of the layering in Figure 5–27 was done with the Paste Into command.

Paste Behind

The Paste Behind command pastes an image behind the current selection area. The pasted image will appear to be masked by the image in front of it as can be seen in Figure 5–28. After the nineteenth-century engravings were scanned and filtered with the Despeckle filter (to eliminate moiré

Figure 5–27 The background (center) was selected with the Magic Wand tool and saved as a channel. Using the Paste Into command, the model (left) was pasted into the selected background. The two lower ferns and the lava background were also pasted into the selected area to create the final image (right).

Figure 5–28 To produce "Ant Stomp" (right), Ellen Landweber used the Paste Behind command to place the figures (left) behind the leaves (center).

patterns), they were isolated from their backgrounds with the Pen tool and converted to selections. One at a time they were pasted into the ant scene behind the selected leaves using the Paste Behind command.

Composite Controls

Normally, a selection pasted into a document from the clipboard floats on a plane over the underlying image. This floating selection can be moved around and modified until it is deselected. Any selection moved from its original position is also a floating selection. Once deselected, a floating selection replaces the original image that lies underneath.

The Composite Controls option under the Edit menu opens a dialog box (Figure 5–29) that allows you to control the interaction between the pixels of a floating selection and the pixels of the background behind it. When composited, the pixels of the two images combine using the numerous options available in the dialog box. The Composite Controls command becomes active in any one of four situations: when pasting an image into a document, immediately after moving any selected area, by choosing the Float command after making a selection, and when text created with the Type tool appears on the screen.

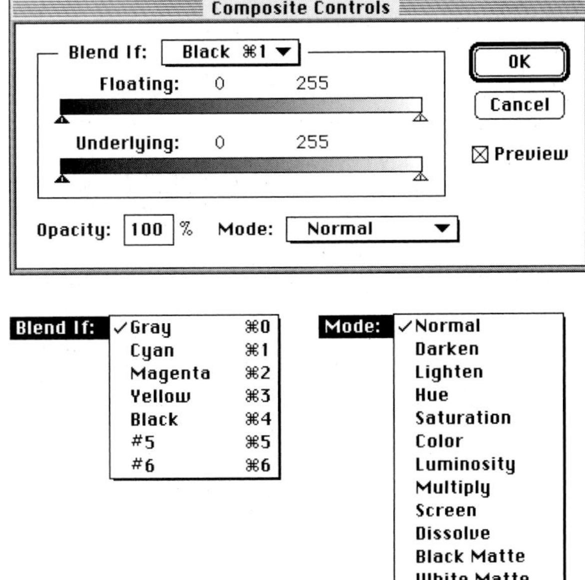

Figure 5–29
The Composite Controls dialog box with its submenus

Tip: Hold down the Option key when pasting an image and the Composite Controls dialog box will open automatically.

Click on the Preview button to see any modifications prior to committing the change to the image. The Composite Controls affects the color or channel specified in the Blend If pop-up menu and the value range specified between the triangles in the Floating slider. Only active channels (selected in the Channels palette) appear in the Blend If pop-up menu. The Gray option controls all colors in an image.

Tip: Apply the Composite Controls to a channel by selecting it in the Blend If pop-up menu or by selecting the channel in the Channels palette before choosing Composite Controls.

The Floating sliders determine the value range of either the floating selection or the underlying image that will be affected. The full range of tones varies from 0 (white) to 255 (black). The space between the triangles determines which pixels will be changed. Pixels with values outside of the specified range will not be affected.

To see the effects of the Floating sliders, Opacity and Mode controls, create a new square grayscale document and fill it with a blend from black to white. In another document of the same size, or in another channel, select a circle with the Elliptical marquee, apply a radial blend, then copy and paste it over the square as shown in Figure 5–30. Choose Composite Controls and click the Preview box. Use this configuration to test the various options and to follow the examples below:

- Try various Opacity settings between 1 and 100% (Figures 5–31 and 5–32). Lower percentage numbers make the Floating selection more transparent.
- Experiment with the Floating slider, moving it to various positions. For example, move the right triangle to the 127 setting (Figure 5–33). Only values between black (0) and middle gray (127) of the Floating selection will be pasted onto the Underlying image when deselected. Next, move the right triangle back to its original position (255) and move the left triangle to middle gray (128) (Figure 5–34). Only values between middle gray (128) and white (255) of

Figure 5–30
A circular selection with a Radial blend pasted over a square with a Linear blend. Use this configuration to test the Composite Controls options.

Figure 5–31
A 60% Opacity setting applied to the Floating selection

Figure 5–32
A 30% Opacity setting applied to the Floating selection

Figure 5–33
Only values between black (0) and middle gray (127) of the Floating selection will be pasted onto the Underlying image when deselected.

Figure 5–34
Only values between middle gray (128) and white (255) of the Floating selection will be pasted onto the Underlying image when deselected.

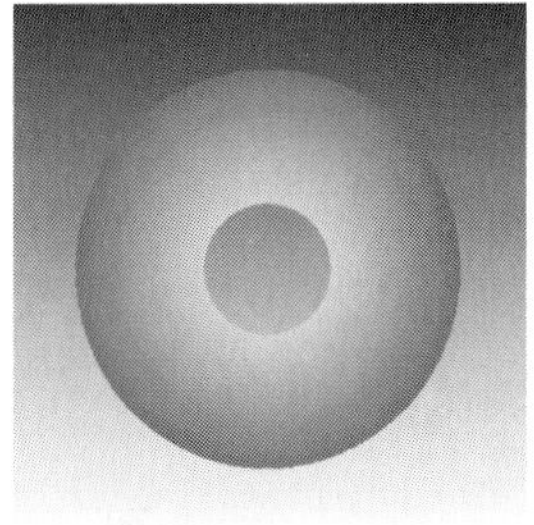

Figure 5–35
Only values between dark gray (64) and light gray (192) of the Floating selection will be pasted onto the Underlying image when deselected.

the Floating selection will be pasted onto the Underlying image when deselected. Finally, move the left triangle to dark gray (64) and the right triangle to light gray (192) (Figure 5–35). Only values between dark gray (64) and light gray (192) of the Floating selection will be pasted onto the Underlying image when deselected.

- As above, experiment with the Underlying slider, moving it to various positions. For example, move the right triangle to the 127 setting (Figure 5–36). The values between black (0) and middle gray (127) of the Underlying image will be changed to the pixels of the Floating selection when deselected. Next, put the right triangle back to its original position (255) and move the left triangle to middle gray (128) (Figure 5–37). The values between middle gray (128) and white (255) of the Underlying image will be changed to the pixels of the Floating selection when deselected. Finally, move the left triangle to dark gray (64) and the right triangle to light gray (192) (Figure 5–38). The values between dark gray (64) and light gray (192) of the Underlying image will be changed to the pixels of the Floating selection when deselected.
- Finally, choose the various Mode options to learn how the pixels of the Floating selection change or combine with the Underlying image. (Figures 5–39, 5–40, and 5–41 are Modes that work in black and white.) The choices in the Mode pop-up menu function the same as those available for the painting and editing tools, with the exception of the Black Matte and White Matte modes. These two additional options assist in eliminating the halo that occurs when pasting images with soft edges. Use the Black Matte Mode when

Figure 5–36
Only values between black (0) and middle gray (127) of the Underlying image will be replaced by the Floating selection when deselected.

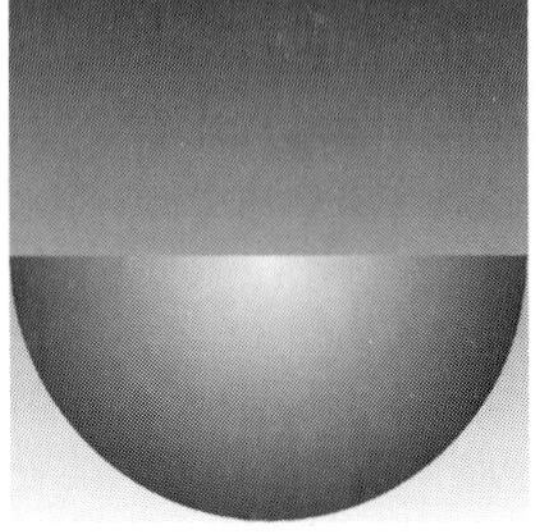

Figure 5–37
Only values between middle gray (128) and white (255) of the Underlying image will be replaced by the Floating selection when deselected.

Figure 5–38
Only values between dark gray (64) and light gray (192) of the Underlying image will be replaced by the Floating selection when deselected

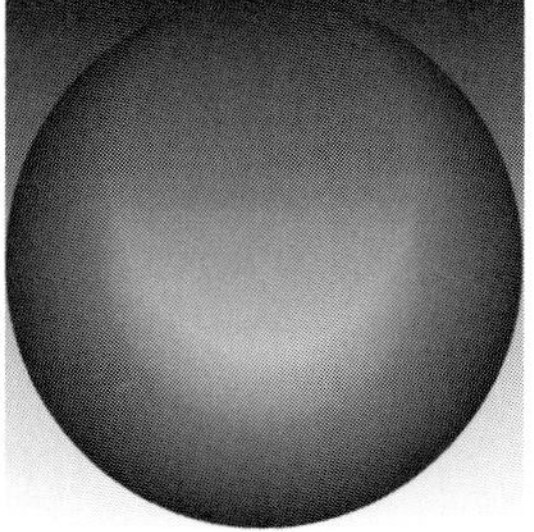

Figure 5–39
The Darken Mode changes (darkens) only pixels of the Underlying image that are lighter than the respective pixels of the Floating selection.

Figure 5–40
The Lighten Mode changes (lightens) only pixels of the Underlying image that are darker than the respective pixels of the Floating selection.

Figure 5–41
The Screen Mode lightens the composited pixels based on the combined values of the Floating selection and the Underlying image pixels.

pasting an image originally created on a black background. Use the White Matte Mode when pasting an image originally created on a white background.

Masking and Channels

Anytime a selection is made it becomes a mask, and manipulations can only be made within its boundaries. Use masks to isolate certain portions of an image and apply color changes, filters, or any other image manipulation command. To use a selection at a later time, it can be saved as a Channel or Quick Mask. When activated, a Channel or Quick Mask becomes a normal selection.

Channels

Although any selected portion of an image is a temporary mask, a selection converted to a channel can be saved with an image file for later use. Use channels to isolate and mask parts of an image, to overlap shapes, to collage various images, and to apply image processing effects to specific areas. A channel, which is sometimes referred to as an alpha channel, can be viewed or edited by activating it in the Channels palette (Figure 5–42). Open the Channels palette by choosing Show Channels under the Window menu.

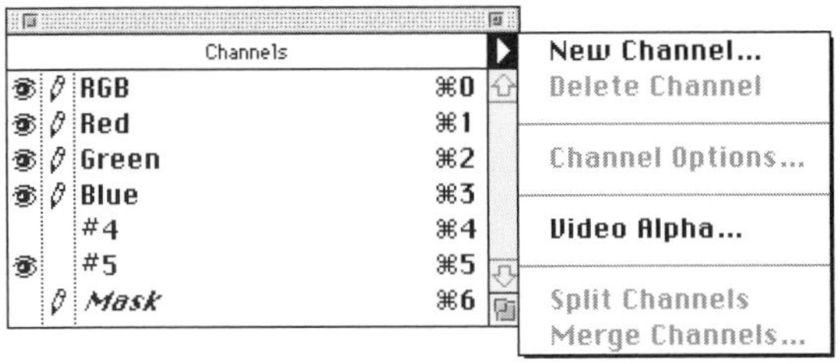

Channels	
RGB	⌘0
Red	⌘1
Green	⌘2
Blue	⌘3
#4	⌘4
#5	⌘5
Mask	⌘6

New Channel...
Delete Channel
Channel Options...
Video Alpha...
Split Channels
Merge Channels...

Figure 5–42
The Channels palette

As introduced in Chapter 1, all Photoshop documents (except for Grayscale and Bitmapped) consist of multiple layers, called channels, each of which is an 8-bit image. When in the RGB Color mode, you can create and edit full 24-bit color pictures because the image is actually made up of three 8-bit channels, red, green, and blue. When viewed as a composite image, these RGB layers display the full spectrum of viewable colors. Photoshop has the ability to work with documents containing up to 16 channels. In a 24-bit RGB image, three channels are occupied (for the RGB layers), leaving 13 channels that can be used for masking and special effects. A document in CMYK Color mode uses four channels, one each for cyan, magenta, yellow, and black, leaving 12 channels available for other uses.

> **NOTE: Channels use memory, and each new channel is equal in size to an existing channel. In a grayscale document, adding a channel doubles the size of the file. In an RGB image, each channel occupies one-third of the document's size. Each channel maintains the same resolution of the main image.**

Channels can be combined in various ways by using the Calculate Commands under the Image menu. Refer to Chapter 7, "Advanced Photoshop Techniques," for information on the Calculate commands.

Creating and Using Channels

Create a new blank channel by choosing New Channel from the pop-out menu in the Channels palette. The Channel Options dialog box will appear (Figure 5–43). You can also create a new channel by making a selection with any of the selection tools and choosing Save Selection under the Select menu. Use any tool, filter, or control that normally works in the Grayscale mode in a channel (Figure 5–44).

Channel Options

Name: #2

OK

Cancel

Color Indicates:
- ◉ Masked Areas
- ○ Selected Areas

Color

Opacity: 50 %

Figure 5–43
The Channel Options dialog box

Figure 5–44
A channel was used in this composite image by Joseph Tracey to mask the child from the background in order to manipulate them separately.

To view, edit, or manipulate a channel, click on it in the Channels palette or use its keyboard command (next to the channel number). When a channel is visible on the screen, you see an eye symbol in the far left row. To make any channel invisible, click on the eye symbol. The pencil symbol in the row next to the eye indicates that a channel can be modified. To disallow modification of a channel, click on the pencil icon. To view or modify a channel, click in the appropriate row and either the eye or pencil icon will appear. Any number of channels can be viewed or modified simultaneously. You can even view one channel while modifying another.

***Tip*: Be careful to view and edit the desired channels. It is very easy to accidentally manipulate a channel other than the one being viewed.**

The pop-out menu in the Channels palette allows you to delete channels, set channel options, split and merge channels, and even copy a channel to a 32-bit video card.

- To delete a channel, click on it in the Channels palette list and choose Delete Channel from the pop-out menu.
- Select New Channel or click on a channel in the list and choose the Channel Options command to open the Channel Options dialog box (Figure 5–43) that allows you to name new channels, select what color indicates either a masked area or a selected area, and set the opacity of the channel's color.
- The Video Alpha command in the pop-out menu allows you to copy a channel into the extra 8 bits provided by using a 32-bit video card that supports the use of an alpha channel. This command will control the transparency of an image when combining it with a video source.
- The Split Channels command separates each channel into a Grayscale document that can be edited and saved under its own name.
- Choose Merge Channels to combine separate documents into one file, with each document becoming a channel. When Merge Channels is selected a dialog box appears allowing you to specify the Mode and number of Channels. Click OK and the Merge MultiChannel dialog box appears (Figure 5–45) in order to specify the channel that each document will become.

***Tip*: When merging channels, each channel must be exactly the same size and resolution.**

The Quick Mask Mode

The Quick Mask mode is a temporary channel that lets you see both the image you are working on and the mask at the same time. After making a selection, click on the Quick Mask icon in the Toolbox to create a Quick

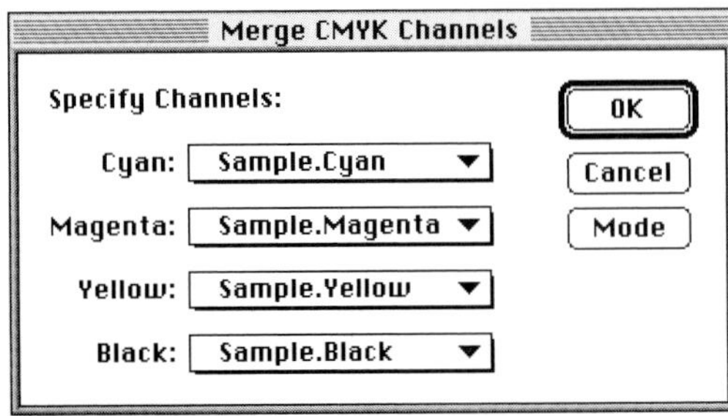

Figure 5–45 The Merge MultiChannel dialog box allows you to specify which channel each document will become.

Mask. Double Click on its icon to open the Mask Options dialog box, which is identical to the Channel Options dialog box (Figure 5–43).

The specified color shows either the selected areas or the masked areas. The default overlay color, red (similar to a rubylith), masks the image from editing and the clear areas represent the selection. Any changes made to the image will only occur in the clear areas.

CHAPTER 6

Image Processing

Image processing is a term loosely thrown around in the computer graphics world. It can mean many things. In scientific circles, image processing is used to analyze images in order to "see" things that are not immediately apparent. The prepress industry uses image processing to make color corrections on images. Photographers and artists use image processing tools and techniques to manipulate and combine images. In this chapter, we will discuss the tools, commands, and controls to change (or process) an image in Photoshop.

Image-processing controls found under the Image menu include the Map controls, which allow you to invert, equalize, and posterize an image, as well as to create high-contrast images using the Threshold command. The Adjustment controls offer precision color balancing and alterations by changing the data in the Levels, Curves, Brightness/Contrast, Color Balance, Hue/Saturation, and Variations windows. You can control the angle and distortion of an image by using commands found under the Flip, Rotate, and Effects submenus. The Image Size command allows for the resizing and resampling of images, whereas Canvas Size changes the dimensions of the working area. The Histogram choice plots out the tonal distribution of the pixels for part or all of the image.

The Calculate commands, also found under the Image menu, combine channels in numerous ways. Refer to Chapter 7, "Advanced Photoshop Techniques," for more information regarding the practical uses of the Calculate commands.

This chapter looks at image-processing functions and concludes with a look at the multitude of filters available for Photoshop. In addition to the many native filters that come with Photoshop, we will survey several third-party "plug-ins" that add further to the power of the program.

Image Processing Basics

Photoshop's image-processing controls have a number of features:

- All of the image-processing controls, with the exception of the Image Size and Canvas Size commands, affect only the selected portion of an image. If nothing is selected, the image-processing controls affect the entire image.
- Many of the image-processing control dialog boxes have Preview buttons. Click on the Preview button to see the changes exclusively in the currently active document or selection area. By using the Preview button, you can experiment with different effects without leaving the dialog box. Some filters have a small preview within their dialog boxes.

***Tip*: A quick way to compare a manipulation to the original is to select a small area and then apply the color adjustment, value change, or filter effect. Select Undo to get back to the original.**

- Cancel the changes made in a dialog box (except for filters) without closing it by holding the Option key and clicking on the Cancel button.
- When working on an 8-bit video display, the image-processing slide controls work in real time. On 24-bit displays, some of the image-processing controls work in real time, but others do not. If you turn on Video LUT Animation in the General Preferences dialog box, all open Photoshop documents will show changes as they are being made (except for filters), if the Preview button is deselected. With Video LUT animation off, no changes will be seen unless the Preview button is selected.

Tip: If you are using a 24-bit or 32-bit video card and are having problems previewing, try resetting the Monitors control in the Control Panels by clicking another display mode and then reselecting the desired mode. Video LUT in the General Preferences also should be deselected.

Tip: Before you press the Preview button after changing a slider or other control, you can do quick before-and-after comparisons of the change by pressing on the Title Bar of the control dialog box that you are using (with Video LUT Animation on). The screen will temporarily revert to the normal, unaffected display mode.

- While you are in an image-processing dialog box, the current document's Scroll Bars, as well as the Grabber and Zoom tools, are active. You can scroll around a document and zoom into an area to see the effects of an image-processing change without closing the dialog box.
- Moving the cursor over the active document turns it into the Eyedropper tool, which displays readouts in the Show Info window.
- If you are running Photoshop on a black-and-white machine (Macintosh SE or Plus), most of the interactive map and adjustment controls are not interactive; you have to use the Preview command to see the changes made. Although you cannot see color, you can work with it on a black-and-white system by using numerical color values.
- If you work in an environment where you must apply the same color corrections or value adjustments to a number of images, use the Save and Load features which are in many of the image-processing dialog boxes. After making a color correction or value adjustment, save the settings for later use by clicking the Save button. Name and file the settings in the resulting dialog box. When you want to apply the same settings to another image, select the method you used and click the Load button in the dialog box to locate and apply the settings.

Tip: **If you would like to automate redundant work to an even greater extent, check out software that allows you to record a series of keystrokes to perform a function. QuicKeys, a popular program of this type, provides a number of options for speeding through repetitive work. If you have many images that require the same types of color corrections and adjustments, you can use an application called Debabelizer. This helpful program allows for batch processing of multiple images that require the same changes.**

The Map Commands

The commands found in the Map submenu under the Image menu allow simple modifications to the colors or brightness levels in an image. In the Map submenu you will find the Invert, Equalize, Threshold, and Posterize commands.

Invert

This command inverts the values of the pixels in an image or selection area. You can make a positive image negative, or take a scanned negative and create a positive image. With a color image, the Invert command will change all the colors to their opposites or complementaries on the color wheel (Figure 6–1).

Equalize

The Equalize command balances the brightness and contrast values of an image to what Photoshop analyzes as the optimum settings. For example, if a scanned image appears darker than the original, you might want to use the Equalize command to automatically redistribute the balance of

Figure 6–1
Lightning Dancer by Cher Threinen-Pendarvis (left) was inverted to create the negative version (right).

brightness and contrast values, resulting in a lighter, more balanced image. The Equalize command sets the darkest value to black, the brightness value to white, and redistributes the in-between values to an even range of tones (Figure 6–2).

The Equalize command can be used in conjunction with the Histogram in order to observe before-and-after brightness values in an image (see the discussion of the Histogram later in this chapter).

Besides applying the Equalize command to the entire image, additional tone controls become available by selecting a portion of an image (Figure 6–3). In the Equalize dialog box, the values in the entire image can be equalized based on the values in the selected area. Conversely, the selected area itself can be equalized without affecting the rest of the document, as in Figure 6–4.

Figure 6–2
The Equalize command was applied to the original boats by Michael Roney (left), to automatically adjust the tones and produce the version on the right.

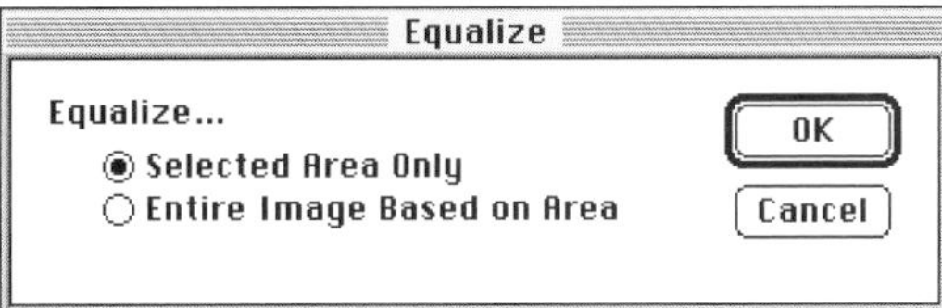

Figure 6–3
The Equalize command dialog box

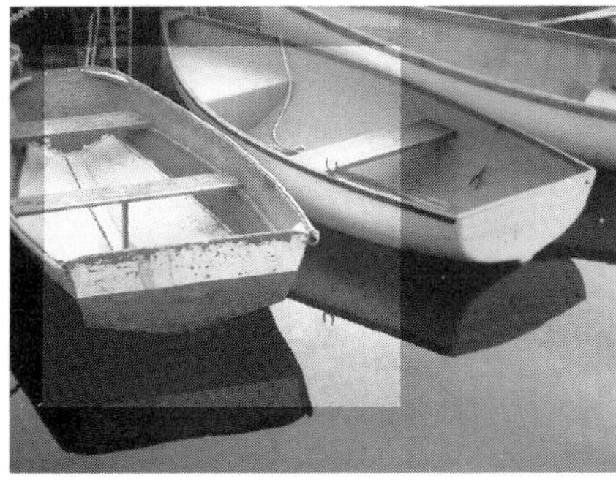

Figure 6–4
The Equalize command applied to the selected area only (left) and then to the entire image (right), based on the selected area

***Tip*: Although Equalize facilitates the correction of a scanned image, you might find the results to be brighter or darker than you expect, and therefore unusable. In this case, try using the more accurate Curves or Levels commands instead. The Variations command might also be a help with its ability to show thumbnail versions of your image in a before-and-after fashion. The Curves, Levels, and Variations commands are discussed in more detail later in this chapter.**

Threshold

Threshold allows you to create high-contrast black-and-white versions of a grayscale or color image. Selecting Threshold temporarily converts the screen into a 1-bit, black-and-white display mode and opens the Threshold dialog box (Figure 6–5).

This dialog box displays a Histogram and a Threshold Level text field showing the values in the current document or selected area. The position of the slider represents the brightness level at which tones will become either white or black. A lower Threshold Level will produce more white areas. A higher Threshold Level will produce more black areas. The midpoint is 127 in a range of 0 to 255.

The position of the slider determines the brightness level that Photoshop uses to determine whether a pixel should be converted to black or white when Threshold is applied. (The numerical brightness value is displayed at the top of the Threshold dialog box, and changes as you drag the slider.) Try dragging the slider back and forth—the functionality will become obvious (Figure 6–6).

Posterize

The Posterize command (Figure 6–7) allows you to specify the number of colors or gray levels (brightness values) used to represent the value range of an image or selection area. Typically, the Posterize command is

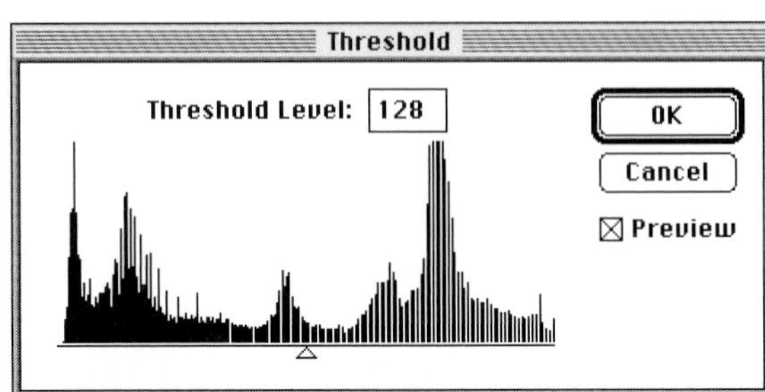

Figure 6–5
The Threshold dialog box

Figure 6–6
In this photograph (courtesy of Varden Studios), the Threshold slider was set to a light (left), medium (center), and dark (right) Threshold Level.

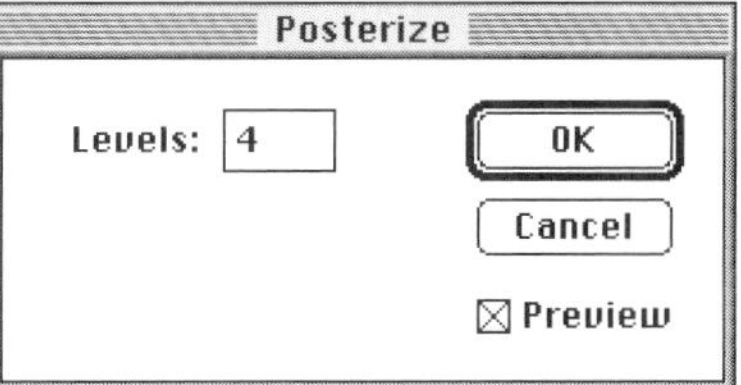

Figure 6–7
Enter the number of gray levels in the Posterize dialog box.

Figure 6–8
Posterizations with 4 levels of gray (left) and 6 levels of gray (right).

used to reduce the number of levels of gray in a grayscale image, but it also can be useful for special color effects. The tones in the image will appear in distinct steps (Figure 6–8).

The Adjust Commands

The commands found in the Adjust submenu under the Image menu include commands that are used for value adjustments, color correction, and color changes. These include Levels, Curves, Brightness/Contrast, Color Balance, Hue/Saturation and Variations.

Levels

Use the Levels command (Figure 6–9) to precisely adjust the brightness and contrast values in an image. It also allows you to control the gamma, which relates to the contrast of the midtones of an image.

The Levels dialog box displays a Histogram for the current document or selection area. The pop-up menu allows control for each of the channels in the image. The left side of the Histogram represents the darker areas of the image, and the right side represents the lighter areas. Remember, a value of 0 is black, 255 is white, and numbers in between correspond to varying degrees of brightness.

Along the bottom line of the Histogram are three triangular sliders. The black slider represents the darkest value (shadows), the gray triangle is for the midtones (gamma), and the white triangle is for the brightest values (highlights). At the top of the Levels dialog box, you will find three numbers, which correspond to the values of the three triangular slider controls. The positions of the sliders in relation to the Histogram represent the Input Levels. In an optimum situation, the darkest actual value in the image (pure black) would be right over the black triangle, and the lightest value in the image (pure white) would correspond to the position of the white triangle. For example, an image that appears too dark might display a Histogram in the Levels dialog box showing the brightest mapped value in the image to the left of the white triangular indicator (Figure 6–10).

To lighten the image, drag the white triangle slider to the left until it lines up with the right end of the Histogram. The image will have a more balanced brightness component. You may also need to adjust the gray midtone triangle to compensate for the newly brightened image, as in Figure 6–11.

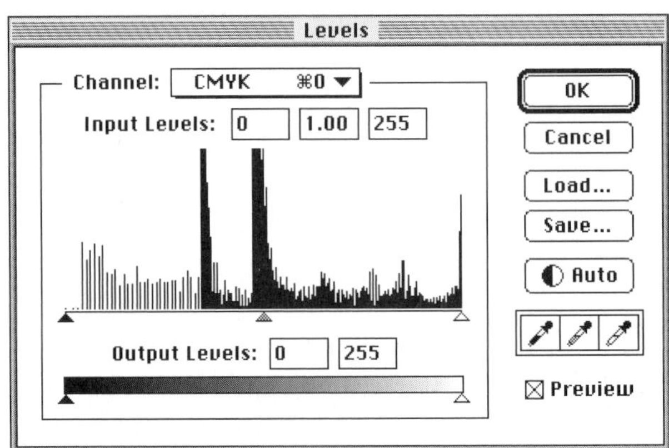

Figure 6–9
The Levels dialog box

The Output Levels slider at the bottom of the Levels dialog box allows for the adjustment of the output contrast of the image. The slider represents the range of tones in the image after performing this function. To achieve the highest contrast, set the triangles at the extreme ends. Move them in to lower the contrast or decrease the value range.

To reproduce well, an image should have a full range of tones from black to white. Click on the Auto button to have the black and white points set automatically. The darkest pixels in the image will be adjusted to black and the lightest pixels will be adjusted to white. This function is preset to clip the values by .5% in order to base the values on more than one tone. To change this default value, hold the Option key and click on the Auto button. The Auto Range Options dialog box will appear (Figure 6–12). Type in a percentage between 0 and 9.99.

To set the black and white points manually, click on the black Eyedropper in the dialog box and then click on the darkest part of the image. That point will become black. Set the white point with the white Eyedropper tool by clicking on the lightest part of the image.

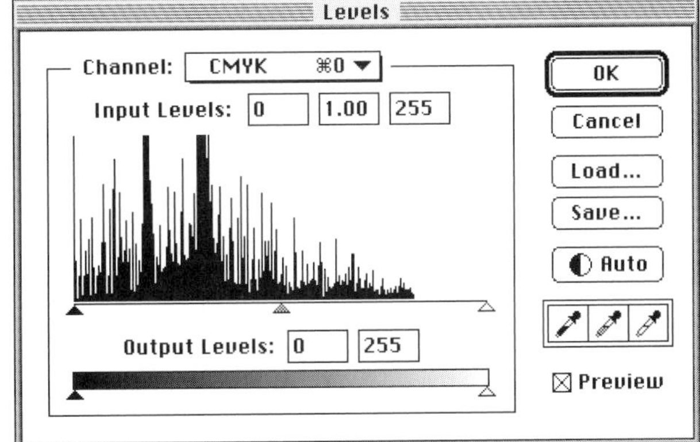

Figure 6–10
This Levels dialog box represents an image that lacks good highlights.

Figure 6–11
The dark car on the left was lightened with the Levels command to produce the car on the right.

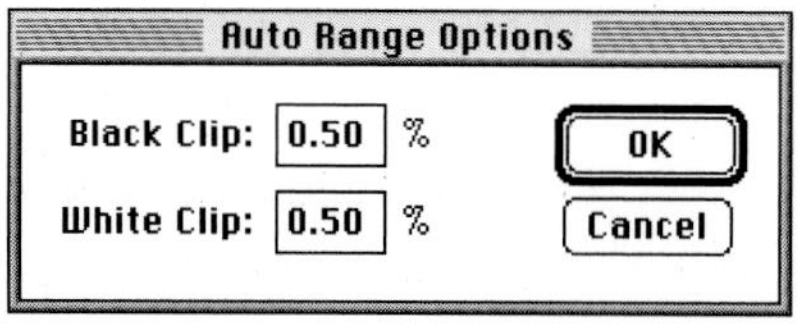

Figure 6–12
The Auto Range Options dialog box

That point will become white. To change the value that the black or white points will be set to, double-click on the Eyedropper tools to open the Color Picker. You can then set the values to be other than pure black or white.

***Tip*: Printers often want a halftone dot in the highlights and shadows. Provide this by setting the black and white points to be other than pure white or black. Consult your printer in advance to find out what values should be set for the highlights and shadows.**

To remove a color cast from an image quickly (set a neutral gray), click on the middle Eyedropper tool in the dialog box and then click on the desired middle gray point in the image. The colors at that point will be adjusted to middle gray and, along with it, all colors in the image will be adjusted accordingly toward the neutral color. To change the color setting of the Middle Eyedropper, open the Color Picker by double clicking on the tool.

Curves

The Curves command provides a visual graph (map) to precisely control and adjust the input to output relationship of the contrast, brightness, and gamma values of an image. When opened, the Curves dialog box appears (Figure 6–13). The dialog box displays a pop-up menu for the separate channels in the document. You can adjust the map for the overall image or for each individual color channel. A straight diagonal line from the lower-left to the upper-right corners represents a normal distribution of brightness values.

When you move the cursor into the map area, it turns into a crosshair by default. You can change the curve with this crosshair by dragging any point on the line to a new position. This new curve changes the way brightness values are represented in the image. Selecting the Pencil tool at the bottom of the mapping (Arbitrary Map option) area allows you to draw lines with the Pencil in the map area. Try drawing the following line: Click the Pencil in the upper-left corner of the map area, hold down the

Shift key (this constrains the lines drawn with the pencil to 45° and 90° angles), and click the Pencil in the lower-right corner of the map area. This will draw a straight line that is exactly the inverse of the normal map, resulting in an inverted, or negative image (Figures 6–14 and 6–15).

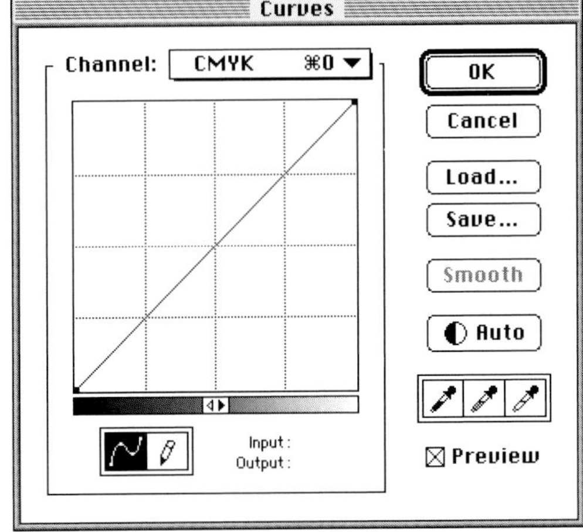

Figure 6–13
The Curves dialog box showing a normal distribution of brightness values

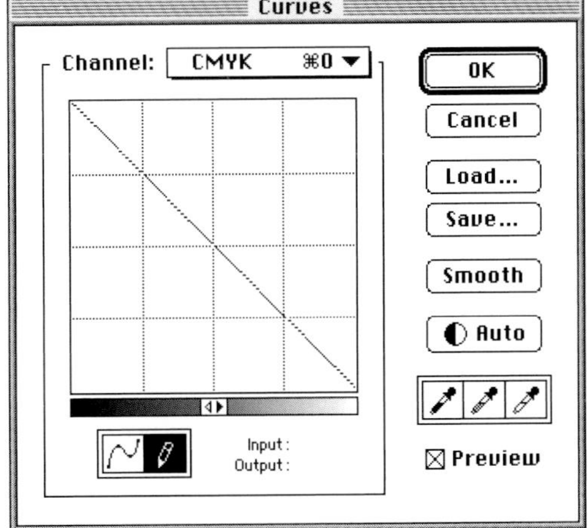

Figure 6–14
The Curves dialog box showing a reversed 45° line

Figure 6–15
Reversing the 45° line creates a negative image.

By using the Pencil to draw irregular maps (Figure 6–16), you can achieve a wide variety of solarization effects (Figure 6–17). To smooth out the abrupt, jagged, straight lines drawn with the pencil, click on the Smooth button. This will create smoother transitions between colors and tones.

Setting the black and white points, as well as the neutral gray point in the Curves command dialog box, is identical to the method used in the Levels command dialog box.

Brightness/ Contrast

Use the Brightness/Contrast command to control the overall brightness and contrast values of either an entire image or a selected area. The current numerical values are displayed above the respective sliders in the Brightness/Contrast dialog box (Figure 6–18). Although this command works well for simple adjustments (Figure 6–19), the Levels or Curves command provides greater control.

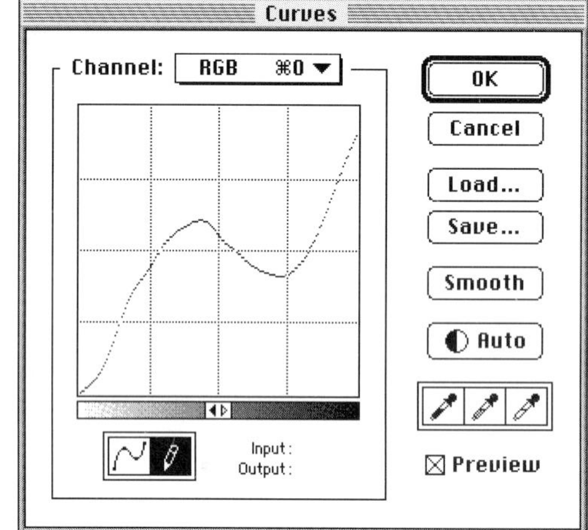

Figure 6–16
The Curves dialog box showing an irregularly drawn map

Figure 6–17
Examples of effects you can achieve by drawing an irregular Curves map

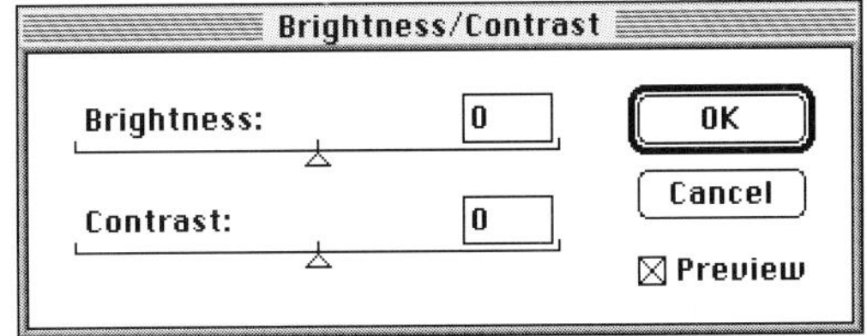

Figure 6–18
The Brightness/Contrast command dialog box

Figure 6–19
A low-contrast, light image (left) and a high-contrast image (right)

Color Balance
Color Levels: 0 0 0
Cyan Red
Magenta Green
Yellow Blue
Shadows Midtones Highlights
OK
Cancel
Preview

Figure 6–20
The Color Balance dialog box

Color Balance

The Color Balance command adjusts the balance of the colors that make up an entire image or selection. You can remove undesired color in an image or brighten dull colors. The controls can be used to affect changes in the shadows, midtones, or highlights. Choose Color Balance to open its dialog box (Figure 6–20).

The Color Balance command works with RGB, CMYK, Lab, and Indexed Color images. When used with a Lab Color image, the sliders represent the **a** (Green/Magenta) and **b** (Blue/Yellow) channels. The Color Balance can be changed by moving the slider controls or by entering numbers between +/–100 in the boxes above the sliders. Each slider represents colors directly across from each other on the color wheel. Moving a slider toward a color increases the amount of that color and decreases the amount of the opposite color.

You can remove unwanted color casts from an image with the Color Balance command. For example, a photographer may shoot a photo of a child wearing a bright yellow jumper surrounded by big red balloons.

Light bouncing off the red balloons will adversely affect the yellow color of the jumper. This reaction of light and color is known as color contamination. With Color Balance, these areas of color contamination can be corrected by pulling out the unwanted colors.

Hue/Saturation

With the Hue/Saturation command (Figure 6–21), you can change the hue (color tint), the saturation (purity of color), or the lightness (value) of an image or selection area. You can also tint an image or selection area with a solid color by using the Colorize command (found in the lower-right side of the dialog box). This is similar to filling an area with the Color Only option (except that you can dynamically change the color by using a slider control).

Adjustments can be made to all of the colors in an image or to specific primary color components. You can adjust all colors by clicking on the Master radio button or select individual primary colors to adjust along the left side of the dialog box. The Sample box displays the current foreground color, showing how changes in this dialog box will affect it.

The Hue slider shifts the colors around the color wheel. As you move the Hue slider, all of the colors change with respect to one another. This rotation, measured in + or – degrees is displayed in the text field next to the slider. The Saturation slider controls the purity (intensity) of the colors. Move the slider to the right for brighter, richer colors and to the left for duller muted colors. The text field uses numbers between +/–100. The Lightness slider controls the brightness (values) of the colors. Move the slider to the right for lighter colors and to the left for darker colors. The text field uses numbers between +/–100.

The Hue/Saturation command can make subtle color shifts or major color changes. We used it in two projects to achieve the correct colors.

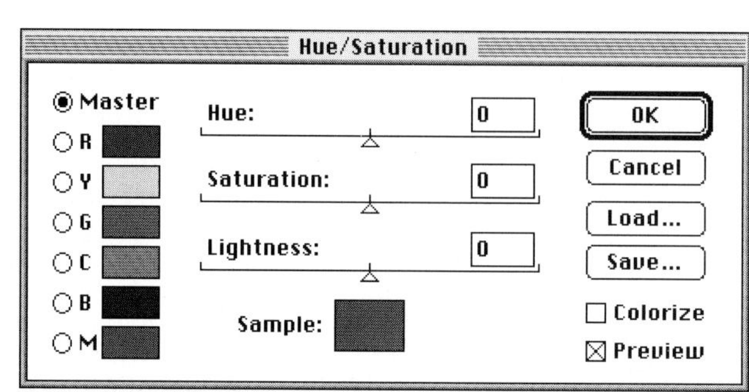

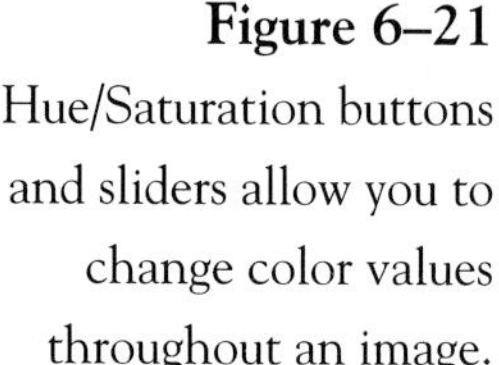

Figure 6–21
Hue/Saturation buttons and sliders allow you to change color values throughout an image.

We photographed a shoe care kit. The shoe bags were made of a lime-green nylon. The polishing cloth was the same lime-green but made of felt. In the photograph, the shoe bags were the correct shade of lime-green but the cloth appeared a brownish green. By selecting the cloth and adjusting the Hue slider, the proper green tones were regained.

You might need to totally change the color of an object. We had to photograph a sweater for inclusion in a mail-order catalog. The manufacturer, meanwhile, discontinued the particular color used in the shot, requiring a total change in color. With the Colorize option chosen, the sweater was selected and the color was completely changed.

Variations

The Variations command, introduced in version 2.5, allows you to adjust the color balance, contrast, and saturation of an image or selected area by using small, thumbnail images with corrections applied as a reference (Fig 6–22). If you have ever made test strips in a traditional darkroom, you will appreciate the options in the Variations dialog box. You not only see how changes you make will look as they are applied to an image, but you will also be presented with a number of optional sample corrections that are updated as you make changes.

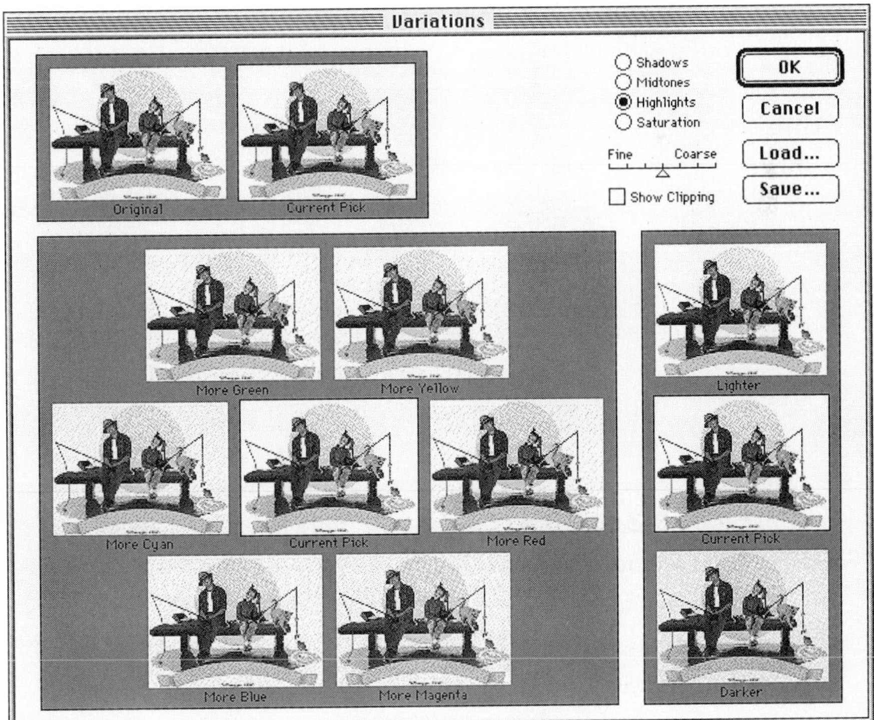

Figure 6–22
The Variations command displays different color and value options.

Although not as accurate as the Levels or Curves commands, the Variations command does provide an obvious method of seeing your options. The dialog box looks sort of like a wall of television screens with your image each of them. Each screen displays a representation of your image showing subtle differences in color, saturation, or contrast settings. For example, to make a color correction that adds red to your image, click on the thumbnail image that says More Red. The redder image slides in next to the original image to show you a comparison. The top left thumbnail, Original, is your image before corrections, and the thumbnail on the right, Current Pick, is your image with the current color adjustment. The color options correspond to the position of the colors in the Apple Color Picker.

The radio buttons to the right of the top two thumbnail images give you the choice of adjusting the Shadows, Midtones, Highlights, and Saturation of your image. The slider below these radio buttons controls how small or large these incremental changes will be displayed and applied.

The Variations command window changes its controls when using grayscale or duotone mode images. The only options available are for the adjustments of the highlights, midtones, and shadows. You cannot use the Variations command with Lab Color, Index Color, or Bitmapped modes.

The Show Clipping checkbox controls whether or not you want to preview the areas in an image that will be clipped (changed to black or white when an adjustment is applied). Since highlights and shadows can get too light or too dark, the Show Clipping checkbox allows you to ask Photoshop to show you which areas are being clipped. Photoshop will show you the clipped areas by substituting neon colors in these areas when you are pushing things too far.

***Tip*: After experimenting with Variations, if you want to get back to the original, simply click on the Original image to return the Current Pick back to the original.**

As you go through the selection process, you should come to a point where you are satisfied with the changes that have been made. This may take only one selection, or it may take 5 or more selections. You will always have the reference thumbnail view to check against your original. At this point you could save your settings for future image adjustments or click OK to apply the changes to your image.

For the Variations command to be visible under the Image menu, the Variations plug-in must be located in Photoshop's Plug-ins folder.

Tip: The Variations command can be used for color separation insurance. Bill Niffenegger from Chicago offers the following advice: "When using a new printer or color house, strike an agreement with them to run an 8 × 11 inch-film and match print test at no cost. Make a composite image using the most sensitive areas of all the image files that will be used in the final job. Use the Variations command to bracket different saturation levels and color casts of the composite file (similar to a photographer bracketing a photo shoot) and place it into the page layout software that will be used for the printing job. Note the settings used for each step in the test. When the match print test is returned and the most accurate strip picked, apply the same settings to images throughout the job." Refer to the color section (Figure C–6) to see an example of Niffeneger's test strip.

The Histogram Window

The Histogram window (Figure 6–23) displays a visual analysis of the brightness and darkness components of the current selection or of the currently active document (if nothing is selected). The Histogram plots out the distribution of the pixels in a given area at their respective brightness or darkness levels, shown numerically as 0 through 255. Use the Histogram in conjunction with other color correction tools as a gauge to check for optimum brightness and contrast settings in an

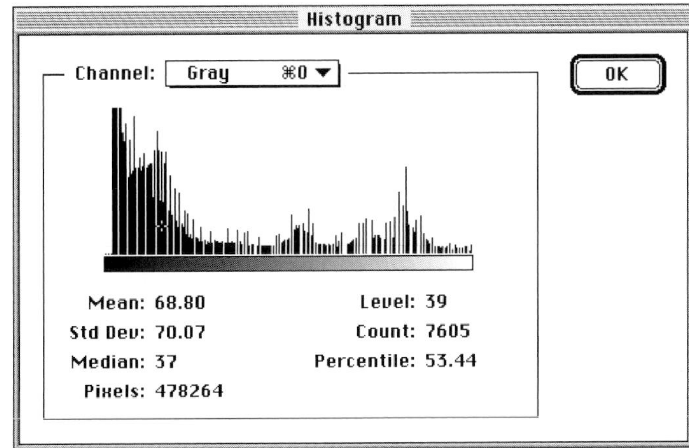

Figure 6–23
The Histogram window shown with the cursor selecting a pixel that activates the Level, Count, and Percentile displays

image. A Dark image typically has a Histogram with a heavy emphasis on the left side of the graph. Lighter images display uneven balances toward the right side of the graph.

As you move the mouse over the Histogram, the numerical readouts in the lower right informs you of the brightness value (Level), number of pixels (Count), and percentage of pixels less than the Level displayed (Percentile) of the current pointer location. Selecting the appropriate channel in the pop-up menu changes the display to show information for each of the channels. Select Gray to show information on all pixels (all channels combined).

The information in the lower left refers to brightness values of the entire selected area or document. The Mean takes into account the entire range of values and shows the middle value in a selection or document. The Standard Deviation (Std Dev) displays how much the values in the image vary. The Median gives a middle value.

Working with Resolution and Size

The essential relationship between the size and resolution of an image is not immediately obvious to the casual user. To control resolution and size of an image, use the Image Size and Canvas Size commands under the File menu.

The physical size of an image is measured by the number of pixels, inches, or centimeters that make up the dimensions of an image. The resolution of an image refers to the pixel density of an image. For example, a 3 × 4-inch image can vary in the number of pixels in that area, even though the size is fixed. An image with a resolution of 72 pixels per inch (ppi) has fewer pixels, takes up much less disk space, and contains far less detail, than the same size image at 300 ppi. The optimum resolution of an image to be printed on a press usually is determined by three factors:

1. The resolution at which the image is scanned
2. The resolution of the output device
3. The halftone screen frequency of the final output

For offset printing, the optimum resolution of an image should be twice the desired line frequency of the halftone screen that will be used. For example, if you are going to print an image at 150 lines per inch (lpi), you should be working with a 300 ppi image. Keep in mind that the 300 ppi is relevant to the final size. If the photo you scan is 2 × 3 inches and you want to print it at 4 × 6 inches, then you need to scan the original at a 600 ppi. When you double the size of the scan to make your printable size, the resolution will be 300 ppi.

Image Size

Use the Image Size command to resize an image while controlling its resolution or to change an image's resolution while controlling its size. Keep in mind that as you work with images on your computer, you are only able to see a 72-dpi representation of your image. Any manipulations you make to the resolution or size of an image may not be correctly displayed on your monitor, but will show when printed to a high-resolution imagesetter.

The Image Size dialog box under the Image menu (Figure 6–24) contains the current information on the width, height, and resolution of the image as well as choices for a new width, height, and resolution.

Choose the measurement units you would like to use from the pop-up menus next to the New Size values. The Width pop-up menu (introduced in Photoshop 2.5) includes a Columns measurement choice that is based on the values entered in the Width and Gutter fields found in the Units Preferences dialog box.

The Constrain options, located under the New Size options area, allow for scaling an image in proportion, without losing resolution or file size. Click in the Proportions box to keep width and height relationship constant when making size or resolution changes. The File Size option allows changes to the dimensions or the resolution without resampling

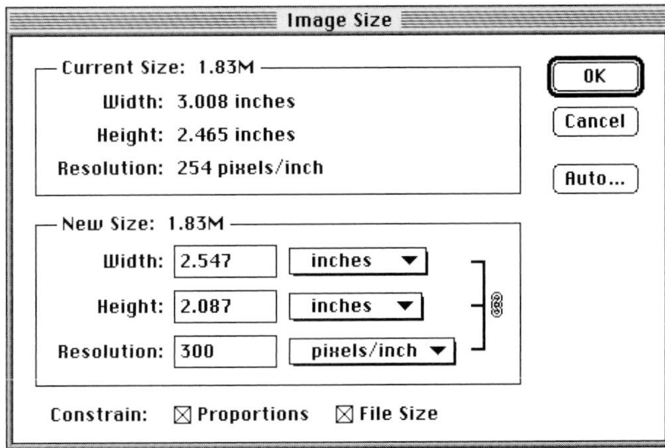

Figure 6–24
The Image Size dialog box

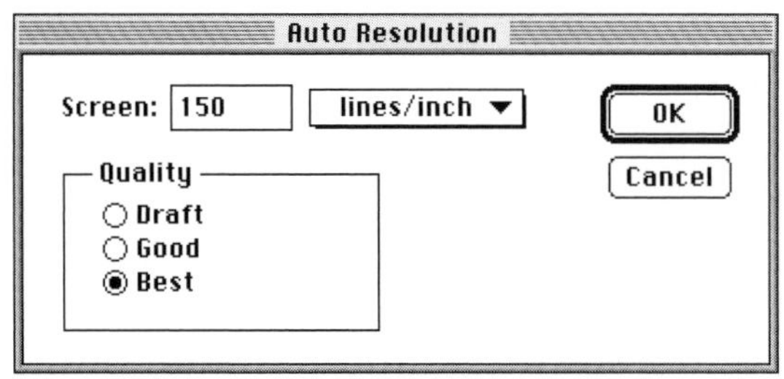

Figure 6–25 The Auto Resolution dialog offers an easier method for calculating the resolution of an image.

the image (see "Resampling" below). Photoshop will automatically update the parameters based upon entries so that no information is removed from or added to the original image.

By clicking the Auto button in the Image Size dialog box, you can have Photoshop automatically determine the resolution for an image. Click the Auto button to open the Auto Resolution dialog box (Figure 6–25). You may enter the final output halftone screen resolution in the Screen value box and select a measurement from the pop-up menu. Remember that the value you enter will only be used to calculate a resolution value for the image. If you want to set a halftone screen frequency for final output, use the Halftone Screens dialog box in the Page Setup dialog box.

The Quality options include the following:

- Draft, for a resolution that is one times the screen frequency up to 72 and results in the lowest resolution
- Good, for a resolution setting that is one and one-half times the screen frequency, which may be used for noncritical situations
- Best, which results in a resolution two times the screen frequency and is the optimum setting for standard printing procedures.

After you enter the desired Auto quality and click the OK button, you will return to the main Image Size dialog box, with the new resolution entered in the resolution field. Remember, once a file has been resampled down in resolution, pixel information is lost and can never be retrieved in its original form.

Resampling

Resampling means increasing or decreasing the resolution of an image through interpolation. When the resolution is increased, Photoshop inserts a new pixel with an intermediate value between existing pixels.

When you resample an image with the File Size checkbox deselected, the document's printed size (dimensions) will not change, but the amount of information (number of pixels) in the image changes. Therefore, the file size changes.

When the resolution of an image is decreased, there is a loss of data, thereby creating a smaller file size. In other words, pixels are removed from the document.

You can see the results of a resampled image by holding down the Option key and clicking on the Size Indicator in the lower-left corner of a document window immediately before and after resampling. Any changes in physical dimensions and file size will be reflected in this window. Resampling will also be evident when viewing an image at a 1:1 zoom factor, as displayed in the Title Bar, because at a 1:1 ratio every pixel of the monitor displays a pixel of the document.

***Tip*: When resampling, keep an original version of the image and resample it as necessary for output. If you resample an image down in resolution, and then resample it back up again, degradation of image quality will result.**

When you resample, rotate, or apply special effects filters such as Perspective or Skew to an image, Photoshop sometimes needs to create new pixels to fill in areas. Photoshop decides where to place these new pixels based upon one of three methods of interpolation specified in the General Preferences dialog box under the File Menu. (Refer to the General Preferences section of Chapter 2, "Setup and Document Management," for a detailed discussion of interpolation methods.)

Canvas Size

In most cases, the Canvas Size reflects the exact size of the image. Use the Canvas Size command to add extra working space outside the image area or to crop an image to a specific size without changing its resolution (Figure 6–26).

The Canvas Size dialog box displays the current canvas size in the measurement units specified in the Units Preferences dialog box under the File menu. Enter the desired size in the New Size area and select the unit of measurement from the pop-up menus.

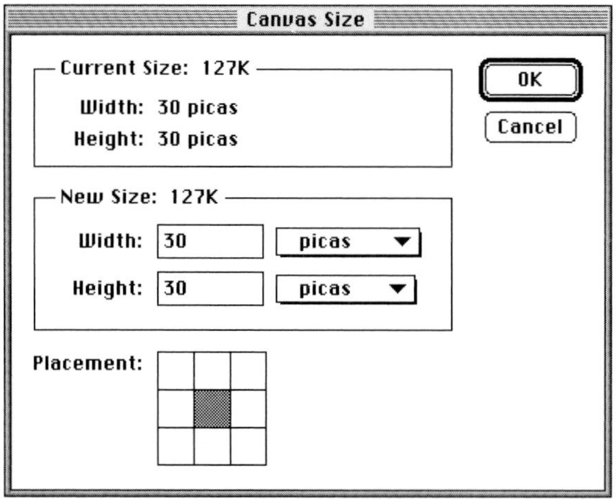

Canvas Size

Current Size: 127K
Width: 30 picas
Height: 30 picas

OK
Cancel

New Size: 127K
Width: 30 picas
Height: 30 picas

Placement:

Figure 6–26
The Canvas Size dialog box

The nine squares below the New Size selection area show where the image will be placed on the new canvas. You can change this location by clicking on one of the boxes.

Dynamic Effects

Under the Image menu you will find the commands that allow you to flip, rotate, scale, stretch, skew, change the perspective, and distort portions of images. Although the function of these commands is fairly obvious (we will not, therefore, discuss each command individually), there are some basic rules to remember.

- The Interpolation method specified in the General Preferences dialog box under the File menu affects the rendering quality of the dynamic effects. Remember that Nearest Neighbor is the fastest method but gives the poorest results; Bilinear is a reasonably fast method with reasonable quality; and Bicubic is the slowest method with the best quality. (Refer to Figure 2–11 to compare the visual differences in these methods.)
- The Flip, Rotate, and Effects commands, otherwise referred to in this section as the Dynamic effects commands, can be applied to any selection.
- To flip or rotate an entire image, apply the command without making a selection. Photoshop will automatically adjust the document area to accommodate the image. If you select the entire image

(with the Select All command), and apply an arbitrary or a 90° rotation, the resulting image will be cropped.

- In any of the dynamic commands, CW stands for "clockwise" and CCW means "counterclockwise."
- The acceptable value range for the Arbitrary Rotate command is –359.99° to 359.99°. Note that you can specify fractions of a degree.
- When using the Free Rotate command, determine the axis of rotation by dragging one of the four handles.
- When using any of the Effects commands, you can continually change a selection by dragging the handles to new positions. If you Undo the effect, all of the consecutive changes of the specific command will be undone, returning the image to its initial state. Pressing Command-Period achieves the same result.
- When applying any of the manual dynamic effects (Free Rotate, Scale, Distort, Perspective, and Skew), handles appear on four corners of a selection's bounding box. As you drag the corner handles into the desired position, the image redraws itself when you release the mouse button. If you hold down the Option key while dragging handles, the image will not redraw itself until all of the handles have been placed and the Option key is released. This improves efficiency when distorting a high-resolution image to a predetermined shape.
- The Skew command allows you to slant an image in a vertical or horizontal direction. The first time you use this command, the horizontal and vertical pairs of handles are coupled. Moving one handle also moves the coupled handle. The handles are then decoupled, allowing you to choose an individual handle, causing the Skew command to behave like a constrained Distort. You can recouple the handle pairs by pressing the Shift key while dragging a handle.

Filters

The variety of filters found in Photoshop can be overwhelming, but exploring the creative possibilities is satisfying and fun. Some filters are subtle, others are useful in everyday production tasks, many yield unexpected artistic effects, and a few are downright strange. To appreciate the power of the filters, practice using them individually and in combinations on many types of images.

There are two types of filters: *built-in* and *plug-in* modules. The built-in filters (the standard filters) are programmed directly into Photoshop and cannot be removed. Modular filters (plug-in modules) are separate little programs that can be added to the Photoshop Filter menu (Figure 6–27) at any time by placing a filter module in Photoshop's Plug-ins folder. No special installation procedure is required.

NOTE: If a filter module does not appear in the Filter menu, make sure that the filter file is in the Plug-ins folder. If it still does not appear, chances are that the filter file has been corrupted. (It's unlikely but possible.) Try installing a fresh copy of the filter file.

The Photoshop package includes some fantastic Distortion Plug-in modules that should be placed in the Plug-ins folder: Displace, Pinch, Polar Coordinates, Ripple, Shear, Spherize, Twirl, Wave, and ZigZag. You can verify which plug-in effects modules are currently loaded by opening the About Plug-in command under the Apple menu. Credits for each plug-in will appear on your screen.

***Tip*: Holding down the Option key while choosing any of the Photoshop Distortion Plug-in modules in the About Plug-in submenu will open a dialog box that has a Show Preview and Sliders check box. When you subsequently select any of the Distortion filters you will get an image preview and a wire frame representation of the filter effects.**

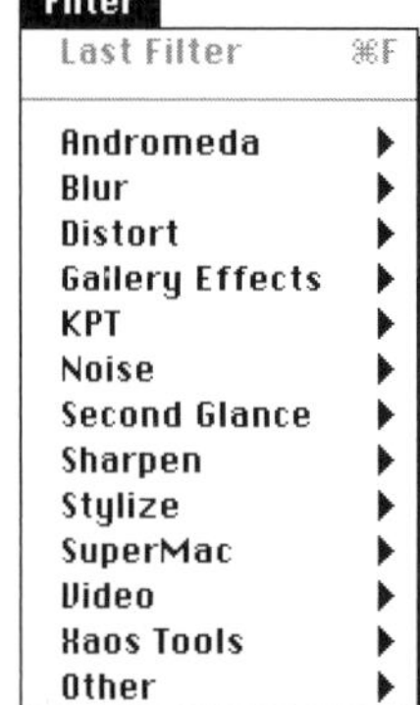

Figure 6–27
The filter submenus under the Filter menu

Some filters perform immediately while others have user-specified parameters. For example, Blur and Blur More begin processing immediately after you select them from the menu, but Gaussian Blur has a control dialog box that asks you to specify the degree of blurring.

Keep in mind the following when working with Photoshop filters:

- Filters do not work in Bitmap and Indexed Color modes. To apply a filter to an image in Bitmap mode, you must first convert the image to Grayscale. To apply filters to an Indexed Color image, you must first convert it to RGB Color mode, apply the desired filters, and then convert the file back to Indexed Color mode.
- Filters can be applied to any selected portion of an image, including masked areas and channels. If nothing is selected, the filter will be applied to the entire image.
- When applying a filter to a selection, feathering the selection might give it a smoother transition into the background.

***Tip*: Try applying filters to individual component channels of color images for glowing special effects.**

- After the Mac starts processing an image through a filter, the process can be instantly halted by pressing the Command-Period keys. When this is done, the image reverts to its prefiltered state.
- Use the Undo command to get a quick before-and-after appraisal of an applied filter effect.
- To reapply the same filter twice in a row, use the keyboard shortcut Command-F. By applying a filter multiple times, you can simplify and abstract an image quickly.

***Tip*: Paint with a filter using the Rubber Stamp tool. Open the file you want to work with and make a copy. Apply the filter to the new image. With both the original file and the modified file open, select the Rubber Stamp tool (make sure it is set to Clone Aligned). With the Info palette open, move the Rubber Stamp tool to the upper-left corner of the document. Try to place the cursor so the reading in the Info palette is 0,0, and hold down the Option key and click once. This registers the image from which to clone. Next go to the document on which you wish**

to paint and place the Rubber Stamp tool on the same spot by using the Info palette to register the two files. Click when the palette reads 0,0. If you do not want to start applying the filter to this section of the image select Undo. Now you can paint the filtered image onto the unaltered image in exact alignment.

Native Filters

The native filters that are included with Photoshop are categorized in the submenus under the Filter menu. The basic filter categories are Blur, Distort, Noise, Sharpen, Stylize, Video, and Other.

Blur

The Blur filters can soften an image or eliminate unwanted textures (Figure 6–28).

Use the **Blur** filter for subtle smoothing and softening of images (Figure 6–29). Blur works by lightening the pixels found next to the hard edges of well-defined lines and shaded areas. The Blur filter effect is subtle, when compared to Blur More and Gaussian Blur. The Blur filter can smooth out regions of noise (grain) from a less than optimum scan. By using the Blur filter in conjunction with the Defringe command under the Select menu, you can effectively blend the edges of a pasted image with the background.

Blur More is equivalent to multiple passes of the normal Blur command (Figure 6–29). Use the Blur More filter for a stronger and faster blurring effect.

Gaussian Blur smoothes in variable amounts. Unlike the other blurring filters, you can specify the degree of blurriness. Accepted Radius values range between 0.1 to 250. Using this filter, you can create very subtle or overwhelmingly blurred variations of an image (Figure 6–29).

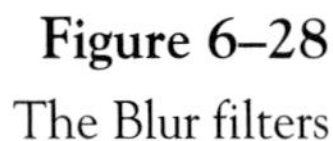

Figure 6–28
The Blur filters

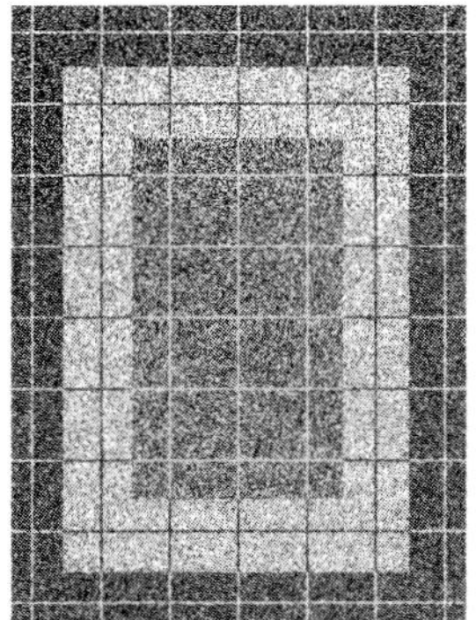

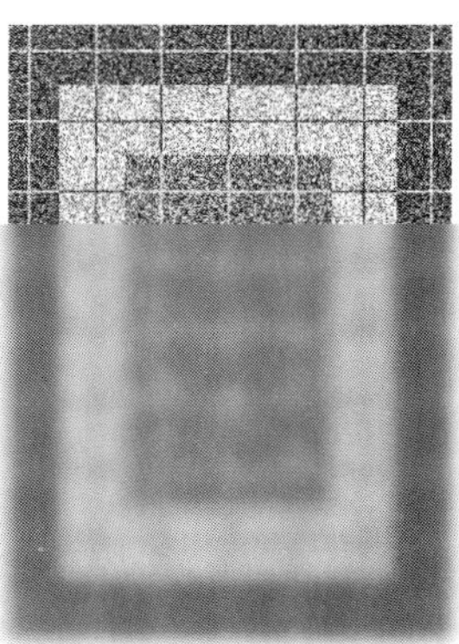

Figure 6–29 The lower sections of these four examples show various degrees of blurring. Shown from left to right: Blur, Blur More, Gaussian Blur with a 2-pixel Radius setting, and Gaussian Blur with an 8-pixel Radius setting.

Motion Blur creates the illusion of movement by distorting the image. The human eye does not perceive a moving object in focus. Motion Blur allows you to simulate movement at various speeds, in a specific direction (Figure 6–30).

The two variables, Angle (measured in degrees between –90° and 90°) and Distance (measured in pixels between 1 and 999), control the direction and amount of blurring (Figure 6–31).

The **Radial Blur** filter creates the effect of zooming or moving a camera rapidly. There are two blur options, Spin or Zoom. Spin blurs along circular lines while Zoom blurs back and forth. The Amount field can accept values from 1 to 100. This controls the direction of rotation if the Spin option is selected or the amount of the blur if Zoom is selected. A higher value causes more blur. The Quality field has three options: Draft, Good, and Best. Draft is the fastest method but does produce additional grain. Good and Best produce less grain and a smoother blur, but they take longer to apply. By dragging on the small dot in the Blur center box, the origin of the blur can be moved (Figure 6–32 and Figure 6–33).

Distort

Geometry forms the basis of the Distort filters. When any of these filters is chosen, a dialog box appears showing the control parameters (Figure 6–34).

Figure 6–30
The Motion Blur filter was used to simulate the movement of this old car.

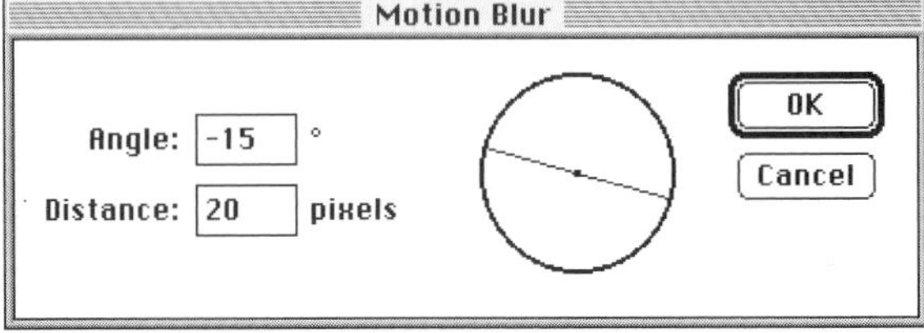

Figure 6–31
The Motion Blur dialog box

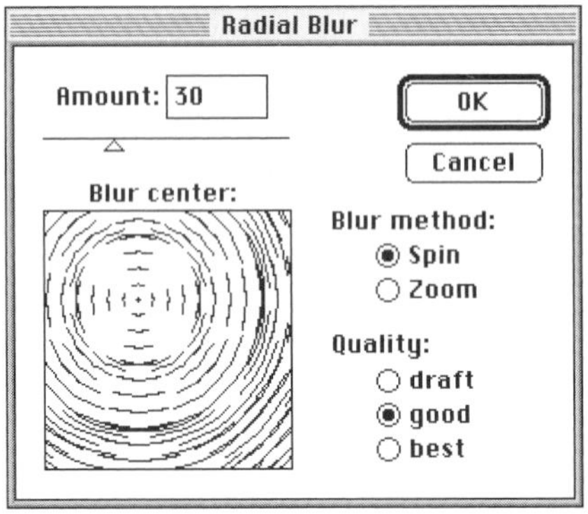

Figure 6–32
The Radial Blur dialog box

Displace refers to another image to control the distortion. Color values read from this displacement map (reference image) displace the values in the affected image. Values range from 0 (negative displacement) to 255 (positive displacement) with no affect at 128. After setting the parameters in the Displace dialog box, you will be prompted to choose a file to use as a reference image. Any Photoshop file (it must be in Photoshop format) except for bitmapped images can be used as a displacement map (Figure 6–35).

Pinch distorts an image toward or away from the center of a selection area. Accepted values range from –100% to +100%. Negative values pinch the selection toward the center and positive values push it outward (Figure 6–36). Try the Pinch filter on faces and type (Figure 6–37 and Figure C–8 in the Color Section).

Polar Coordinates converts an image from a horizontal and vertical coordinate orientation to a polar orientation. It can also look at the image as if it were in a polar orientation and convert it to rectangular coordinates. You can create an anamorphosis with this filter. To view this popular art form from the eighteenth century, use a mirror formed as a cylinder (Figure 6–38).

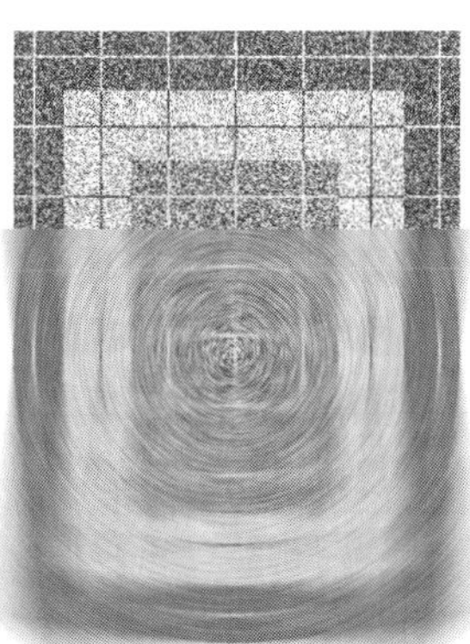

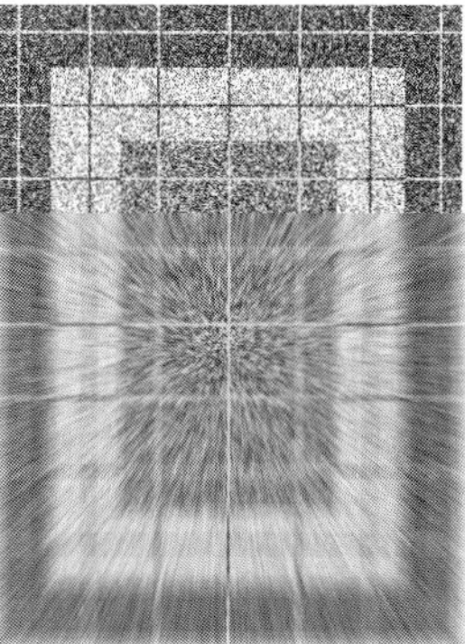

Figure 6–33 The lower sections of these four examples show various methods of applying the Radial Blur filter. From left to right: Spin with Amount set to 3, Spin with Amount set to 15, Zoom with Amount set to 8, and Zoom with Amount set to 25.

Distort ▶
- Displace...
- Pinch...
- Polar Coordinates...
- Ripple...
- Shear...
- Spherize...
- Twirl...
- Wave...
- ZigZag...

Figure 6–34
The Distort filters

Figure 6–35 The Displace filter was applied to the Blends image (center), using the silhouetted figure (left) to create the final image (right).

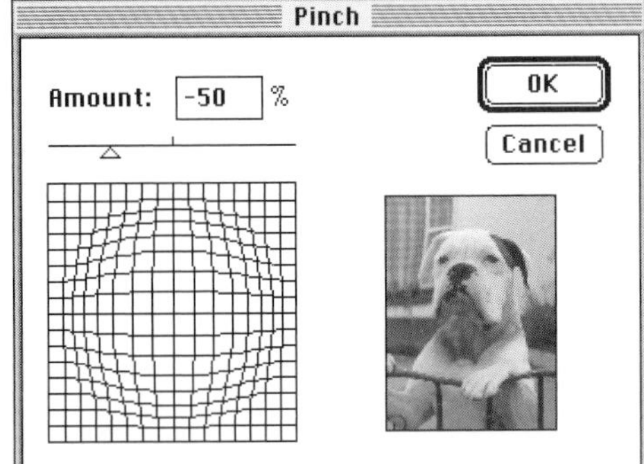

Figure 6–36
The Pinch dialog box

Figure 6–37
The Pinch filter was applied to the two dogs in this photograph. A positive value was used on the left and a negative value on the right.

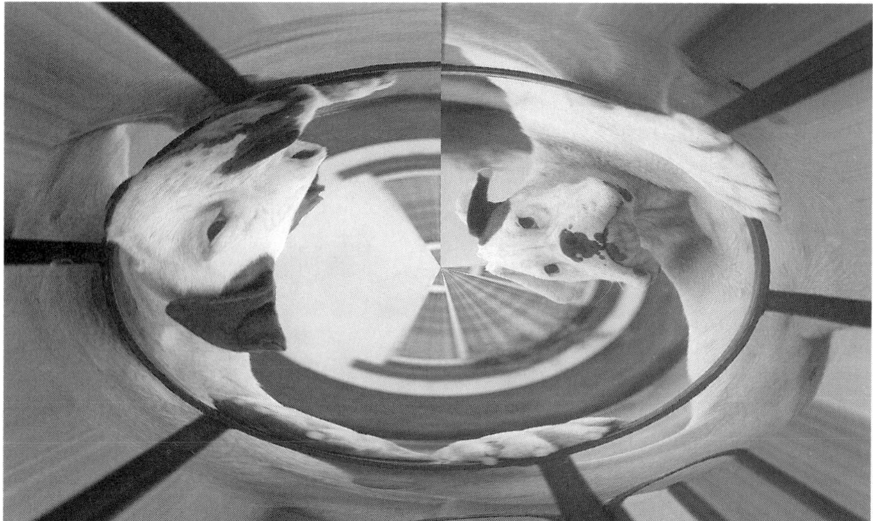

Figure 6–38
The Polar Coordinates filter was applied to the photograph of the two dogs. To view this anamorphosis, place a mirrored cylinder in the center of the picture.

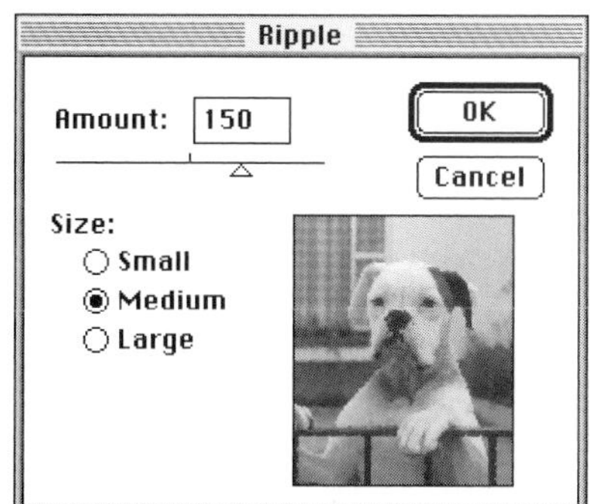

Figure 6–39
The Ripple dialog box

Ripple breaks up an image with a fluid, liquid effect. The accepted values range between –999 and 999. You can also choose the Size of the ripple effect, Small, Medium, or Large (Figure 6–39). Use this filter to create textures and patterns (Figure 6–40).

The **Shear** filter allows you to wrap or distort an image along a curve created in the Shear dialog box. The line (band) running along the grid can be moved along any point to create a curve that sets the direction of the distortion. (Figure 6–41). Wrap Around fills empty space with imagery from opposite sides while the Repeat Edge Pixels extends the pixels along the edge of the image (Figure 6–42).

Figure 6–40
The Ripple filter was applied to the photograph of the two dogs at a Small size (left) and a Large size (right).

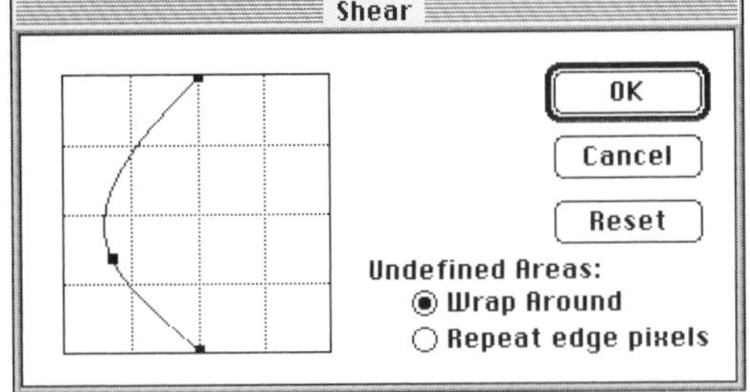

Figure 6–41
The Shear dialog box

Figure 6–42
The Shear filter was applied to the two dogs in this photograph at different settings.

Spherize maps a selected area onto an imaginary spherical surface, similar to a photograph taken with a fisheye wide-angle lens. Values between –100% and 100% can be specified in the Spherize dialog box (Figure 6–43). Negative percentages render a concave effect and positive a convex effect (Figure 6–44).

Twirl spins an image toward the center of the selection area. Down the digital drain! The rotation is greater nearer the center. You can specify values between –999 and 999. Positive values yield a right-hand twist, and negative numbers result in a left-hand twist (Figures 6–45 and 6–46).

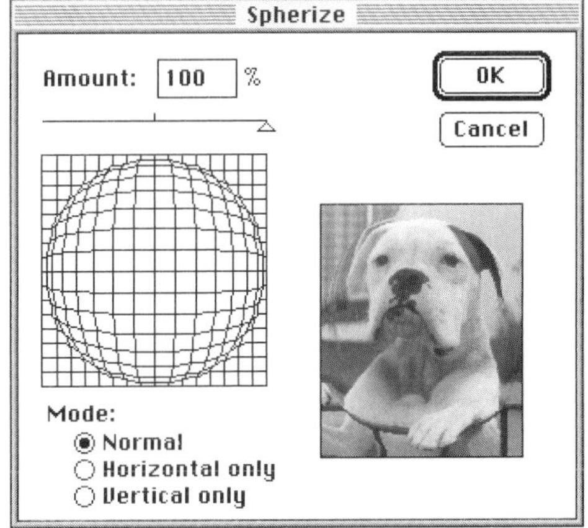

Figure 6–43
The Spherize dialog box

Figure 6–44
The Spherize filter was applied to the dogs in this photograph.

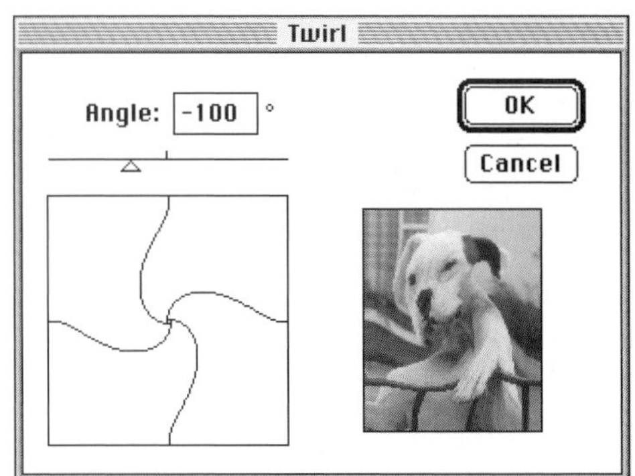

Figure 6–45
The Twirl dialog box

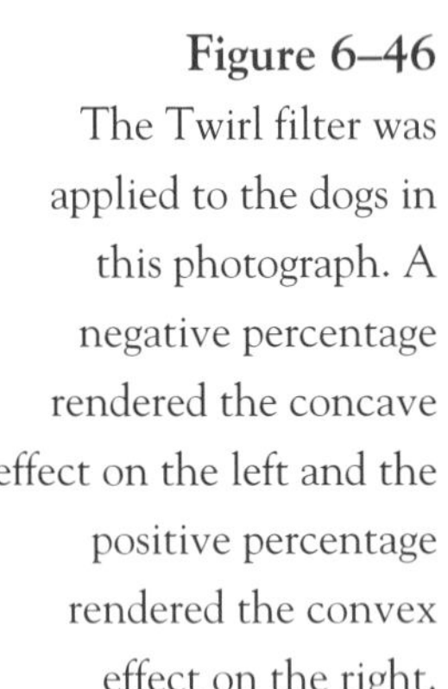

Figure 6–46
The Twirl filter was applied to the dogs in this photograph. A negative percentage rendered the concave effect on the left and the positive percentage rendered the convex effect on the right.

Wave works like a programmable Ripples filter through which you can create rich organic textures. The turbulence effect is a mathematical concept based on chaos theory. Turbulence abounds in the natural world—wisps of smoke, patterns formed by pressurized water, mixing oil and water.

The Wave dialog box has a number of controls (Figure 6–47). The Number of Generators specifies how many strange attractors will be used for a wave pass. You can specify up to 999 generators. Higher numbers of generators produce more complex patterns.

***Tip*: The Wave filter is similar to the Ripple filter when applied once, but multiple passes yield smooth, liquid effects. Each pass modulates the previous pass. Think of a pond of water into which you drop many**

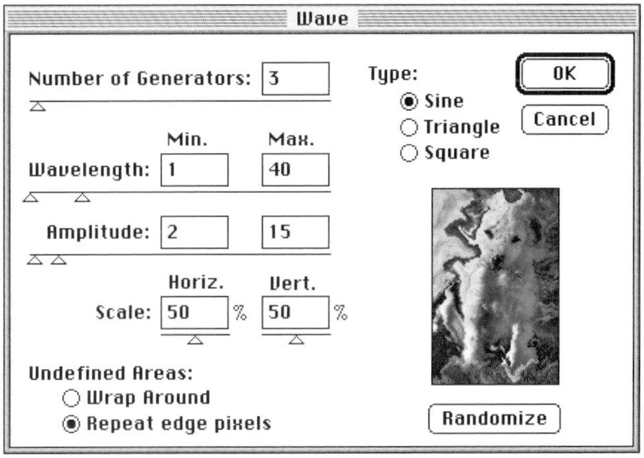

Wave

Number of Generators: 3

Type:
(•) Sine
( ) Triangle
( ) Square

OK

Cancel

	Min.	Max.
Wavelength:	1	40
Amplitude:	2	15

	Horiz.	Vert.
Scale:	50 %	50 %

Undefined Areas:
( ) Wrap Around
(•) Repeat edge pixels

Randomize

Figure 6–47
The Wave dialog box

pebbles into the water at the same time. Even though each splashing pebble produces a simple radial wave pattern, the combined effect of many radial waves crashing into each other produces more complex patterns.

The Wavelength and Amplitude fields allow you to enter minimum and maximum values ranging from 1 to 999. Photoshop uses the values within the specified range on each of the generators. A greater range between the minimum and maximum values yields a more random and chaotic effect. The Random Start Phase checkbox causes each pass of the filter to be based on a different set of locations for the generators. The Scale values allow you to determine the separate horizontal and vertical emphasis of the filter effect. Specify the type of waveform used by the effect: Sine, Triangle, or Square. Each yields an entirely different effect. You can also choose to Wrap Around the pixels in a selected area or Repeat Edge Pixels. This determines what happens on the edges of the selected areas. Most of the time you will probably want to use Wrap Around, as this preserves the visual continuity of an image (Figure 6–48).

ZigZag is like dropping a rock into the center of a glass disk filled with water which is on top of an image. The waves ripple away from the point where the rock hits the water (Figure 6–49).

You can specify the Amount of the effect (–100 to 100) and the Ridge of the waves (1–20). The larger the amount, the more evident the waves; the larger the ridge, the more wavy the edges of the waves. You also have three different types of ZigZag: pond ripples, out from center, and around center (Figure 6–50).

Figure 6–48
The Wave filter was applied to the background in this photograph.

Figure 6–49
The ZigZag filter was applied to this photograph.

Noise

Noise refers to the random texture that appears in an image. This texture, referred to as grain in photography, can be smooth, subtle, or extreme. The noise filters can add, emphasize, subdue, or eliminate the grain in an image (Figure 6–51).

The **Add Noise** filter introduces random pixels to an image. It can be used after blurring, softening, or combining images from different sources to simulate the grain usually found in photographs. When processed through some of the other filters, such as Blur, Gaussian Blur, and Find Edges, noise becomes a useful source for organic patterns otherwise difficult to create from scratch. Applying small amounts of noise (amount set between 10 and 40) to grayscale images enhances the overall texture, producing a stippled effect.

Specify the amount of noise applied by entering numbers ranging from 1 to 999. Uniform noise tends to be more ordered than the more chaotic Gaussian method. Gaussian noise also slightly lightens the image (Figure 6–52).

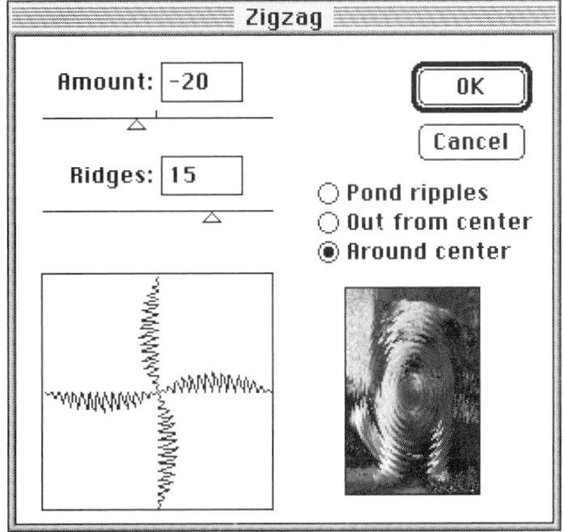

Figure 6–50
The ZigZag dialog box

Figure 6–51
The Noise filters submenu

The **Despeckle** command subtly blurs an image without affecting distinct areas of contrast. Use this filter for removing unwanted noise (grain) from an image without affecting major areas of detail. Grainy or old photographs are prime candidates for the Despeckle filter. It can also help stabilize images captured from video sources with a frame grabber.

The **Median** filter can be used to reduce the amount of noise in an image. Specify a Radius (1–16) for it to blend and discard pixels. Pixels that vary too much from adjacent pixels are discarded. Higher values cause more averaging, which makes the image look more blurred (Figure 6–53).

Figure 6–52
The Noise filter was applied to these blends in varying amounts. Shown from left to right: 8 Gaussian, 25 Uniform, 80 Gaussian, and 200 Uniform.

Sharpen

By adjusting the contrast of pixels next to each other, especially at edges, the sharpen filters give the illusion of increased sharpness (Figure 6–54).

***Tip*: Although the Sharpen filters can improve the apparent sharpness of an image, they are not a substitute for a high-quality scan of a focused photograph.**

The **Sharpen** filter sharpens blurry images by increasing the contrast of adjacent pixels (Figure 6–55).

Sharpen Edges applies a sharpening filter only to the areas of major brightness change, the same edges that the Find Edges filter picks up (Figure 6–55). It sharpens an image without affecting smooth soft areas.

Sharpen More is equivalent to applying the normal Sharpen filter several times (Figure 6–55).

Figure 6–53
The Median filter was applied to the dog photograph at various radius settings. Left to right: 1 pixel, 4 pixels, 8 pixels, and 16 pixels.

Sharpen ▶ Sharpen
Sharpen Edges
Sharpen More
Unsharp Mask...

Figure 6–54
The Sharpen filters dialog box

Figure 6–55
The Sharpen filters at various settings. Left to right: Sharpen, Sharpen Edges, Sharpen More, and Sharpen More applied three times.

Unsharp Mask is the most accurate way of controlling the sharpening effect. It has its origins in the traditional noncomputer techniques developed to sharpen images on film. The process essentially consisted of taking a film negative, creating a blurred positive version of the image, sandwiching the two together, and shooting the results onto a higher-contrast photographic paper.

Photoshop's Unsharp Mask filter essentially does the same, only digitally. The image is copied, made negative, blurred, and averaged with the original image. The resulting image is brightness balanced and appears sharpened only in areas of substantial brightness differentiation (you control the threshold value).

The Amount of the blur controls the weight of the blend between the blurred and normal images. Higher percentages result in more pronounced sharpening (within the areas affected based on the radius setting). The acceptable range of values for Amount is 1% to 500%. When specifying the Radius of the blur (0.1 to 250 pixels), higher Radius values render stronger sharpening effects. Lower radius numbers produce less noticeable sharpening. The value specified in Threshold (0 to 255) controls the brightness level used. Lower numbers yield a stronger effect (Figures 6–56 and 6–57).

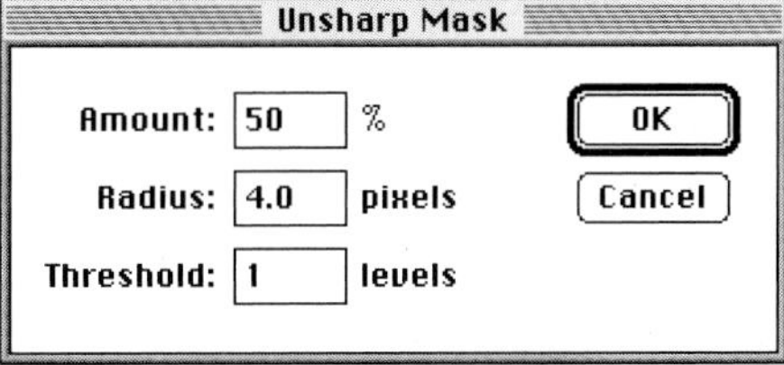

Figure 6–56
The Unsharp Mask dialog box

Figure 6–57
The Unsharp Mask filter. Amount, Radius, and Filter settings, left to right: 50%, 2 pixels, 5 levels; 50%, 4 pixels, 0 levels; 100%, 4 pixels, 0 levels; 500%, 2 pixels, 40 levels.

Stylize

Use the Stylize filters to distort and abstract images or selections. Some create the appearance of drawings, paintings, or photographic filter effects (Figure 6–58).

The **Color Halftone** filter creates the effect of enlarged halftone screens. The filter converts each CMYK channel of the image into a series of halftone dots. The dialog box has a field for entering the maximum radius of the halftone dots from 4 to 127. The angle for the screens can be configured for each channel (Figure 6–59).

The **Crystallize** filter groups pixels into a polygon shape. The actual size or cell is set using the Slider or by entering a number (3 to 300) into the Cell Size box. Smaller numbers render more subtle effects. (Figure 6–60).

Diffuse randomly jitters the pixels in a selected area by shifting the pixels in various directions. Repeated application of this filter gradually breaks up the image, until it looks as if it were drawn with crayon or charcoal.

There are three options in the Diffuse dialog box. Normal breaks up all of the pixels in the image. Darken Only breaks up darker parts of the image more than lighter areas. Lighten Only breaks up lighters parts of the image more than darker areas (Figure 6–61).

The **Emboss** filter makes images appear engraved or raised by darkening the traced edges of an image, and subduing the colors and tones. The Emboss dialog box has three parameters (Figure 6–62): Enter the desired angle in the Angle field or move the line in the circle to a new angle.

Figure 6–58
The Stylize filters submenu

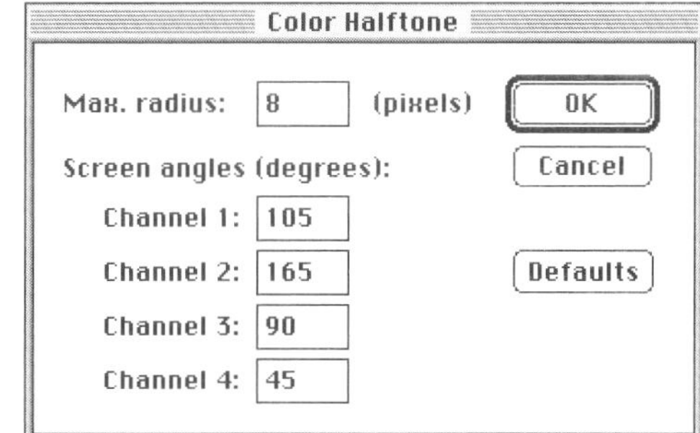

Figure 6–59
The Color Halftone dialog box

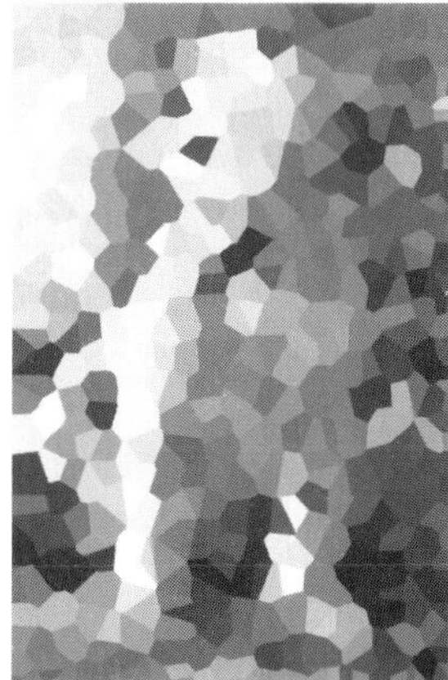

Figure 6–60
The Crystalize filter was applied to the dog photograph at various Cell Sizes: 8 (left), 16 (center), and 32 (right).

Figure 6–61
The Diffuse filter was applied to the dog photograph at Normal (left), Lighten Only (center), and Darken Only (right) settings.

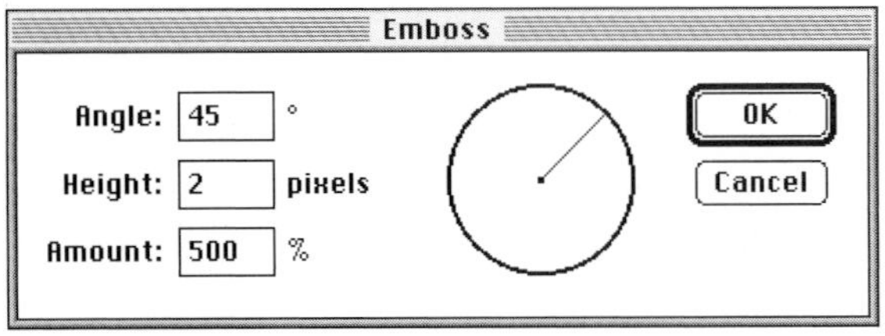

Emboss

Angle: 45 °

Height: 2 pixels

Amount: 500 %

OK

Cancel

Figure 6–62
The Emboss dialog box

Figure 6–63
The Emboss filter was applied to the photograph of the two dogs. On the left, the settings were Angle 45°, Height 2 pixels, Amount 500%; and on the right, Angle 155°, Height 10 pixels, Amount 150%.

Use a positive angle or move the line clockwise to raise the surface. Use a negative angle or move the line counter clockwise to lower the image.

The Height field can accept a value from 1 to 10 pixels. This sets the depth of the emboss. The Percentage field can accept values from 1 to 500% with the lower figure producing the least amount of color or tonal changes around the emboss edges, and the higher figure producing a more pronounced color effect (Figure 6–63 and Figure C-7 in the Color Section).

The **Extrude** filter creates 3-D shapes in Blocks or Pyramids. The dialog box has several options for setting the parameters (Figure 6–64). The Size box, in pixels from 2 to 255, sets the length of the selected shape's base. A higher number will produce fewer but larger objects. The Depth box, in pixels from 0 to 255, controls how far the shapes appear to protrude from the surface. The Random button will create the depth effect indiscriminately. The Level-Based check box matches the depth of the shapes to the overall brightness of the image (darker shapes will appear deeper). The Mask Incomplete Blocks masks blocks at the edges of a selection so they do not appear cut off (Figure 6–65).

The **Facet** filter analyzes an image, determines major areas of solid or similar colors, and emphasizes them using flat, geometric color, shapes (Figure 6–66).

Find Edges finds the significant brightness transitions (edges) in an image and darkens them, lightening the flat areas (Figure 6–67).

Fragment makes four copies of an image and places them slightly offset from each other. It is similar to a photographic star filter.

The **Lens Flare** filter creates an effect similar to the circular refractions that appear when bright light shines into a camera lens. There are several parameters in the dialog box (Figure 6–68). Enter a value (10% to 300%) for Brightness or use the slider. Drag the crosshair in the thumbnail to set the center of the Flare. The Lens type changes the size of the

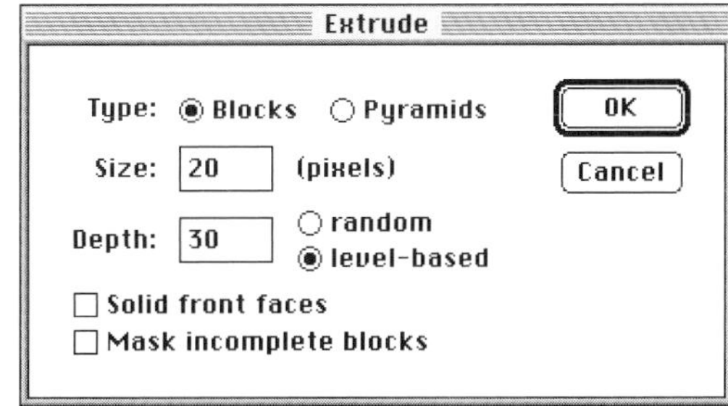

Figure 6–64
The Extrude dialog box

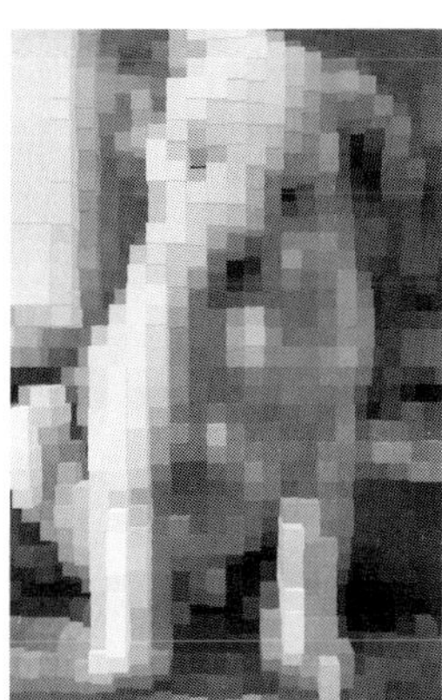

Figure 6–65
The Extrude filter was applied at various settings. Left to right: Size 30 pixels, Size 15 pixels, and Size 15 pixels with Solid front. The Type was set to Blocks and the Depth at 30 (level based) on all three.

Figure 6–66
The Facet filter was applied several times to this photograph.

Figure 6–67
The Find Edges filter was applied to this photograph.

flare and the number of refractions. Flare only works on color images (Figure 6–69).

The **Mosaic** filter turns an image into pixelated squares. In the dialog box, you can set the Cell Size in pixels from 2 to 64.

You can create variations on the square cell by resizing the image by 50% horizontally or vertically, applying the Mosaic filter, and then resizing the image back to the original size. Another method is to rotate the

Figure 6–68
The Lens Flare dialog box

Figure 6–69
The Lens Flare filter was applied to this photograph with Brightness set to 100% and the Lens Type at 50–300mm zoom.

image, apply the Mosaic filter, and then rotate the image back to the original orientation (Figure 6–70).

The **Pointillize** filter creates random dots throughout the image. The size of the cell can be from 3 to 300 pixels. Note that the background canvas color is used between the dots (Figure 6–71).

Figure 6–70
Mosaic filter examples. Left to right: Cell Size 10 pixels; Cell Size 10 pixels (45° rotation, then rotated back to original angle); Cell Size 20 pixels (horizontal stretch, then returned to original proportions.

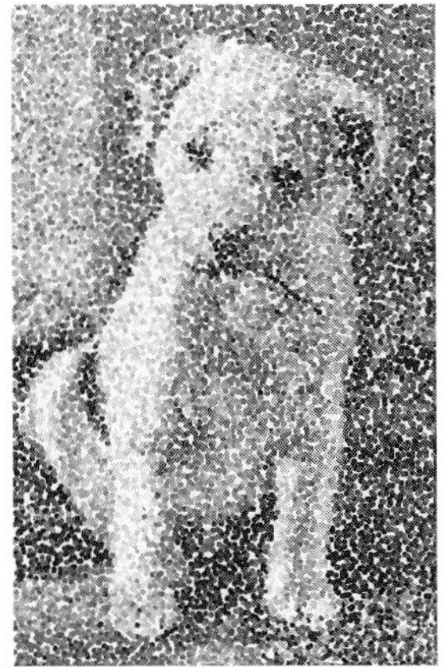
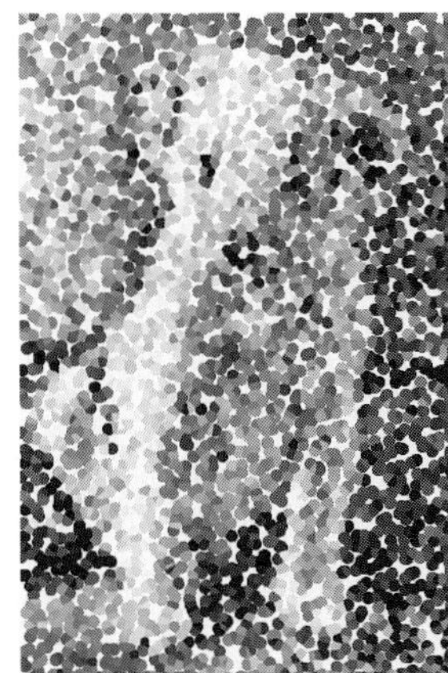

Figure 6–71 The Pointillize filter was applied to the dog photograph. Shown from left to right: Cell Size at 3 pixels, 6 pixels, and 12 pixels.

Figure 6–72
Solarize filter applied, then image lightened

The **Solarize** filter has its roots in the photographic darkroom as a technique for altering the tones on a photograph to achieve special effects. The print or film is exposed with a flash of light in the development process. This exposure quickly darkens only the lighter portions of the image causing a reversal of the tones. The shadow areas retain normal values.

Since the Solarize filter darkens the lighter values in an image, it usually appears too dark after applying the filter. To adjust the values after applying the filters, use the Levels, Curves, or Brightness/Contrast commands under the Image menu (Figure 6–72).

The **Tiles** filter fragments an image into square shapes. The first parameter in the dialog box (Figure 6–73) specifies the number of tiles to be generated. Maximum Offset sets the distance the tiles should be offset from each other. The last option, Fill Empty Area With, controls how the areas between the tiles are filled (Figure 6–74).

Trace Contour finds major brightness changes (edges) and draws thin lines around them, changing the remainder of the image to white. You can specify the threshold level and which side of the edge to highlight (Figure 6–75).

The **Wind** filter gives the illusion of wind blowing by creating small horizontal lines across an image (Figure 6–76). In the dialog box, choose the strength of the filter, Wind, Blast, or Stagger, as well as its direction.

Video

Images captured from a video source might not appear correct on a computer, and computer images might not appear correct when output to video. The following filters can help correct images transferred from one to another (Figure 6–77). For more information on working with video refer to Chapter 9, "Animation."

Tiles

Number of Tiles: 4

Maximum Offset: 50 %

OK

Cancel

Fill Empty Area With:

○ Background Color ◉ Inverse Image

○ Foreground Color ○ Unaltered Image

Figure 6–73
The Tiles dialog box

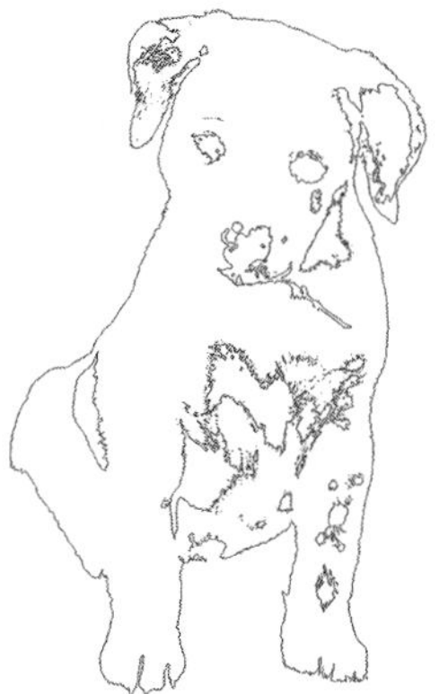

Figure 6–74 Tiles filter examples. Left to right: Number of Tiles 10, Maximum Offset 10%, Foreground Color; Number of Tiles 8, Maximum Offset 20%, Background Color; Number of Tiles 4, Maximum Offset 50%, Inverse Image.

Figure 6–75
After applying the Trace Contour filter, the background was erased.

Figure 6–76
The Wind filter was applied to the dogs photograph.

De-Interlace smoothes an image by removing either the even or odd interlaced lines. Specify whether the lines should be replaced by Duplication or Interpolation.

NTSC Colors remaps the colors in an image to match the gamut of colors that can be reproduced by a television.

Other Filters

These filters allow you to make custom filters, abstract images, affect masks, and offset images (Figure 6–78).

The **Custom** filter opens a programmable matrix to create special effects, custom blurring, and sharpening filters. The text fields multiply individual pixel's brightness values by the number entered (–999 to 999). By using the Save and Load buttons, custom filters can be saved for use at another time.

Figure 6–77
Video filters submenu

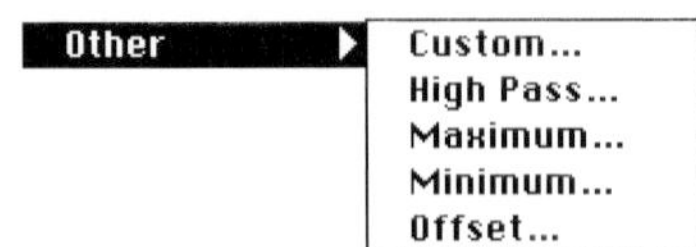

Figure 6–78
The Other filters submenu

High Pass is a filter that originated in engineering. It allows the high-frequency portion of a signal to get through, blocking out lower frequencies. The High Pass filter finds areas of major brightness changes (edges) and highlights them, while it softens and neutralizes areas of low contrast. In the accepted range of 0.1 to 250, lower numbers emphasize the edges more and remove more color. Higher numbers retain more colors and affect the edges less.

Maximum spreads lighter areas by converting darker pixels adjacent to them to lighter ones. Specify the number of pixels to be converted from 1 to 10.

Minimum is the opposite of the Maximum filter. Darker areas are spread by converting lighter adjacent pixels to darker ones.

Offset shifts the image by the number of pixels set in the dialog box. Move images precisely with this filter.

Other Plug-In Filters

The technology Adobe used to create Plug-ins has become a standard for the Mac graphics industry. This plug-in format is used not only by Photoshop, but by other programs such as Adobe Premiere, Aldus SuperPaint, EFI Cachet, ColorStudio, Fractal Design Painter, QuarkXPress, and StrataVision 3-D. Although Adobe has created some Plug-in filters, most must be purchased from third-party vendors. Following is a brief discussion of some of the most popular plug-in modules.

Aldus Gallery Effects

Gallery Effects Volume 1, a set of 16 filters, imitates various art styles. All filters share a common interface involving a preview dialog box that is accessed after selecting a filter from the Gallery Effects submenu (Figure 6–79). The dialog box previews the filter's effects on a selected portion of the image. In the larger box there is a small frame that can be moved around to the exact spot on which you wish to preview the filter. Two smaller windows are shown that match the small selection frame on the larger image; Original is unaltered and the other shows the filter's effect. Most filters have sliders to adjust settings, which you can

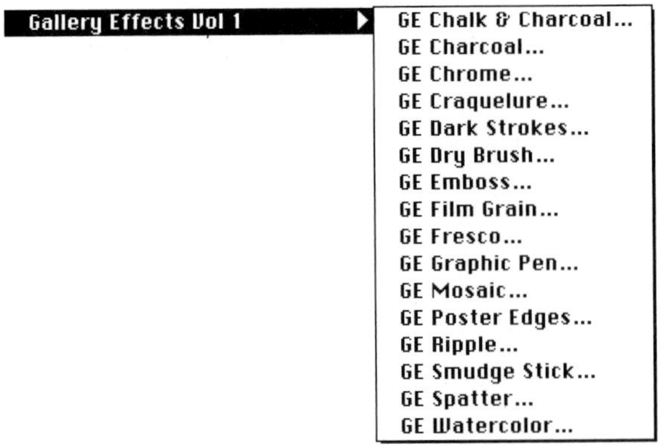

Gallery Effects Vol 1 ▶

- GE Chalk & Charcoal...
- GE Charcoal...
- GE Chrome...
- GE Craquelure...
- GE Dark Strokes...
- GE Dry Brush...
- GE Emboss...
- GE Film Grain...
- GE Fresco...
- GE Graphic Pen...
- GE Mosaic...
- GE Poster Edges...
- GE Ripple...
- GE Smudge Stick...
- GE Spatter...
- GE Watercolor...

Figure 6–79
The Aldus Gallery Effects Volume 1 submenu showing the 16 available filters

change and preview before applying the filter to the actual image. In addition, the filter parameters can be saved and named for later use.

The Gallery Effects **Graphic Pen**, **Dry Brush**, **Chalk & Charcoal**, and **Charcoal** are similar because they reduce a color image to simple shades and tones to create a stroked effect. The **Water Color** filter transforms a color photograph into a pseudo watercolor painting style, and the **Poster Edge** filter creates a somewhat similar effect. The **Smudge Stick** filter is a more intense alternative to the standard motion filter. (See Figures 6–80, 6–81, and 6–82, and also Figures C–9, C–10, and C–11 in the Color Section.)

A second set of filters, **Classic Art, Volume 2**, contains an additional 16 filters using the same interface as the original set (Figure 6–83). The Volume 2 filters have excellent on-line help and useful tips accessible

Figure 6–80
The Graphic Pen filter

Figure 6–81
The Mosaic filter

Figure 6–82
The Ripple filter

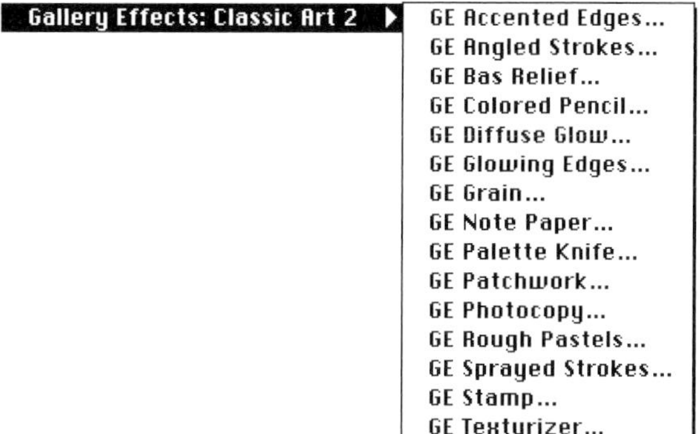

Figure 6–83
The Aldus Gallery Effects Volume 1 submenu showing the 16 available filters

from within each filter's dialog box (Figure 6–84). Several of the filters create striking effects with continuous tone images, such as the **Diffuse Glow** and **Grain** filters. Although Volume 1 had a Film Grain filter, the Grain filter in Volume 2 creates a much nicer effect with color images, producing colorful noise. **PhotoCopy**, **Stamp**, **Note**, and **Bas Relief** reduce continuous tone color images to simple graphic images, textures, and shapes much like Graphic Pen, Dry Brush, and Charcoal filters in Volume 1. Another feature of Volume 2 is the ability to apply a texture using three of the filters: Rough Pastels, Texturizer, and Underpainting. From within their dialog boxes, by clicking on Texture Controls button, you can access an additional dialog box that has a pop-up menu of several textures such as Brick, Canvas, or a PICT file that can be loaded as a texture to be applied by the filter. (See Figures 6–85, 6–86, 6–87, and 6–88, as well as Figure C–12 in the Color Section.)

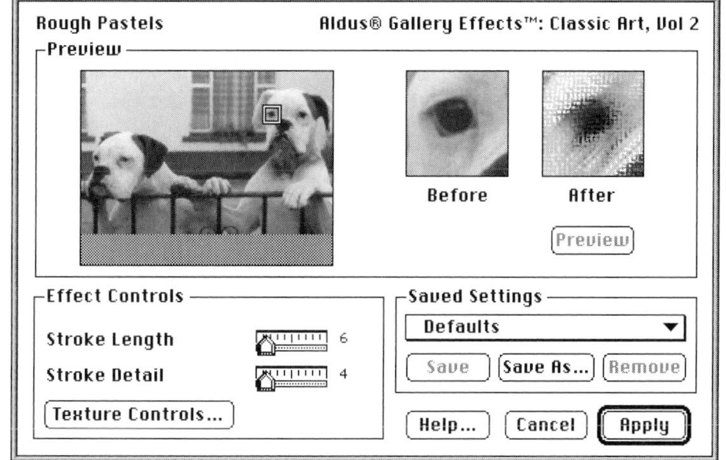

Figure 6–84
The Aldus Gallery Effects Volume 2 dialog box for the Rough Pastels filter

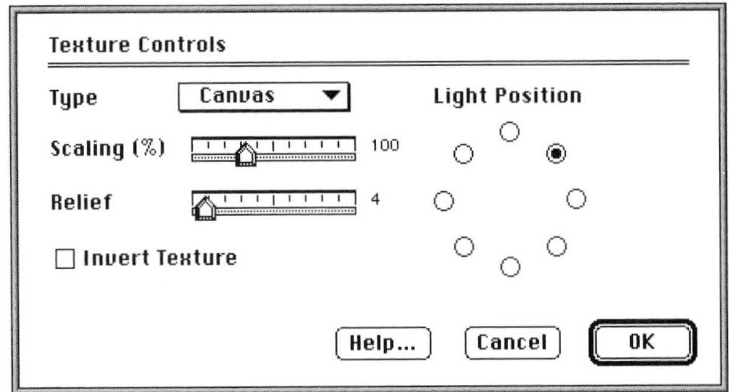

Figure 6–85
The Texture Controls dialog box—accessed by clicking on the Texture Controls button in the previous dialog box

Andromeda

Andromeda Series 1 Filters are a set of ten plug-in filters (Figure 6–89). If Gallery Effects filters can be said to mimic the look of various art styles, the Andromeda filters mimic photographic optics and camera filters. **Diffract**, **Prism**, **Star** and **Reflection** are special effects that traditionally are accomplished with optical filters over a camera lens at the time the picture is taken. The number of possible effects created with the Andromeda filters far exceeds those possible with a camera filter.

As the GE filters, the Andromeda plug-ins open with a large dialog box and a preview of the image being manipulated (Figure 6–90). Numerous sliders and controls can be used to modify the filters, and the effects can be previewed or reverted on one large image preview window. A smaller, mini window, called the Parameter Proxy window, is used to further refine the parameters visually. Changes are shown in the larger window; you do not see a "before" image unless you click on the

Figure 6–86
The Bas Relief filter

Figure 6–87
The Glowing Edges filter

Figure 6–88
The Palette Knife filter

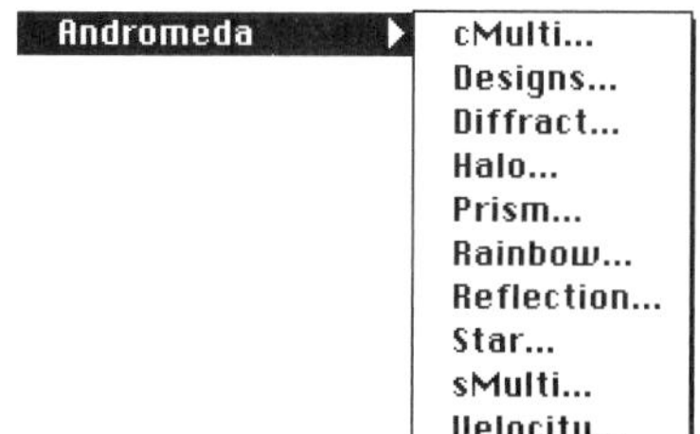

Figure 6–89
The Andromeda Series 1 submenu showing the 10 available filters

revert button. Unfortunately you cannot save custom named effects as you can with the GE filters.

The **Velocity** Filter creates wonderful Motion Blur effects with a large number of parameters, such as one or two way smears. You also have control over the angle, height, and width of the blur. The **Halo** filter is used to diffuse and spread highlights into darker portions of an image giving the illusion of a halo. If set with a low cut off (the parameter that specifies the tonal ranges affected by the filter), the effect can look very much like a painting. The **Star**, **Rainbow**, and **Diffract** filters create image elements. For example, the Rainbow filter creates a colorful translucent rainbow in the image. Several filters are used for breaking up and repeating the image. The **sMulti** filter breaks up image area's into multiple straight lines or patterns while the **cMulti** filter does the same thing with circular elements. The **Reflection** reflects part of the image in a pool of water (Figure 6–91). The **Prism** breaks up the image slightly while intensifying the spectral colors (like looking through a prism).

The **Andromeda Series 2** Filter is a single, powerful plug-in that allows creation of true 3-D surface mapping from within Photoshop. The plug-in can produce these effects with variable viewpoints and shading controls, and map a Photoshop image onto shapes such as a sphere, cylinder, plane, or box.

Upon choosing the filter, a single dialog box appears in which all the parameters for the filter are applied while viewing their effect in a low resolution preview (Figure 6–92). The viewpoint control allows you to "fly" around the surface, select a camera viewpoint, and take snapshots of the 3-D scene. The surface, or image on the surface, may be resized, shifted, rotated, or scaled. A movable light source allows you to control the object's lighting and shading. In addition to controlling the ambient light, the light source has a specular (hot spot) associated with it which may be moved onto the surface for special glossy or matte shading

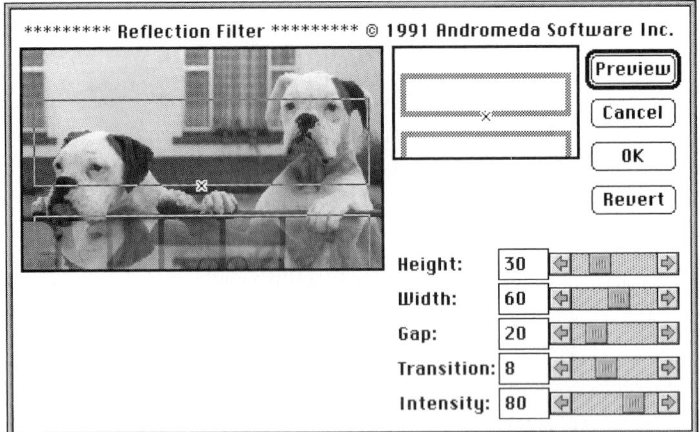

Figure 6–90
The Reflection filter dialog box

Figure 6–91
The Reflection filter was applied to this photograph of the dogs.

effects. This allows control of the depth and shading of the object. Choice of surfaces, shading effects, viewpoint, and distance provide the flexibility to create quick 3-D scenes and single animation frames (Figure 6–93 and Figure C–15 in the Color Section).

XAOS Tools Paint Alchemy

Paint Alchemy takes the idea of the filter preview dialog box even farther. This single Photoshop plug-in is actually composed of five different control cards for customized effects: **Brush**, **Color**, **Size**, **Angle**, and **Transparency**. Paint Alchemy is described as a painting system in the form of a plug-in. It applies brush strokes to selected areas of the image

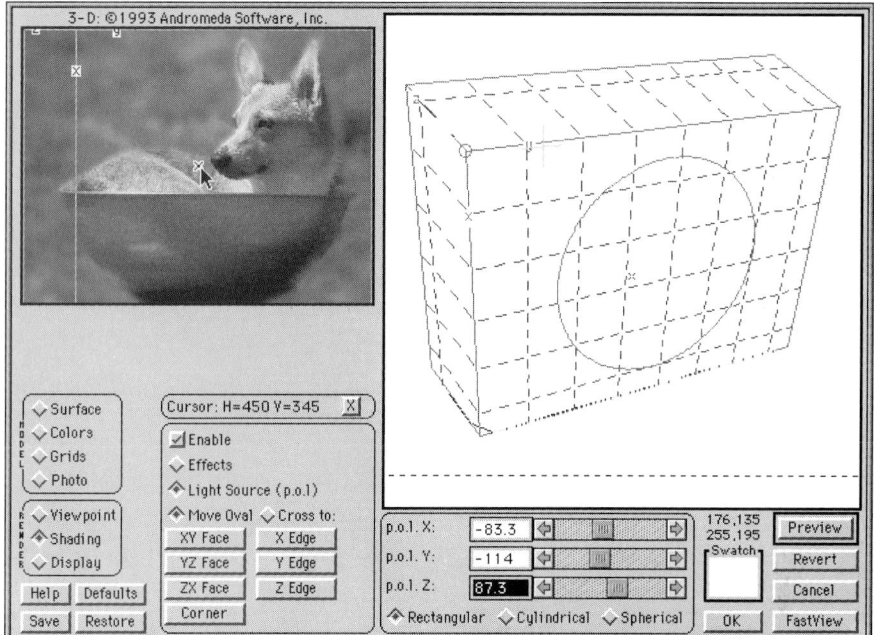

Figure 6–92
The Andromeda Series 2 Filter dialog box

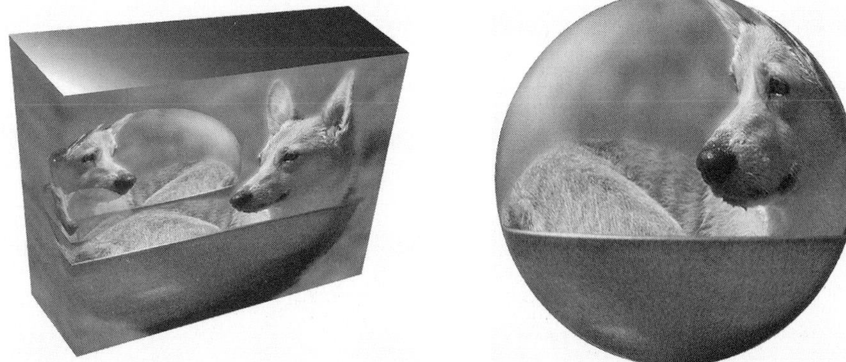

Figure 6–93
The Andromeda Series 2 Filter applied to a box (left) and to a sphere (right)

using the control cards to generate an unlimited set of parameters. The sheer number of different parameters available in Paint Alchemy for manipulating an image is staggering! Not only does it allow custom, user-defined styles to be saved, but it comes loaded with 75 styles already installed. Paint Alchemy has a preview similar to Gallery Effects with a larger window showing the entire image and two smaller windows showing the unaltered and manipulated images. Move from card to card in any order; and configure the parameters and preview the changes until the ultimate effect you want is created (Figure 6–94).

Figure 6–94
The Oil Detail style in Paint Alchemy was applied to the dogs in the foreground, while the Watermarker style was applied to the background.

Since, in principal, Paint Alchemy applies brush strokes to an image, the **Brush** card is the first to appear and generates the greatest effects on the image (Figure 6–95). Although there are six standard brushes, any PICT file of any size can loaded as a brush. Brush controls include Density, Positioning, Randomizing, and Layering.

The **Color** card is used for basing the color of each brush stroke. You can apply a solid color or a color from the image and adjust its hue, brightness, and saturation.

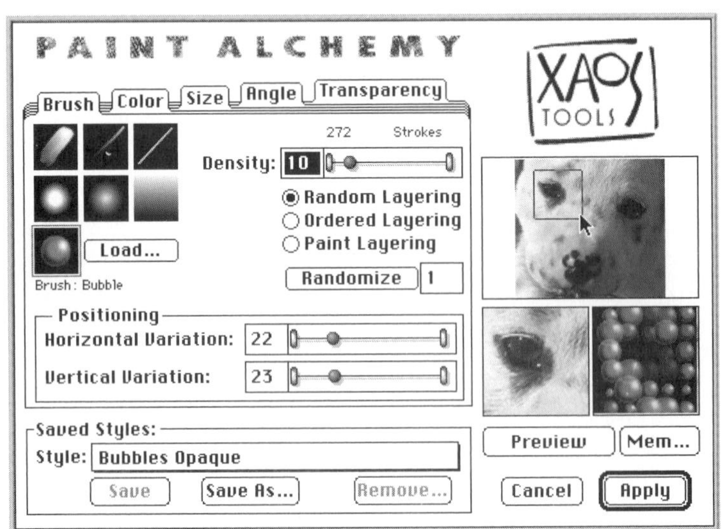

Figure 6–95
The Paint Alchemy Brush card

The **Size** card sets the size of the brush strokes through a pop-up menu. For example, by setting the size to Radial Distance, the brush strokes will change in size in a circular fashion from the center gradually outward to the edges.

The **Angle** card is used to specify the orientation or rotation of the brush strokes, from no variation to random strokes. A pop-up menu similar to that of the size card allows for variance like the radial distance, and vertical or horizontal position variation controls.

The **Transparency** card sets brush stroke transparency with controls similar to those already mentioned.

Paint Alchemy only works in RGB Color mode. To manipulate an image in another mode, convert it to RGB Color mode, apply the filter effects, and then convert it back to its original mode. An interesting feature of Paint Alchemy is the ability to assign a fixed amount of memory to speed up its performance. (See Figures C–17 and C–18 in the Color Section.)

Kai's Power Tools

Kai's Power Tools (KPT) is a group of 33 filters broken down into seven groups within Photoshop's Filter menu. In the latest release, version 2.0, the largest group appears in KPT's own submenu while the other filters are scattered about in various native filter submenus. For example, the Noise menu includes Hue Protected Noise, Grime Layer, and some special noises. In addition, there are Distort filters, Blur filters, Stylize filters, and Video filters (see Figures C–13 and C–14 in the Color Section).The KPT submenu contains filters that are the core of the entire set (Figure 6–96), or as some have called them, "The really killer filters."

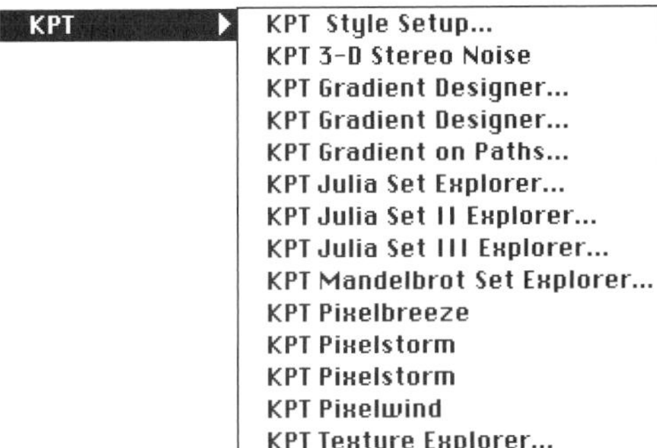

Figure 6–96
The original KPT (Kai's Power Tools) submenu showing available filters. KPT 2.0 features a new, improved set

Many of the filters have real-time previews showing you how an effect will apply to the image. In version 2.0, these function efficiently in CMYK color mode as well as in RGB. They have also been optimized for greater speed.

The KPT **Texture Explorer** dialog box opens with a graphic of a tree with 3-D balls that control the mutations of the texture based on the balls' locations (Figure 6–97). Next to the tree is a series of previews that change or mutate as you click on them. The higher up in the tree that a button is selected, the more dramatic the changes appear on the center preview. Most of the filters come with a tremendous number of preset parameters that you can add to, save, and name as custom effects.

The KPT **Gradient Designer**, a filter used to create blends or gradients, goes far beyond Photoshop's blend tool. The Blend tool can create a gradient with two colors, but with the KPT Gradient Designer you can

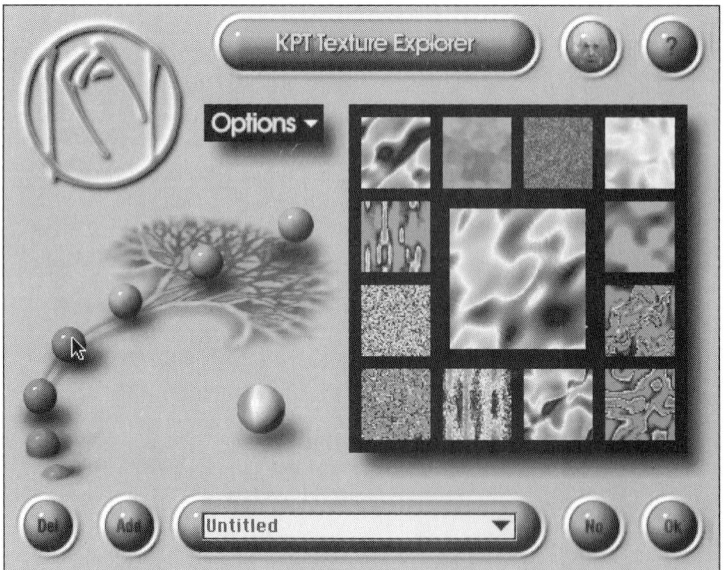

Figure 6–97
The KPT Texture Explorer dialog box

assign any number of colors throughout the blend, as well as control the transparency, direction, origin, number of repetitions, and more.

PixelStorm, **PixelWind**, and **Pixel Breeze** filters diffuse and displace pixels (Figure 6–98). Within the native Photoshop Blur filter submenu are four KPT **Smudge** filters: Darken Left, Darken Right, Lighten Left, and Lighten Right. Each creates subtle motion blur effects with control over direction and density.

In the Noise submenu, you will find seven different noise filters including the KPT **Special Red**, **Green**, and **Blue** that add intense noise with a dominate color. The three Hue-protected filters, **Maximum**, **Medium**, and **Minimum**, each generate noise based upon the hue of the selected image that causes random noise. The **Fractal Explorer** navigates through the expanse of fractal space, coloring images using presets from the Gradient Designer.

The three filters in the Distort submenu, called the KPT **Glass Lens** (Bright, Normal, and Soft) create 3-D spheres using a special ray tracer (Figure 6–98). The intensity of the spectral highlight in the sphere depends on the filter used and the direction set using the keyboard, with 10 different directions possible.

Chromassage

The Chromassage plug-in remaps colors in an image. After choosing the filter, a preview appears with two palettes: a small tool set and a large single image preview (Figure 6–99).

Figure 6–98
KPT filters effects. Shown from left to right: Pixel Breeze, Pixel Wind, and Glass Lens Soft with Hue Protected Noise Maximum.

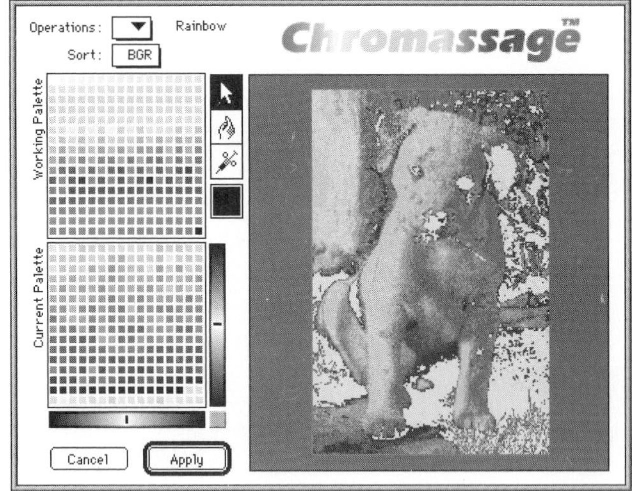

Figure 6–99
The Chromassage dialog box

The Current color palette contains 256 of the most common colors in the image while the working palette contains 256 color squares that you can use to define the changes to the original image. When they are first opened, both palettes have the same 256 color squares and are arranged in a sorted order that can be changed using the Sort pop up menu. For example, the colors can be arranged by RGB, GRB, BGR, etc. The resorted palettes affect how you control the remapping of colors. Next to the Current palette are two Jog Wheels, one horizontal and one vertical. The vertical Jog Wheel shifts the hue of the current palette much like a color wheel. The horizontal jog wheel cycles the color squares; each square is replaced by the one before it. In addition, a pop-up menu contains many preset palettes such as rainbow, pastel, and so on. With selection tools, move some or all of the colors of an existing color palette to your palette, and view the color changes on the preview (Figure C–16 in the Color Section).

DSP Accelerators

Waiting for a filter to process a high-resolution image can be exasperating. DSP Accelerator cards are available to speed up Photoshop filters and functions. We were able to speed through the revision of this book because we used Supermac's ThunderStorm and Thunder II cards.

Many of the DSP Accelerators made specifically to speed up Photoshop functions have their own filter versions, which appear under the Filter menu. The DayStar Charger DSP, for example, has a plug-in called the PowerPreview. When selected, a large dialog box appears with an adjustable preview similar to those previously discussed. All nine Charger filters can be accessed from a pop-up menu and sliders are available to change the various filter parameters.

Some DSP Accelerators speed up Photoshop's filters without adding filters to the menu. The Image Processing Accelerator Software that comes with SuperMac's Thunder II card transparently accelerates many filters and several Image Processing effects.

CHAPTER 7

Advanced Photoshop Techniques

In this chapter we present tips, techniques, and tricks that we think many of you will find interesting and helpful for your own work. We cover drawing and filling shapes, creative options for type, and duotones, as well as channel effects, including calculate commands. Some of these procedures are not easily discovered through experimentation alone. Keep in mind that there is never a single solution to a creative problem—be painterly or mathematical as you like.

Creating Basic Shapes

Although Photoshop does not have basic primitive shape tools, you can draw rectangles, circles, and other geometric and organic shapes with the selection tools, filling them with any solid color or gradient.

In a new document select an area with the Marquee tool and choose Fill under the Edit menu. The selection will fill with the current Foreground color (Figure 7–1). Then try filling the selection using the Gradient tool. Set the Foreground and Background colors to the desired

Figure 7–1
Basic shapes with various fills drawn with the Rectangular Marquee, Elliptical Marquee, and Lasso tools

values. With the Gradient tool chosen, drag across the selected area in the direction that you want the blend to follow.

***Tip*: One drawback of this technique is that the rectangular and circular Marquees are always anti-aliased. To create a basic shape that is not anti-aliased, draw it with a selection tool and fill with black. (If you zoom in and examine the edges you will notice that they are anti-aliased.) With the shape still selected, choose the Brightness/Contrast command and slide the contrast slider to the right, increasing the contrast. This will take the gray anti-aliasing away from the shape.**

In addition to fills, shapes can have an outline. Choose the Stroke command under the Edit menu after making a selection. You can Stroke with one color and Fill with another (Figure 7–2).

Using the Composite Controls and Fill modes, various transparency effects can be achieved when overlapping shapes (Figure 7–3).

The 3-D Sphere with a Shadow

Using the above techniques with some simple channel operations you can create a 3-D sphere with a soft shadow, a basic exercise for any art student.

1. Open a new grayscale document that is at least 600 pixels square. Set the Foreground color to white and the Background color to black.
2. Double-click on the Elliptical Marquee tool and choose a Fixed Size marquee of 300 × 300 pixels. Click the Elliptical Marquee tool on the page to create a selection at the specified size.

Figure 7–2
Shapes with various strokes applied

Figure 7–3
Various transparency effects using the Composite Controls and Fill modes

3. Double-click on the Gradient tool. Choose the Radial Fill option with a 60% midpoint skew, and a 10% radial offset. Drag the Gradient tool across the selection, starting at the point that will be the highlight and ending at the shadow. Leave the sphere selected (Figure 7–4).
4. Under the Select menu choose Save Selection to save it as a new channel. Make sure to leave it selected.
5. To create the reflection on the underside of the sphere, double-click on the Elliptical Marquee tool and choose a Fixed Size of 400 × 400 pixels with a feather radius of 10 pixels. While holding down the Command key, press the mouse button and position the marquee over the original selection so that a thin crescent at the lower edge

Figure 7–4
The selection filled with a Radial blend

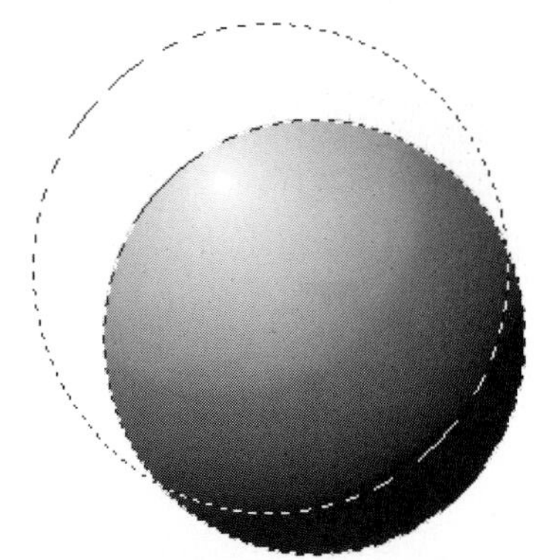

Figure 7–5
By holding down the Command key while selecting with the Elliptical marquee (left), a circular section is subtracted from the original selection, leaving a crescent shaped selection (right).

of the sphere remains selected (Figure 7–5). Release the mouse button and choose Save Selection under the Select menu to save it as a new channel. Leave it selected.

6. Set the Foreground color to black and the Background color to 60% gray. Double-click the Gradient tool and choose 85% Radial offset. Drag the Gradient tool from the existing highlight to the outer edge of the selection (Figure 7–6).
7. Now that you have created the sphere, make the shadow cast on the surface beneath it. Select New Channel in the Channels palette. Click on the new channel to make it active (the pencil should appear) and leave the others inactive. Leave the eye showing on the Black channel in order to use it as a guide.
8. Using the Elliptical Marquee tool, draw an oval for the shadow. Set the foreground color to black and the background color to white. Double-click the Gradient tool and choose a Radial Offset of 10%. Drag the gradient tool from an off-center point to the edge of the oval. Leave it selected (Figure 7–7, left).
9. Choose Perspective in the Effects submenu. Alter the shape of the shadow until it appears to lie on a flat surface. If the shadow is too small, use the Scale command in the Effects submenu to alter its width and height. Apply the Gaussian Blur filter with a pixel radius of 7 (Figure 7–7, right).

Figure 7–6
The sphere with a subtle reflection on its underside

Figure 7–7
Figure 7–7 After applying a Radial fill with the Gradient tool (left), the circular selection is distorted with the Perspective and Scale commands, and then softened with a the Gaussian Blur filter (right) to create the shadow.

10. You can now put all the parts together: Make the channel with the shadow active; select the shadow with the Marquee tool; and copy it.
11. Click on the Black channel to make it active (all the other channels should be inactive). Load Channel 2 from under the Select menu to select the sphere, and choose Paste Behind under the Edit menu. The shadow will appear behind the sphere. Drag the shadow into position beneath the sphere and deselect (Figure 7–8).

Figure 7–8
The completed sphere with its shadow

***Tip*: Three-dimensional shapes are easily created in 3-D programs such as Alias Sketch, Ray Dream Designer, Strata Vision 3-D, Swivel 3D and Infini-D. Once created in the 3-D program with lighting, surface modeling, and textures, the images can be opened in Photoshop to be edited or combined with other images.**

Drawing and Painting

A scanned drawing or photograph can be used as a template to draw and paint in Photoshop. With some practice you can draw freehand directly into the computer with the mouse or preferably with a pressure-sensitive digitizing tablet such as the Wacom ArtZ tablet. To introduce some drawing and painting techniques, we present two case studies.

Anna Stump scanned the drawing "Fieldbrook General Store" as a template to create the final color version (Figure C–22 in the Color Section).

1. After scanning the drawing (Figure 7–9) into Photoshop, Stump selected the entire image and copied it to the Clipboard.
2. Stump opened a new document in the Lab Color mode and then she pasted the Clipboard image into the Lightness channel. With the **a** and **b** channels active and Lightness inactive, yet viewing all three, she could paint over the drawing using colors without affecting the grayscale values in the original drawing.

Figure 7–9
The original black-and-white drawing was scanned and then pasted into the Lightness channel in the Lab Color mode.

Tip: A scanned drawing or photograph can be pasted into a new channel in any color mode (including Grayscale). In the Channels palette, make the new channel inactive (no "pencil" icon) but visible ("eye" icon showing), to trace or paint over the template without affecting it. When finished, delete the template.

3. After roughing in the desired colors, Stump converted the file to RGB Color mode and made further refinements. By painting with the Paintbrush and Airbrush tools in the Multiply mode (set in the Brushes palette), she was able to build the colors in transparent layers in the same way that she applies washes with traditional watercolors.
4. After she achieved the desired colors, she applied various filters as the final step.

Francois Guerin sketched and painted freehand without using a template to create "Iced Tea" (Figure C–23 in the Color Section).

1. Guerin began by drawing with the Paintbrush tool on a Wacom Tablet to develop some ideas, sketching loosely.
2. Using the Lasso tool to draw basic shapes, he filled them with various colors, paying particular attention to the balance between brights and darks. Guerin repeated this step many times to develop a complex painterly image.
3. He used the Airbrush to achieve transparencies and the Blur tool to mix adjacent colors. For depth and softness he applied the Gaussian Blur to specific elements and areas.

Special Effects

Glow Effect Around Text or Objects

Some higher-end computer graphics systems have specialized commands to create glowing shapes and text. In Photoshop you can achieve this popular effect by combining the Border and Feather commands.

1. Start by filling the background color to a dark gray or black.
2. Make a selection using the Elliptical Marquee; fill it with a dark gray or color. Choose the Save Selection command under the Select menu to save it as a channel.

3. With the shape still selected, choose the Border command under the Select menu and enter a value of 20. Choose the Feather command and enter a value of 10.

Tip: When using this technique, the size of the border determines the range of the glow. A good starting point for the Feather value is usually slightly less than half that of the Border value.

4. Choose a light gray as the Foreground color, and Fill the selected area to achieve the glow (Figure 7–10, left). Choose Load Selection under the Select menu to retrieve the original selected circle. Fill it with black (Figure 7–10, right).

You can use this technique with any selected shape. The shapes can be against a solid or complex background. The glow technique also works well with type (Figure 7–11).

Smooth Drop Shadows for Text and Graphics

You can create soft, realistic drop shadows for any shape or type with a few simple steps.

1. Open an image that you want to have as a background.
2. In the Brushes palette, set the Opacity slider to 1. With the Type tool selected, click on the image to open the Type Tool dialog box. Enter the desired text. Set the size to 80 points, and click Anti-aliased.

Figure 7–10
The Border and Feather commands create the glow (left), and then the original circle is filled with black to create the final image (right).

Figure 7–11
The Glow Effect can be used on any selected shape or type against a dark background.

3. Move the selection to the desired position, copy it to the Clipboard, and then choose the Feather command under the Select menu. Set the Feather Radius to 5 pixels.
4. Set the Foreground color to a dark color and choose the Fill command under the Edit menu. In the pop-up menu set the Fill mode to Multiply. The fill color will combine with the background to give it a transparent effect.
5. Paste the Clipboard selection and move it over the shadow, slightly offsetting it. Change the Foreground color to a darker color and choose the Fill command. Set the Fill mode to Normal to make it opaque (Figure 7–12).

Figure 7–12
The "smooth drop shadow" technique is a simple method to give the illusion of floating type.

Custom Contour Fills

Thomas Cushwa, a Photoshop artist, creates a custom contour fill using the Lasso, the Feather command, and the Paintbucket. The technique lends a three-dimensional look to rounded shapes or type. Compare the two effects shown in Figure 7–13.

1. In a new file select white as the Foreground color.
2. Using the Type tool, click on the page to open the Type Tool dialog box and select a desired font. (Palatino was used in the example) Set the size to 150 points and the style to Bold and Anti-aliased.
3. Type in the letters "3D," click OK, and save the selection as a channel.
4. To give the type a rounded appearance, make the new channel active, apply the Feather command, and increase its contrast with the Brightness/Contrast command (Figure 7–14).
5. Make the master channel active and choose Load Selection under the Select menu. Fill it with light gray and then deselect.
6. Double-click on the Lasso tool and enter a low value as the Feather setting with Anti-aliasing on.

Figure 7–13
Left: The drop shadow usually applied to achieve a three-dimensional quality. Right: A custom contour fill adds more dimensionality.

Figure 7–14
Left: Hard edged type. Right: The type is rounded with the Feather and Brightnesss/Contrast commands.

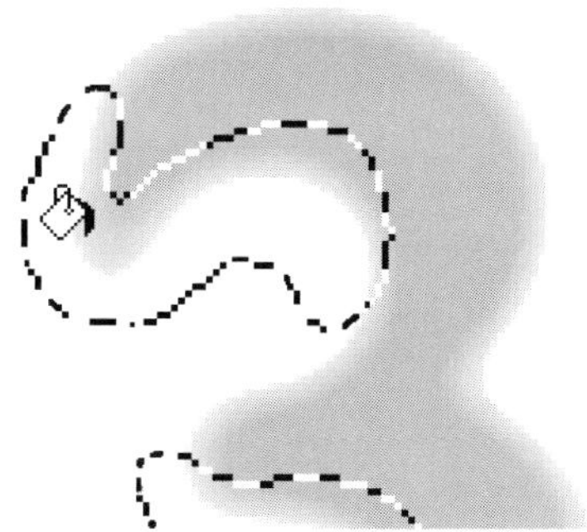

Figure 7–15
The Lasso tool is used to select portions of the type (left) and then the gray areas are filled with black using the Paint bucket tool (right).

7. With the Lasso tool, select the edges of the type (use the Shift key with the Lasso tool to add to the selected areas). Be sure to select a portion of the white surrounding the edges (Figure 7–15, left).
8. Select black or a dark color for the Foreground color. With the Paint Bucket tool, click within the gray portion of the letters in the selection (Figure 7–15, right). Although the white of the page is also selected, the fill will extend only to the outside edge of the type and not venture into the white.
9. For the highlight, choose the Airbrush tool with a small size and spray some soft lines along the edges opposite the shadows, as in Figure 7–13.

The Molten Metal Effect

Using a combination of filters, you can make a detailed image look like stamped or molten metal (Figure 7–16 and Figure C–24 in the Color Section). This technique works especially well with scanned, highly detailed, black-and-white line art.

1. Open the desired image, Select All and copy the image to the Clipboard. Apply a Gaussian Blur with a Radius of 3 to 6 pixels to the entire image.
2. Apply the Find Edges filter to the entire image. Use the Levels, Curves, or Equalize command to bring out the detail and balance the brightness in the newly filtered image.
3. Paste the Clipboard image back on top, open the Composite Controls, and apply Color mode. You also can experiment with the Sliders and Opacity.

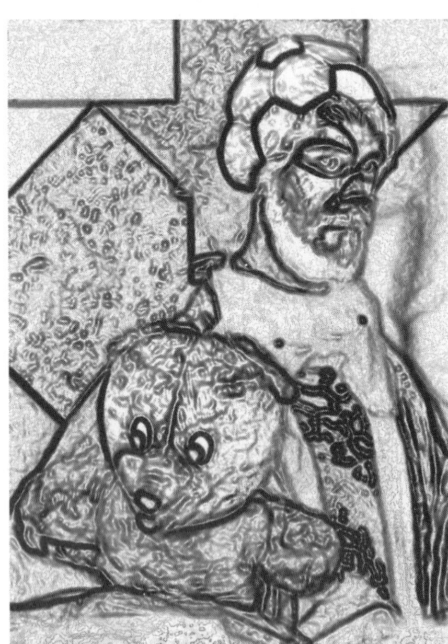

Figure 7–16
The original image (left) and the Molten Metal Effect (right)

Try the above steps while the image is in the Lab Color mode with the Lightness channel isolated. When the **a** and **b** channels are made inactive, and the Lightness channel is the only one manipulated, the original colors will be intact.

Duotones, Tritones, and Quadtones

Traditional printing methods utilize the duotone, or two passes of ink, to increase the tonal range and add depth to a photograph. Duotone also can add colorful effects to black-and-white images. The halftones needed to produce a duotone of a continuous-tone image require two photographic negatives with different value and contrast ranges. Refer to Figures C–19 through C–21 in the Color Section to see examples of duotones and quadtones.

To produce a monotone (one color), duotone (two colors), tritone (three colors), or quadtone (four colors) on the desktop, open a scanned image in Grayscale mode and then choose Duotone from the Mode menu to get the Duotone Options dialog box (Figure 7–17). In the Type pop-up menu, choose Monotone, Duotone, Tritone, or Quadtone. The Type choice will activate the ink color fields and boxes.

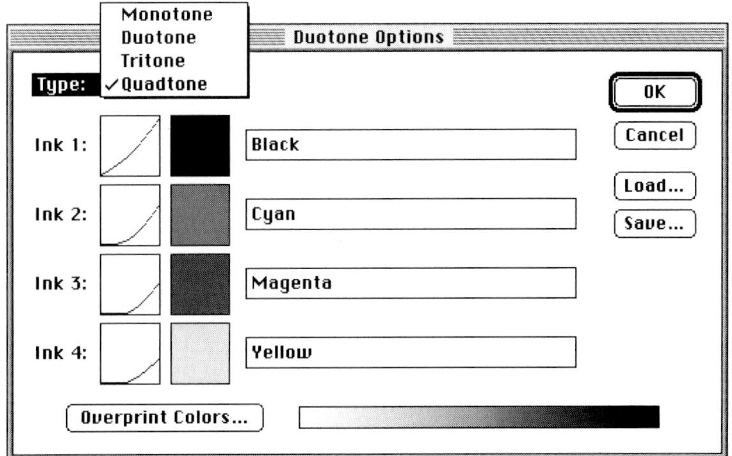

Figure 7–17
The Duotone Options dialog box

Colors can be picked from any of those in the Custom Colors pop-up menu (Figure 7–18). To choose an ink color from the Custom Colors dialog box, click on the solid color square for the desired ink. Click on the Picker button to mix your own color. Whether you're using a custom color or defining your own, the spelling of the color names must match the spelling of the same colors used in any other programs that will be used in combination with Photoshop to separate the file. Not all programs spell the custom colors identically. Check the naming conventions in the various programs that you are using or type in your own simple color names such as Color 1 and Color 2. For more information on the Custom Colors refer to Chapter 4, "Using the Tools and Palettes."

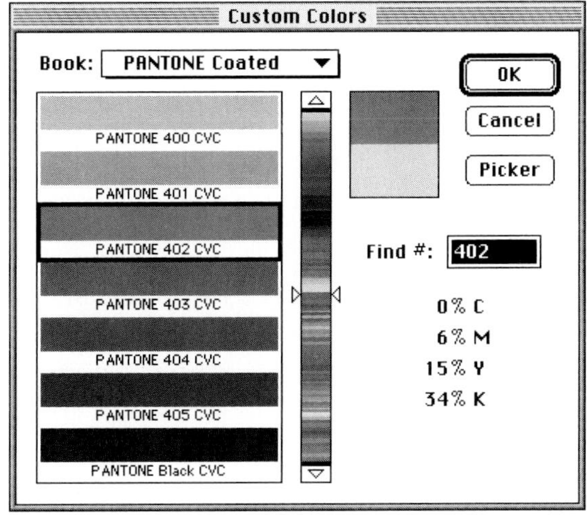

Figure 7–18
The Custom Colors dialog box

***Tip*: When using Pantone colors, you can choose Use Short Pantone Names in the General Preferences dialog box to ensure that the spelling will match most other programs. Be sure to check the spelling; misspelled names could be a costly mistake.**

> **NOTE: Some of the custom colors in the menu, such as the Trumatch selections, are mixed with process colors (CMYK). Others, such as Toyo, are mixed with custom inks. In either case, be aware that the color on the monitor often does not match the printed ink color. Always refer to a printed swatch book when specifying ink colors.**

Next you can adjust the relationship between input gray values and the output values for each of the inks by clicking on the curve icon next to the ink color. This opens the Duotone Curve dialog box (Figure 7–19), where you can make adjustments by clicking points on the graph or by entering numbers in the percentage boxes. The x-axis (horizontal) refers to input values and the y-axis (vertical) refers to output values. Usually, you set darker colors to print heavier in the shadows (toward the right) and lighter colors to print heavier in the highlights (toward the left).

When you are satisfied with the effect on your monitor, print a color composite or output color separations. Either can be printed directly from Photoshop, but often images need to be included in other programs to be combined with graphics and text. When saving a file from the Duotone mode, save it in the EPS file format. A dialog box will appear

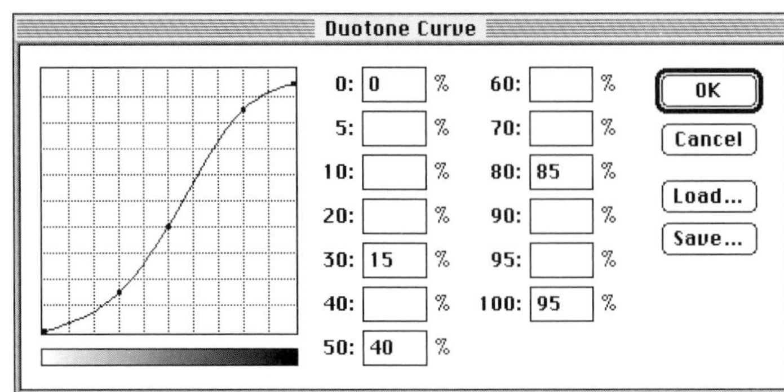

Figure 7–19
The Duotone Curve dialog box

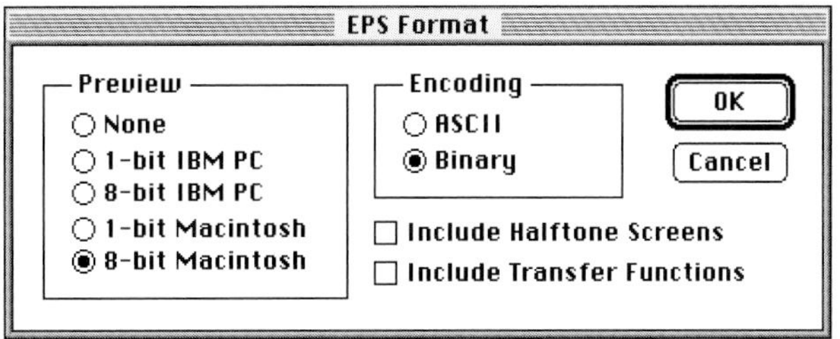

Figure 7–20
The EPS Format dialog box for duotones

with various options (Figure 7–20). Set the Preview to the computer platform that you are using (Mac files can be used on a IBM PC). If you want to see the colors, choose 8-bit. Set the Encoding to Binary for most situations (some older programs only accept ASCII). Click Include Halftone Screens only if you have specified a halftone frequency and angle in the Page Setup dialog box. Check with your service bureau to find out how you should handle the halftone screens. Refer to Chapter 8, "Output," for more information on printing composites and separations.

Halftone Screen Alternatives

To print tones on a printing press, an image needs to be broken up into dots to simulate values. The normal method of generating a halftone screen produces a series of dots that vary in size but remain constant in frequency (See Chapter 8, "Output," for more on halftone screens). Photoshop can produce halftone screens with various dot shapes at any angle (Figure 2–26). In addition, dot shapes can be created by using the Define Pattern command under the Edit menu. Any pattern or texture can be defined as a Custom Pattern and then be used as a custom halftone screen by converting a grayscale image to the Bitmap mode.

Another halftone screen alternative is to break the image into dithered pixels, also achieved by converting to Bitmap mode. Define a resolution, but not a dot shape. The size of the dithered pixels remains constant while their position (frequency) varies.

Since the conversion to Bitmap mode must be from the Grayscale mode, color images must be separated into individual grayscale documents, one for each channel component. When defining a custom pattern to use as a screen, any color in the pattern will be ignored. Three exercises showing this technique are described in the next sections.

Dithered Pixels

When converting to the Bitmap mode, a Grayscale document can generate a pattern dither (Figure 2–23) or diffusion dither (Figure 2–24). Refer to "The Display Modes" section in Chapter 2, "Setup and Document Management," for an explanation of the conversion process. The following example illustrates the process using a color image. See Figures C–25 and C–26 in the Color Section for examples.

1. Starting from a CMYK Color image, open the Channels palette and choose Split channels from the Pop-out menu (Figure 7–21). This creates four separate grayscale documents.
2. Convert each of the documents to Bitmap mode, choosing Diffusion Dither and the desired resolution in each dialog box (Figure 7–22). Use a resolution equal to or less than the resolution of your output device.
3. Each of these bitmap documents must now be converted back to Grayscale mode at a Size Ratio of 1. After converting all four files back to the Grayscale mode, choose Merge channels from the pop-out menu in the Channels palette (Figure 7–23). Choose CMYK

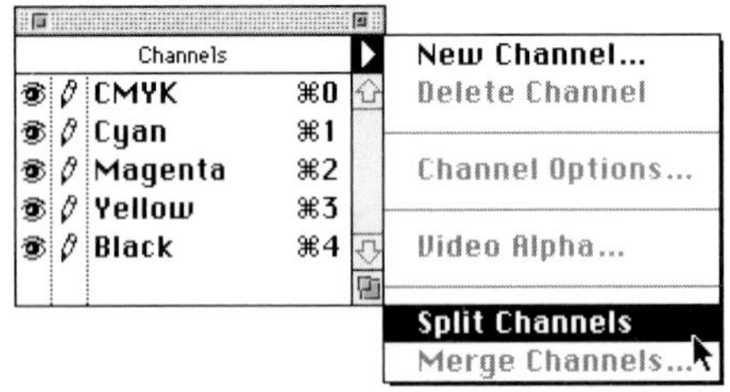

Figure 7–21
Choose Split Channels from the pop-out menu in the Channels palette to create four separate grayscale files from a CMYK document.

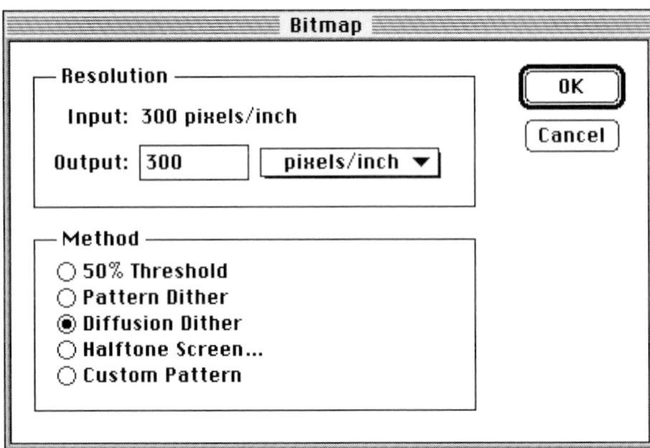

Figure 7–22
Specify Diffusion Dither and the desired resolution in the Bit Map Dialog box

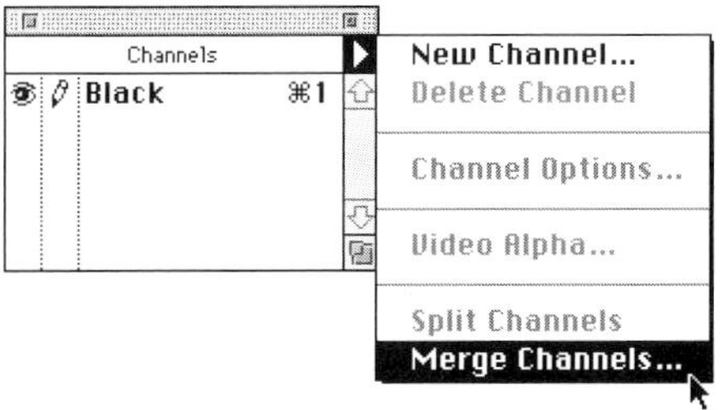

Figure 7–23 Choose Merge channels in the Channels palette to combine the four separate files into one.

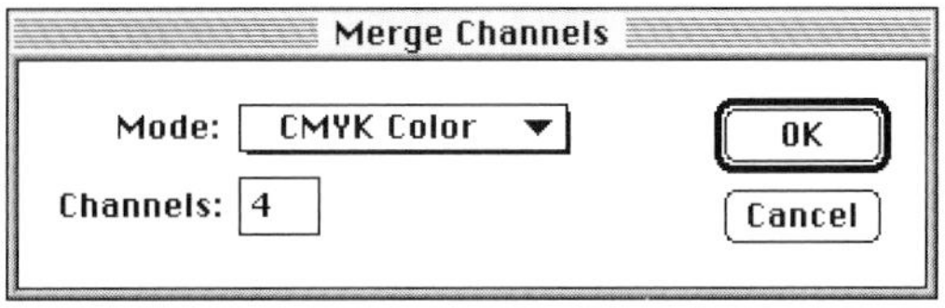

Merge Channels

Mode: CMYK Color

Channels: 4

OK

Cancel

Figure 7–24 Specify the color mode in the Merge Channels dialog box.

Merge CMYK Channels

Specify Channels:

Cyan: Maile.Cyan

Magenta: Maile.Magenta

Yellow: Maile.Yellow

Black: Maile.Black

OK

Cancel

Mode

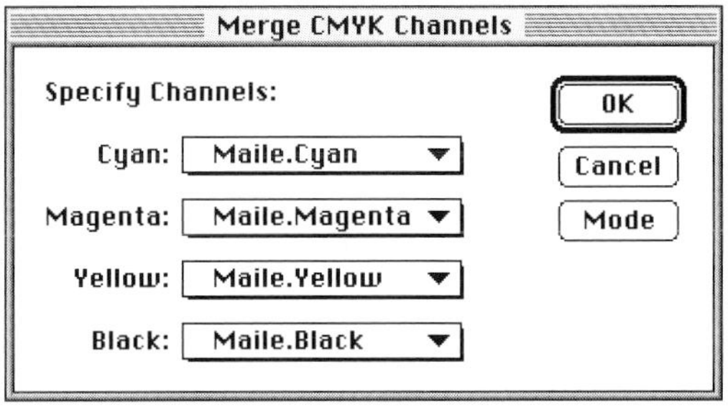

Figure 7–25 In the CMYK Channels dialog box, link each document with its corresponding channel.

Color mode from the pop-up menu in the Merge Channels dialog box (Figure 7–24). The Merge CMYK Channels dialog box will open (Figure 7–25). Make sure that the proper document appears in the pop-up menu next to each corresponding channel.

4. You can now print color separation of the resulting document; each separation will have the dithered effect. Refer to Chapter 8, "Output," for more on making color separations.

Mezzotint

A mezzotint is another type of halftone screen with irregularly shaped dots. When you create a mezzotint screen a defined Custom Pattern breaks up the tones in an image into random shapes. Included with Photoshop are some pattern documents that can be used as custom patterns. Two of them, Mezzotint dot and Mezzotint shape, can be used to define a pattern that will simulate a mezzotint. Use the following method to create your own pattern and resulting mezzotint on a color image. See Figures C–25 and C–27 in the Color Section for examples of mezzotints used as screens.

1. Open a new grayscale document to be used as a pattern. Make it the same size as your image. Choose Add Noise in the Noise submenu under the Filter menu. In the dialog box, set the desired amount and the distribution to Gaussian. Apply the Blur filter to soften the pattern.
2. Choose Select All under the Select menu and then choose Define Pattern under the Edit menu.
3. Open the Grayscale image to be screened, and convert to Bitmap mode, found under the Mode menu. In the dialog box click on the Custom Pattern option and enter a resolution. (Adobe recommends a higher resolution than the input value.)

To apply a mezzotint to a color image, follow the above steps under Diffusion Dither, substituting the Custom Pattern option for Diffusion Dither in the Bitmap mode dialog box.

Texture as a Custom Screen

You can define any pattern or texture as a Custom Screen by doing the following:

1. Start with a scanned texture (Figure 7–26). Select the entire pattern, and choose Define Pattern under the Edit menu.
2. Open an image to be processed through the defined pattern. A color image must be converted to Grayscale mode.
3. Choose the Bitmap mode from the Mode menu. Select the Custom Pattern option and enter the resolution in the dialog box (Figure 7–27).

Channel Tricks

The channel capabilities of Photoshop are an endless source of special effects. Some techniques for exploiting the channels are explained below.

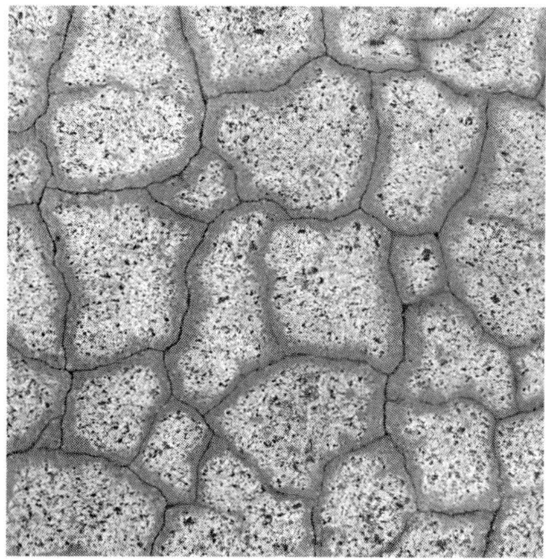

Figure 7–26
Original scanned texture used to define a custom screen

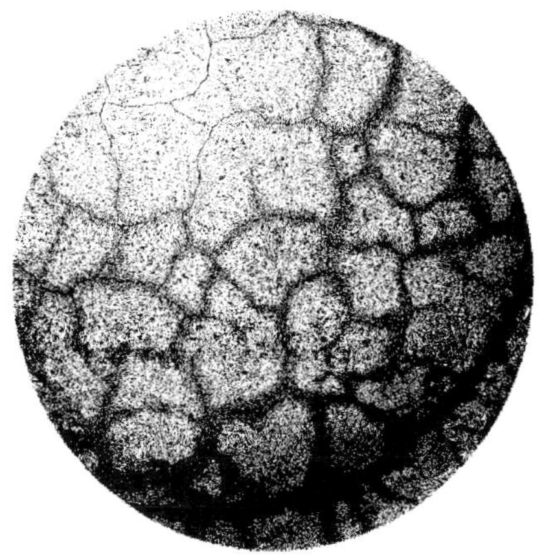

Figure 7–27
Image with Custom Screen applied

Creating Smooth Crossfaded Images

By using gradient fills in channels, you can create smooth crossfades between images.

1. Begin with two grayscale images of approximately the same size. Make a new channel in the Channels palette of the first image.
2. With the Foreground color black and the Background white, double-click on the gradient tool and choose Linear as the blend type.
3. Drag in a vertical direction to create a linear gradient from the top of the window to the bottom.
4. Click the Black channel to make the image visible.
5. Choose Load Selection under the Select menu. The new channel (with the blend) will appear as a selection in the image, with the lighter side of the gradient selected.
6. Click on the window of the second document, select the entire image, and copy it to the Clipboard. Click on the window of the first document (the original selection should still be active). Choose the Paste Into command under the Edit menu. The clipboard image is pasted through the gradient channel into the first image. The result is a verticle crossfade (Figure 7–28).

The same technique also can be used to crossfade between different modified versions of the same image, and between color and black-and-white versions of the same image.

Figure 7–28
Two images combined using crossfading

Channel Gradients and Filters

Variations of the previous technique can be used to selectively apply filters to an image.

Starting with a grayscale image, create a new channel in the Channels palette and fill it with a black-to-white gradient (Radial blend). Click on the black channel to make it active. Choose Load Selection from under the Select menu and apply the Gaussian Blur filter, entering a value of 5.

This effect works well with both grayscale or color images using any type of gradient or filter effect (Figure 7–29).

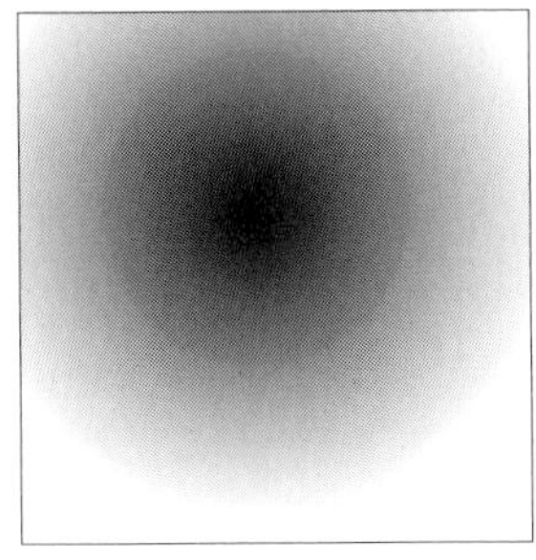

Figure 7–29
Channel Gradient technique used to blur and filter portions of the these images using the channel in the first frame as a mask.

Special Effects with the Lab Mode

Use the Lab mode for special effects that cannot be created easily in the RGB display mode. The Lab mode consists of three channels: Lightness (gray component), **a** (red/green component), and **b** (yellow/blue component).

In the Lab mode, the tones of an image can be altered without affecting the colors by manipulating the Lightness channel only.

1. Open a color image and convert it to Lab Color mode.
2. Open the Channels palette under the Windows menu. Click on the Lightness channel to activate it (make sure that both the "eye" icon and the "pencil" icon appear).
3. Open the Curves dialog box in the Adjust submenu under the Image menu, and make changes to the curve, altering the image. Click on the Lab channel in the Channels palette to view the composite. The gray values in the image will appear distorted, but the colors will remain intact (Figure C–5 in the Color Section).

The color of the image can be manipulated without altering its Lightness channel by using the above method and altering the **a** and **b** channels. The final image will have altered colors, but the value range will remain intact (Figure C–4 in the Color Section.).

Listed below are tips and suggestions for using the Lab mode.

- Colorize black-and-white images by converting to Lab mode, isolating the **a** and **b** channels, and adding colors without affecting the gray values (Figure C–1 in the Color Section).
- Tools commands and filters that keep the channels in register, such as Pointillize, Median, the Threshold and the Airbrush tool, and the Paintbrush tool, seem optimal when working on multiple channels.
- Invert the **a** or **b** component of an image to substitute negatives (complements) of the colors, leaving the main detail of an image positive (Figure C–2 in the Color Section).
- Invert the Lightness channel only to create a negative of the image, leaving the original colors intact (Figure C–3 in the Color Section).
- Posterize the image with the Lightness channel isolated, and then apply the median filter. When you activate the color channels, the image will look hand-painted.

- Apply the Molten Metal Effect, seen earlier in the chapter, to the Lightness channel, leaving the original colors and their placement untouched.
- Experiment with other filters and commands on the Lightness channel: Solarize, Find Edges, Invert, Brightness/Contrast, Gaussian Blur, and the various tools in the toolbox.

The Calculate Commands

Photoshop's ability to manipulate the individual channels of an image is extended by the commands in the Calculate submenus under the Image menu (Figure 7–30). The Calculate commands combine channels by comparing their brightness values, and then move channels from one document to another. For example, the Subtract command diminishes the brightness value of the pixels in one channel from the brightness values of the pixels in another channel, and puts the resulting pixels in a third channel.

NOTE: The Calculate commands work only if the channel sizes are identical. If you try to blend two files that are off by even a single pixel you will not be able to see them in the pop-up menus.

Caution: **Do not resize the main image in any way after creating a separate corresponding channel document. If you do, the channels can no longer be superimposed onto the main image because the registration is lost.**

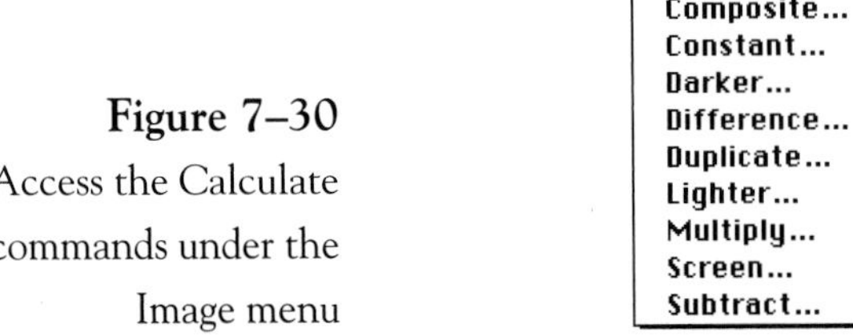

Figure 7–30
Access the Calculate commands under the Image menu

You can use the Calculate commands on both color and black-and-white images, but they are not accessible to images in the Indexed Color mode (convert to RGB Color mode) or the Bitmap mode (convert to Grayscale mode). Some of the commands have a field for a Scale and Offset value—compensation factors for more complex calculations. Read the description in the User Manual for a detailed discussion of the mathematics behind the Calculate commands. Practical applications for some of the Calculate commands are listed below.

DUPLICATE COMMAND: CREATING A SEPARATE MULTICHANNEL DOCUMENT

When a channel is created for an image with the Save Selection command, the resulting channel is added as a new channel to the document. There are times, however, when you might not want to place the channel into the document. This is especially true when working with large, high-resolution files. Use the Duplicate command to create a separate multichannel, grayscale document containing only defined channels.

1. Starting with the desired color image (saved to the disk with the name "Color Image"), select a portion of the image using any of the selection tools.
2. Choose the Duplicate command in the Calculate submenu. A dialog box appears (Figure 7–31).
3. The Source file is the document from which you are creating the channel. Beneath it, you will see the current channel as RGB. Press on the pop-up menu and choose Selection. Leave the Destination Document and Channel as New.

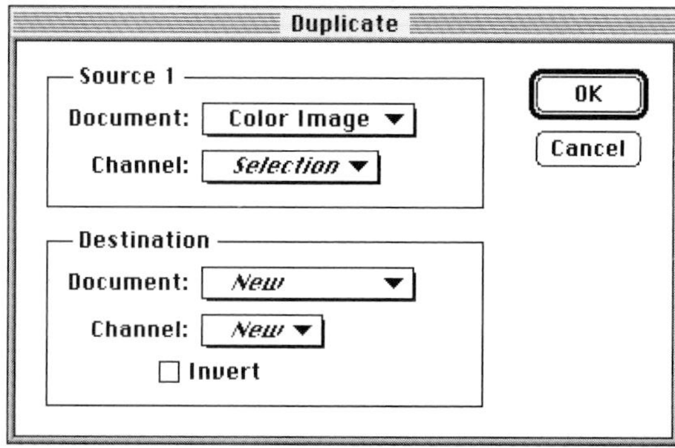

Figure 7–31
The Duplicate Dialog box

4. You now have a new untitled document open on the screen, showing the channel created with the selection from the original RGB image. Save the file to disk, naming it "Color Image Masks."
5. Go back to the original RGB image, select another area from which to make a channel, and open the Duplicate command.
6. Add this new channel to the existing "Color Image Masks" file. Make sure that "Color Image" is still the selected Source channel. Choose "Color Image Masks" as the Destination file, and "New" as the destination channel.
7. Your two "Color Image Masks" channels can be used in the original color image, even though the channels are in a different document. Select a channel to overlay onto the "Color Image" document, and choose the Duplicate command again.
8. Make sure that the "Color Image Mask" file is the source. Set the Destination to the "Color Image" document, and the Channel to Selection. (Although you might think that the destination channel should be the RGB channel, this is incorrect; duplicating the channel to the RGB channel in the destination image would completely replace the color image with the channel.)

With this technique, you can create channel documents that are not part of the actual image, allowing you to keep the size of your main image relatively smaller than it would be of you had all of the image's channels stored with it.

SUBTRACT COMMAND: EXTRACTING LAYERS FROM EXISTING GRAPHICS

If you need to make modifications to a channel of a masked image that lies behind an overlapping image that is placed with another image mask, use the Subtract command.

1. Create a feathered, circular selection on an RGB image, and select the Save Selection command. This will make a channel with the feathered circular selection.
2. Create a new channel, and place some type into the channel, overlapping the circular selection.
3. Overlay the text channel onto the image, filling with a solid color.

4. Overlay the feathered circle onto the image, filling with a different solid color. It should overlap and obscure part of the colored text created in Step 3.

   Now you can change the color of the type, without disturbing the colored and feathered circle in the foreground. An easy method would be to subtract the feathered circle channel away from the text channel, resulting in another channel that contains the text without the feathered circle overlap.

5. Select the Subtract command. The Source files are the image documents that contain the channels to be manipulated. In this case, both are both from the same document. Specify Source 1 as the Text channel and Source 2 as the feathered circle channel. Apply the results to the original color image, choosing the original document as the destination, and the Selection as the destination channel.
6. Now you are returned to the original RGB image, with the text that is not underneath the feathered circle selected. Any command or filter will be applied only to the selected text area.

You can use Subtract to create more complex composite masks by placing the results of the calculations into new channels, instead of automatically overlaying them onto the target color image as in the example above.

SUBTRACT COMMAND: CREATING A RAISED SHADOW EFFECT

Another application of the Subtract command is to add a raised shadow effect to an image. The trick is to create two channels, one with the actual shape and one with an offset version of the shape, and subtract the first from the second (Figure 7–32).

ADD COMMAND: COMBINING MULTIPLE CHANNELS INTO ONE

The Add command combines multiple channels into a single channel. The overlapping white areas from the two or more channels remain pure white (transparent), while the luminosity values of overlapping gray areas are added together. The Add command saves time when you need to apply the same color correction or brightness increase to several channels.

THE CONSTANT COMMAND

The Constant command is useful for placing a solid gray value (from 0 to 255) into a channel. It is like filling a channel with a solid shade of gray except that you can specify the shade numerically.

THE COMPOSITE COMMAND

Use the Composite command (Figure 7–33) to overlay a channel onto a complex background, maintaining smooth anti-aliased edges between the channel image and the background. If the image and the background are large, high-resolution files, the Copy and Paste commands might take too much time and memory.

Figure 7–32
Create this drop-shadow effect with the Subtract command.

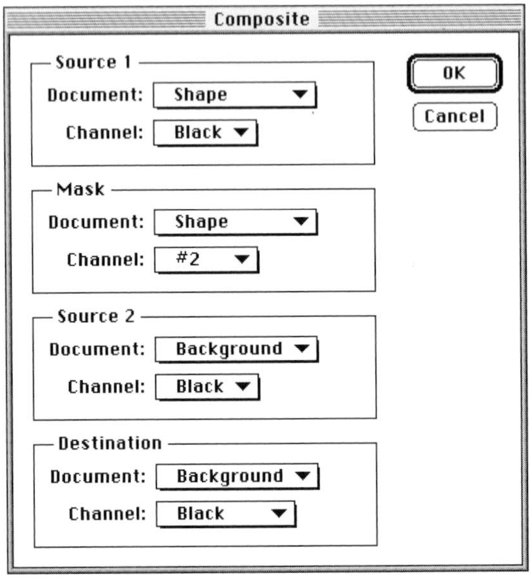

Figure 7–33
The Composite dialog box

1. Start with two grayscale documents of exactly the same size—one with a complex background and the other with a distinct shape defined as a mask in a channel. Save them as "Background" and "Shape" (Figure 7–34).
2. With both documents open, choose the Composite command.
3. Choose the Black channel of the "Shape" document as Source 1, choose Channel #2 of the "Shape" document as the mask, choose the Black channel of the "Background" document as Source #2, and choose the Black Channel of the "Background" document as the Destination (Figures 7–33 and 7–34).

THE MULTIPLY AND SCREEN COMMANDS

The Multiply and Screen commands are related but different. Multiply is comparable to two transparencies on a light table. The common light areas are light; overlapping dark and light areas are medium dark; and overlapping dark areas are the darkest. The Screen command, with an opposite effect, is like projecting two slides onto a wall—overlapping light areas become lighter.

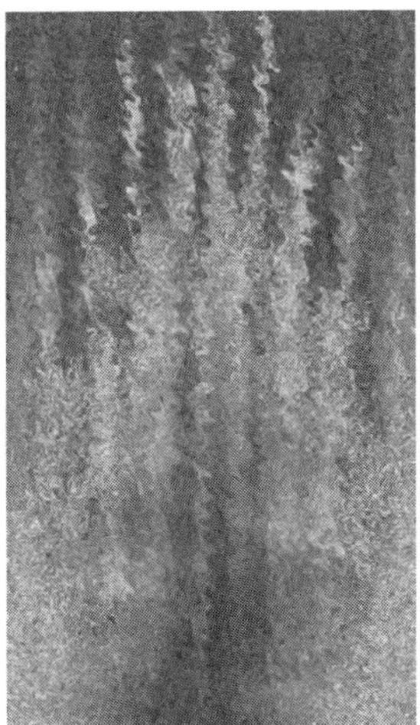

Figure 7–34 Use the Composite command to overlay an image onto a background in another document. Shown from left to right: The original shape, the channel for the shape, the background in another document, and the final composite.

Kai's Chops

Kai Krause, Photoshop wizard and developer of Kai's Power Tools, offers a series of techniques for using the Calculate commands.

Secrets of Channel Operations: You Need Chops . . .

Channel operations are powerful methods to create effects that could not be created in any other way, no matter how good you are with that Wacom airbrush. These operations involve images as sources, destinations, and masks. Most compare two channels, but Duplicate works on only one, and Composite on three.

Shadow and Highlight Multipliers

We begin with the drop shadows. The effects can be generated at any size, but exact numbers are the only examples provided because they offer repeatable results.

1. Select New under the File menu and create a new document that is 400 pixels wide and 300 pixels tall; set the Mode to Grayscale and the Resolution to 72 ppi.
2. Draw some lines similar to Figure 7–35 with the Paint Brush tool. Keep it black for now, but crisscross any way you like.
3. Select Duplicate from the Calculate submenu. The default settings will create a copy of the first window as a new untitled document.
4. This copy will become our shadow. From the Filters menu, select Blur, Blur More, or the Gaussian Blur filter set to 5 (Figure 7–36).

Figure 7–35
Scribble created with the Brush tool

Figure 7–36
The Gaussian Blur applied to the scribble

5. For more realism, move the shadow by selecting Offset filter from the Other submenu under the Filter menu. Enter 6 pixels for the Horizontal value and 4 pixels for the Vertical value.

> ***Tip*: Try not to use identical offset values; a displacement of exactly 45° can create artifacts such as moiré patterns. Furthermore, clean diagonal lines would not have any visible shadows along their length.**

6. Select the Calculate Subtract command to see the dialog box shown in Figure 7–37.
7. Basically you have two images, Sources 1 and 2, and a Destination. Each has a Channel pop-up menu underneath it. With full color images these channels could be RGB (Red, Green, and Blue). In Grayscale the pop-up shows only black. Note that the currently active window name is already inserted for you. If you press on the document name you will see all the files that can be accessed with the Calculate commands (those of equal dimensions and compatible modes).

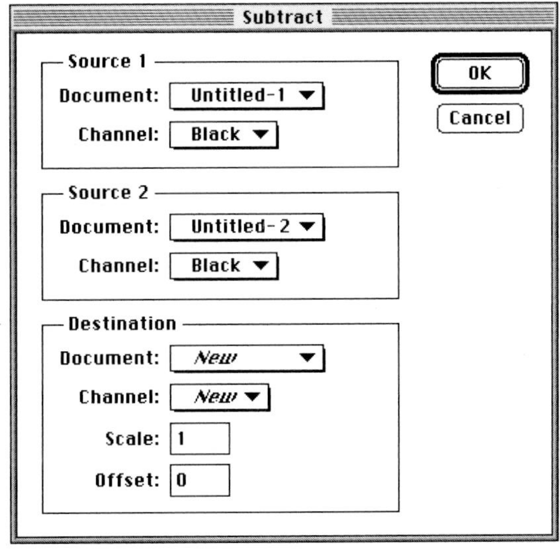

Figure 7–37
The Subtract dialog box

Tip: If the image you want to blend, add, etc., does not show up in the pop-ups, it's because the size does not match the currently active window or it is in an incompatible mode (e.g., Indexed or Bitmapped).

8. To subtract the shadow from the clean original, select the original document in the top pop-up menu (Source 1) minus the second document in the bottom pop-up menu (Source 2) which will be saved into the Destination document (in this case a New file).
9. Apply the Invert command in the Map submenu under the Image menu (Figure 7–38).
10. Select the Calculate Multiply command. Multiply Untitled 1 by Untitled 3 to create a new destination document (Figure 7–39).

All's Well That Blends Well

The Calculate Blend command will add together the brightness values of each pixel in two images (similar to Add) and allow you to shift the relative dominance of either one, expressed as a percentage. At 50% they are usually equally strong (Figure 7–40).

Duplicating and inverting the original image, a capital letter "G," produces the exact opposite in the second document (Figure 7–41.)

Use the Blend command to combine the original G with the duplicated and inverted version. Combining each corresponding pixel pair results in the average of the two, which in this case is an even shade of gray: white (256) plus black (0) equals gray (128) (Figure 7–41).

Figure 7–38
The Shadow Multiplier applied to the scribble pattern

Figure 7–39
The final scribble with a displaced soft shadow

Blend

Source 1
Document: Untitled-1
Channel: Black
Weight: 50

Source 2
Document: Untitled-2
Channel: Black

Destination
Document: New
Channel: New

OK
Cancel

Figure 7–40
The Blend dialog box

The original G blended with gray yields a toned version of the original (Figure 7–42). Black (0) and gray (128) produces a lighter value (64) as in Figure 7–42.

In Figure 7–43, the inverted G (left) blended with gray produces a toned version of the inverted G (the rightmost G is lighter). White (256) and gray (128) produces a lighter value (192).

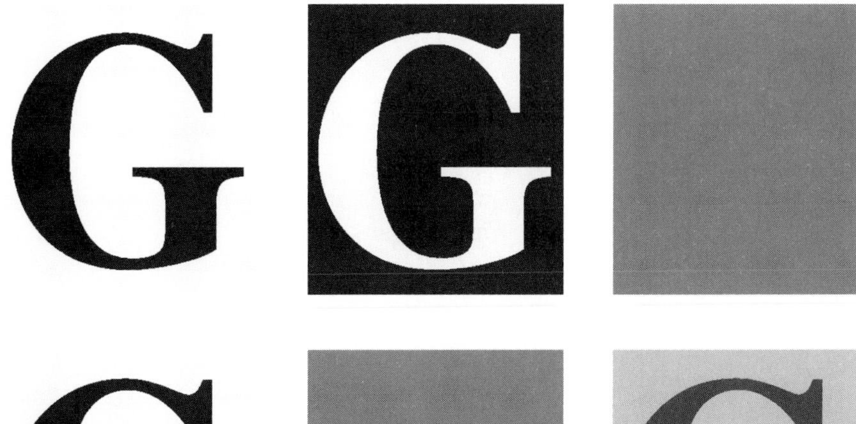

Figure 7–41
Duplicating and inverting the original G (left) produces the G in the center. Blending the two yields gray (right).

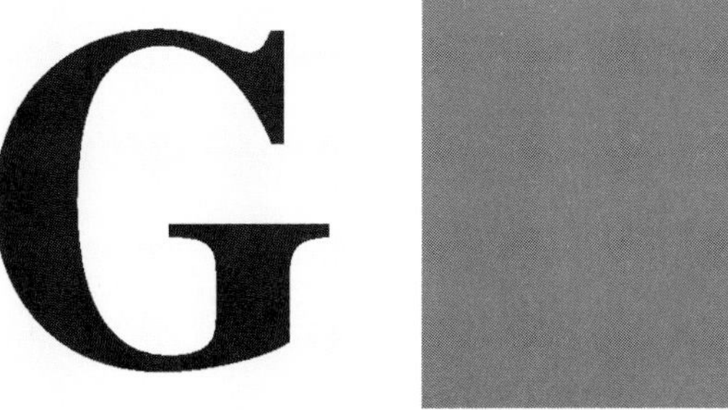

Figure 7–42
Blending the original G (left) with the gray in the center yields a toned version of the original (right).

The original G blended with a gradient yields a version toned by the gradient (Figure 7–44).

In summation, if the two images blended (Sources 1 and 2) are exactly matching duplicates, but one is inverted, they cancel each other, producing 50% gray. If they are not exactly registered but slightly offsetting one from another, the result will be embossed (Figure 7–45).

The middle image is the inverted duplicate and is moved up and left 1 pixel. After applying the Calculate Blend command you get the Relief on the right (which is almost identical to the Embossing filter set at 1 pixel).

Figure 7–43
Blending the inverted G (left) with the gray in the center yields a toned version of the inverted G (right).

Figure 7–44
Blending the original G (left) with the gradient (center) yields a version toned by the gradient (right).

Figure 7–45
Blending the original G (left) with the inverted offset version (center) produces a relief effect (right).

Figure 7–46
Blending the original G (left) with the inverted, blurred, offset version (center) produces a soft relief effect (right).

Figure 7–47
Continue to blend the various resulting images for more possibilities.

We will now discuss more powerful uses of Blend. The original G will be our main image, "Source 1," in all these examples. Take the inverted duplicate of the G and apply the Gaussian Blur set to 4 and Offset the resulting blurred shape by –4x, –3y (left and up). Apply the Blend command to the two images. The result has a light corona effect and a shadowed curve on the right (Figure 7–46).

Any of the resulting files can also be used for further blends for many possibilities (Figure 7–47).

Another Chopping Spree, Close to the Edge

Using Border under the Select menu to create an outline border region that is then blurred (an often desired effect) can cause problems which can be avoided with masking using Chops. Try creating a border around an area (here at 8 pixels), and apply the Invert command in the Map submenu under the Image menu. Notice the jagged artifacts that are produced (Figure 7–48).

Using the Border command may not work as expected because it feathers equally both in and out. To make a border with Chops, as shown in Figure 7–51, make a duplicate document of the original shape, blur it slightly once, and run the Find Edges filter (Figure 7–49). Apply the Gaussian Blur filter and then use the Brightness/Contrast command to increase the contrast (Figure 7–50).

Figure 7–48
Apply the Border command to the selection, use the Blur filter, and then invert the selected border.

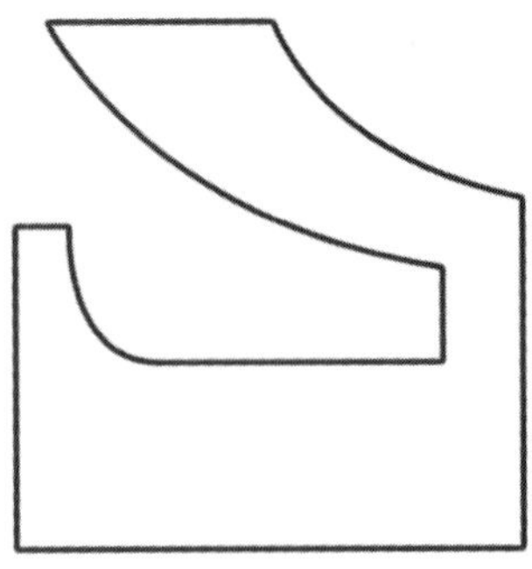

Figure 7–49
Blur the original shape and then apply the Find Edges filter.

Figure 7–50
Apply the Gaussian Blur filter and increase the contrast.

Figure 7–51
The final version created with the Difference command

Use the Calculate Difference command with the original shape as Source 1, the blurred version as Source 2, and New as the destination. Invert the document and there you have it, a border made with Chops (Figure 7–51).

The Calculate Difference command uses one image as a source and a second image as a "selective inverter." Solid black areas are inverted, white areas will be left alone, and gray values will be inverted proportionally (Figure 7–52).

Figure 7–52 The Difference command applied to "Art" (left) as Source 1 and "Pop" as Source 2 (center) to arrive at the final image (right)

A Case Study by Kai Krause

The Leonardo Pix series of images (Figure C–28 in the Color Section) illustrate various principles of channel operations, as well as examples of Algorithmic Painting, such as gold and silver textures.

Krause started with a small scan of Leonardo daVinci's famous study of anatomy (Figure 7–53). He created a duplicate copy on which he applied the Levels command to whiten the light gray outside shades and darken inside shades to black. Then a mask was built to isolate the figure from the background, creating a clean shape with anti-aliased edges. This black mask made it easier to composite the final figure onto any background later (Figure 7–54).

GOLDEN TEXTURE

Here's how Krause created the distinctive golden texture of the image:

1. In order to retain some of the figure's features he used the black mask to isolate the inside of the man onto a plain white background in a new separate image (Figure 7–55). This grayscale man was then processed with the Levels and Curves commands, and filters such as blurring and ripples to produce grayshades with the meandering curve look that is perceived as metallic (Figure 7–56).
2. He then switched to RGB mode and used a combination of Arbitrary maps, Curves, and Levels to get the proper spectrum of "golden" colors: white, yellows, oranges, greens, browns, and black. (This gold curve was saved as a file and applied to other images later.)

Figure 7–53
Kraus started with a drawing by Leonardo DaVinci.

Figure 7–54
The mask used to isolate the figure from the background

Figure 7–55
Using the mask, the figure was isolated from the background.

Figure 7–56
Levels, Curves, and filters were applied to distort the image.

3. To create metal, Krause drew small horizontal segments in the Curves dialog, isolating a small range of grays to become solid white and others solid black, applying Smooth once or twice. He focused first on the distinct shape and contrast of the reflection, disregarding the colors altogether. Later he employed Color Mixing and Hue Adjust to get the proper range of metal hues.

A less saturated version of the Gold can produce a convincing Silver or Chrome appearance.

PLAIN GOLD ON GRAY

In the case of the plain gold on gray, a small copy was chosen for a tiled background and the colorized figure was composited with the Composite Calculate command, using the original black mask. The Chops trick for subtracted shadow-only information was used; a copy of the black mask was blurred heavily, offset down and right and then subtracted from the original mask, leaving a cut-out dark piece of diffused offset shadow. This shadow was then multiplied into the composite image, adding only the darkness and lifting the figure from the background.

To create the thin edgeline around the figure he ran the anti-aliased KPT version of Find Edges on a copy of the black mask, yielding a thin white line on black, which was screened as a white outline.

SURREAL VERSION

Krause hid copies of the figure in the surreal version, reminiscent of the M. C. Escher picture titled "Three Worlds." There are copies of the man in the inside area, another in the rainbow, color-only shape, and small tiled copies in the shadows.

TILED VERSION

The background is a tiled version of the figure, colorized to resemble a greenish marble with pink veins. The shadow information was twirled in one of the pictures and then a clean copy was composited into the original position.

In each case the foreground element and the background were created or tiled separately until the black mask shape composited it all together. Krause multiplied the shadows and screened in the highlights.

As Krause recommends: "Let yourself be guided by the process and let it come back to surprise you all by itself! Rather than trying to achieve a precontemplated effect, be open to merely steering the path of the process and with complex combinations of the elements it will reach completely unexpected results. To that end, first create a number of ingredients to work with: a plain mask, maybe several shrunken or expanded sharp masks, blurred copies—which can be blended—and Difference, outlines, shadows, highlights, depthy curvature, and maybe some preferred textures or scans. Then plug and play with the elements, or rather plug and pray you have enough time and disk space to see it all and keep all the good stuff. . . ."

CHAPTER 8

Output

Once you have created your masterpiece in Photoshop, the final step is to get the image out of the computer and onto paper or other media. Of course, you do not have to wait until your project is completed to output. Several methods can be utilized as a project progresses, such as creating comprehensives or proofs. You have the following options:

- You can prepare your image for a slide film recorder (see Chapter 3, "Input").
- You can prepare your image for presentation graphics, video, or animation (see Chapter 9, "Animation").
- You can print black-and-white halftone prints on a laser printer or on a high-resolution imagesetter.
- You can print color prints directly to an RGB, CMY, or CMYK digital printer.
- You can separate color images into four-color process separations for offset printing.
- Finally, you can import your Photoshop image into a page layout or illustration program, combine it with text and vector graphics, and output either a color digital print or color-separated film as a composite finished document.

This chapter will discuss how to set yourself up for whatever kinds of output you choose. It will introduce you to the concept of four-color process separation, and discuss output from within Photoshop and from within other applications.

Quality and Technology

The technology used to import, manipulate, and print your work in Photoshop directly affects the final quality of your product. There is a qualitative difference between images scanned from a newspaper with a handheld scanner and those scanned from large color transparencies or carefully developed 35mm slides on professional prepress laser drum scanners. To get the best output, you need to get high-quality input at the appropriate resolution (see Chapter 3, "Input").

To assure the highest quality for your job, there are four steps you should take before beginning to work.

Calibrate Your Monitor

A key issue that arises in the discussion of quality is calibration. Original artwork, the scanned artwork viewed on the computer screen, and a color proof print will all probably end up looking slightly different in terms of color saturation and consistency.

The issues of calibration in the production process are very complex. They are most important when you are using Photoshop to separate a color image into four process colors, that is, to convert to CMYK. The way your monitor is calibrated significantly affects the way your image is separated. Monitor calibration affects all the work you do in Photoshop. Even if you purchase your scans from a high-end drum scanner already separated into CMYK, your monitor calibration affects how your image is displayed on the screen.

Monitor calibration software primarily achieves consistency and predictability in the way a monitor displays images and how its display relates to the colors of the original scanned artwork and those generated by your output device. As it warms up, a monitor's display color changes. As a monitor ages, it will display color differently. Monitor calibration can also help remove color cast and adjust the gamma (brightness curve) to make it closely resemble the effect of light reflected off paper (for digital color proofs or film separations) or to match the gamma of a slide film recorder or television screen (for video).

***Tip*: An image displayed on a monitor will always appear different from a color proof or press sheet. The former displays with projected light and has the larger color gamut of RGB; the latter is seen with reflected light and shows the smaller gamut of CMYK. Don't drive your-**

self crazy trying to make them match exactly. However, as you develop an experienced eye on a calibrated monitor you can begin to use the monitor appearance as an indication of how an image will print.

There are two approaches to monitor calibration. You should do one, but not both. One way is to use the Gamma Control Panel device (CDEV) that comes with Adobe Photoshop (Figure 8–1). This utility allows you to precisely set the gamma levels of any monitors you have attached to your Macintosh, for optimum screen brightness calibration in Photoshop and any other applications. It can also be used to calibrate monitors among various workstations so that each displays the same color images with consistent color representation from screen to screen. By adjusting the Gamma adjustment slider so that the gray bars above it appear to be equal, you can "normalize" the monitor gamma to its optimum setting. Refer to Chapter 15 in the Photoshop 2.5 manual for a full description of the Gamma CDEV.

The second way to calibrate your monitor is to use third-party monitor calibration utilities. There are several available that offer more sophisticated capabilities than the utility that comes with Photoshop. Each uses a suction cup device that you attach to your screen. The device measures the light produced by your monitor phosphors and adjusts the output through software. (See the manual with your third-party calibrator for more details.)

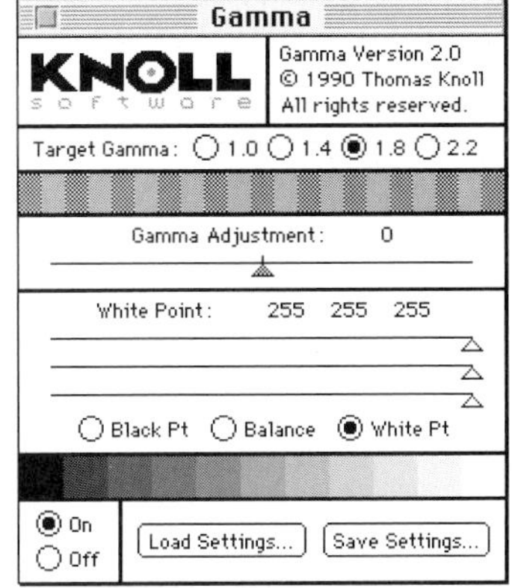

Figure 8–1
The Gamma Control Panel Device

We used the Kodak Color Sense Color Manager software to calibrate a Quadra 800 using a Hewlet Packard Scan Jet IIc. The Color Sense calibrator and target (a reference image) allowed us to synchronize the colors to output consistently to printers.

Enter Monitor Setup Information

After you have calibrated your monitor, choose the Monitor Setup submenu from Preferences under the File menu (Figure 8–2). Then, choose your monitor from the Monitor pop-up menu, and enter the Gamma value you entered in the Gamma utility or that was set by your third-party calibration software.

***Tip*: The Photoshop manual suggests a value of 1.8 to best match printed output. If your final output is slide film or video, you will need to set a higher gamma to match the gamma of the film slide recorder or of television sets. Use a Gamma value of 2.2 unless your slide or video service bureau recommends a different value.**

Choose the White Point value established by your calibration software. If you are using the Gamma utility, leave the default value at 6500K. Next, choose the monitor type in the Phosphors pop-up menu. (If you don't see your monitor listed, you will need to set Custom values, which you can get from your monitor manufacturer.) Finally, choose a setting for Ambient Light that reflects the lighting in the room where your Macintosh is located.

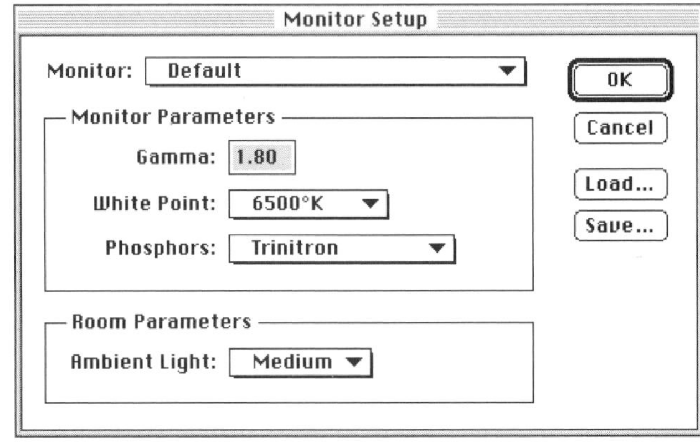

Figure 8–2
The Monitor Setup dialog

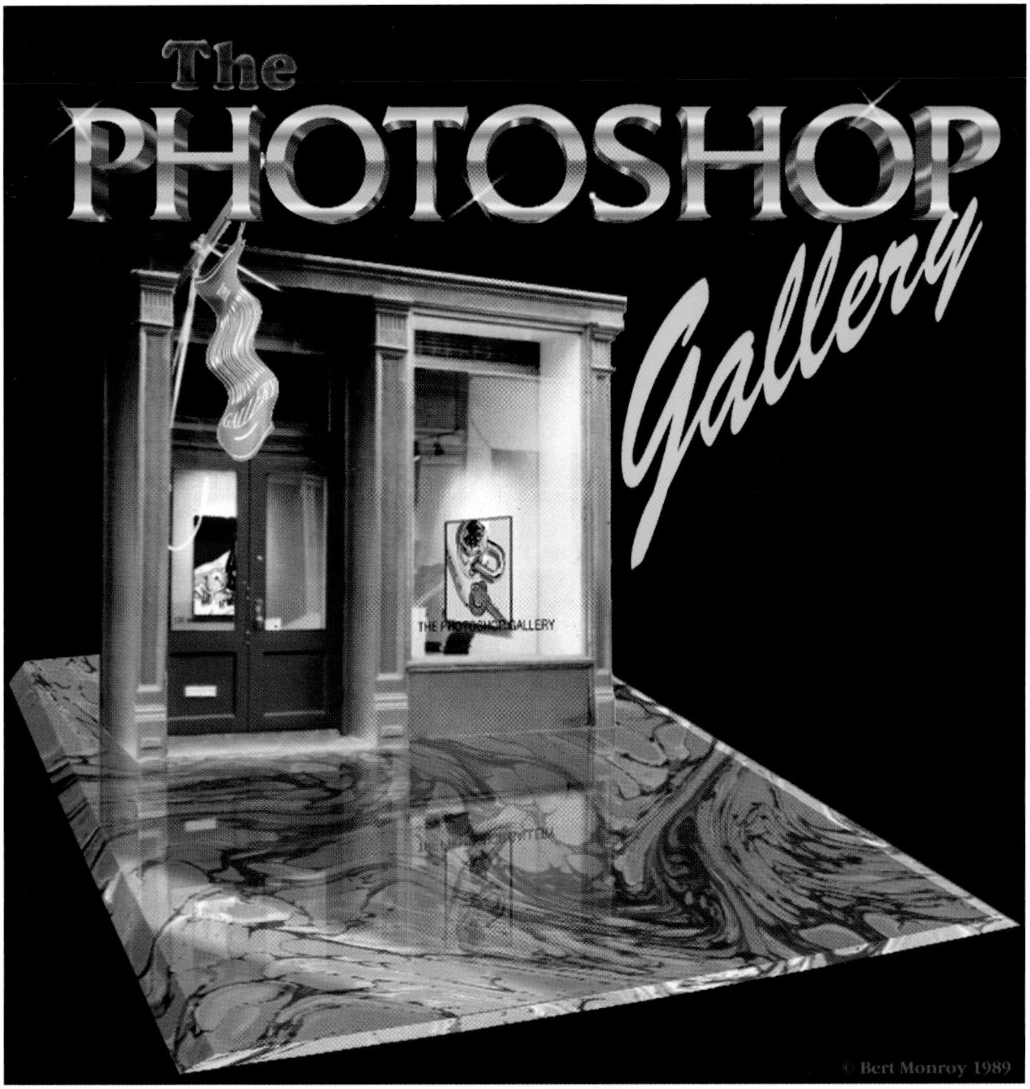

Gallery Intro
Bert Monroy

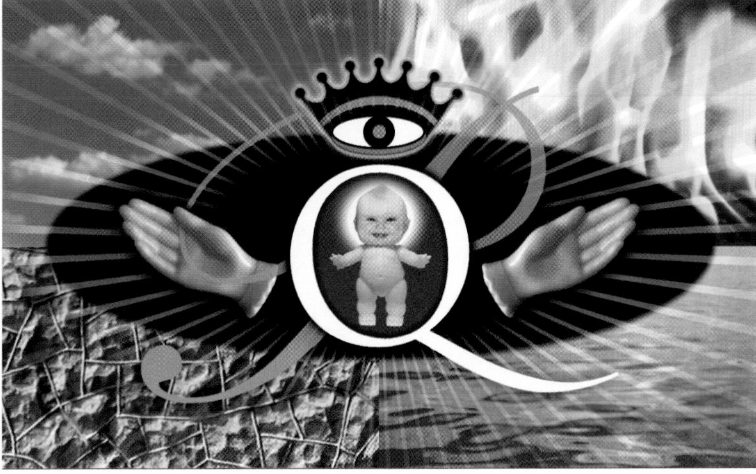

Q.P. Doll
Louis Fishauf

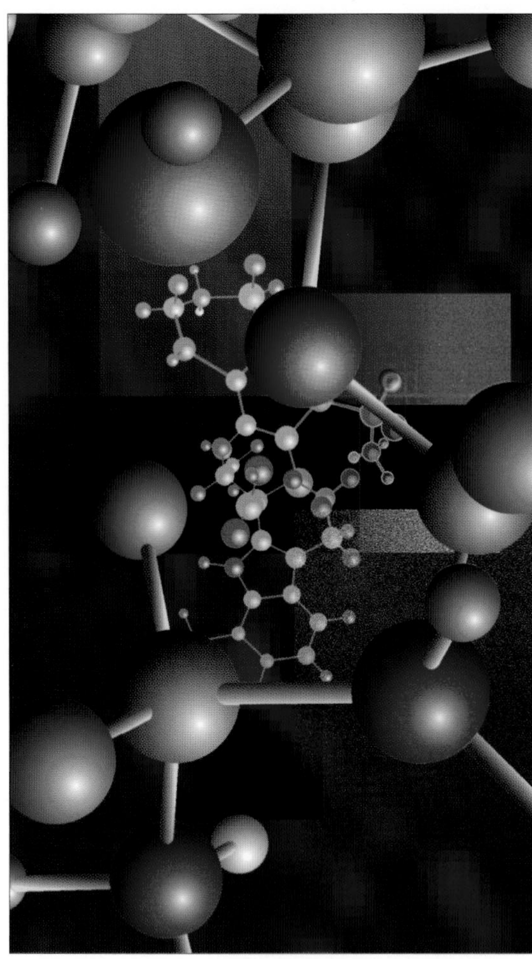

Anodyne Cover
Michael Colanero

Tosh
Andrew Rodney

Orbital World
Bert Monroy

Summer Fishing Fun
Bill Niffenegger

Proposal Cover
Howard Tiersky

Brooklyn Dreams
Eve Elberg

Thoughts of My 10 Year Old
Elaine O'Neil

1993 Cincinnati Symphony Orchestra Poster
Alan Brown

Day Eight/Hour of the Wolf
Diane Fenster

November
Nick Fain

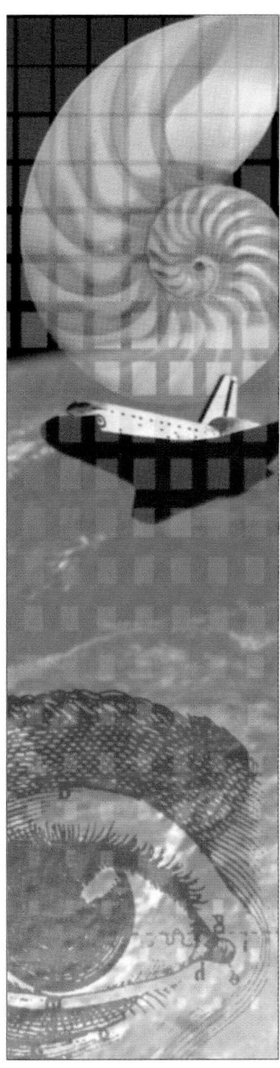

GFX Strip
Chris Swetlin

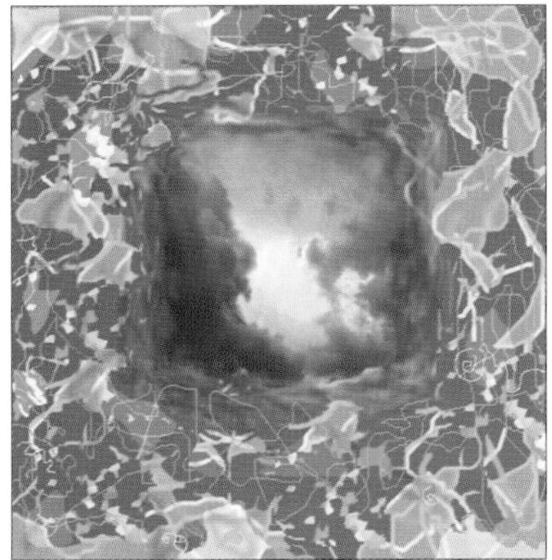

The Window
Joseph Bellacera

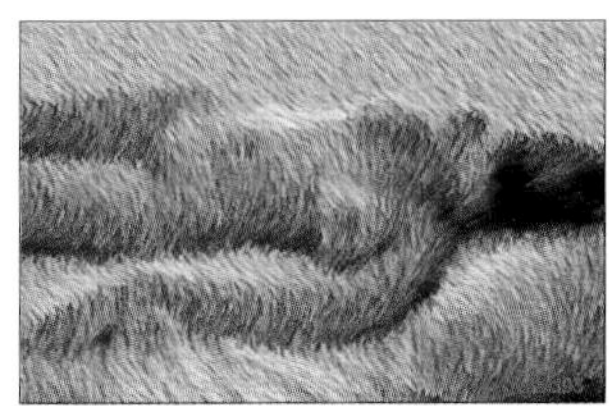

Fiery Lover
Mark Gould

Future City
Bert Monroy

Regalia
Bill Niffenegger

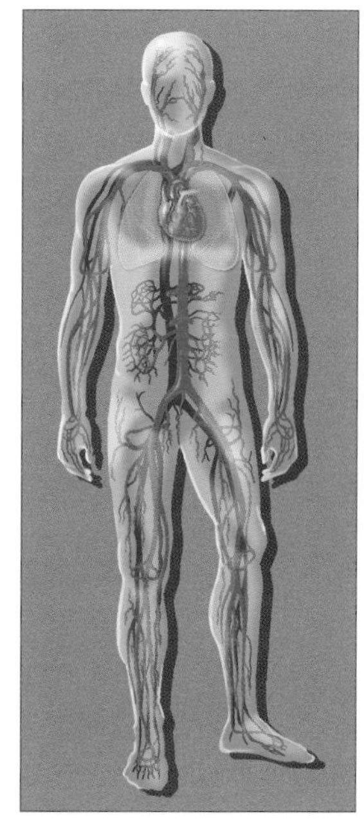

Vascular Man
Fran Milner

Urban Landscape
Adam Cohen

Maile on the Rocks
Mark Siprut

Untitled
Marc Yankus

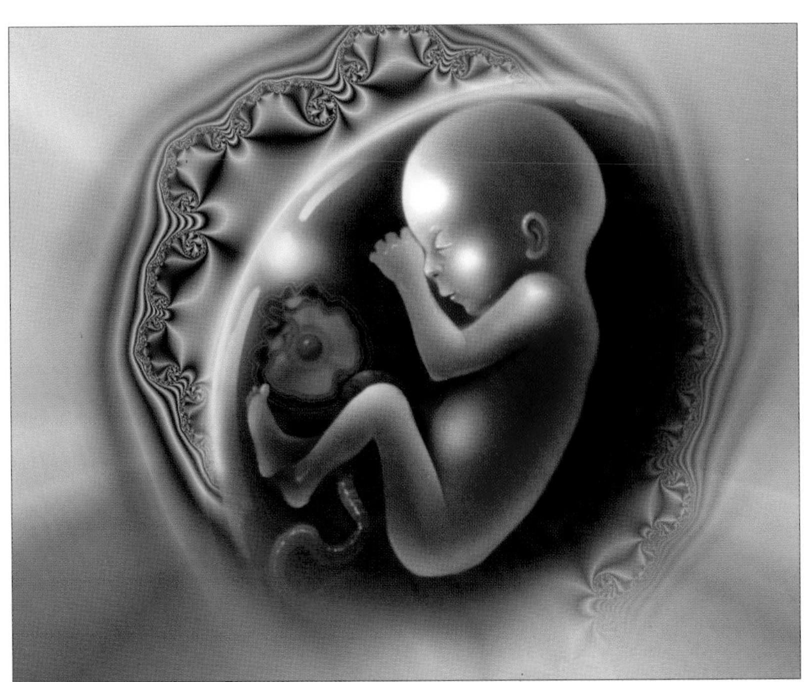

A Womb with a View
Ellen Van Going

***Tip*: The type and amount of room lighting can make a significant difference in the color you see. When you are viewing an image, always keep the room lighting consistent.**

Plan the Steps to Get to Output

Depending on the source of your image and how you output it, you may have to change the display mode (color model) to achieve the best results. (See Chapter 2, "Setup and Document Management," for a discussion of display modes.)

Consider the display mode of your source image. If your source image came from a desktop scanner, digital still camera, or video capture, you are starting in RGB mode. If your source image came from Photo CD, you may be starting in either Lab or RGB mode, depending on the software you used to bring your image into Photoshop. (See Chapter 3, "Input," for a discussion of Photo CD options.). If your source image was a drum scan that you purchased from a color service bureau, you are probably starting in CMYK mode. (Some drum scanners can also give you a corrected RGB scan for use with a film recorder.)

Consider the mode conversion that will be necessary to achieve the best output. For printing to a black-and-white laser printer, you can be in any mode. For printing to an RGB or CMY digital printer, you usually need to be in RGB mode to get the best results. (Check with the documentation that came with your printer to make sure.) For printing to a CMYK digital printer, you need to be in CMYK mode to get the best results. For printing to a film recorder or working with video, you need to be in RGB mode. For printing four-color process separations, you need to be in CMYK mode.

Plan what stage in the work you will be doing the mode conversion (if it is necessary). Usually you should to stay in one mode throughout the color correction and image manipulation stages, and mode conversion will only happen immediately before output. For example, if you scanned your images on a desktop scanner, you would usually stay in RGB mode until you use Photoshop or third-party color-management software to convert to CMYK Color mode prior to printing CMYK digital prints or color separations. (See the discussion on color separation in the next section.) If you received a CMYK scan from a drum scanner, you would usually stay in CMYK.

Tip: Mode conversion, especially between RGB and CMYK, is a complex process. Do not casually convert your image back and forth between modes because this will adversely affect the color quality.

Choose Your Target Printer in Printing Inks Setup

This final step in preparation for output is essential. The way Photoshop outputs your image is dependent on settings that you make in the Printing Inks Setup submenu from Preferences in the File menu (Figure 8–3). Photoshop uses this information when converting from RGB to CMYK (or converting from Lab to CMYK for Photo CD images).

Choose the Ink Colors (the type of digital printer or printing press setup) from the pop-up menu. There are many printers on the list. However, your digital color printer may not be there. If not, choose another make or model of a similar type. Leave the Dot Gain values and Gray Balance values alone unless you are going through the full calibration process described below. If you want to adjust the display of grayscale and duotone images, click the Use Dot Gain for Grayscale check box.

Tip: In both the Monitor Setup and Printer Ink Setup you can load and save settings for different monitors and printing inks. This can save time and ensure consistent results.

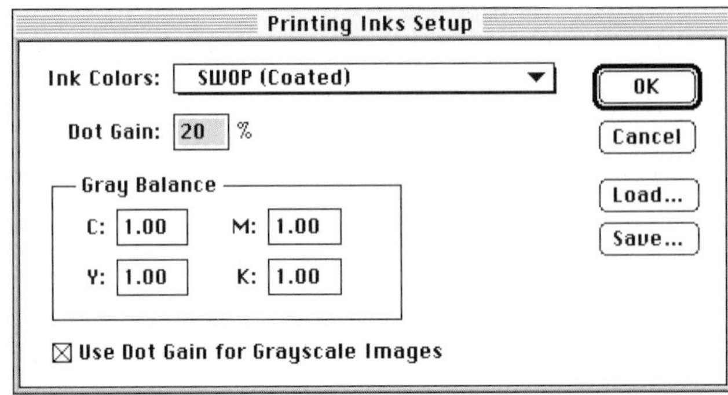

Figure 8–3
The Printing Inks Setup dialog box

Digital Halftones and Four-Color Separations

A Primer on Digital Halftones

Any photograph, illustration, or scene that consists of a wide range of tones or gradation of tones is called *continuous-tone*. In letterpress and offset lithography, tones cannot be reproduced by varying the amounts of ink. A printing press can only lay solid ink for image areas and no ink for nonimage or white areas. To reproduce gradients, or different tones, within an image, you must convert to what is commonly known as a *halftone*.

The halftone principle relies on patterns of small dots of different sizes (printed with ink of uniform density) to simulate different shades of gray or color. Halftoning is the process by which varying tones are converted into patterns of clearly defined dots in various sizes.

The size of the dots determines the tonal values. For instance, a cluster of large dots that leave little white space between them will reproduce an area that is dark. On the other hand, an area composed of tiny dots where the white area is stronger will produce a light gray area. Varying the size of haltone dots results in a print with multiple tones (Figure 8–4).

Traditionally, halftones are created photographically using screens. Digitally produced halftones and screens are essentially equivalent to traditional screens. The major difference is that the computer digitally simulates the halftone screens. The technology of digital screening has developed rapidly in the past few years, and professionally produced digital screening can now exceed the quality of halftones produced traditionally.

Figure 8–4
Halftone screen closeups

Halftone screens, measured in lines per inch (lpi), vary in frequency in order to meet the critical requirements of various forms of printing. Newspapers, for instance, require a coarse dot screen. Newsprint paper is very absorbent and cannot reproduce screens that are too dense; the ink will spread and mix together, thus muddying the images. The coated or glossy stock on slick magazines can hold a small tight dot without the ink spread, thus attaining much finer detail in reproduction. This spreading of the ink, commonly known as *dot gain*, can also be affected by other variables, such as the type of press used or amount of humidity.

The halftone screen is also known in the industry as the *screen ruling*. Some common screen rulings for offset printing are 65 and 85 lpi for newspaper; 100, 120, and 133 lpi for uncoated papers; 133 and 150 lpi for slick magazines and high-quality coated papers.

Halftone screens are set at different angles. In black-and-white, you are dealing with only one screen, in black, which can be set to any angle. In color separations these angles are crucial. Without the correct configuration, you run the danger of getting what is known as moiré patterns (pronounced mwa-ray). These are wavy patterns that interfere with the clarity of the image.

Traditionally the screen angles for process colors are set 30° apart, except for yellow which differs by 15° (Figure 8–5). Imagesetters and laser printers using pixels on a grid to create halftone dots potentially conflict with the angle of the halftone screens to create moiré patterns. To avoid this additional problem, the angles and screen frequencies are adjusted slightly to compensate. This adjustment can happen at various stages in the output process. They can be set manually or automatically in Photoshop or in a page layout program. We recommend that you let the service bureau handle these settings at output stage.

The Complexity of Four-Color Printing

Four-color process separation and printing has traditionally been done by professionals with many years of color experience. This was necessary because of the complexity of the process.

Theoretically, it should be possible to convert from the RGB to the CMY color model easily for printing on a digital color printer or printing press. However, the inks and pigments used in the printing process are impure. If you printed full saturation (100%) each of cyan, magenta, and yellow, you should theoretically get black. Real inks, however, will print a dirty brown. A black plate must be generated to produce a true black and to improve the appearance of shadow areas.

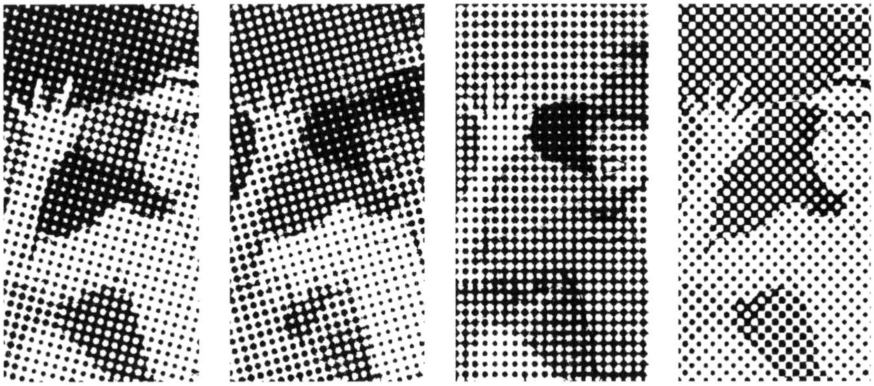

Figure 8–5
Conventional halftone screen angles for cyan, magenta, yellow, and black (left to right)

Another constraint is that you cannot print the full saturation of several inks on top of each other without creating press problems. Most printers request that print jobs have no more than 240 to 300% ink coverage to prevent these problems. This number is called the *total ink limit.*

These dual problems have created two broad solutions. Traditionally, certain amounts of cyan, magenta, and yellow are removed from neutral gray areas wherever black is going to print to reduce the ink coverage. This approach is called *undercolor removal* (UCR). The second approach, called *gray component replacement* (GCR), sees a neutral component wherever a pixel contains cyan, magenta, and yellow. Some or all of this component is printed with black, and the CMY components are reduced.

Finally, the problem of dot gain (as mentioned above) must be compensated for by setting a dot-gain value for the printing process. Set the default values for dot gain in the Printing Inks Setup submenu (described above). However, to get the best result you must find out the actual dot gain for the particular press on which your job will be printed.

NOTE: The dot gain settings in Printing Inks Setup only affect the conversion to CMYK mode or printing to a CMYK printer from other than the CMYK mode. If you are already in CMYK or are working in Bitmapped, Grayscale, or Duotone modes, the dot gain settings will have no affect on the output. If you are in RGB mode and are outputting to an RGB output device, the dot gain settings will also not affect the output.

Strategies for Doing Color Separations

Photoshop has the power to do very high-quality color separations. The controls for doing this are in the Printing Inks Setup and Separation Setup dialog boxes. Choose the Separation Setup submenu from Preferences in the File menu (Figure 8–6). Here you may set Separation Type—either UCR or GCR. For GCR separations, you select the degree of Black Generation—Medium (the default), None, Maximum, or Custom. The Custom option allows you to adjust the black generation curve manually. You can choose the Black Ink Limit and the Total Ink Limit as percentages. You may also select *undercolor addition* (UCA) to reduce the amount of undercolor removal in very dark areas.

Making these choices can be daunting to anyone who is new to working with color images! All of these settings will affect the final quality of your color separation. You must decide whether to take on the responsibility for making these choices or to find another way of handling color separations. Fortunately, there are now at least three strategies for handling color separations in Photoshop.

STRATEGY 1: LEARN TO DO COLOR SEPARATIONS IN PHOTOSHOP

If you choose to do your own color separations in Photoshop, it is essential that you calibrate the image you see on the screen to printed output. Usually this is done by printing a film separation and having an integral proof made from the film (such as DuPont Cromalin, 3M MatchPrint, or Hoechst/Enco PressMatch). Photoshop 2.5 includes a sample image, *Olé no moiré*, which you can use, or you can use your own color image. You examine the proof and adjust the Gamma setting in Monitor Setup or adjust dot gain and ink colors in Printer Ink Setup and then print another proof. The process is fully described in Chapter 15 of the

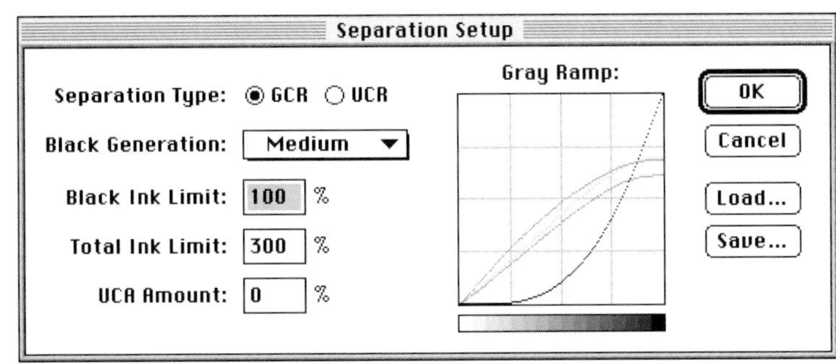

Figure 8–6
The Separation Setup dialog box

Photoshop 2.5 manual, which discusses calibration and producing a color separation.

If you are doing your own separations, you must gather some essential information from your commercial printer to make the proper settings in Photoshop:

- You will need to find out what *screen frequency* the press can handle in printing your image. Use this information at the scanning stage to scan at the proper image resolution (see Chapter 3, "Input").
- Ask the printer how much *dot gain* to expect from the *film stage* to press sheet in the midtones. Printers are used to talking about dot gain from *proof stage* to press sheet, but this is not the correct value to use for Photoshop. If you cannot determine this, use the default values for your paper stock in Printing Inks Setup preferences.
- Your printer can also tell you what the recommended *black ink limit* and *total ink limit* are for the press that will be used to print your image. Enter this information in the Separation Setup dialog box. A small print shop may not be able give you this information. If you cannot determine this, use the default value.
- Ask your printer whether they prefer you to use GCR or UCR to generate the black plate. You make this choice in the Separation Setup dialog preference.

STRATEGY 2: USE A COLOR MANAGEMENT SYSTEM

Recently a new class of software has become available on the Macintosh: color management systems (CMS). While the components of these systems vary, they have much in common: (1)They make use of a device-independent color space, which is conceptually similar to the Lab mode in Photoshop; (2) they have profiles (or they allow you to generate profiles) that record the exact color-gamut and color-rendering characteristics of devices like scanners, monitors, and printers; (3) they have an "engine" that is capable of transforming color from one color space to another.

It is easiest to understand this new software by considering an example. Electronics for Imaging (EFI) has produced a product called EfiColor for Adobe Photoshop, which uses a proprietary color management system. The same EfiColor profiles are also used in Cachet, EFI's color correction and separation product, and EfiColor XTension for QuarkXPress 3.2.

(Cachet also gives you a very visual method of color-correcting images that is similar, in some ways, to the Variations dialog box found in Photoshop 2.5.) What is significant for Photoshop users is that you can use EfiColor's Separation Tables to replace the selections that you would usually make in Monitor Setup, Printer Ink Setup, and Separation Setup. You choose the digital color printer or press setup that matches your output, and the separation table converts the image to CMYK, taking into account the color gamut and dot gain for that printer or press.

After installing the EFI software, to convert an RGB or Lab color image to CMYK using EfiColor for Adobe Photoshop, you must first select the EFI Calibrated RGB Table in the Monitor Setup dialog box. Photoshop will use this table when converting images to and from RGB mode. Second, you must choose Preferences from the File menu and Separation Tables from the submenu to select the table for your target printer (Figure 8–7). Photoshop will use the table you load whenever you convert to and from CMYK mode. The Core Pack for EfiColor offers profiles for a number of digital color printers, as well as profiles for printing with Standard Web Offset Press (SWOP) coated and uncoated stocks. Other profiles may be purchased separately.

There are several other color management systems available from vendors, and many others are being introduced at this writing, including the Precision Color Management System from KEPS Inc., Kodak's ColorSense, and Agfa's Photoflow. All of these systems take advantage of the new, system-level color management architecture developed by Apple for the Macintosh, called ColorSync. Photoshop 2.5 is able to use ColorSync and, when they are available, you can use ColorSync profiles through the separation table mechanism.

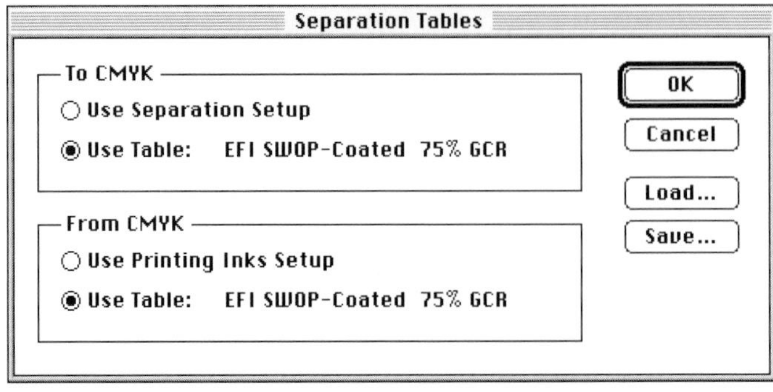

Figure 8–7
The Separation Tables dialog box with EfiColor for Adobe Photoshop installed

STRATEGY 3: GET A CMYK SCAN FROM A DRUM SCANNER

Another strategy is to pay for the expertise and to buy color scans from a color service bureau that uses a drum scanner. This is the best choice for critical prepress work. Your service bureau will provide you with a high-quality CMYK image that you can manipulate in Photoshop. Therefore you can take advantage of the scanner operator's years of experience and the sophisticated color computers built into the drum scanners.

Remember that this scan is already preseparated, so you should keep it in CMYK as you work. You will lose some of the quality if you convert it to RGB and back again. (The mode conversion process uses the settings for Monitor Setup, Printer Ink Setup, and Separation Setup.)

Trap Control

Current printing technology, although quite good, still can not ensure perfect registration. There are instances where two or more areas of solid distinct colors butt up against each other. A plate shift will cause these areas where colors abut to leave a gap between the colors. To avoid this discrepancy, a slight overlap is typically created to prevent these gaps from appearing.

The preparation of these overlaps is called *trapping*. Traditionally, print shops used methods called "choking and spreading" to overexpose an image in the film process in order to create the necessary overlaps. Photoshop prints directly to film, thereby making these former processes impossible. The trapping in Photoshop is controlled with the Trap command.

***Tip*: The Trap command works only in the CMYK mode—it's only relevant when color-separating an image, and has no effect on onscreen editing.**

When an image has been converted to CMYK Color mode, the Trap command, found under the Image menu, becomes active. When selected, the Trap dialog box appears.

To use the Trap command, simply enter the value to compensate for misregistration. You can specify the amount of trapping in pixels, points, or millimeters. Your print shop will be able to supply the necessary numbers based on their particular equipment, as they know (through experience) the amount of misregistration expected from their presses.

Applying the Trap command would normally be the last step before you print color separations.

> **NOTE: Unless there are sharp transitions of flat color in your image, trapping may not be necessary. Consult your commercial printer to see if they think trapping should be applied.**

Printing from Within Photoshop

If you are printing an image from within Photoshop, you will make the most of your settings in the Page Setup dialog by choosing Page Setup from the File menu (Figure 8–8).

The top portion of the dialog is the standard LaserWriter Page Setup, giving the selection of paper size, scaling, orientation, and effects. For further detailed information on these commands, refer to your Macintosh manual. In this section we will concentrate on the section below the dotted line.

A collection of buttons and options is available at the bottom of this dialog. These commands give Photoshop the capability to output the color image and separations with precise control. We will focus on the most important choices here; for the others refer to Chapter 14 in the Photoshop 2.5 manual.

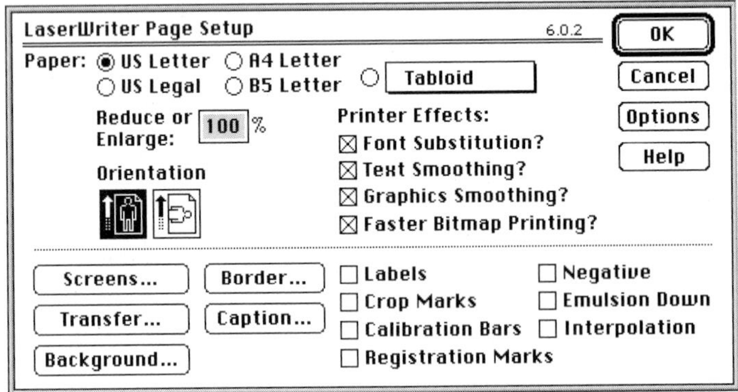

Figure 8–8
The Page Setup dialog box

Screens

As described in the Digital Halftone section above, halftone screens have a screen frequency, or ruling, and an angle. To print a grayscale halftone, you can set these values in the Halftone Screens dialog box, which you access by clicking the Screen... button in the Page Setup dialog. You can also set the shape of the halftone dot. Check with your commercial printer for the preferred frequency, angle, dot shape.

To print a color separation, set the screen frequencies and angles of each ink color in the Halftone Screens dialog box. Dot shape also may be set here. Check with your printer for the preferred frequency, angle, and dot shape. You may either: (1) choose the color of the screen from the Ink pop-up menu and enter the frequency and angle values manually; or (2) click the Auto button and enter the resolution of the printer and the screen frequency you wish to print. Photoshop will calculate the values automatically. Different high-resolution imagesetters use different screening technologies to eliminate moiré problems. You should consult the documentation that comes with your imagesetter (or consult your color service bureau) for the values to use for best results. If you are using an imagesetter equipped with PostScript Level 2 or an Emerald controller, make sure the Use Accurate Screens option is checked.

Transfer

Clicking the Transfer... button takes you to the Transfer Functions dialog box. Normally this function is only used to calibrate imagesetters in order to make sure they produce accurate gray values. See Chapter 15 in the Photoshop 2.5 manual for more information.

> **NOTE: Most people should never have to use Transfer Functions, since it is primarily used for calibrating imagesetters. Most service bureaus use other methods for calibrating their systems.**

Calibration Bars

A Calibration bar is an 11-step grayscale bar that represents the transition in density from 0 to 100% in increments of 10%. When printing color separations, a gradient tint bar and a progressive color bar are also printed. These bars can be measured with a densitometer during the color calibration process.

Registration Marks

With this option activated, registration marks and star targets are printed. These are used to line up the four individual plates to ensure that they will print in the correct registration to avoid any moiré patterns or ghosting colors.

Negative

If you are printing separations directly to film, it is advisable to print in negative. This process will give you the best results. This is something that should be discussed with your printer to verify their particular requirements. If you are printing to paper, then printing a positive is best. When the Negative option is used, the printed image is inverted, but the screen image will remain in positive form.

Emulsion Down

The emulsion side of the film or paper is the side that is sensitive to light and that will record the image. When the emulsion is up, any type on the image is readable. Emulsion down is the opposite; and the text reads as a mirror image. This is often the preferred format when printing to film; however, check with your printer to see which emulsion direction they prefer.

The Print Dialog

There are some additional printing options available from the Print dialog box in Photoshop (Figure 8–9). Choose Print from the File menu.

When you are in CMYK or Duotone Color mode, there is a checkbox below the dotted line for Print Separations. Check Print Separations to print a color-separated image to your imagesetter or printer. Uncheck this option to print a composite print to a black-and-white or digital color printer. When you are in RGB Color mode, you have the option of printing the file as a grayscale, RGB, or CMYK image.

There are two choices for Encoding: ASCII and Binary. Binary produces a file that is half the size of ASCII and prints faster. Binary is the best choice in most cases. Old versions of Aldus applications, like PageMaker and FreeHand and some spooling software, cannot use Binary, so ASCII must be used.

You may print a selected part of an image by selecting the area with the rectangular marquee tool. Then click Print Selected Area in the Print dialog box. The file may also be printed to disk as a PostScript file by checking the PostScript button.

***Tip:* To print an individual channel, select the channel in the Channel palette and make it the only visible channel. Then choose the appropriate commands in the Page Setup and Print dialog boxes.**

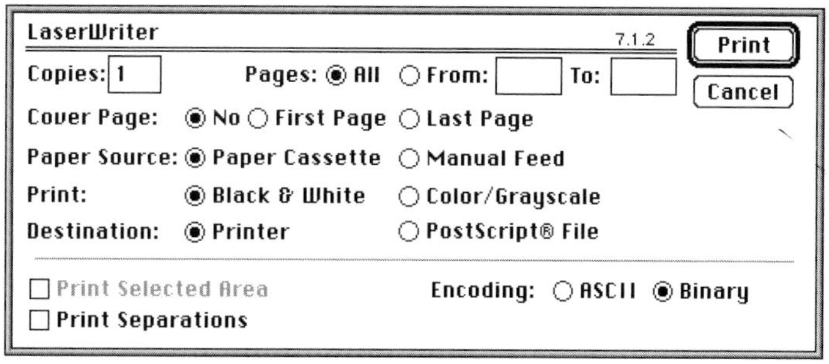

LaserWriter 7.1.2 Print
Copies: 1 Pages: ◉ All ○ From: To: Cancel
Cover Page: ◉ No ○ First Page ○ Last Page
Paper Source: ◉ Paper Cassette ○ Manual Feed
Print: ◉ Black & White ○ Color/Grayscale
Destination: ◉ Printer ○ PostScript® File
☐ Print Selected Area Encoding: ○ ASCII ◉ Binary
☐ Print Separations

Figure 8–9 The LaserWriter Print dialog box for printing from the CMYK Color mode

Printing Photoshop Images in Other Applications

Choose the Appropriate File Format

Often images to be printed from Photoshop are placed into an illustration program like Adobe Illustrator or Aldus FreeHand or a page layout program like QuarkXPress or Aldus PageMaker. To do this successfully you must make sure that you save your Photoshop file in the correct file format. (File formats are discussed in Chapter 2, "Setup and Document Management.")

If your image is grayscale, the ideal file format to use in another program may be the TIFF format. It is recognized on both the Macintosh and PC platforms by many applications. Grayscale TIFF files can be monochromatically colorized in applications like QuarkXPress or Aldus PageMaker.

However, if your image requires color separation, or if you are placing your image into Adobe Illustrator, you should use the EPS (Encapsulated PostScript) format. Color service bureaus have generally found that this gives the best results. Adobe Illustrator only accepts this format. (Be sure to always convert your images to CMYK before saving them in the EPS format in order to separate them correctly by Adobe Separator or by page layout applications like QuarkXPress or Aldus PageMaker.

There are other cases when you *must* save your image in EPS format:

- If you have created a clipping path using the Paths palette, you must save that information in EPS format in order to have it print correctly in another application.
- If you have created a duotone, tritone, or quadtone, you must save in the EPS format for it to correctly separate into the desired colors. (See Chapter 7, "Advanced Photoshop Techniques," for more information on Duotones.)

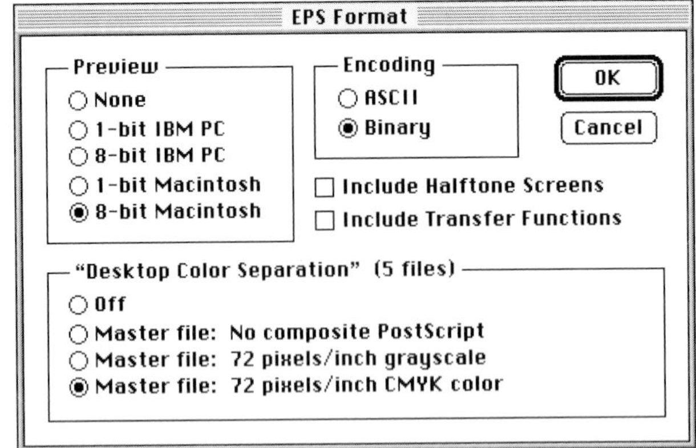

Figure 8–10 The EPS Format dialog box

When you save a file in EPS format, you are presented with a dialog box (Figure 8–10) that gives you many choices for how to save your file. (If you save a grayscale image, you will only see the top portion of this dialog box.)

- The Preview option gives you choices for 1-bit (black-and-white) or 8-bit (color) preview on Macintosh or IBM PC-compatible computers. If you plan to place the EPS file in another application, Preview will provide a representation of the way the image will look. See the discussion above in the Print Dialog about the choices for Encoding.
- If you select Include Halftone Screens, the choices you make in Screens in Photoshop (see above) will be saved with the EPS file; otherwise the image will print with the screen frequencies and angles that are set in the application that is printing the color separations.
- Any adjustments made in the Transfer Functions dialog (see above) will be saved with the EPS file, if Include Transfer Functions is checked.

Check with the service bureau that will output your file as to whether you should save this information with your file. It is usually safer *not* to save with either Halftone Screens or Transfer Functions. If you are saving a CMYK image as an EPS file, you have additional choices in the dialog box:

- If you are printing four-color separations, choose the option labeled "Desktop Color Separations (DCS)." This will create five separate EPS documents. This option preseparates the high-resolution image data so that it can be printed more efficiently by applications like Adobe Separator, QuarkXPress, Aldus PageMaker, and Aldus PrePrint. Import the low-resolution "master" file into your illustration or page layout program. The other four files contain the high-resolution information that will be sent to the imagesetter when the color separation is printed.

- When using the DCS option, you have the option of selecting a low-resolution grayscale or color image with the "master" file if you wish to make a low-quality grayscale or color proof. You may also select no image.
- If you want a higher quality digital color print of your image placed into another application, *do not* select the "Desktop Color Separation" option. This way the high-resolution image information can be used to produce the color print. This choice produces a single file, instead of five files.

It is a good practice, if you require a high-quality digital color print (before producing film separations) and color-separated film, to make two versions of your image—a sampled down version saved as a single file for the color digital print, and the full-resolution version, saved in DCS format for the final film separations.

Mixing Photoshop Images with Illustration Programs

Often you may need to incorporate some sharp-edged objects with a photograph. Illustration programs like Adobe Illustrator and Aldus FreeHand have the ability to create smooth objects. Photoshop has the ability to import Adobe Illustrator EPS files. The one problem is that when the objects come into Photoshop, they lose vector properties (clean edges) and become part of the bit-map (raster).

Bringing Vector Art into Photoshop

There are some special reasons why you might want to bring smooth illustrations to be rasterized into Photoshop files. Ordinarily you cannot see overprinting information either on a computer monitor or on a digital color proof (such as the overprinting strokes that may be created in Illustrator or FreeHand to build traps). However, when Photoshop rasterizes an Illustrator file, it shows two overprinting colors as a third color (as they would print on a printing press). You can use this feature as a way of previewing trapping.

Blends created in Illustrator and FreeHand are limited to 256 shades of color (this is a limitation in PostScript). But the bands of color they create are too perfect. When there are an insufficient number of steps, they appear as shade-stepped (banded) when to output to film. If you open the Illustrator file in Photoshop, it will open in CMYK mode. You can open each channel, one by one, and apply the Add Noise filter to each channel that has an image. (Do not add noise to a channel if there is no image.) Usually an Amount setting of 2 or 3 is sufficient. The added noise will break up the regularity of the steps, making them look smoother (Figure C–25/left in the Color Section). Be aware, however, that there is a penalty. The resolution necessary for high-quality printing the file size will now be much larger!

Occasionally, because of complexity, an Illustrator file may be impossible to RIP (print) on an imagesetter. Converting it to a Photoshop bit-map at the appropriate resolution will often solve the printing problem.

Working with Adobe Illustrator

There are two ways to bring Adobe Illustrator documents into Adobe Photoshop.

- The Open command in the File menu allows you to open an Adobe Illustrator file as a new Photoshop document. When you open an Illustrator EPS file, it is rasterized into a bit-map—the pattern of pixels on a grid in Photoshop. You are asked to specify the file dimensions and resolution. Select the Anti-aliased option to improve the quality of the image being rasterized.
- The Place command in the File menu places an Illustrator file as a floating selection on top of an existing Photoshop document. You are given the choice of what dimensions the Illustrator file will be rasterized to when it is placed, and you can select the Anti-aliased option. Like any other floating selection, you can resize and move the selection. Once you have positioned it, clicking inside the selection box (the pointer becomes a gavel) confirms the placement. To cancel, move the pointer outside the box and click (the pointer becomes a No symbol). Then the Illustrator graphic can no longer be edited.

Tip: Be aware of some limitations of the rasterizing process: You cannot import patterns, stroked text, or any graphic that has been placed in the Adobe Illustrator document.

Working with Aldus FreeHand

Adobe Photoshop will only reliably open or place Adobe Illustrator EPS files. If you use Aldus FreeHand, another popular illustration program, there is a commercial utility, called EPS Exchange from Altsys, which adds Export options to FreeHand for exporting into Illustrator formats (it also allows FreeHand to open Illustrator documents). Then you can use the process described above to work with FreeHand files in Photoshop.

Tip: If there is any text in the FreeHand document, after exporting, open it in Illustrator and resave the file. If you do not have Illustrator, export it in the Illustrator 88 format.

Bringing Photoshop Art into Illustration Programs

Sometimes you may want to bring Photoshop images into illustration programs like Adobe Illustrator and Aldus FreeHand. As long as you save your image as an EPS file, you can place it in Adobe Illustrator. To use the file in Aldus FreeHand you need to use EPS Exchange.

A very common situation is that you want to create a silhouette around an image you have created in Photoshop. The best choice for doing this is to use the Pen tool on the Paths palette to draw the silhouette (see Chapter 5, "Image Selection and Masking"). Save the path you create as a Clipping Path. As noted above, you must save the Photoshop image in the EPS format to save the path with the image. When printed to a PostScript printer, the smooth vector path will clip out the silhouette.

Tip: Always set the Flatness setting for complex clipping paths from 6 to 8 for output to a high-resolution imagesetter. The difference will usually not be visible, but it greatly increases the chances of the file printing successfully.

Exporting Paths to Illustrator

Another way to bring Photoshop art into Illustrator is to export a path to Illustrator. Choose Export in the File menu and select Paths to Illustrator from the submenu. You can then open the path in Illustrator and enhance it (for example, you might add type effects). The enhanced path can then be returned to Photoshop and made part of the bit-map.

Case Study

A clever use of this technique is to create a trap for a silhouetted image when it is placed against a background color. The background could be in Illustrator or it could be created in a page layout program like QuarkXPress.

1. In Photoshop create a path around an object that you want to be silhouetted using the Pen tool on the Paths palette. Select Save Path from the Paths palette pop-up menu. A dialog box appears. Enter a path name.
2. Choose Export from the File menu and Paths to Illustrator from the submenu and Save the path.
3. Select the path name you just created in the Paths palette and select Delete Path from the pop-out menu. (Do a Save As if you want to keep a copy of the file with the path.) Now save the image as an EPS file using the DCS option; this contains the image *without the path*.
4. Open Illustrator and then open the path you exported from Photoshop. It will appear with crop marks set at the bounding box of the path.
5. Choose Release Crop Marks from the Arrange menu. This will change the crop marks into a bounding box with no stroke or fill. Now choose Make Guides from the Arrange menu which will turn the bounding box into guide lines.
6. Choose Place Art from the File menu. Open the Photoshop image that you saved without a path.
7. Carefully align the bounding box of the image with the guidelines of the path.
8. Select the path you created and choose Style from the Paint menu. Set the Flatness to 6 to 8 pixels and click OK. (You cannot save flatness when you export the path. Also, this will usually eliminate printing problems with a high-resolution imagesetter.)

9. With the path still selected, choose Copy from the Edit menu. This copies the path to the Clipboard which will be used later for creating the trap.
10. With the path still selected, again choose Style from the Paint menu. Leave Stroke and Fill at None but check the Mask checkbox. Click OK.
11. Choose Send to Back from the Edit menu. This sends the path behind the placed image. Shift-click the bounding box of the image to add it to the selection. Choose Group from the Arrange menu. This masks the image with the path.
12. Choose Paste in Front from the Edit menu to paste a second copy of the path in the Clipboard in front of the masked image.
13. With the second path still selected, choose Paint from the Style menu. Stroke the path with the background color. Use a Weight that is twice the value of the trap that you are creating. Be sure to check Overprint for the Stroke. This creates a choke with the background color. Choking is the only option for trapping bitmapped images to a background.
14. If you will be placing the Illustrator file into a page layout program, be sure to Save the file with Include Placed Images selected.

CHAPTER 9

Animation

Although primarily designed as a print-production tool, Photoshop's screen dithering capabilities and special effects make it an essential multimedia production resource for creating animated special effects. Most effects can be created with filters: the Stretch, Perspective, and Distort commands, and channel masks. In this chapter, we'll explore these effects and show how they can be applied to animation and video. We'll also discuss how Photoshop can be used with Macromedia Director, VideoFusion, Adobe Premiere, DiVA/Avid VideoShop, and other video and animation programs.

As in print production, the secret to preparing images for animation is to know the final medium on which the project will play, and how to use Photoshop's nearly infinite capabilities to properly prepare the images for optimum clarity in that environment. Many animation applications that do not require a great deal of memory, such as a touch screen kiosk or interactive games, utilize images that look great on a 72-dpi color computer screen. Others require special adjustments because they are to be output to broadcast-quality videotape. Existing images may be fine as they are, or they may need to be cropped, touched up with a filter, and saved to a specific size, color depth, and format. As we mentioned in Chapter 3, "Input," find out what the image requirements are for the chosen output device and authoring program before starting on a project.

***Tip*: Work in the RGB Color mode (24-bit). When creating any kind of animation effects using Photoshop, apply all effects to 24-bit versions of the images, then sample down to 8-bit (Indexed Color mode) as required. Do this even if 8-bit indexed images were imported for processing. This will ensure maximum final image quality. Also note that the filters and some tools do not work in the Index Color mode anyway.**

If 24-bit animations are to be created for use on accelerated 24-bit display systems, remember that a 24-bit image requires three times the RAM and disk space of a comparable 8-bit image, therefore limiting the length of the accelerated 24-bit animations.

Creating smooth movement in animation is usually a long, laborious process requiring the creation of many images to become progressive "frames" in the sequence. With some patience, persistence, and an open mind to explore Photoshop's capabilities, fascinating animations and effects will emerge from the many hours of invested time.

Custom Animated Filter Effects

Photoshop's special effects filters do wonders with still images, but they truly come to life in creating animation. Most useful are filters that have adjustable parameters. The concept is to gradually modify an image over time by processing it through a filter, and increasing (or decreasing) the parameter increments with each pass while saving each iteration.

The general flow of the process is as follows:

1. Open an image into the RGB Color mode and then select, crop, and size it as required.
2. Save the image to a disk in the Photoshop format.
3. Determine how long the animated effect will be. For example, if it's 2 seconds long at 30 frames per second, you will want to create 60 individual frames. Thus you have 60 incremental changes you will want to make over 60 separate files. Then, determine the increments you will use for the filter, choose the desired filter from the Filter menu, and enter the desired parameter values in the filter dialog box.
4. Once the filter effect has been applied to the image, convert the image to Indexed Color mode under the Mode menu, and choose

the appropriate options (Resolution, Palette, and Dither) from the dialog box.

5. Select the Save As command under the File menu. Choose the PICT format from the Format pop-up menu and name the file, adding a sequence extension number to keep the files in numerical order.

Tip: Good file-naming habits save time and frustration in the long haul. For example, if more than 100 and less than 999 images are to be used, begin the numbering with 001 instead of 1 (e.g., Animation.001). Also indicate which files have channel files attached.

6. After saving the file, close it and reopen the original RGB Photoshop document.
7. Apply the next filter pass, and repeat the conversion and saving process above. Repeat these steps for as many frames needed for a sequence.
8. Sequence these frames in an animation program such as Macromedia Director or Adobe Premiere.

Most filters in Photoshop can be used for animation effects. (Refer to Chapter 6, "Image Processing," for more information on using filters.) Filters can also create an infinite range of amazing backgrounds for your presentations (Figure 9–5). Experiment and use your imagination, starting with the following suggestions.

Gaussian Blur Dissolves

By taking advantage of the programmable Gaussian Blur filter, you can create a stunning, animated "blur-on" effect that is distinctly different from the various dissolve transitions found in animation programs. Enter different amounts into the Radius factor in the Gaussian Blur filter dialog as follows: Start by determining the number of steps for the dissolve (5 to 10 frames work well); use a Gaussian Blur setting of between 20 and 30, and in increments of 4 to 5, gradually decreasing the blur factor until the image is normal. You can also reverse this sequence starting with a normal image and going to a full blur (Figure 9–1).

Motion Blur

Motion blurring gives the illusion of something moving past you at high speed; instead of a solid detailed image, you see a blur. This filter can compensate for large pixel jumps in frame-by-frame animation to give the appearance of smoother motion. The Motion Blur filter allows you to determine the angle and distance of the blur effect. The longer the distance, the more of a "trail" is left behind the moving object. The angle relates to the motion of the object, so if the object is moving at a 45° angle with respect to the horizontal plane, then the blur should also be at 45° (Figures 6–31 and 9–15).

Radial Blur

Similar to the Motion blur, the Radial Blur gives the illusion of rotation around a definable center point or a zooming-in effect on the defined point (Figure 9–2).

Twirl

Down the digital drain! Use increments of 10 to 50 in this dialog, and take it all the way to 999. The effect is quite dramatic and unique. Generally the more increments used, the smoother the overall effect (Figure 9–3).

An alternative is to use the twirl filter in reverse sequence, creating an animation that starts with a fully twirled image and ends with the original untwirled image. Words can twirl onto the screen out of a misty background by gradually building up the brightness or transparency of the twirling image as it unfurls.

Figure 9–1
The Gaussian Blur technique (at 4, 10, and 30 pixels) was applied to this image by Sally Everding.

Figure 9–2
The Radial Blur technique was applied with the Amount set at 10, 50, and 100.

Figure 9–3
The Twirl filter was applied at 60°, 100°, and 500°.

Mosaic Filter

Starting with the normal image, gradually increase the mosaic effect by a single step on each pass (4, 5, 6, etc.) to yield the best results. The Mosaic filter accepts any number between 2 and 64.

Plug-in Filters

Plug-in filters, such as Andromeda, Kai's Power Tools, Aldus Gallery Effects, Second Glance Chrommassage, and Xaos Tool's Paint Alchemy, add tremendous flexibility and power to Photoshop. Placed in the Photoshop plug-ins folder, they become available under the Filters menu. An example of one of these plug-ins, Paint Alchemy, has sliders that can yield a different result when manually changed over time (Figure 9–4).

Dynamic Effects

Three-dimensional shapes can be created with one of the various 3-D programs available. The objects can then be rotated at single-degree increments, and each movement captured as an individual frame for the animation. However, when not using a 3-D program, a reccurring problem is how to change the viewing angle of a two-dimensional image. Some examples are turning a page in a book with a picture on it or spinning a plate with an image mapped onto its surface. In this case, the image must go through a series of distortions to appear that it is moving in three-dimensional space (Figure 9–5).

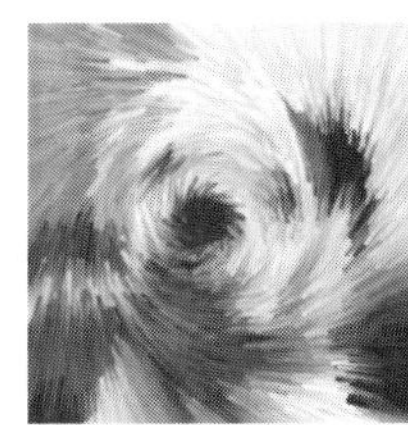

Figure 9–4
An animation sequence created with Xaos Tool's Paint Alchemy

   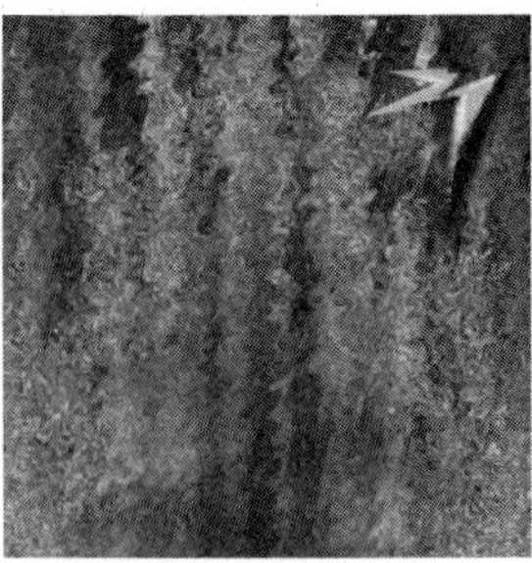

Figure 9–5 An animation sequence created by using the Rotate, Scale, Perspective, and Distort commands. The background was created using various filters.

***Tip*: The interpolation method selected in Photoshop's Preferences dialog will affect the quality of animation sequences created with any of these commands. Nearest Neighbor interpolation yields the lowest quality effect with the fastest processing speed, while Bicubic interpolation provides better quality but slower processing.**

For example, a kiosk created for the Oldsmobile division of General Motors required the visual effect of a rotating plate of glass with a picture of a car on its face. Each time the opposite side of the plate appeared it would have a different car on it. To ensure smooth movement of the plate of glass, a rectangular object of a narrow thickness was created using a 3-D program. On the vertical axis, the plate was rotated in 15° increments. Each movement was recorded as an image. Twenty-one of the movements were at an angle in which a car would be visible. A file was created in Photoshop for each of the 21 movement images of the plate. The original images of the cars were scanned from 4 × 5 color transparencies on a Howtek color scanner and saved as 24-bit color Photoshop files. The following process was used to get each car image on the rotating plate surface:

1. Using the Marquee tool, the image of a car was selected and copied into the clipboard.
2. The car image was pasted into the first of the 21 plates files.
3. Using the Distort feature in the Effects submenu under the Image menu, each corner of the car image was matched up to a respective corner of the 3-D plate and then saved as the first image in the PICT format.

4. The above steps were repeated for the other 20 plates, changing the car images sequentially, more with each step.

When the full sequences of rotating plate images were put together in Director, the result was a smooth transition. The plate appeared to move in space. The plate was suspended over a field of Oldsmobile logos under a blue sky. To simulate the reflective edges with a continuous sensation of movement, the following steps were employed:

1. A portion of the background was copied into the clipboard.
2. The edge of each plate was selected. Using the Paste Into command, the contents of the clipboard were pasted into the selected areas only.
3. The pasted background was shifted slightly for each plate so that each would be different. When animated, this gave the impression that the plate moved within the environment over which it was suspended.
4. To heighten the dimensional effect, a white glare was placed on the edge of the plate using the Airbrush tool. This gave the impression that a light source was being picked up as the plate turned. The position of the glare was offset on each plate so that when the plate moved, the glare seemed to travel up the side. These small details help to add life and realism to an animation.
5. The final animation files were assembled in Macromedia Director, accelerated with Macromedia Accelerator, and played back from within HyperCard with the Director Player software.

Any of these dynamic effects can help create smooth, transforming images such as text in perspective rolling in from the background, images mapped onto the sides of flying shapes, smooth camera moves around two-dimensional images, and more.

Channel Animation

Channel Mask and Layer Effects

Photoshop's channel and masking capabilities are key for creating complex layered image effects. The techniques for creating channel animation are often labor-intensive, but the results are well worth the effort.

Channel animation techniques can be used to move a shape inside a selected area, masked by loading it from a channel (Figure 9–6). Visualize yourself sitting in a train, looking at the scenery that appears to flow past the window. This effect might be used for a logo, in which the text of the logo is like the train window and the image you want viewed is like the moving scenery.

1. Select an image that you want to animate inside some type and copy it to the Clipboard. Use an image at least twice the size of the type.
2. Open a New RGB Color document and create a new channel in the Channels palette. Click on Color Indicates: Selected Areas. Click OK.
3. Make the Foreground color black and create some large bold type in the new channel.
4. Return to the RGB composite channel and save the file.
5. Choose Load Selection under the Select menu and paste the clipboard image into the selected type (Paste Into under the Edit menu).
7. Use the Offset filter (Other submenu under the Filter menu) with the Wrap Around option selected, to shift the image horizontally about 2 to 5 pixels.
8. Convert the image to the Index Color mode (8-bits/pixel, System Palette, and Diffusion Dither). Save this image as an 8-bit PICT file, naming it "LogoWindow.1."
9. Close "LogoWindow.1" and reopen the original RGB Color image. Reload the channel selection, and again paste the clipboard image into the type selection.

Figure 9–6
A channel used as a mask to paste the shape into the selected area, moving it to a new position for each file.

10. Repeat the Offset, but this time double the offset amount specified in step 7. Repeat step 8 by saving the image in PICT format, calling it "LogoWindow.2."
11. Continue this process to create more images. As the offset amount is continually doubled and saved through a full rotation, the result is a series of images showing the picture moving from left to right within the text. The Wraparound feature causes a duplicate of the selected picture to come in as the original moves out of the logo to the right. It is like having an unlimited number of duplicate pictures butted together horizontally, and moving by within the logo. Only one full cycle is needed.
12. Import the sequence of PICT files into an animation program and loop (repeat) the sequence to produce a logo (the type) with a picture continually passing by inside it.

Other Complex Combination Effects

Here is another example using two effects at the same time. You distort one image with the Twirl filter while at the same time dissolving it into a second image. Getting the second image to fade in can be somewhat challenging. One way is to use the Threshold command from the Map submenu under the Image menu with a channel mask presenting increments of the second image over the first image. Adjustments of the Threshold command in each increment will cause a little more of the second image to appear in the first with each step (Figure 9–7).

1. Open two different color 24-bit, 72-dpi, RGB images of the same (or similar) size (images A and B for reference). It will be easier if they are cropped to exactly the same size. Although any pictures can be used, a good test might dissolve a picture of a person or a simple shape (image A) into a text logo (image B).
2. Choose Show Channels under the Windows menu and note the four open channels listed from #0 to #3 (RGB, Red, Green, Blue). Use this window throughout this exercise.
3. Make image A the active window and choose Select All. Apply the Twirl filter from the Distort submenu under the Filters menu with an angle of 50. Copy the image to the Clipboard.
4. Use the pop-up menu in the Channels window to select New Channel. The Channel Options dialog box will appear. Leave the settings as they are and click on OK. The new channel, #4, automatically opens as an active window (grayscale).

Figure 9–7 In this animation by Bruce Powell, an image ("Blocks" type) with the Twirl filter applied, pasted into a channel using the Threshold command at various settings, creates the mask to let the "Blocks" image show through in varying increments.

5. Paste the image from the Clipboard into channel #4.
6. Open the Threshold dialog box from the Map submenu of the Image menu. Move the adjustment triangle at the bottom of the graph to several different positions, letting up on the mouse each time to preview the effect on your channel image. With the slider all the way to the right, all pixels in the image become black; all the way to the left makes all the pixels white. When the pointer is set anywhere else, it identifies the point at which all pixels to the left of it become black and all to the right are white. This is called the Threshold level. Set the slider to where the image is mostly black with some white pixels showing. Note the Threshold level number and record for reference when making new settings.
7. Click on the RGB channel in the Channels window. Choose Load Selection under the Select menu. The selected area (dancing ants) represents the mask or channel selection where image B will be pasted.
8. Click on image B. Select all and copy it to the Clipboard.
9. Click on image A. Select Paste Into under the Edit menu.

10. Convert the image to the Index Color mode (8-bits/pixel, System Palette, and Diffusion Dither). Save this image as an 8-bit PICT file, naming it "Dissolve 1." Since only one channel can be saved in the Indexed mode, a dialog box will appear saying some channels cannot be saved. Click OK since only the one channel is needed anyway.
11. Close Dissolve 1 and reopen the original RGB image A.
12. Use the same procedures as above (steps 3 through 5) again but increase the Twirl filter setting by 50 more points.
13. Go through the procedures at step 6 again, noting where the Threshold was set last time. As six more dissolve images will be created including this one, figure the distance remaining to the left of the slider and adjust it one-sixth of that amount. (In the last image in this series the slider will be almost all the way to the left making the channel mask nearly all white, with most of image B showing. The final picture will be only image B with no effects.)
14. Execute steps 7 through 11. Save the resulting image as "Dissolve 2."
15. Go through the same steps six more times, increasing the Twirl filter in increments of 50, moving the Threshold slider in increments described above, and saving each image with the name "Dissolve" with the appropriate sequence number.
16. Convert the original images A and B to Index Color as in step 10, saving image A as "Dissolve 0" and image B as "Dissolve 9."
17. Load all the Dissolve images (0 to 9) into an animation program and play.

This process can be applied with many different filters and more intermediate steps for smoother transitions. We have barely scratched the surface of the creative potential of this technique. Through experimentation you can discover other variations of this technique that are much more exotic.

Soft Explosion Technique

This technique is especially useful for video. Using the selection tools and the feathering command, a gradually growing soft-edged "burst" can be created from any portion of the screen. The trick is to make an increasing centered selection, with an increasing soft feather, and fill the feathered selection with a solid color. As the selection increases, the brightness and saturation of the color can also be adjusted to enhance the effect. Keep in mind that larger burst frames will slow down the animation speed and increase the "screen tearing" effect.

One problem encountered with this effect is that as the feathered selection grows toward the edges of the document, it becomes "flattened out," or restrained, by the document boundaries. To avoid this problem, create a larger canvas size (using the Resize command to enlarge the current image area without changing the actual image size, and placing the image in the center of the resized document), with the final document area masked in a channel. The burst can grow beyond the edges of the active area of the document, and the feather will not be distorted.

Photoshop with Other Programs

A variety of methods can be used to exchange images between Photoshop and other programs in the process of creating animations or multimedia presentations. Single images saved in the PICT format usually can be imported by most programs. Multiple images can be copied to a scrapbook file which can be imported all at once by some programs. Use a scrapbook management program such as Smartscrap from Solutions Inc. to create and file separate scrapbook files. Each scrapbook file can contain the specific series of images needed for a project. For example, Swivel 3D Professional can save a series of in-between frames as a Scrapbook file which can be accessed in Photoshop by choosing the PICT Resource command in the Acquire submenu under the File menu. In the dialog box that appears a preview of each image can be seen (Figure 9–8). Click

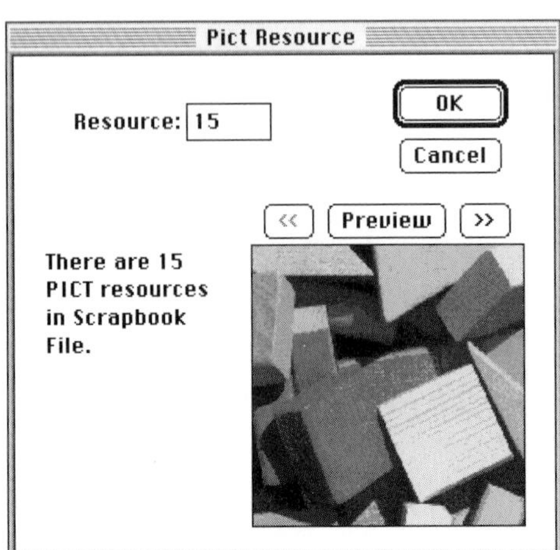

Figure 9–8
The PICT Resource Acquire command opens this dialog box to click through, preview, and open a series of images saved as a scrapbook or in the PICS format.

on the arrows to scroll through the images and then open each as an independent file. Other programs can save in the PICS format (see "Photoshop and 3-D Animation Programs" toward the end of the chapter), as well as in the Filmstrip format (Adobe Premiere) and QuickTime movies. PICS files open the same as scrapbook files described above. Files can also be transferred to and from the IBM PC, Amiga, workstations, and other platforms in various file formats. Completed animations can be output directly to video using specialized hardware and software. Before starting on a project, learn which formats will be needed to transfer images among the various programs and platforms to be used.

Photoshop and Macromedia Director

As a two-dimensional animation authoring program, Director provides up to 24 layers, or channels, of independent movable objects (sprites) on the screen at once, as well as simultaneous sound effects from two sound tracks. It also has an extensive English-like programming language, called Lingo, which allows you to create elaborate interactive presentations that can also control external devices such as laser disc players and CD-ROM drives. Director can import MacPaint, PICT, scrapbook files, and QuickTime movies along with sound files that can then be orchestrated into an animation or movie.

An important issue to consider when creating graphics for Director is the use of color palettes. You can manually resample 24-bit images to 8-bit with Photoshop, or you can import them directly into Director for automatic, multiple-frame resampling.. Director can also play in the 24-bit mode if you have a fast computer system with a 24-bit monitor. Since most CD-ROMs need to be playable on 8-bit color systems, animations and movies created in Director are normally done in the 8-bit (256-color) mode. Director can handle colors other than the standard Macintosh system color palette by creating different palettes, but there are drawbacks. Palette changes drastically slow down the overall flow of the animation, use up valuable castmember positions, consume more memory, and usually cause visual discomfort during the palette transitions. Therefore, the best animations tend to have the fewest palettes. An efficient method of managing the color palette situation, without having to use the system palette, is to set the color palettes in Photoshop first. If you have many images to remap to a custom palette, the program DeBabelizer can process them efficiently. (See the "Photoshop and DeBabelizer" section below.)

Tip: When an RGB Photoshop file is converted to Indexed Color Mode, the number of bits of color information per pixel can be specified from 3 bits (8 colors) to 8 bits (256 colors). While 8 bits are normally used for images ending up in Director, it is sometimes useful to convert images to 6 or 7 bits to reserve color palette positions for consistent or recurring colors in the Director animation (such as control buttons for interactive presentations that are always the same color). Additionally, 24-bit color images can be converted to a usable format for standard 4-bit (16-color) Apple video cards.

PICT files, PICS files, QuickTime movies, Scrapbooks, and sounds are imported into Director through the Import command found under Director's File menu (Figure 9–9). For efficiency, import images into Director in the order they are to be played back. When importing a Scrapbook file into Director, use the Centered command in the Import dialog; this will assure that incoming images center on a central axis. After importing the desired files into Director, select all the images in the Cast window by clicking on the first one, holding down the Shift key, and clicking on the last image in the sequence. Choose Cast to Time from the Cast menu to place all the images, in their proper order, onto the score. At this point, the movie can be played by pressing the Play command in the Panel dialog box (Figure 9–10).

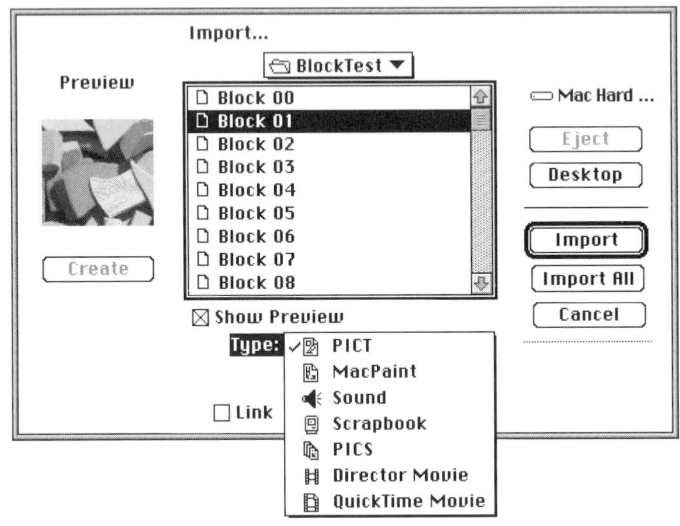

Figure 9–9
The Macromedia Director Import command accesses a variety of formats including sounds.

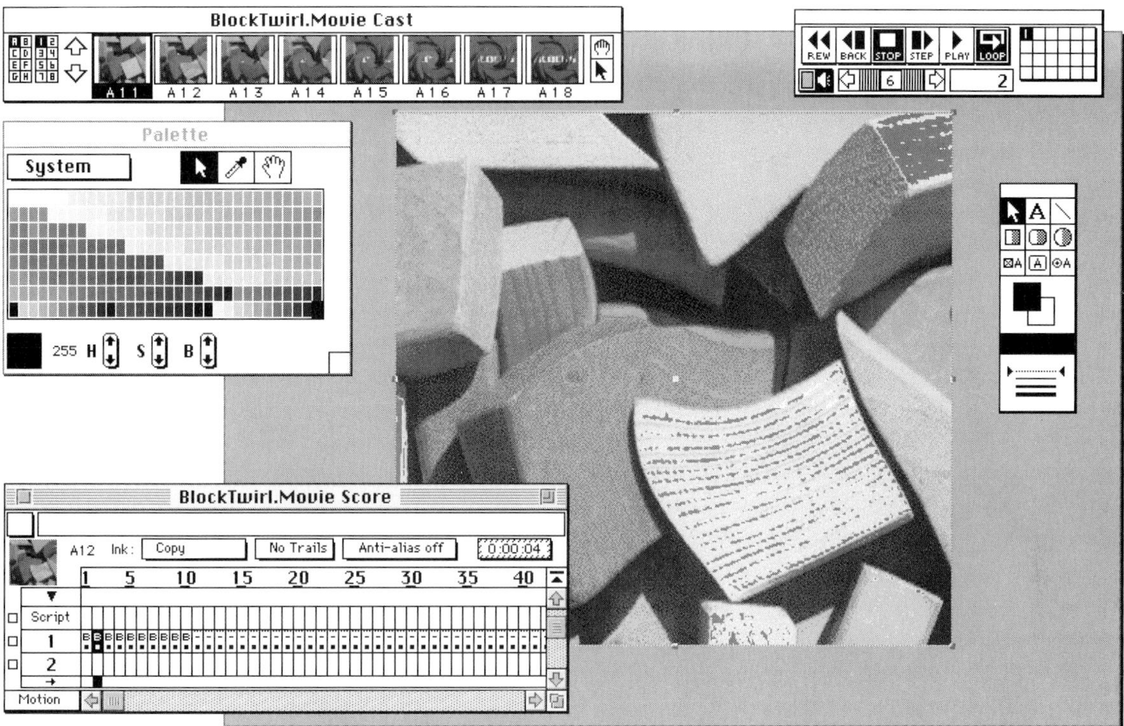

Figure 9–10 Macromedia Director showing the Stage, Cast, Panel, Palette, and Score

Photoshop and Adobe Premiere

Premiere, a powerful editing program that combines video, audio, animation, still images, and graphics into QuickTime movies, interfaces effectively with Photoshop (Figure 9–11). Besides employing Photoshop to touch up still images and filters to create animation or transitions, you can use it to add custom effects and images to existing QuickTime movies. Movies may also serve as templates to draw cartoon-type animation. This type of frame-by-frame editing is called Rotoscoping. For this process to work, the Filmstrip plug-in from Premiere must be installed in the Photoshop Plug-ins folder.

The following Rotoscoping technique uses a sequence from Adobe Premiere, saved in the Filmstrip format. The RasterOps 24XLTV card was used to digitized the original video into the QuickTime format (Figure 9–12).

1. Begin in Premiere by creating or opening a QuickTime movie to be edited. Use the Clip window to locate the section of the movie you want to edit. Mark the "In" and "Out" points to specify the

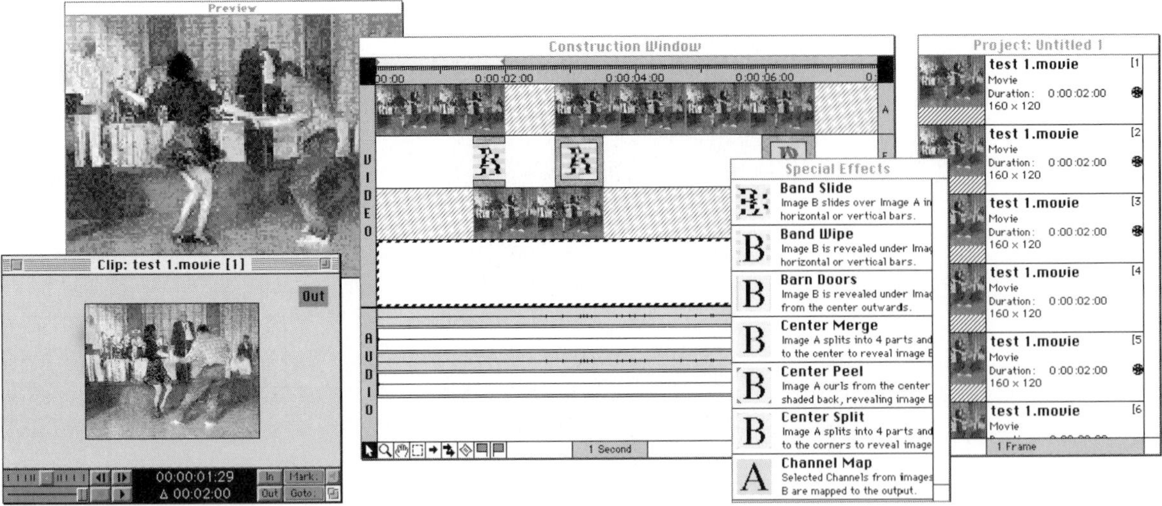

Figure 9–11 Adobe Premiere with the Preview, Clip, Construction, Special Effects, and Project Windows open

sequence to be exported. With the Clip window still open, use the Export command to create a Filmstrip export file.

2. Open the file in Photoshop as you would any other file. It will display as a series of frames with a scrolling window (Figure 9–12a). If you do not mark the "In" and "Out" points, the entire movie will become loaded, which might require a very large amount of RAM. Filmstrips automatically open in the RGB Color mode with an additional fourth channel masking each frame (Figure 9–12b).

Caution: You can edit and manipulate a Filmstrip file in Photoshop with most tools and commands, but do not scale, crop, or change the resolution of the document.

3. With the RGB Channel active, lighten the entire image by using the Brightness/Contrast command.
4. In the Channels palette, select New Channel in the pop-out menu.
5. In addition to an active Channel #5 (with both the "eye" and "pencil" visible), make the RGB Channel visible but inactive (with only the "eye" showing). The original frames in the RGB channel will appear as a light template behind Channel #5 (Figure 9–13).

Figure 9–12
An example of the Rotoscoping technique: (a) The original Filmstrip from Adobe Premiere open in Photoshop. (b) Filmstrips automatically open in the RGB Color mode with a fourth channel masking each frame. (c) The RGB composite channel is lightened, made inactive, and traced over in a new channel. (d) After drawing the main characters, the background is drawn and pasted into each frame.

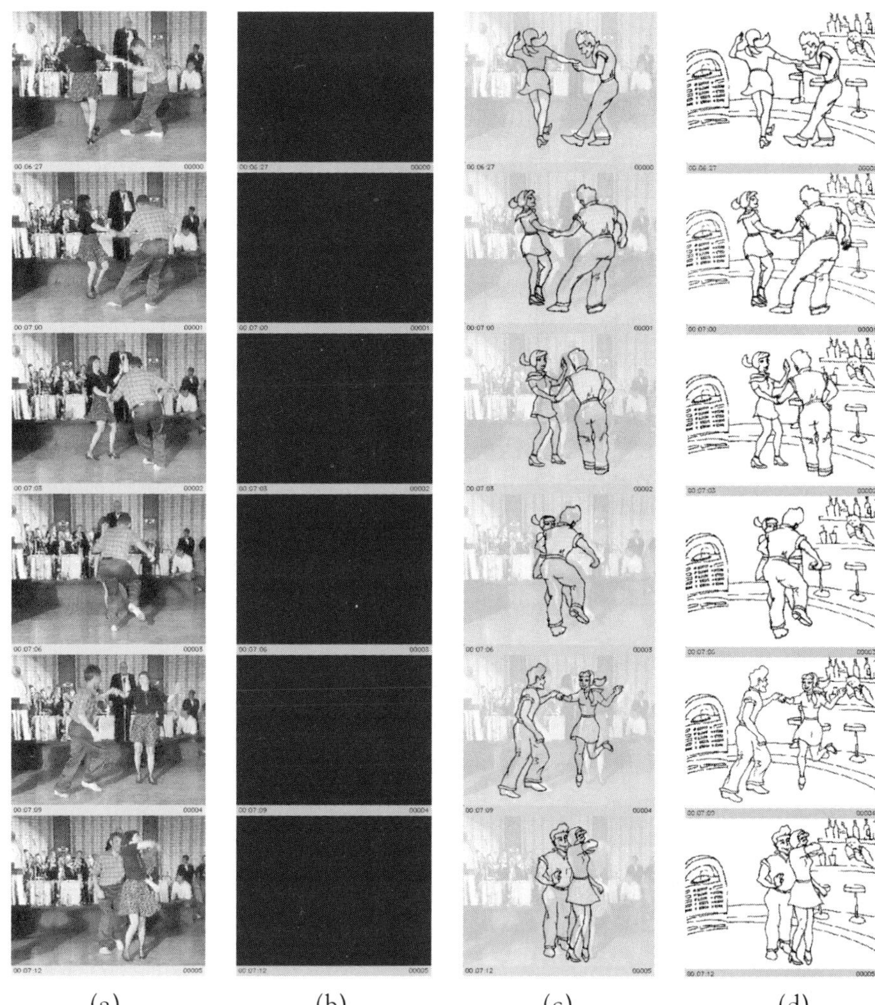

(a) (b) (c) (d)

Figure 9–13
Channel #5 is active and visible; the RGB channels are visible but inactive.

Channels	
RGB	⌘0
Red	⌘1
Green	⌘2
Blue	⌘3
#4	⌘4
#5	⌘5

6. You can now trace over each frame without affecting the original. In this case, animated cartoon characters are traced over the dancers (Figure 9–12c). Using this tracing technique, any type of character can be drawn over the template. The new images can be dramatically different. For example, you can turn people into animal characters and place them into new environments.
7. Draw any common elements and a background and paste them into each frame in exactly the same position. Touch up as needed.
8. Choose Select All and copy the tracings in channel #5 to the clipboard. Click on the RGB Channel to make it active and paste the clipboard. This will eliminate the original images.
9. Click on Channel #5 to make it active and then choose Delete Channel from the pop-out menu in the Channels palette (in addition to the RGB Channel, make sure to end up with four channels, Red, Green, Blue, and #4).
10. The line drawing can now be colorized with any of Photoshop's tools and commands. Use your imagination.
11. After completing the rotoscoping, save the file in the Filmstrip format, and reopen in it in Adobe Premiere.
12. Since the sounds, if any, are not transferred in this format, they will have to be readied in Premiere. As long as the length of the movie has not changed, the sounds will link up with the new movie identically as in the original.

***Tip*: Determine the length of the effect and the frames-per-second playback rate. Multiply these together to determine the number of frames to edit. For example, if a hand-drawn animated character is to appear for 3 seconds on a filmstrip that will play at 15 fps, then 45 frames will require editing. Frame-by-frame editing is very tedious, so prepare yourself to invest some time. If filters and other common effects are to be used frequently, consider using a batch processing program like DeBabelizer from Equilibrium to speed up the process.**

Photoshop and VideoShop

DiVA/Avid's VideoShop can add rotoscoping to QuickTime movies in a way similar to Adobe Premiere's method. Instead of a Filmstrip filter plug-in, a "QTime" plug-in filter provided by Diva is placed in Photoshop's Plug-ins folder. Select a portion of a QuickTime movie in

VideoShop, and copy it to the Clipboard. The movie opens within Photoshop by first opening "QTime" from the Acquire menu and choosing Clipboard. After editing the segment in Photoshop, choose "QTime" from the Export menu. This saves the strip as a standard QuickTime movie. It can be brought back into VideoShop for further editing along with other movies, images, effects, and sounds.

Photoshop and Morph

Morph, an authoring program from Gryphon Software, looks at two different images and creates a series of in-between images that can be animated as a QuickTime movie. These in-between images appear as a gradual metamorphosis or transformation between the two. To produce the best-looking Morph, the beginning and ending images should be exactly the same size, with the same or similar backgrounds in the PICT format. Use Photoshop to prepare (retouch, edit, scale, and crop) the two images before "in-betweening" them in Morph (Figure 9–14).

Photoshop and 3-D Animation Programs

Use Photoshop to edit or manipulate images created in 3-D programs. Most of the current programs such as Infini-D, Swivel 3D, and Stratavision 3-D can save animation sequences as a series of PICT files, a scrapbook, a QuickTime movie, or in the PICS format. Three-dimensional images created on other platforms such as IBM PCs and high-end systems can also be used in Photoshop (Figure 9–15). Use Photoshop also to create backgrounds to paste into a 3-D program prior to generating an animation sequence.

At first glance, the PICS format seems inaccessible. The PICS format, which is a type of PICT Resource file, is a common file format designed to exchange animation sequences between programs. PICS files from Infini-D, Swivel 3D, Stratavision 3-D, and other PICS supporting 3-D

Figure 9–14 Create in-between frames between two images with Morph.

Figure 9–15
The airplane was created in Topaz on an IBM PC by Chris Swetlin. It was saved in the TGA format and then pasted on the farm photograph by Mark Siprut. The Motion Blur filter was applied in increasing amounts on each subsequent frame to the background only.

programs can be opened just like any other PICT Resource file (e.g., Scrapbook files and Startup Screen files). Use the Acquire submenu under the File menu in Photoshop and choose PICT Resource. Select a PICS file (or scrapbook) and Open. All frames of the PICS file (or scrapbook) are now available for editing one at a time in Photoshop (Figure 9–8). After clicking the Preview button in the dialog, click the arrow buttons to view each of the pictures in the file. Stop at the picture to be edited and click OK. Each image will open as an independent file. After manipulating or editing, save each picture into any format (usually PICT), except the PICS format (Photoshop cannot save in the PICS format). As previously mentioned, this process is identical for opening scrapbook files. To return images to the scrapbook, they must be copied and pasted one at a time back into the scrapbook.

Photoshop and DeBabelizer

DeBabelizer from Equilibrium provides automated graphics batch processing, manipulation, and file translation. This powerful program, with its steep learning curve, indexes (converts 24-bit images to 8-bit images) and creates a Superpalette that works for all the 8-bit images in a chosen file.

All image work is first done in 24-bit color in Photoshop and then transferred to DeBabelizer for batch processing to reduce each image to its own 8-bit adaptive palette (indexing). DeBabelizer creates a single Superpalette, optimized to work for all images in project (an improvement over using the standard System Palette).

Another of its many effective features is Batch Export, which uses third-party Photoshop Export plug-ins to process and save a series of images.

Video Capture and Recording

Some video capture cards manage a full 32 bits of information (like NuVista and RasterOps). This means that along with 24-bit RGB information they can store an additional 8 bits that can function as a channel (i.e., 32-bit board). The extra 8 bits can be used from Photoshop by selecting Video Alpha from the pop-out menu in the Channels palette.

Serious animators who already have a Macintosh II or higher with a video-capture board, a video to NTSC output device, and a videotape recorder (VTR) can add a DQ-Animaq video animation controller (NuBus board) and QuickPass software with Photoshop plug-ins from Diaquest. By working through these special plug-ins, frames can be captured directly from videotape. They can then be edited, and recorded back to a different place on the same videotape without leaving Photoshop.

Animation for Television

Color TV screens and computer color monitors function differently. Otherwise we would not pay up to 10 times more for the latter. Knowing just a little about the technical differences in the two will better prepare you to create images that will transfer from your computer and play well on a television screen.

Both types of monitors use red, green, and blue (RGB) electron guns to paint the dots (pixels) on the screen creating a color image. Both paint one line of pixels at a time, from left to right, starting at the top and going to the bottom of your screen. The similarity ends there.

The National Television System Committee (NTSC) sets the standard and defines how color is encoded for television playback in the United States, Mexico, Canada and Japan. We will now point out some pitfalls that can occur when transferring from computer (RGB) to television (NTSC) or vice versa, and how to avoid them.

***Tip*: Consider purchasing an output device for your computer that will allow viewing of images in real time on an NTSC monitor. You will be able to see problems as they are occur and make corrections on the spot.**

Fixing Flickering Images

When running an animation, the computer monitor displays each frame in passes of 1-pixel lines from top to bottom. A regular television set works in a similar manner but uses two passes to paint each frame. The odd-numbered lines are painted first, and then even numbered ones are painted as the odd ones fade out. This is called interlacing. If 1-pixel-width lines or very small serif type are present, there will be a flicker on the screen because the 1-pixel-wide parts of the image are being painted on every other pass. Since this occurs very fast, it appears as flickering or shimmering.

If those lines were 2 pixels wide, at least half of the line would show up each time, greatly reducing the flickering effect. So when developing images that will go to Television or NTSC format (i.e., computer to videotape), avoid 1-pixel horizontal lines and fine serif typefaces.

When working with an image captured from NTSC with something less than a frame-accurate video deck, use the Photoshop De-Interlace filter from the Video submenu under the Filter menu to remove either the odd or the even lines. This filter will then replace the lines removed by duplicating the existing lines or by interpolating between lines. Try it both ways and see which works best for your file.

Avoiding Bleeding Colors

NTSC uses a small selective set of colors (gamut) to produce the best possible images within the medium's inferior capabilities (60% green, 30% red, 10% blue). Computers can use millions of colors and some are too bright when played on an NTSC system. The color gamut of RGB Color does not match the gamut of NTSC Color. Either the colors will change to a different hue or the color from one bight pixel may bleed over and impact on neighboring pixels, causing the image to look fuzzy. Greens, blues, and yellows are also easily oversaturated. The NTSC Colors filter, in the Video submenu under the Filters menu, restricts the colors to those acceptable for the television standard.

Normally, the relative lack of resolution of standard NTSC video is a drawback in terms of quality. For creating animation files using the standard Macintosh system color palette, the softening effects of NTSC actually improve overall image quality.

If you wish to optimize hard disk space when creating lengthy animation, use 8-bit palettes, especially when outputting to low-end video peripherals. However, note that there is a major drawback to working in 8-bit when designing for video: dithering. Dithered 8-bit images often look fine when viewed in RGB, but can become really obnoxious on video. Dithering creates many single pixels, very much like the fine serifs and single-pixel lines mentioned earlier. It will cause the same offensive flickering or shimmering, even in relatively low-end video formats such as VHS or Hi-8.

Creating Readable Type

Computer screens have a higher resolution than TV screens. Small text may look fine on a computer screen but when transferred to NTSC (TV) it might be unreadable. Use at least 18-point type for text; 24- to 96-point type is even more desirable. For smaller type use sans serif fonts instead of serif. Use drop shadows or 3-D lettering to set titles apart from the background.

Using the NTSC Safe Area

When images transfer from computer to NTSC, 10 to 20% of the image will crop. To ensure that an image is properly displayed, it should be designed appropriately. When using the Macintosh standard 640 × 480 pixels (13-inch) monitor, anything outside 576 × 432 pixels will not show up on an NTSC monitor. Stationary text should be limited to a 504 × 384 pixel area. Consider using a channel mask as a visual reminder of these borders.

CHAPTER 10

Case Studies

When we put out a call for contributions to the Color Gallery of this book, the response was tremendous. We received wonderful images from both well-established and emerging artists. We have tried to publish a cross section of work by Photoshop users, illustrators, graphic designers, educators, medical illustrators, photographers, and fine artists. Originally this chapter was to contain only selected step-by-step procedures on how some of these images were created. But the artists were so helpful with hints, how to's, and ideas, that we decided to have explanations from each of them. We thank these busy people for their contributions.

"Q/P Doll" by Louis Fishauf

Color Gallery Page 1
Software: Adobe Photoshop and Adobe Illustrator

This image is one of a series of promotional postcards for a printer, representing "Quality Printing" (Q/P).

1. The sky, fire, and earth are still video images taken with a Canon Still Video camera. A FV 540 Video Disk Drive/Digitizer read the 2-inch floppy disk from the camera. SV Scan software read the images and saved them in PICT format. The Photoshop plug-in SV Scan was used to access the Video Disk Drive via the Acquire submenu. Fishauf scanned the water, background, and face of the baby on a Sharp JX 300 flatbed scanner. The two hands and the

Q/P doll body were digitized with the Canon Video Visualizer (a video camera on a copy stand).

2. Fishauf created the typographic elements and the rays in Adobe Illustrator. To save time, he set up the Illustrator file with crop marks exactly the same size as the Photoshop document. This allowed him to create objects in Illustrator and import them one at a time, in the correct position, using the Place command. The rays, imported as a channel, were softened by selecting the edges and feathering them. The channel was then loaded and filled with 40% white to give it a transparent quality. The artist formed the oval by making a selection with the Elliptical Marquee, feathering the edge 8 pixels, and filling with 100% black.
3. Fishauf then composited the elements in the following order: the four background elements—clouds, fire, earth, and water; the black oval; the hands; the typographic elements; and the Q/P doll body with the baby's face collaged on top.

"Anodyne Cover" by Michael Colanero

Color Gallery Page 2
Software: Aldus Freehand andAdobe Photoshop

1. The first step in creating this image was to make accurate models of the molecules to be portrayed. Colanero's client supplied two PICT files ("etodolac.PICT" & "hydrochlorathiazide.PICT"), which were placed into a Freehand document and used as a template. The artist made simple line drawings of the molecules and the connecting structures. He then color-coded the molecules and corrected all the elements in relation to their scale and construction. Next, he copied each completed molecule and pasted it into a new document. When all the molecules were in this new document, he arranged them in a visually appealing manner, added a mock light source, and saved the file as "Freehand Molecules" (Figure 10–1).
2. In the second phase of the project, Colanero scaled up the molecules 300% and rearranged them. The resulting image was saved as the file, "Freehand Molecules 300%." The two Freehand files, "Freehand Molecules" and "Freehand Molecules 300%," were then

exported with the help of EPS Exchange to create two EPS files that would now be readable to Photoshop.

3. Colanero created a background in Photoshop using a series of somewhat random filter combinations until the desired pattern emerged. This was converted to grayscale to strip away everything but the luminance. He then converted the file back to CMYK and colorized it. Selecting the entire image, he applied a mosaic filter. Several other effects were also applied, most of them processed through channel selections to blend them together.
4. The file "Freehand Molecules.eps" was opened, scaled, copied to the clipboard, and then pasted onto the background file. The Composite Controls were used to drop out the pure white areas of the selection. A few more filters were applied as in the previous step.
5. In the final step, Colanero opened "Freehand Molecules 300%.eps," copied the image to the clipboard, and pasted it into the background. This time, however, he paid more attention to the individual elements of the molecules. Because the parts were already color-coded and had an approximate light source, he provided himself with a reference. One at a time the individual atoms of the molecule were selected and filled with a radial gradient of black to

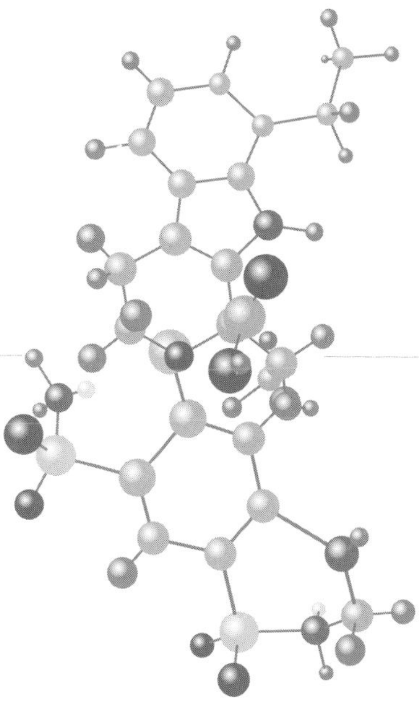

Figure 10–1
The molecules were first drawn in FreeHand from a template.

white (offset to approximate the light source) which produced a 3-D effect. Retaining the selection, each was colorized to match the predefined color pattern. The connecting sticks were selected individually as well. Because they were filled with a linear gradient, they did not need to be colorized.

"Dog and Mac" by Andrew Rodney

Color Gallery Page 2
Software: Adobe Photoshop and Adobe Sonata

1. This image was photographed in black and white with T-Max/100 120 film and scanned in grayscale on a Crosfield drum scanner. Rodney first deleted the cables from the computer, to avoid cutting holes into his studio background screen, and then converted the image to RGB. Next he selected the background and applied several filters in different combinations: Motion Blur, Wave, and Twirl.
2. Rodney did not want to use the image on the computer monitor original, so he modified it through cloning (he did not have permission to use a specific brand name program, so he altered it to be unrecognizable). Then he colorized it using Hue/Saturation with the Colorize option. Some color was added to the background as well. Rodney then created the notes using Adobe Sonata and applied numerous effects to each note, such as translucent gradations and distortions.
3. In the last and most agonizing step, he "neutered" the dog—digitally, that is.

"Future City" and "Orbital World" by Bert Monroy

Color Gallery Pages 2 and 6
Software: Ray Dream Designer, Adobe Illustrator, and Adobe Photoshop

1. Monroy began "Future City" in a 3D program, Ray Dream Designer, where the basic shapes were constructed and positioned in relation to each other, forming city blocks. Two light sources were employed:

an orange light from above, a blue light from below. The rendered PICT files were then imported into Photoshop.

2. In Photoshop, a black-and-white bitmap was saved as a PICT file to use as a template in Illustrator. Using this template, Monroy created all the windows and their contents. Next, the EPS Illustrator files were imported back into Photoshop, where the artist added color and texture to the image. The streets and building windows feature miniature scenes of people, which were designed directly in Photoshop.

Monroy followed a similar procedure in making "Orbital World," with the exception of the 3D elements, which were produced in Illustrator. He developed the land mass on the earth using a series of Calculate functions, and he created the clouds in a separate channel.

"Summer Fishing Fun" Calendar Art by Bill Niffenegger

Color Gallery Page 3
Software: Adobe Illustrator and Adobe Photoshop

1. Niffenegger began this Norman Rockwell–inspired image by posing the "dad" and the "daughter" during separate shoots on a white background, which he frame-grabbed with a Sony TR101 High 8 camcorder. The tackle box, flashlight, and cat were also frame-grabbed images. The fish was colorized from a black-and-white scan taken from a public-domain source. The pier, circular sky, water, and parchment for the banner were manipulated, or fabricated, in Photoshop (Figure 10–2).

> ***Tip*: The use of camcorders for this kind of work allows for hundreds of pose choices while involving very little model-fee time. Frame-grabbed images are generally of poor quality for print work, but the roughness actually seems to encourage more vigorous painterly manipulation.**

2. Niffenegger produced the line art for the banner at actual size in Adobe Illustrator and placed it into Photoshop. To make the parchment pattern that fills the interior of the banner, light tan

Figure 10–2
Dad, daughter, tackle box, cat, fish, flashlight, pier, and water were digitized from a variety of sources.

was used to fill a new file and a darker tan was painted in a random pattern over the base color. Niffenegger applied the ripple filter at a setting of 552, selecting the Large ripples and a gaussian blur set at 12 pixels (Figure 10–3).

3. Several logical elements were needed. The water (Figure 10–4) lacked a shadow corresponding to the pier and the splashes from the fish. Niffenegger began with a base color that filled the entire area. He formed the main shadow areas by airbrushing with a 100-

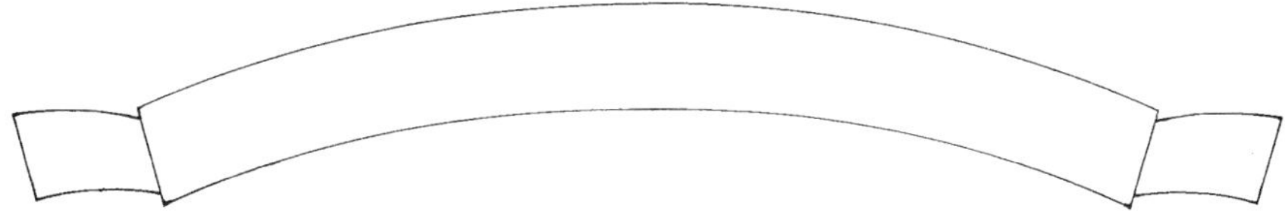

Figure 10–3
The banner was created in Illustrator and then placed into Photoshop.

Figure 10–4
The water before the filters were applied

Figure 10–5
The pier

pixel brush set at 27% opacity, then set the add noise filter to 22 gaussian and applied it to the entire file. A custom setting of the wave filter was applied. He then applied the Gallery Effects Ripple filter and reapplied the wave filter. By painting away the corners of the rectangle with an airbrush (with white), he produced the irregular edges of the water. The ripple of the water from the fish was also painted with white, and refined with the rubber stamp tool.

4. Niffenegger produced the pier (Figure 10–5) by frame-grabbing an old wooden chest with a camcorder, and rotating and saving a piece of the lid. This selection, once despeckled and stretched, became the entire pier. For the pier pilings, he selected, duplicated, and rotated a section of this extended wood sample. The shadow portions of the pier were selected using the rectangle marquee, feathered, and darkened by using levels. The artist made further

refinements to the shadows using the burn tool set at 50%, and created the old worn edges using the smudge tool set at 95%.

5. The circular sky was created with the circular selection of the gradient tool, blending from yellow to orange-gold. Niffenegger painted thin clouds in the lower portion of this sky using a translucent setting of the airbrush, and then the dodge and burn tools for slight variations. The diffuse filter was applied to homogenize the effect.
6. Finally, Niffenegger simplified the daughter and dad by posterization, despeckling, and diffusion-filtering before he began the painterly manipulation. All elements were composited together. To complete the effect, he painted in the fishing lines and color-corrected the entire image for final print output.

"Proposal Cover" by Howard Tiersky

Color Gallery Page 3
Software: Adobe Photoshop

Tiersky began by scanning and pasting the photograph of the workman onto the house using the Composite Controls set to Lighten Only. The next step involved resizing and adjusting with Perspective, in the Effects submenu. Finally, he used the Command key and the Lasso tool with a feather of 5 pixels to deselect unwanted areas of the worker's body.

"Brooklyn Dreams" by Eve Elberg

Color Gallery Page 3
Software: Adobe Photoshop

"What Photoshop gives me," says Eve Elberg, "is the freedom to draw on historical and archival images from the past and combine them with images captured in the present using tools of the future."

1. Elberg started with slides of original photography. She decided that the scan size would be 1290 × 1886 to provide enough data to create a satisfactory halftone screen. The sky, lake, and foundry images

were scanned on a Nikon 3510AF, cleaned, resized, and cropped for the background.

2. The artist also produced some graphic effects. Using the Calculate Duplicate command, she created three same-size grayscale files. She went into the first document and created a vertical black-and-white gradient fill, which she repeated on the second document, but reversed the direction. In the third document she created a horizontal black-and-white gradient fill. Then she went to Merge Channels from the Channel window. She now had a multicolored image, to which she applied a twirl filter set at 100 for added pizzazz.
3. Leaving the multicolored file open, Elberg opened the lake image and, using Calculate Blend command, she also made it multicolored. Opening the sky, she returned to the Calculate Duplicate command to create a same-size grayscale document that she would use as a mask. This was filtered with a vertical black-and-white gradient. She now had three working files to composite: the multicolored lake, the vertical crossfade, and the sky. The Calculate Duplicate command yielded Elberg's desired result of a multicolored sky gently fading toward the middle.
4. Elberg then closed everything except the last composite. Next she opened the Foundry image and used the pen tool for optimum control to silhouette the desired elements, turning them into selections. Using the Calculate Duplicate command, she saved these selections into a new document, thus creating a perfectly registered mask. At this point she was ready to composite the final elements, so she returned to the Calculate Composite command to create the final background.
5. In the final steps, Elberg opened the image of a sunrise, scans of a dried leaf, and a New York City subway token that had been placed on a Microtek color flatbed scanner. Using the feathered Elliptical Marquee tool, she copied the sun and pasted it into position on the final composite, using Composite Controls. This process was repeated with the leaf three times, rotating and scaling it to the desired position. To create the rows of tokens, Elberg pasted the first one, then, using the Shift and Option keys, she dragged the selection across and down to produce the illusion of an army of tokens.

"Thoughts of My 10 Year-Old" by Elaine O'Neil

Color Gallery Page 4
Software: Adobe Photoshop

1. O'Neil began her collage by scanning photographs of herself and her husband holding their daughter (Figure 10–6), calling the file "portraits." She repositioned them in relation of each other and to the frame. Next she selected everything except the image of the child, inverting the tones to make the selection a negative. Through this shift, O'Neil wanted to portray the change of the parents' position in their daughter's world.
2. Next O'Neil placed three butterflies (Figure 10–06) on a flatbed scanner and scanned them. Switching the number and position within the frame, and inverting the color of the insects, several different files were generated. O'Neil placed them into the final

Figure 10–6 Elaine O'Neil's original scans

image using masks and channels. Thee butterflies represent the daughter's readiness to explore the world for herself.

"Fiery Lover" by Mark Gould

Color Gallery Page 5
Software: Adobe Photoshop 2.5 and Fractal Design Painter 2.0 with a 6 × 9 Wacom Tablet

1. In creating this image, Gould was inspired by Vincent van Gogh. The original was a continuous-tone photograph of a model shot with 35mm film and scanned into Photoshop using a Howtek flatbed scanner. Using the Pen tool, Gould drew a path around the model and the bed, and then this selection was loaded, inverted, and the background was deleted. The artist touched up the image with various brushes.
2. To produce the high contrast, which is most effective for Fractal Design Painter's impressionistic effect, Gould employed the Levels dialog box to give extra luminance to the image. In the final steps in Photoshop, he created a palette of reds and yellows, and using the Color Only mode, tinted the image in various percentages of opacity using several brushes.
3. Painter 2.0's biggest strength comes from its simulation of conventional media, such as charcoal, chalk, crayons, oil, airbrushes, and its ability to apply natural-looking "paper" textures using a convenient interface. The program also includes a selection of brushes called "Van Gogh" and "Seurat," which attempt to simulate those great masters by replicating their brush strokes in the program. Although it is possible to Auto Clone the Van Gogh brush stroke and apply the effect to an entire image with one mouse click, Gould did not take this approach with "Fiery Lover." Painter allowed the artist to apply changes to the image in brush size, direction, number of bristles, contact angle, etc., while cloning. In this case, Gould protected the original hue of the image, but created a "plus or minus" percentage of change for saturation and value while "painting" with the stylus on the Wacom tablet.

"1993 Cincinnati Symphony Orchestra Season Poster" by Alan Brown

Color Gallery Page 4
Software: Adobe Photoshop, Adobe Illustrator, and QuarkXPress

1. The poster began as a 4 × 5 color transparency of the violin with the stickers and handle attached. The background was a piece of art board with sky and clouds airbrushed on it. Brown made an initial overall exposure and an additional exposure using a flashlight to bring out more dimension and color in the base of the violin and the shape of its neck; both exposures were on the same sheet of 4 × 5 inch film.
2. He scanned a Polaroid of the photo on a Howtek flatbed scanner within Photoshop and saved the image as a TIFF file. He then imported it into QuarkXPress (the program he uses for electronic paste-up) to determine the final size of the image. Armed with that information, he sent the transparency to a Scitex separation house to do a high-resolution scan (Res 12–120 pixels per centimeter or approximately 304.8 pixels per inch), which was 75% of his intended size. He chose 75% to keep the file size reasonably manageable without sacrificing quality. The separator provided the scan back to Brown on a 44 megabyte Syquest cartridge in Scitex CT format. These files come in the CMYK Color mode, so there is no need to go through the Photoshop conversion process.
3. On his approach to this piece Brown notes, "One of the features of Photoshop that not too many people take advantage of or fully understand is that you can work on an individual color channel and do various things to each with some very interesting results. In the case of this image, I wanted to create a Mezzotinty soft feeling." He went to the cyan and yellow channels to add noise, diffusion, and with the help of Andromeda plug-in filters, he texturized just those two channels. He then went to the Magenta channel and, using Andromeda filters again, added a soft, diffused glow. "Understand that you can open a second window that can be left in Composite mode so that you can work on an individual channel in one window and simultaneously see the effects in the composite window."

4. Finally, a logo type (not shown) was created in Illustrator by a designer for the Symphony and was imported into QuarkXPress. The final image was saved in a CMYK EPS format and brought back into QuarkXPress to be sent back to the separator for final plate-ready films run out at 150 lpi.

"Day Eight/Hour of the Wolf" by Diane Fenster

Collor Gallery Page 4
Software: Adobe Photoshop

Fenster's primary image sources for this piece were still video frames that she photographed using the Canon Xapshot still video camera. The 72 pixels per inch (ppi) video frames are instantly available to the computer without having to process, print, and then scan the film back into the computer.

1. The still video frame of the people in the grocery store was opened in Photoshop on an accelerated Macintosh FX computer by using a frame grabber board to capture the image. First, a Gaussian Blur of 1 pixel was applied to the color image. Next, the artist made a duplicate copy and converted it to grayscale. She then inverted and solarized this copy, and changed it back to RGB mode. The color image was copied and pasted onto the solarized grayscale image with the Composite Controls function set to Color Only.
2. The hand was originally a black-and-white engraving from a clip art book. Fenster scanned it in grayscale and added color by using the Adjust Curves function. Then it was duplicated and flipped.
3. The top part of "Day Eight" is car lights photographed in a tunnel at night. The artist opened the still video frame in Photoshop and applied a Gaussian Blur of 1 pixel.
4. Fenster put the three sections together by creating a new document 10 × 13 inches, 150 ppi. She copied each of the image elements and pasted them into this new document, scaling them to fit. She then opened the file "RGB Table," copied a section of it, pasted it into a new document, and rotated it 90 degrees. This was then selected, copied, and pasted into the image file. It was scaled and color-adjusted (while still a floating selection) using Composite Controls

and Lighten Only, and enhanced with Color Balance and Hue Saturation. Finally, she dropped this onto the hands. For fine art exhibition, the file was output to a 4 × 5 transparency, then enlarged to a 20 × 24 inch Fujichrome print.

"November" by Nick Fain

Color Gallery Page 5
Software: Photoshop, Sculpt 3-D, and Adobe Illustrator

"November" is part of a continuing calendar series by various artists and photographers for Paragraphics, Fine Printing.

1. Fain began this image by creating a new file at full resolution for the largest format to be used (approximately 43 megabytes). The ground evolved through intuition and trial and error of a sequence of noise and motion blur filters on random pixels. He advises artists that, "Experimentation will often provide exciting surprises especially when employed in new ways (as a wordsmith fashions language and metaphors to enhance verbal imagery; conversely, haphazard reliance of filters to enhance weak images is like uninspired reliance on the thesaurus). Learn to utilize filters as tools to accomplish specific tasks. . .as opposed to simply pressing buttons in hopes that magic will occur."
2. Next, Fain scanned the sky and the man in the suit on a high end drum scanner. "I try to scan all transparencies on the best systems available (budget permitting). The next option is to scan the main images on a better scanner and run the incidental images through more affordable systems." He retouched the "folding" sky in Photoshop using masked gradients and pasting over a drop shadow.
3. Three transparent grids and the "NOVEMBER" graphic were rendered entirely in Photoshop, then pasted in using perspective and rotation controls. The numeric graphics were created in Sculpt 3D, with additional enhancement in Photoshop. Fain originally rendered the dates a solid pale blue, but then selected them with the magic wand, and added a gradient fill in Linear mode utilizing a broad color spectrum.

Figure 10–7
Detail of the man in the lower left corner of the "November" calendar

Says Fain, "Working in 3-D presents the hazard of transforming synthetic RGB files into CMYK color space. The illustrations must also be consistent with the target scene which is often photographic. My theory is, 'Don't put in what you can't output.' By recognizing and avoiding unprintable video colors, users can prevent disappointing CMYK conversions and loss of detail. By running the cursor through the upper-right corner of the color field in the Photoshop Color Picker, users can learn to spot the illegal color range when the alert (!) appears. Awareness of this unusable range of colors will become second nature with experience."

4. Fain corrected the skin tones of the man in the suit and colorized the images. Using the anti-aliased pen tool for cleanest edges, he silhouetted the figures and wind-up keys (also created in Sculpt 3-D), and pasted them into the main image (Figure 10–7).
5. The original printed version of this image, which is larger than the cropped area presented in the Color Gallery, had matte and gloss varnishes. Fain created masks for the varnish plates in Photoshop and exported them to Adobe Illustrator as clipping paths.

When merging elements of a composite image, Fain pays special attention to mask edges and scrutinizes the entire image for errors, artifacts, and inconsistencies. His personal guidelines follow.

Murphy and Your Monitor

Visible flaws in a screen image will not be lost in the platemaking process; they will most likely be enhanced. When something appears wrong on the monitor, it probably is. . .Only experience and critical observation (comparison of screen images to printed results) will enable the user to correctly interpret the true visual information, which is, at best, mimicked by the monitor. Important projects should be proofed in stages...on the target imagesetter prior to publication to avoid facing catastrophic results when time has run out.

The Pixel Is Not Always Your Friend

Transforming squares (pixels) into circles (dots) requires finesse. Ragged edges and banded gradients can be avoided by doing the following:

1. Take advantage of powerful anti-aliasing available with the improved Pen tool. (Selected paths can now be "stroked" at 1 to 999 pixels wide!)
2. Reduce banding of feathered edges and gradients with a careful choice of blends, and the subtle application of "noise" (usually 3- or 4-pixel setting) and a minimum of blurring.
3. The now-archaic terms "cut and paste" (which are the primary functions in compositing montage images) are delicate procedures that require close attention for detail and execution. Imprecise outlines drawn with the feathered lasso will often result in a blurry-edged object being pasted with an irregular halo of background pixels. With practice, the Pen tool (anti-aliased setting) can be used efficiently to trace edges with precise paths, which can be feathered, reused, altered, and saved with a minimum of disk space. Another trick is to trace slightly inside an object's outline to further avoid unwanted halos when copying and pasting.

Compositing Layered Montages Is Not As Simple As It Sounds

The blending of images (especially transparent elements) calls for resourceful solutions and artful manipulations. As in mixing multitrack audio recordings, two or more images blended together can, in effect, cancel each other out, resulting in dull, undersaturated confusion. Experiment with enhancing colors and contrast while pasted objects are still floating. The Photoshop masking, selection, and channel features offer flexibility with virtually no practical limitations. Explore the calculation options under the Image menu, especially Duplicate, which instantly transfers selections to related files. The interface may appear complex at first, but with familiarity and some guidance it will become as intuitive and powerful as the advertising on the packaging promises.

"GFX Strip" by Chris Swetlin

Color Gallery Page 5
Software: Adobe Photoshop and Adobe Illustrator

"GFX Strip" was one of five chapter headings produced for an interactive marketing video. The collages were originally produced in 8-bit color because they were to be imported into Macromind Director.

To produce this image in layers,

1. The globe was scanned, as were all the objects in the piece, on a Howtek flatbed scanner. Swetlin adjusted the Levels and Color Balance in each visually.
2. The Nautilus and Shuttle (Figure 10–8) needed very few changes. They were extracted from their backgrounds using the Magic Wand tool and pasted into the collage at 90 and 100% opacity.
3. In Adobe Illustrator, Swetlin produced the rectangular dots and scaled them vertically by 125% (Figure 10–8). They were placed into Photoshop and pasted at 40% opacity into the collage.
4. The artist then applied a linear blend over the entire image, with the Lighten only mode selected in the Brushes palette and the opacity set at 50%.

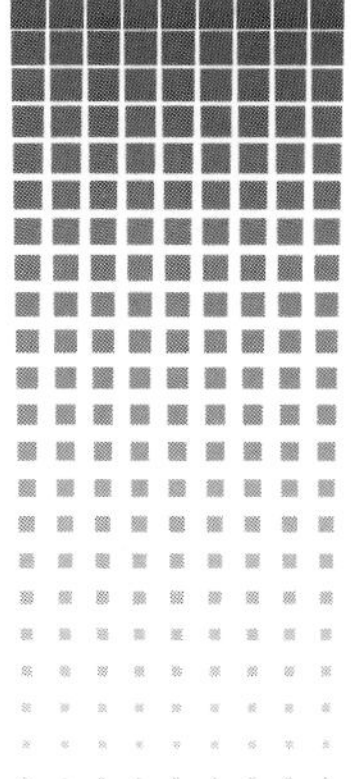
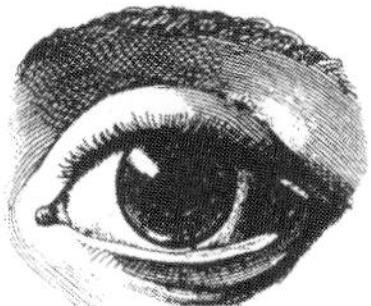

Figure 10–8 The elements Swetlin used to create GFX Strip

5. The color of the Eye (Figure 10–8) was changed to red by pasting the eye over a red rectangle and pasted in at 70% Opacity, in the Lighten mode.
6. Finally, Swetlin adjusted the color balances slightly towards cyan and applied a .5 Gaussian Blur .

"The Window" by Joseph Bellacera

Color Gallery Page 5
Software: Adobe Photoshop

1. Bellacera scanned a photograph of clouds on a Microtek flatbed Scanner.
2. He then altered the RGB curves. The Auto feature created an intense yellow and blue (the original image was basically neutral grays). He then further intensified the color in certain areas with the Airbrush tool.
3. Using the Marquee, Bellacera cut out fragments of the clouds to create an abstract pattern with which to frame the image. Picking up those colors with the Eye Dropper tool, he employed the Pencil, Paintbrush, and Airbrush tools to elaborate on the pattern. Finally, he used the Smudge tool to blend the edges between the clouds and the framing pattern.

"Vascular Man" by Fran Milner

Color Gallery Page 7
Software: Adobe Photoshop

In medical illustration, final art usually needs review by several people, and modifications are the rule rather than the exception. To make changes easier, Milner kept the body outline, arteries, and veins in separate channels.

1. To begin, Milner determined the final size of the document to be $8^1/2 \times 11$ inches, the resolution 120 ppi, and in CMYK. For the background, she created a new document at 100 ppi. Selecting all, she filled a light blue, applied the noise filter (uniform, about 35), and changed the resolution to 120 ppi keeping the same dimensions. This speckled the background so that type and leaders would read well over it.
2. For the figure, she scanned three black-and-white sketches: the body outline, the arteries, and the veins. She created three new documents, each at 120 ppi. Using the sketches as roughs, she redrew each layer with the Bezier curve tool, and saved the paths as selections. These were then copied and pasted into the speckled background, and filled with the same blue.
3. For labeling purposes, the client wanted the veins more prominent on the left side of the body and the arteries more prominent on the right. Milner copied the artery selection and pasted it into the body, filling it with red and airbrushing to add darks and lights for depth. After saving, she copied the vein selection and pasted it on top of the arteries, deleting the right half. The remainder of the selected area was filled with blue. Again she added darks and lights with the airbrush. She reloaded the artery selection, this time pasting veins behind arteries, filling with blue.
4. Milner scanned the heart—a piece of reflective art—then reduced, copied, and pasted it into the body. Using the smudge tool she connected it to the arteries and veins "just like real surgery!" She used the Bezier tool to draw outlines of lung lobes, then airbrushed to make the edges and contours pink.
5. Loading the body outline, Milner airbrushed with white to give the figure volume. For the shadow, she moved the outline selection only using the Command Option keys. Then she loaded the original outline onto this new channel only. The new selection is for the shadow. Feathering it to about 5 to soften the edges, it was filled with blue/black at 60% opacity, set to Darken only.
6. The last step before sending the Syquest off to the client was to make a copy for them without the channels, thus reducing the size of the file considerably.

"Cityscape" by Adam Cohen

Color Gallery Page 7
Software: Adobe Photoshop

Cohen wanted the freedom to experiment and be intuitive, placing spontaneity in his work first and more technical aspects later. He developed a generic procedure using Photoshop to create his images.

1. Cohen began a sketch by opening a window and sizing it according to the client's specifications. For a sketch he always works in RGB color at 150 ppi.
2. He created objects (Figure 10–9), patterns, etc. in other windows which he composed by copying and pasting them into the sketch. At low resolution, the computer can perform fast enough to produce a detailed rough version of the final art, with shadows, selected colors, and special effects. At this point Cohen faxed the sketch to the client for preliminary approval.
3. When the sketch was approved, the artist changed the resolution to 300 ppi, and this sketch became the template used to create the final art. During this slower, more technical Photoshop implementation, Cohen's focus was on producing sharp, clean edges. He copied the entire sketch window and created a new document to maintain the exact proportions of the 300-ppi sketch. This window was saved and named "final art."
4. Next he maked a selection in the template with the Pen tool (Figure 10–10), which is saved as a channel. He opened the channel and used the Calculate Duplicate command to copy the selection from

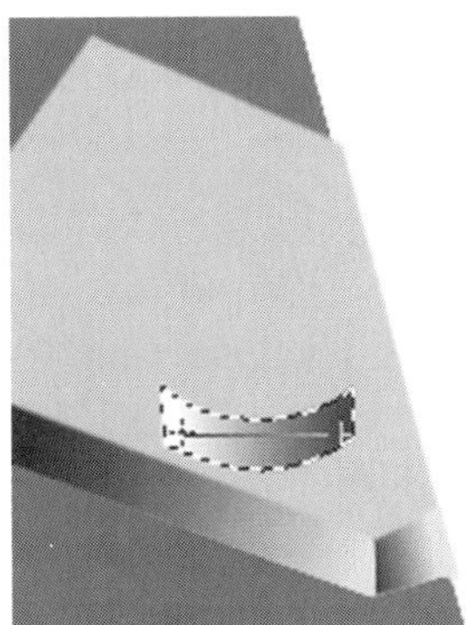

Figure 10–9
These details of the tank show how Cohen creates elements separately.

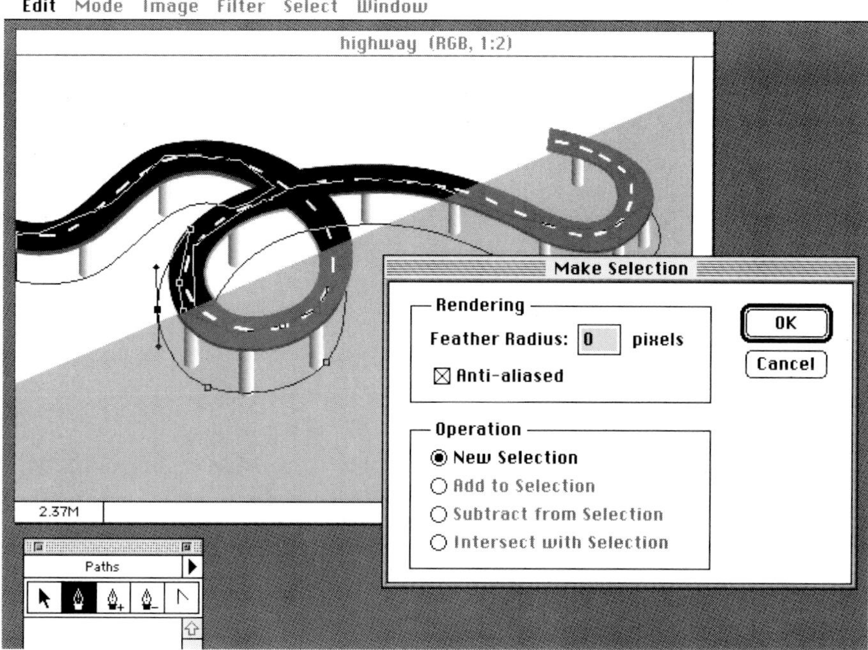

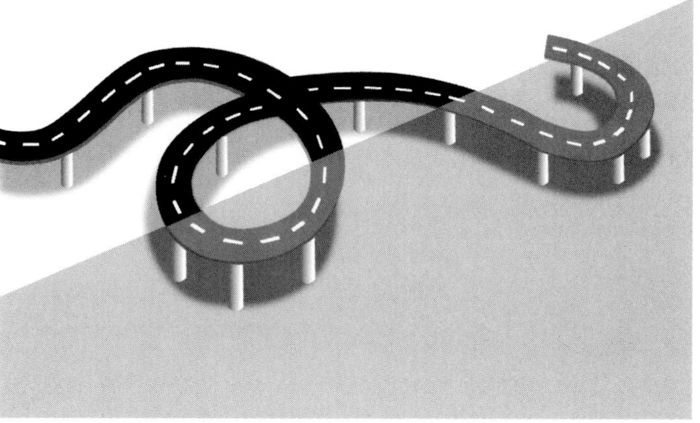

Figure 10–10
The highway shadow is drawn with the Pen tool, converted to a selection, and filled with a gray value.

his template to the final art document. This procedure was repeated over and over, starting with the largest background areas, working in sequence to the smallest objects. As the selections were sent to become the final art, they were filled with color, blends, and special effects. Cohen used the Pen tool to select areas in the template because it has sharp, clean edges. He saved over the same channel each time, unless he needed the channel later on in the painting process. (This way he avoided changing the settings in the Duplicate dialog box). Finally Cohen viewed the finished art at 1:1 to inspect for pixilated edges or flaws, and then at 2:1 for an even closer look.

"Maile on the Rocks" by Mark Siprut

Color Gallery Page 8
Software: Adobe Photoshop

1. The original photographs of the model (Figure 10–11) and the rocks (Figure 10–12) were shot with 35mm Kodachrome 64 film in the Kilawea Crater, Volcano National Park in Hawaii. Siprut had the slides scanned on a Dainippon Screen (DS) Scanner. The experienced color separator at the service bureau color-balanced the two images, making sure that the skin tones matched. They were saved as CMYK TIFF files at 300-ppi resolution on a Syquest 44-megabyte cartridge.
2. Siprut began by painting the rocks (Figure 10–12) in primary and secondary colors with the Paint Brush tool. He set the mode in the Brushes palette to Colors to maintain the value range of the original gray rocks as he applied the colors.
3. The dark background behind the model was selected with the Magic Wand tool. Then the artist added to this selection with careful use of the lasso (using the Shift key), and selected Inverse under the Select menu, leaving the model selected. With the feather set at 2 pixels, Siprut copied the model, pasted her into the rocks document, and saved the selection as a channel.
4. Siprut repeated the same process with a second photograph of the model, but before pasting into the final document, he selected the channel of the first model, and under the Edit menu selected the Paste Behind command. In the Composite Controls dialog, he set the transparency to 50% with color mode set to Normal.
5. Finally, to lighten the midtones in the background, Siprut inverted both of the channels and then selected the Multiply command under the Calculate submenu to create a new channel to mask out both images (Figure 10–13). The new channel was loaded and, in the Curves dialog box, the curve was lowered slightly in the mid-

Figure 10–11
The model was photographed with Kodachrome film against a Lava bed in the Volcano National Park in Hawaii.

Figure 10–12
The rocks were painted with the Paint Brush tool with mode set to Color.

Figure 10–13 The two channels were combined using the Multiply command.

the Curves dialog box, the curve was lowered slightly in the midtone area.

The piece reflects the duality of the model's nature, the dark and light sides of her personality.

"Untitled" by Marc Yankus

Color Gallery Page 8
Software: Adobe Photoshop

1. Using the Acquire submenu, Yankus scanned two images directly into Photoshop with a Microtek Scanner: a color photograph of a man's face from New Guinea and a black-and-white engraving of a butterfly.
2. First Yankus used the Brightness/Contrast submenu to lighten and to increase the contrast of the face, and then he visually adjusted the colors with Color Balance. He then spherized the face at a setting of 100. Placing the circle marquee over this image, he applied a feather radius set to 50 pixels, and copied and pasted it into a new document with a canvas large enough to include the entire composition.
3. The face was again selected with the Elliptical Marquee, but with a feather radius setting of zero, which produces the hard edge. While still selected, Yankus used the Blend tool with the opacity in the Brushes palette set to 35% to gradate (clockwise) from lavender to orange, using a linear blend with the midpoint skew at set 50%.

4. To convert the butterfly to color, one of the black lines was selected with the Magic Wand tool. The artist then applied Similar from the Select menu to select all the black. He used the Blend tool (linear) to gradate lavender to pink, saving the selection as a channel. Finally this channel was rotated counter-clockwise about 45° and pasted into the main document.

"A Womb with a View" by Ellen Van Going

Color Gallery Page 8
Software: Adobe Photoshop and KAI's Power Tools

This image was derived from an original piece of reflective art commissioned by *OMNI Magazine* for the lead story on male pregnancy, a theoretical "Future Birth Scenario" (Figure 10–14). "A Womb with a View" is a combination of a background created in Photoshop with a hand-painted foreground image scanned, edited, and pasted into the background.

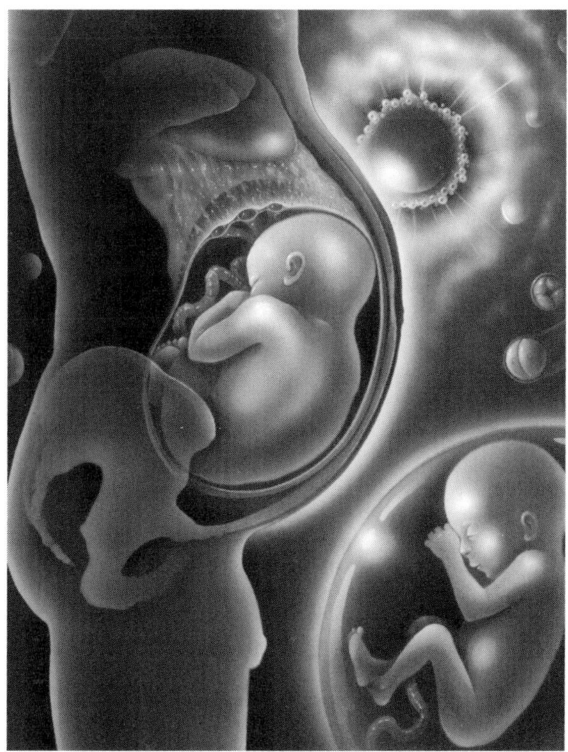

Figure 10–14
"A Womb wth a View." The embryo image was derived from an original piece of reflective art commissioned by *OMNI Magazine* for the lead story on male pregnancy.

1. Van Going's first step was to determine the final reproduction size and resolution of the image. With the aid of pencil sketches, she placed the embryo in relation to the boundaries of the final art image. Creating a new file, she experimented with various blends and gradations that would carry the image of the embryo. She choose a background texture created with Kai's Power Tools plug-in filters, suggesting a sense of protective enclosure, as well as the softness and delicately undulating folds of the endometrial tissue of the uterine lining.
2. The artist scanned the embryo into Photoshop at 300 ppi, and then copied it with the Calculate Duplicate command. Using the Threshold dialog she created a black-and-white, high-contrast image with which to make a mask, isolating the embryo in its amniotic sac from the background of the original scan. This mask was edited and the Calculate Duplicate command was applied to place the mask into the original scanned document. With the mask as a channel, Van Going loaded the selection on the embryo and copied it to the clipboard.
3. Next a feather selection of 25 pixels was applied to the image and filled at 100% with a pale blue, producing a subtle halo effect. She then pasted the original image from the clipboard back into the selection. At this point she enhanced the embryo using the Airbrush, Paintbrush, and Blur tools.
4. The softened and edited image was finally copied and pasted into the background texture. The artist added, as she said, an "advanced egg (magenta) viewed from within the folds of the fallopian tube, as could be seen by the embryo through the transparent fluid-filled amniotic sac, hence the title, 'A Womb with a View.'"
5. Finally, Van Going utilized various Paste Controls, subtracting the selection with the Lasso tool while holding down the Command key, to further soften the married images.

Says Van Going, "Such has been my only experience to date of procreation, and all in Photoshop!"

Appendix A: Complementary Products

This appendix lists some of the most notable products (and their manufacturers) that can be used with Adobe Photoshop. Many of these are discussed in the book.

Accelerator Cards

DayStar Digital Charger

DayStar Digital, Inc
5556 Atlanta Hwy.
Flowery Branch, GA 30542
(404) 967-2077, 800-962-2077 or (404) 967- 3018 (fax)

FastCache

DayStar Digital, Inc.
5556 Atlanta Hwy
Flowery Branch, GA 30542
(800) 962-2077 or (404) 967-3018

Radius DSP Booster (daughter board for the Radius Rocket)

Radius Inc.
1710 Fortune Dr.
San Jose, CA 95131
(408) 434-1010, 800-227-2795 or (408) 434-6437 (fax)

RasterOps Photopro

RasterOps Corp.
2500 Walsh Ave.
Santa Clara, CA 95051
(408) 562-4200 or (408) 562-4065 (fax)

Spectral Innovations Lightning Effects

Spectral Innovations, Inc.
1885 Lundy Ave., Ste. 208
San Jose, CA 95131
(408) 955-0366 or (408) 955-0370 (fax)

SuperMac ThunderStorm and Thunder II

SuperMac Technology
215 Moffett Park Dr.
Sunnyvale, CA 94089-1374
(408) 541-6100

Newer Technology Image Magic

Newer Technology
7803 E. Osie, Ste. 105
Wichita, KS 67207
(316) 685-4904, 800-678-3726 or (316) 685-9368 (fax)

Animation and Video Editors

Adobe Premiere

Adobe Systems Inc.
1585 Charlston Rd.
P.O. Box 7900
Mountain View, CA 94039-7900
(415) 961-4400 or 800-833-6687

After Effects

Company of Science & Art (CoSA)
14 Imperial Pl., Ste 203
Providence, RI 02903
(401) 831-2672 or (401) 831-2675

DeBabelizer

Equilibrium Technologies
475 Gate Five Road, Ste. 225
Sausalito, CA 94965
(415) 332-4343

Avid VideoShop

Avid Technology Inc.
222 Third St.
Cambridge, MA 02142
(617) 491-4147 or (617) 491-2208 (fax)

Macromedia Director

Macromedia
600 Townsend St.
San Francisco, CA 94103
(415) 252-2000

Morph

Gryphon Software Corp.
3298 Governor Dr.
P.O. Box 221075
San Diego, CA 92122-1075
(619) 454-6836

QuickFLIX

Video Fusion
1722 Indian Wood Circle, Suite H
Maumee, OH 43537

Calibration, Color Managment, and Scanning

Cachet

Electronics for Imaging
2855 Campus Dr.
San Mateo, CA 94403
(415) 286-8600 or (415) 286-8686 (fax)

Color Encore

Southwest Software, Inc.
3435 Greystone
Austin TX 78731
(512) 345-2493

Color Sense

Eastman Kodak Co.
343 East St.
Rochester, NY 14653-7300
(716) 724-4000 or 800-242-2424

Scanmatch

Savitar, Inc.
139 Townsend St., Ste 203
San Francisco, CA 94107
(415) 243-3030 or (415) 243-3080 (fax)

Ofoto

Light Source Computer Images Inc.
17 E. Sir Francis Drake Blvd., Ste. 100
Larkspur, CA 94939
(415) 461-8000 or (415) 461-8011 (fax)

Photo CD

Kodak Photo CD Access
Kodak Photo CD Acquire
Kodak PhotoEdge Photo CD Software

Eastman Kodak Co.; CD Imaging
343 State St.
Rochester, NY 14650
(716) 724-4000 or 1-800-242-2424

Color Matching Systems

ANPA-COLOR (NAA Color)

Newspaper Association of America
11600 Sunrise Valley Drive
Reston, VA 22091
(703) 648-1367

Focoltone Ltd.

Focoltone Ltd.
Springwater House
Taff's Well
Cardiff CFF4 7QR
United Kingdom
(44) 0222-81094

Pantone Matching System

Pantone, Inc.
55 Knickerbocker Rd.
Moonachie, NJ 07074
(201) 935-5500

Toyo Ink Co.

Toyo/Dupont Internation Ink Co.
P.O. Box 6099
Newark, DE 19714
1-800-227-8696

Trumatch Colorfinder

Trumatch, Inc.
25 West 43rd St. Ste. 802
New York, NY 10036
(212) 302-9100

Compression

Compact Pro

Cyclos
PO Box 31417
San Francisco, CA 94131-0417

Disk Doubler

Fifth Generation Systems, Inc.
10049 N. Reiger Rd.
Baton Rouge, LA 70809
(504) 291-7221

Stuffit Deluxe

Aladdin Systems, Inc.
165 Westridge Dr.
Watsonville, CA 95076
(408) 761-6200 or (408) 761-6206 (fax)

Picture Press

Storm Technology, Inc.
1861 Landings Dr.
Mountain View, CA 94043
(415) 691-6600

Drawing Tablets/Input Devices

CalComp Drawing Pads and Digitizers

CalComp, Digitizer Products Group
14555 N. 82nd St.
Scottsdale, AZ 85260
(800) 458-5888 or (602) 948-5508 (fax)

Kurta IS, XGT and XLC /ADB Drawing Tablets

Kurta Corp.
3007 E Chambers St.
Phoenix, AZ 85040
(602) 276-5533 or (602) 276-7823 (fax)

Wacom Drawing Tablets

Wacom Technology Corp.
501 S.E. Columbia Shores Blvd. Ste. 300
Vancouver, WA 98661
(800) 922-6613 or (206) 750-8924 (fax)

Illustration and Paint Software

Adobe Illustrator

Adobe Systems, Inc.
1585 Charleston Rd.
P.O. Box 7900
Mountain View CA 94039
(800) 833-6687

Aldus Freehand

Aldus Corp.
411 First Ave. S
Seattle, WA 98104
(206) 622-5500

Canvas

Deneba Software
7400 SW 87th Ave
Miami, FL 33173
(305) 596-5644 or (305) 273-9069 (fax)

Fractal Design Painter

Fractal Design Corp.
335 Spreckels Dr. Ste F
Aptos, CA 95003
(408) 688-8800 or (408) 688-8836 (fax)

Monet

Delta Tao Software, Inc.
760 Harvard Ave.
Sunnyvale, CA 94087
(408) 730-9336

Image Databases/Managers

Aldus Fetch

Aldus Corp.
411 First Ave. S
Seattle, WA 98104
(206) 622-5500

Kudo Image Browser

Imspace Systems Corp.
4747 Morena Blvd. Ste. 360
San Diego, CA 92117
1-800-949-4555 or (619) 272-4292 (fax)

Shoebox

Eastman Kodak Co.
343 State St.
Rochester, NY 14650-0405
(716) 724-1021 or 1-800-242-2424

SmartScrap

Solutions, Inc.
30 Commerce St.
Williston, VT 05495
(802) 865-9220

Page Layout

Aldus PageMaker

Aldus Corporation
411 First Ave. S
Seattle, WA 98104
(206) 622-5500

QuarkXPress

Quark, Inc.
1800 Grant Street
Denver, CO 80203
(303) 894-8888

Kodak Renaissance

Eastman Kodak Co.
343 State St.
Rochester, NY 14650
(716) 724-4000 or 1-800-242-2424

Plug-ins/Filters

Aldus Gallery Effects 1 and 2

Aldus Corp. Consumer Division
9770 Carrol Center Rd., Ste J
San Diego, CA 92126
(619) 695-6956 or (619) 695-7902 (fax)

Andromeda Photography Series 1 and 2 Filters

Andromeda Software Inc.
849 Old Farm Road
Thousand Oaks, CA 91360
1-800-547-0055

Cromassage and PaintThinner

Second Glance Software
25381-G Alicia Parkway, Ste. 357
Laguna Hills, CA 92653
(714) 855-2331 or (714) 586-0930 (fax)

Kai's Power Tools

HSC Softwre
1661 Lincoln Boulevard, Ste. 101
Santa Monica, CA 90404
(310) 392-8441 or (310) 392-6015 (fax)

Paint Alchemy

Xaos Tools
600 Townsend St. #270
San Francisco, CA 94103
1-800-833-9267

Plug-ins/Other

DQ-Animaq

Diaquest, Inc.
1440 San Pablo Ave.
Berkeley, CA 94702
(510) 526-7167

FASTedit/DCS
FASTedit/TIFF

Total Integration, Inc.
155 E. Wood St.
Palatine, IL 60067
(708) 776-2377 or (708) 776-2378 (fax)

Kodak Photo CD Acquire

Eastman Kodak Co.; CD Imaging
343 State St.
Rochester, NY 14650
(716) 724-4000 or 1-800-242-2424

LineWorker
PlateMaker

IN SOFTWARE
2403 Conway Dr.
Escondido, CA 92026
(619) 743-7502 or (619) 743-7503 (fax)

Photospot
Scantastic

Second Glance Software
25381-G Alicia Parkway, Ste. 357
Laguna Hills, CA 92653
(714) 855-2331 or (714) 586-0930 (fax)

Stock Photography

ArtBeats

ArtBeats
P.O. Box 1287
Myrtle Creek, OR 97457
(503) 863-4429, 800-444-9392 or (503) 863-4547 (fax)
(612) 699-1858 (voice/fax) or 800-598-9884 (for ordering)

CD Folios

CD Folios
6754 Eton Ave.
Canoga Park, CA 91303
(818) 887-2003, 800-688-3686 or (818) 887-6950 (fax)

Comstock

Comstock, Inc.
The Comstock Building
30 Irving Pl.
New York, NY 10003

800-225-2727, in New York (212) 353-8600 or (212) 353-3383 (fax)

D'pix

D'pix, Inc.
P.O. Box 572
Columbus, OH 43216-0572

800-238-3749 or (614) 294-0002 (fax)

Husom & Rose Photographics

Husom & Rose Photographics
1988 Stanford Ave.
St. Paul, MN 55105

(612) 699-1858 (phone/fax) or 800-598-9884 (for ordering)

PhotoDisc

PhotoDisc Inc.
2013 4th Ave., Ste. 200
Seattle, WA 98121

(206) 441-9355, 800-528-3472 or (206) 441-9379 (fax)

Three-D Programs

Alias Sketch

Alias Research, Inc.
110 Richmond St. E
Toronto, Ontario, Canada M5C1P1

(800) 447-25427

Infini-D

Specular International
PO Box 888
Amherst, MA. 01004
(413) 549-7600 or (413) 549-1531 (fax)

Ray Dream Designer

Ray Dream Inc.
1804 N. Shoreline Blvd.
Mountain View, CA 94043
(415) 960-0765 or (415) 960-1198 (fax)

StrataVision 3D

Strata Inc.
2 W. Saint George Blvd., Ste. 2100
St. George, UT. 84770
(800) 678-7282 or (801) 628-9756 (fax)

Swivel 3D Professional

Macromedia
600 Townsend St.
San Francisco, CA. 95103
(415) 252-2000

Glossary

Portions copyright © 1993 Adobe Systems, Inc. and copyright © 1993 by Mark Siprut and Steve Werner. Reprinted by permission.

additive primary colors Red, green, and blue, which are the three colors used to create all other colors when direct, or transmitted, light is used (for example, on a computer monitor). They are called additive primaries because when pure red, green, and blue are superimposed on one another, they create white.

alpha channel An 8-bit, grayscale representation of an image, often used for creating masks to isolate part of an image.

analogous colors Colors that are next to each other on the color wheel.

anti-aliasing Smoothing edges created with painting, selection, or type tools.

arbitrary map An option that helps control the amount of black in a color separation by remapping black pixels to white in certain areas of an image, thereby ensuring that cyan, magenta, and yellow will be used in those areas instead of black.

ASCII Acronym for American Standard Code for Information Interchange. A standard that assigns a unique binary number to each text character and control character.

aspect ratio The height-to-width ratio of a Marquee selection.

bitmap-type image A single channel image with 1 bit of color information per pixel, also known as a bitmapped image. The only colors displayed in a bitmap-type image are black and white.

black generation The amount of black generated on the black plate of a color separation.

bleed Printing that extends to the edge of a page after trimming.

brightness One of the three dimensions of color; the other two are hue and saturation. The term is used to describe differences in the intensity of light reflected from or transmitted through an image independent of its hue and saturation.

bull's-eyes (registration marks) Marks that appear on a printed image, generally for CMYK color separations, to help you align the various printed plates.

calibration The process of adjusting equipment to a standard measure to produce reliable, repeatable output. *Monitor calibration* corrects the rendition of color on a monitor to match printed output. *Imagesetter calibration* adjusts the gray values produced by an imagesetter so they are accurately and consistently rendered.

calibration bars The printed 11-step grayscale wedge that appears on printed output. When you print a CMYK color separation, this step wedge appears only on the black plate. On a color image, this refers to the color swatches printed at the sides of the image.

caption Text that appears below a printed image.

channel Analogous to a plate in the printing process, a channel is the foundation of an image. Some image types have only one channel, whereas other types have several channels. An image can have up to 16 channels.

choke To create a trap in which the size of the hole behind the object is shrunk. In computer prepress this is usually accomplished by cloning the original object; the clone has a white fill and a nonoverprinting stroke in the same color as the background.

CMYK Cyan, magenta, yellow, and black, the four process colors.

CMYK image A four-channel image containing cyan, magenta, yellow, and black channels. A CMYK image is generally used to print a color separation.

coated stock Paper with a coating of clay that prevents ink from being absorbed.

color correction The changing of the colors of pixels in an image, including adjusting brightness, contrast, mid-level grays, hue, and saturation to achieve optimum printed results.

Color Keys See *overlay proof*.

color separation An image that has been separated into the four process colors of cyan, magenta, yellow, and black (CMYK), and is then printed on four separate plates, each plate representing one of the four process colors.

comp A comprehensive simulation of a printed piece.

complimentary colors Colors that are directly across each other on the color wheel.

constrain To restrict the movement of a selection.

continuous-tone image An image containing gradient tones from black to white.

contrast The tonal gradation between the highlights, midtones, and shadows in an image.

crop To select part of an image and discard the unselected areas.

crop marks The marks that are printed near the edges of an image to indicate where the image is to be trimmed.

custom color See *spot color.*

DCS Desktop Color Separation. A file format defined by Quark and used by many vendors for the separation of color images on a PostScript imagesetter. A program which creates color images (for example, Adobe PhotoShop) saves five EPS files Four files contain high resolution CMYK separation data. The fifth "master file" is placed in a page layout program (for example, QuarkXPress). The "master" EPS file contains a PICT preview of the image and a low resolution PostScript version for proofing. When output to an imagesetter, the high resolution files are linked and are used for imaging.

densitometer An instrument used to measure the density of printed halftones. A densitometer is used to measure the density levels on the printed calibration bars.

density The ability of an object to stop or absorb light. The less the light is reflected or transmitted by an object, the higher its density.

density range The range from the smallest highlight dot the press can print to the largest shadow dot it can print.

digital Computer data in the form of discrete 0 or 1 digits (on or off), as opposed to continous analog data.

digital proof A process color separation proof in which the digital CMYK data is used directly to produce the proof. It uses no negatives and no film processing. Examples DuPont 4CAST, QMS ColorScript 100.

dithering The technique of making adjacent pixels different colors to give the illusion of a third color. Dithering can give the effect of shades of gray on a black-and-white display, or more colors on an 8-bit color display.

dodge and burn Dodging an area lightens the tones and burning darkens the tones. Photoshop goes beyond conventional darkroom printing by allowing dodging and burning to selectively affect only highlights, midtones, or shadows.

dot gain A defect in printing that causes dots to print larger than they should, causing darker tones or colors. Dot gain is reflected in an increase in the density of light reflected by an image.

dpi Dots per inch; a measure of resolution.

emulsion The photosensitive layer on a piece of film or paper.

EPS Encapsulated PostScript. A popular and flexible graphic format for storing object-oriented graphics and bit-mapped, gray-scale and RGB images, used on both Macintosh and PC-compatible computers. The EPS file usually consists of two parts—the PostScript description for printing resolution-independent graphics on a PostScript printer, and a low-resolution bit-mapped preview. On a Macintosh the preview image, used for cropping and scaling in a page layout program, is stored as PICT.

fade-out rate The rate at which the paint brush and airbrush tools fade out as you paint with them to simulate an actual brush stroke.

feather edge The area along the border of a selection that is partially affected by changes you make to the selection.

fill To paint a selected area with a gray shade, a color, or a pattern.

Filmstrip A file format developed by Adobe allowing sequential images from a movie to be transferred between Premiere and Photoshop.

filter A filter normally is placed in front of the lens on a camera to distort or modify the light rays. The filters in Photoshop simulate these effects, plus more...

Focoltone A trademarked standard for specifying and producing colors using *process color inks*. It attempts to guarantee that a color chosen during the design process will match the ink used to produce the final product.

fringe The pixels along the edge of a selection. The fringe pixels contain a mixture of the colors in the selection and the background color(s) around the selection.

fuzziness A parameter that controls how much anti-aliasing is applied to the edges of a selection.

gamma A measure of contrast that affects the mid-level grays (midtones) of an image.

gamut The available range of colors for a particular stage of a color production process. For example, color monitors have a different gamut than that of CMYK inks.

gradient fill A fill that displays a gradual transition from the foreground to the background color. Gradient fills are made with the blend tool.

grayscale image A single-channel image that consists of up to 256 levels of gray, with 8 bits of color information per pixel.

gray-component replacement (GCR) The removal of a mixture of cyan, magenta, and yellow, and replacement of them with black.

halftone The reproduction of a continuous-tone image, made by using a screen that breaks the image into various size dots.

halftone cell The pattern of device pixels which is repeated in a digital halftone screen. The shape of the pattern may be round, elliptical, linear or other shapes, and the halftone cells are equally spaced.

highlight The lightest part of an image, represented in a halftone by the smallest dots, or the absence of dots.

histogram A graphic representation of the number of pixels with given color values. A histogram shows the breakdown of colors in an image.

HSB image An RGB image that is displayed in three channels: hue, saturation, and brightness. Only one channel is displayed at a time.

HSL image An RGB image that is displayed in three channels: hue, saturation, and luminance. Only one channel is displayed at a time.

hue Color; the main attribute of a color that distinguishes it from other colors.

imagesetter A device used to output computer-generated pages or images at high resolution onto film or paper.

indexed color image A single-channel image, with 8 bits of color information per pixel. The index is a color lookup table containing up to 256 colors.

kern To adjust the character spacing in type.

Lab color The Lab Color mode is based on visual color perception using a standard created by the Commission Internationale de L' Éclairage (CIE). International standards for color measurements were established by this organization in 1931. Color values are defined mathematically so that they can exist independent of any device. Lab colors will not vary among different monitors and printers, as long as they are calibrated correctly.

labels A printing option that prints the document and channel name on the image.

laminate proof A proof created from process color separation negatives in which four process color pigment layers are laminated to a sheet of white paper to create the color image. Examples Cromalin (DuPont), Matchprint (3M), Color Link (Enco).

leading The line spacing for type measured from baseline to baseline of the lines of text.

linear fill A fill that is projected from one point to another in a straight line.

lpi Lines per inch; a measure of resolution.

luminance Lightness; the highest of the individual RGB values plus the lowest of the individual RGB values, divided by two; a component of an HSL image.

luminosity A color parameter that measures the brightness of color. Luminosity is expressed as a value computed as the weighted average of the pixel's individual RGB values, expressed as a percentage (.30 × red + .59 × green + .11 × blue).

MacPaint A graphic file format on the Macintosh for storing 1-bit bitmapped images. It originated with the program of the same name.

midtone Tonal value of a dot; located approximately halfway between the highlight value and the shadow value.

moiré pattern An undesirable pattern in color printing, resulting from incorrect screen angles of overprinting halftones. Moiré patterns can be minimized with the use of proper screen angles.

multichannel image Any image that has more than one channel.

noise In an image, pixels with randomly distributed color values.

object-oriented graphic A graphic made up of distinct objects which can be individually edited and transformed. When printed with the PostScript language, these objects are imaged at a finer quality on high resolution printers and imagesetters.

overlay proof A proof created from process color separation negatives which uses four sheets of acetate that are placed on top of each other to create the color image. Each film layer represents one of the process colors. Examples Color Keys (3M), Chromacheck (DuPont).

pattern A selection that repeats in tiles to form a regular design.

PICS The PICS format, a type of PICT Resource file is a common file format designed for the exchange of animation sequences between programs.

PICT2 A extension of PICT, this is a graphic file format for storing RGB images. It consists of two subtypes—*24-bit PICT2*, a 16.8 million color version, and the more common *8-bit PICT2*, which holds a palette of 256 colors. It is a good choice for presentations work, but this format is poorly supported by page layout and process color separation applications.

PICT The oldest generic graphic file format on the Macintosh. It can store any combination of bit-mapped images and object-oriented graphics, in black and white or in a palette of eight colors. It is not suitable for high-quality object-oriented graphics or bit maps.

pixel A single dot on a computer display or in a digital image.

plug-in module Software developed by a third-party vendor in conjunction with Adobe Systems that lets you use a function that is not available in the standard Adobe Photoshop application.

PMS Pantone Matching System. A trademarked standard for specifying and producing *spot colors* using proprietary ink mixes. It attempts to guarantee that a color chosen during the design process will match the ink used to produce the final product.

posterization Graduated tones converted into a specific number of steps. Conventionally, a posterization is made with a series of high contrast line shots (threshold).

PostScript A computer language developed by Adobe Systems specifically designed to describe text, object-oriented graphics, and bit-mapped, gray-scale and RGB images. Using this language, the same page can be imaged on a computer screen (for computers which have Display PostScript) or printed on output devices of different resolutions and color capabilities.

primary colors When mixing paint or pigments the primary colors are red, yellow and blue. When mixing colors with light, either the additve or subractive system is used. The additive primary colors are red, green and blue. The subtractive primary colors are magenta, yellow and cyan. See *additive primary colors* and *subtractive primary colors*.

process color The four color pigments—cyan, magenta, yellow, and black—used in color printing.

process color separation An image that has been separated into the four process colors—cyan, magenta, yellow and black (CMYK). When a computer application produces this separation, it prints a separate plate for each of these colors.

progressive color bar A bar printed on process color separations, showing all possible combinations of cyan, magenta, yellow and sometimes black. It is used to ensure proper ink coverage and color.

Quarter (1/4) tone Tonal value of a dot, located approximately halfway between highlight and midtone.

radial fill A fill that is projected from a center point outward in all directions.

random access memory (RAM) The part of the computer's memory that stores information temporarily while you're working on it.

rasterize To convert digital information into a series of pixels on an output device—computer screen, printer or imagesetter.

registration marks (bull's-eyes) Marks that appear on a printed image, generally for CMYK color separations, to help you align the various printed plates.

remap colors When changing palletes the computer will attempt to match the original colors in a document with similar colors in the new palette.

repeat rate The rate at which paint is deposited on an image by the painting and editing tools when the mouse is stationary.

resample To change the resolution of an image. Resampling down discards pixel information in an image; resampling up adds pixel information through interpolation.

resize To change an image's size while maintaining its resolution.

resolution The number of pixels per inch in an image, or the number of dots per inch used by an output device. Resolution can also refer to the number of bits per pixel.

RGB image A three-channel image containing a red, green, and blue channel.

RIP Raster image processor The processor in an output device that rasterizes the PostScript description of a page so it may be imaged onto film or paper.

rosette The tight cluster of halftone cells which is created when two or more halftone screens are properly oriented.

saturation The amount of gray in a color. More gray in a color means lower saturation; less gray in a color means higher saturation.

scanned image The image that results when a photograph, slide, paper image, or other two- or three-dimensional image is converted into a digital image.

scanner An electronic device that digitizes and converts photographs, slides, paper images, or other two-dimensional images into bitmapped images. A video camera is a scanner that converts three-dimensional objects into digital, bitmapped images.

screen angles The angles at which the halftone screens are placed in relation to one another.

screen frequency The density of dots on the halftone screen, commonly measured in lines per inch.

screen tint A screened percentage of a solid color.

shadow The darkest part of an image, represented in a halftone by the largest dots.

spacing The distance between the pixels that are affected by each painting and editing tool.

spot color A method of color reproduction where the printer mixes an ink to create each of the colors used on the page. In a computer application, spot colors can usually be specified using any of several color models—including RGB, CMYK or PMS colors. When the application prints *spot color overlays*, it prints a plate for each specified spot color.

star targets The printed pinwheels, used primarily in printing color separations, to align the different plates, and measure dot doubling, grain, and slurring during printing.

subtractive primary colors The inks—cyan, magenta and yellow—which are combined together in process color printing to render different colors. When cyan, magenta and yellow are combined they produce darker colors.

Three-quarters (3/4) tone Tonal value of a dot, located approximately halfway between midtone and shadow.

TIFF Tag Image File Format. A graphic file format widely used as an interchange format for images on both Macintosh and PC-compatible computers. One of the most flexible and reliable formats, it has subtypes capable of storing 1-bit images, 8-bit gray-scale images, and RGB images up to 16.8 million colors. It is well supported by page layout and color separation programs.

tolerance A parameter of the magic wand and paint bucket tools that specifies the color range of the pixels to be selected.

toolbox The set of tools normally displayed to the left of an image. The toolbox is a floating palette that you can move or hide.

total ink density The maximum amount of ink a printing press can handle. It is measured as a percentage representing the sum of percentages of the process color inks. It will vary according to the paper stock used.

trap An overlap that prevents gaps from appearing along the edges of an object in a separated image, due to slight misalignment or movement of the separations onpress.

uncoated stock Paper which is not coated with a layer of clay and which absorbs ink more readily.

undercolor removal (UCR) The technique of reducing the cyan, magenta, and yellow inks from the darkest neutral shadow areas in an image, and replacing them with black.

value The relative lightness and darkness of a color or tone.

virtual memory The memory space that is separate from the main memory (physical random access memory), such as hard disk space. Virtual memory allows you to work on large documents without requiring you to have large amounts of RAM.

zoom To magnify or reduce your view of the current document.

Index

D

E

F

G

H

I

J

K

N

O

P

Q

R

S

T

U

V

W

X

Y

Z

For more information about how Optronics' ColorSetter series of imagesetters and ColorGetter II series of desktop color scanners can improve your performance, please photocopy, then fill out the form below and mail or fax it to: Optronics, An Intergraph Division, Marketing Services Department, 7 Stuart Road, Chelmsford, MA 01824. Fax: (508) 256-1872.

Please send more information on:

_____ DeskSetter 3000 imagesetter

_____ ColorSetter series of imagesetters

_____ ColorSetter XL series of imagesetters

_____ ColorGetter II series of scanners

_____ ColorRight software

Name ____

Title ____

Company ____

Address ____

City ____

State ________________________________ Zip___________

Phone _______________________________ Ext.___________

Facsimile___________________________

Performance in Precision Imaging